Perspectives in Total Quality

Perspectives in Total Quality

Edited by

Michael J. Stahl
University of Tennessee at Knoxville

in association with
ASQ Quality Press

American Society for Quality

ASQ

611 East Wisconsin Avenue
P.O. Box 3005
Milwaukee, Wisconsin 53201-3005

Copyright © Blackwell Publishers Ltd 1999

First published 1999

2 4 6 8 10 9 7 5 3 1

Blackwell Publishers Inc.
350 Main Street
Malden, Massachusetts 02148
USA

Blackwell Publishers Ltd
108 Cowley Road
Oxford OX4 1JF
UK

Library of Congress Cataloging-in-Publication Data

Perspectives in total quality / edited by Michael J. Stahl.
        p.   cm.
    Includes bibliographical references and index.
    ISBN 0–631–20884–4 (alk. paper)
    1. Total quality management.   I. Stahl, Michael J.
HD62.15.P47   1998
658.4′013—dc21   98–8587
                                            CIP

British Library Cataloguing in Publication Data

A CIP catalogue record for this book is available from the British Library

Typeset in Baskerville 10/12pt
by Graphicraft Limited, Hong Kong
Printed in Great Britain by TJ International, Padstow, Cornwall

This book is printed on acid-free paper

Contents

List of Figures   vii

List of Tables   ix

List of Contributors   x

Acknowledgments   xiv

Introduction
Michael J. Stahl   1

PART I CUSTOMERS   5

1 Building Advantage Through Customer Value
Robert B. Woodruff and Sarah Fisher Gardial   7

2 The Emerging Academic Research on the Link
between Total Quality Management and Corporate
Financial Performance: A Critical Review
George S. Easton and Sherry L. Jarrell   27

3 Academic Culture and the American Quality
Movement: Linking Fundamental Research and
Quality Practice
Marietta L. Baba   71

PART II SYSTEMS   103

4 High Performing Organizations
Garry J. Huysse and Sheron Kennedy   105

5 Organizational Culture and the Total Quality
Organization
*Kyle M. Lundby, Jacquelyn S. DeMatteo,
and Michael C. Rush*   134

6 An Organizational Model for Implementing a Total
Quality Management System
Andrew G. Kemeny 153

PART III PROCESSES **181**

7 Process Management and Process Reengineering
William C. Parr 183

8 The Role of Process Managers and Understanding
Process Variation
Mary G. Leitnaker 210

9 Design Quality and New Product Development
*Michael E. Kennedy, Carmen J. Trammell,
and Clement C. Wilson* 221

10 Product Development Speed and Quality:
A New Set of Synergies?
*Barbara B. Flynn, E. James Flynn, Susan K. Amundson,
and Roger G. Schroeder* 245

11 Building the Lean Enterprise
Thomas G. Greenwood and Kenneth E. Kirby 272

PART IV CONTINUOUS IMPROVEMENT AND ASSESSMENT **311**

12 Using the Baldrige Framework for Self-Assessment
and Continuous Improvement
John P. Evans 313

13 Using ISO 9000 and the European Quality Award
Approach to Improve Competitiveness
John J. Kirchenstein and Reg Blake 343

14 The Competitive Advantages of the TQM Firm
John W. Mogab and William E. Cole 371

Index 387

List of Figures

1.1	Customer value hierarchy.	13
1.2	Customer value drives customer satisfaction.	16
1.3	Customer value changes over time.	18
1.4	Applying customer value learning.	20
4.1	The functioning of the organization as a system.	109
4.2	Leveraging the higher level capability of workers.	111
4.3	Framework for transition to high performance teams.	121
4.4	Lucent Technologies high performance team implementation education and training curricula.	128
5.1	Representational modes.	144
6.1	Organizational model for quality management system implementation.	160
6.2	Matrix management.	168
6.3	Process inventory.	169
6.4	Institutional strategic direction.	172
6.5	Illustrative roles and responsibilities of teams in the institution.	174
7.1	IRS forms distribution process (old process).	192
7.2	IRS forms distribution process (new process).	193
7.3	Loan flow chart.	198
7.4	Impact on registration process: MDC perspective.	200
7.5	Process for curriculum change.	203
8.1	Process outcomes: "out of control."	214
8.2	Process outcomes: statistical control.	215
8.3	Process outcomes: appropriate, constructive, and verifiable process changes.	215
8.4	Injection molding process flow chart (process parameter classification).	216
8.5	Data collection plan example.	218
9.1	A superior product development process for an innovative product, with milestone goals for each phase.	227
9.2	Selected phases from figure 9.1, illustrating how measurements of critical product characteristics are used throughout the entire product development process.	230

9.3	Illustration of a formal method for transferring critical product characteristic information into the manufacturing process.	231
9.4	An example of an operating space.	234
9.5	The initial product design step of the Product Design and Evaluation phase.	236
11.1	The lean enterprise.	276
11.2	Model-level planning BOM.	279
11.3	Integrating the elements.	283
11.4	Process flowcharting symbols.	285
11.5	Lean enterprise measures.	287
11.6	Aligning the value stream.	295
11.7	First-level planning BOMs.	298
11.8	Component level planning BOMs.	299
11.9	Production scheduling: provide maximum model-mix flexibility.	300
11.10	Objective of rate-based planning techniques.	303
11.11	The factory response profile.	304
11.12	Customer demand profiles by product family.	306
12.1	Baldrige award criteria framework (a systems perspective).	316
12.2	The planning-assessment link.	317
12.3	An assessment process.	318
12.4	Matching maturity and approach to assessment.	320
12.5	Leadership: values, directions, and systems.	332
12.6	Value chain items.	334
12.7	Support items and feedback loops.	335
12.8	Direction setting – input items.	337
12.9	Direction setting – outputs.	338
12.10	Leadership: closing the loop with feedback.	339
12.11	Examples of building blocks.	339
13.1	Meeting the continuous challenge to provide customer satisfaction – applying TQM.	353
13.2	The European model for TQM and self-assessment process.	358
14.1	Cost cutting through downsizing – a one-dimensional strategy.	375
14.2	Simultaneous improvements in net customer value components.	376

List of Tables

7.1   Dimensions on which successful and unsuccessful process management efforts differ.   187

7.2   Examples of reengineering.   204–5

10.1   Case summary.   251

12.1   Three hypothetical levels of maturity for a quality effort: choices.   321

12.2   Three hypothetical levels of maturity for a quality effort: assessments/level of performance.   322

12.3   Three hypothetical levels of maturity for a quality effort: prototypical choices.   323

12.4   Information-gathering matrix for lead and back-up teams.   325

12.5   Three hypothetical levels of maturity for a quality effort: typical choices for different levels of maturity.   326

12.6   Three hypothetical levels of maturity for a quality effort: assessment discussion and feedback.   329

12.7   Summary of the step-by-step approach to designing an assessment process.   330

13.1   The certifiable quality system elements of ISO 9000 (all are contained in ISO 9001; as indicated, some are not in ISO 9002 or ISO 9003).   348

13.2   1992–1995 winners of the European Quality Award and European Quality Prizes.   359

13.3   1996 European Quality Award and Quality Prize winners.   359

List of Contributors

Dr Marietta L. Baba
Professor and Chair
Department of Anthropology
Wayne State University
Detroit, MI 48202

Phone: (313) 577–2935
FAX: (313) 577–5958

Mr Reg Blake
British Standards Institution
8000 Towers Crescent Drive (1350)
Vienna, VA 22182

Phone: (703) 760–7828
FAX: (703) 761–2770

Dr William E. Cole
9912 McCormick Place
Knoxville, TN 37923

Phone: (423) 694–5956

Dr George S. Easton
Goizueta Business School
Emory University
1602 Mizell Drive
Atlanta, GA 30322

Phone: (404) 727–3326
FAX: (404) 727–6313
Email: george_easton@bus.emory.edu

Dr Jack Evans
Professor of Business Administration
University of North Carolina –
    Chapel Hill
Caroll Hall, Box 3490
Chapel Hill, NC 27599

Phone: (919) 962–4602
FAX: (919) 962–5539
Email: evansj.bsacdl@mhs.unc.edu

E. James and Barbara B. Flynn
Wake Forest University
Babcock Graduate School of
    Management
Post Office Box 7659, Reynolda
    Station
Winston, Salem, NC 27109–7659

Phone: (910) 759–1888 – Barbara
Phone: (910) 759–1886 – James
FAX: (910) 759–4514
Email: Jim_Flynn@mail.mba.wfu.edu
Email: Barb_Flynn@mail.mba.wfu.edu

Dr Sarah Fisher Gardial, Professor
Marketing, Logistics and
   Transportation Department
324 Stokely Management Center
University of Tennessee
Knoxville, TN 37996–0570

Phone: (423) 974–5311
FAX: (423) 974–1932
Email: gardial@UTKVX.UTK.EDU

Dr Thomas G. Greenwood
Assistant Professor
Department of Management
608 Stokely Management Center
University of Tennessee
Knoxville, TN 37996–0545

Phone: (423) 974–1739
FAX: (423) 974–3163
Email: tgreenwo@utk.edu

Mr Garry J. Huysee, Assoc. Director
Global Quality Improvement
The Procter & Gamble Company
One Procter & Gamble Plaza, 10-C
Cincinnati, OH 45202

Phone: (513) 983–9949
FAX: (513) 983–1177
Email: huysse.gj@pg.com

Jacquelyn DeMatteo Jacobs
Assistant Professor
Management Department
407 Stokely Management Center
University of Tennessee
Knoxville, TN 37996–0570

Phone: (423) 974–4844
FAX: (423) 974–3163
Email: jjacobs1@utk.edu

Dr Sherry L. Jarrell
Goizueta Business School
Emory University
1602 Mizell Drive
Atlanta, GA 30322

Phone: (404) 727–3462
FAX: (404) 727–6313
Email: sherry_jarrell@bus.emory.edu

Andrew G. Kemeny
President
Kemeny Consulting
190 Gates Avenue
Montclair, NJ 07042

Phone: (201) 783–4596
FAX: (201) 783–4790

Michael E. Kennedy
Lexmark International
Dept. A04/035–1
740 New Circle Road NW
Lexington, KY 40511

Phone: (606) 232–6637
FAX: (606) 232–3900
Email: mkennedy@lexmark.com

Sheron Kennedy
Lucent Technologies
Room C3E05
283 King George Road
Warren, NJ 07059

Phone: (908) 559-3062

Dr Kenneth E. Kirby
Associate Professor
Industrial Engineering
147 Alumni Memorial Building
University of Tennessee
Knoxville, TN 37996-0570

Phone: (423) 974-7648
FAX: (423) 974-0588
Email: kkirby@utk.edu

John J. Kirchenstein
7914 Gleason Road #1166
Knoxville, TN 37919

Phone: (423) 691-0970

Dr Mary G. Leitnaker
Associate Professor
Statistics Department
341 Stokely Management Center
University of Tennessee
Knoxville, TN 37996-0570

Phone: (423) 974-2556
FAX: (423) 974-2490
Email: mleitnaker@utk.edu

Kyle M. Lundby
Questar Data Systems Inc.
2905 West Service Road
Eagan, Minnesota 55121-2199

Phone: (612) 688-1962
FAX: (612) 688-0546
Email: klundby@questarweb.com

Dr John W. Mogab
Department of Finance and Economics
Southwest Texas State University
San Marcos, Texas 78666

Phone: (512) 245-3244
FAX: (512) 245-3089
Email: JM12@academia.swt.edu

Dr William C. Parr
Professor
Statistics Department
332 Stokely Management Center
University of Tennessee
Knoxville, TN 37996-0570

Phone: (423) 974-2556
FAX: (423) 974-2490
Email: wparr@utk.edu

Dr Michael C. Rush, Professor
Management Department
College of Business Administration
418 Stokely Management Center
University of Tennessee
Knoxville, TN 37996-0570

Phone: (423) 974-3161
FAX: (423) 974-3163
Email: mrush@utk.edu

Dr Carmen J. Trammell
Manager of Software Quality Assurance
CTI-PET Systems Inc.
810 Innovation Drive
Knoxville, TN 37932

Phone: (423) 966-0072, ext. 276
FAX: (423) 966-8955
Email: carmen.trammell@cti-pet.com

Dr Clement C. Wilson
11915 W. Fox Chase Circle
Knoxville, TN 37922

Email: clemwilson@utk.edu

Dr Robert B. Woodruff, Professor
Marketing, Logistics and
    Transportation Department
313 Stokely Management Center
University of Tennessee
Knoxville, TN 37996–0570

Phone: (423) 974–5311
FAX: (423) 974–1932

Acknowledgments

It is very easy to write the acknowledgments for this book. First and foremost, justice demands that I acknowledge the contributors. Their hard work and subject-matter expertise made this book possible. I owe them a debt of gratitude.

Rolf Janke at Blackwell Publishers originally conceived of the idea of this book. I also wish to acknowledge the leadership of Al Bruckner at Blackwell Publishers and Dick Sandretti at the American Society for Quality (ASQ). The spirit of cooperation between their two organizations made this joint publishing effort a reality.

I gratefully acknowledge the organizational skills of Tami Touchstone at the University of Tennessee. As a very capable administrative assistant, she administered the schedule and the chapters from authors through the development of this book.

This book would not have been possible without the collective efforts of the above team.

Thank you.

Michael J. Stahl

Introduction

When designing *Perspectives in Total Quality*, we needed to define the users of the book, the theme of the book, its title, and the organization of the chapters.

USERS

The book is aimed at users interested in understanding current issues in Total Quality. The book should help readers become more conversant in TQ. We expect that the primary users will be academic users, and that professors and students will be interested in using the book in courses on Total Quality. A seminar course can be organized with the chapters as readings to stimulate and focus discussion. We also anticipate that academics will use the book as a reference book and as a source book in selected research topics.

The secondary users of this book are practitioners of TQ. Thus, we expect the book to appeal to general managers, quality managers, and quality professionals interested in understanding current issues in Total Quality.

Given that the chapters were written by different authors, the chapters are somewhat independent and can be read independently. Recognizing this dual audience of academics and practitioners, in places, the book has a theoretical, and in other places, an applied flair. The book is not designed as a "how to" book.

TITLE AND THEME

Since there are many discrete topics covered in the field of TQ, we needed to decide if we should attempt to cover all the topics, or just selected issues. Since this book is not meant to be a comprehensive "how to" handbook, it is not necessary to cover all issues associated with TQ. Since we elected to cover selected major topics of interest, we chose the title of this book to be: *Perspectives in Total Quality*.

Defining the theme of the book for a topic as broad as Total Quality is a substantial task. Let us review a definition of TQ to guide the discussion.

Although there are several different definitions of TQ in the literature, it is not important here to decide which definition is best. We only need to pick one to guide our discussion for the theme of the book. "Total Quality Management is a systems approach to management that aims to continuously increase value to customers by designing and continuously improving organizational processes and systems" (Stahl, *Management*, Boston: Blackwell, 1995: 4). Such a definition covers a range of topics. Based on this definition of TQ, we grouped the chapters into four major sections.

SECTIONS

Part I concerns customers. In chapter 1 on Customer Value, "Building Advantage Through Customer Value", Woodruff and Gardial of The University of Tennessee lay out a new framework for the concept of customer focus and the pervasive role of the customer in organizations. In chapter 2, "The Emerging Academic Research on the Link Between Total Quality Management and Corporate Financial Performance: A Critical Review", Easton and Jarrell of Emory University show that the external customer is not the only stakeholder served by TQ. Across many studies, the authors demonstrate that the shareholders or private owners receive substantial financial returns from a well implemented TQ system. In chapter 3, "Academic Culture and the American Quality Movement: Linking Fundamental Research and Quality Practice," Baba of Wayne State University shows how academics and practitioners have been linked as stakeholders of TQ research and practice.

Part II concerns systems as the definition articulates a systems approach to management. In chapter 4, "High Performing Organizations," Huysse of P&G and Kennedy of Lucent Technologies describe how TQ concepts are associated with a holistic model of high performance across the entire workforce of an organization. Lundby, DeMatteo, and Rush of The University of Tennessee describe in chapter 5 the important link between "Organizational Culture and the Total Quality Organization." In chapter 6, "An Organizational Model for Implementing a Total Quality Management System," Kemeny of Kemeny Consulting articulates the importance of information to the TQ System.

Part III concerns processes as the definition of TQ articulates design and continuous improvement of organizational processes. In chapter 7, "Process Management and Process Reengineering", Parr of The University of Tennessee describes the key managerial roles of managing and reengineering processes. Leitnaker, of The University of Tennessee, describes in chapter 8, "The Role of Process Managers and Understanding Process Variation," how understanding of process variation causes managers to manage differently. Chapter 9 by Kennedy of Lexmark, and Trammell and Wilson of The University of Tennessee concerns a key process of new product development and links it to quality: "Design Quality and New Product Development." Flynn and Flynn of Iowa State, Amundson of

Arizona State, and Schroeder of University of Minnesota link product development speed and quality in chapter 10: "Product Development Speed and Quality: A New Set of Synergies?" In chapter 11, "Building the Lean Enterprise," Greenwood of the Carrier Corporation and Kirby of The University of Tennessee describe how a process approach to the entire organization yields a new form of organization referred to as the Lean Enterprise.

Part IV is about continuous improvement and assessment of TQM. In chapter 12, "Using the Baldrige Framework for Self-Assessment and Continuous Improvement," Evans of The University of North Carolina discusses the Baldrige criteria as the most commonly used assessment framework in US. In chapter 13, "Using ISO 9000 and the European Quality Award Approach to Improve Competitiveness," Kirchenstein of UT and Blake of the British Standards Institution describe ISO 9000 and the European Quality Award as commonly used continuous improvement and assessment frameworks in both Europe and the US. In chapter 14, "The Competitive Advantages of the TQM Firm," Mogab of Southwest Texas and Cole of The University of Tennessee, discuss how the TQ Firm is different in the marketplace, and how the TQ Firm is better equipped to compete than other firms. The preceding four parts discuss selected current topics in TQ.

PART

I

Customers

1 | Building Advantage Through Customer Value

Robert B. Woodruff and Sarah Fisher Gardial

Abstract

Events typically drive change in organizations' competitive strategies, and the current shift to competing on superior customer value delivery is no exception. Today's world of business imposes an intimidating array of pressures on organizations and their performance. More demanding customers, more global competition, and slower growth economies and industries have brought the era of the customer. While the logic of competing on superior customer value delivery is compelling, organizations struggle as to how to do it. This chapter discusses the operational challenge for managers to implement customer value delivery strategies and offers three major guidelines. First, re-examine how your organization conceives of customer value. That conception drives how and what managers learn about customers. Second, build your capability to learn about customer value through training in the tools suggested by the customer value concept adopted. Third, develop managers' ability to translate that learning, stemming from the language of the customer, into improvement and innovation in internal processes and products that deliver the value that customers seek.

INTRODUCTION

Today's world of business imposes an intimidating array of pressures on organizations and their performance. Customers are more demanding, intense competition threatens survival, and many economies and industries promise no more than slow long-term growth. Organizations respond in many ways, from plowing forward with the same old strategies to a frantic search for new ways to compete. Looking back on the past decade or two, experience tells us that staying with the status quo is fraught with risks. Many companies, including industry leaders such as IBM, General Motors, and Sears, experienced devastating performance erosions before realizing that the new market realities demand different strategies.

The emerging environment shifts more and more initiative to customers. In channels of distribution for many products, large intermediary customers acquired enormous buying power. Category leaders, such as Wal-mart, Home Depot, and Toys R Us, demand preferential treatment from manufacturers.

Increasingly, end users in both industrial and consumer markets demand more value as they perceive it, including but often going well beyond receiving more quality at lower prices. We have entered the era of the customer, and organizations must find new ways to respond.

TQM's missing link

Nearly two decades ago, US companies discovered total quality management (TQM). It was one answer to the increasingly successful competition coming from outside domestic markets. Organizations began the long process of learning TQM's philosophy and accompanying tools for bringing quality improvements to products and processes. To its credit, TQM asked managers to learn about customers' requirements before deciding what aspects of products and processes needed quality improvements. The philosophy was intended to merge an external focus on customers with an internal focus on quality. In practice, that merging has been slow to occur.

In a sense, TQM's major strength has been that it combined philosophy (e.g., compete on superior quality) with ways to achieve the quality imperative (the quality tools). However, most of the quality tools were aimed internally to help managers understand operations processes and discover ways to tweak them for improved outputs. In comparison, TQM offered few tools for understanding customers and for translating that learning into decisions affecting internal organizational processes. This gap is TQM's missing link. For example, too many managers thought that they already knew what customers wanted. So, they ignored the opportunity to learn directly from customers.

Gradually, we are finding out that assuming you know what customers want is not the best practice. Anecdotal evidence suggests that too often managers from different parts of an organization know different things. For instance, one of the authors participated in a discussion among one organization's managers from sales, marketing, manufacturing, and product design. This group wanted to develop a plan for increasing its percent of a key customer's purchases. The meeting started with great enthusiasm as the managers anticipated the lively discussion over ways to go after that customer. By the end of the day, the mood had turned much darker as it dawned on everyone that what they knew about the customer was inconsistent and fragmented. The group's leader was most distressed about major gaps in the group's knowledge about how the company's products were being used in customers' plants.

Empirical evidence presents a similar picture. Gaps analyses, which compare a supplier's perceptions of what their customers want with what these customers actually want, often reveal significant differences (Parasuraman, Berry, and Zeithaml 1985; Sharma and Lambert 1994). Personal experience with customers does not seem to be sufficient for truly understanding what customers want. A supplier's contact persons look at customers through biased lenses, and their often irregular and infrequent contact with customers hinders the depth and accuracy of learning about their requirements. One manager framed the problem this way, "I always ask sales people what they think their customers' key buying criteria, and they always seem confident in telling me what they are. Yet, when a new sales person takes over those same customers and I ask the same question, I often get a different answer. That bothers me a lot."

More and more companies recognize that TQM practice must include going directly to the customer to learn about requirements. In the 1980s customer satisfaction measurement (CSM) boomed as a tool for doing that (Dutka 1994; Hayes 1992). It brings "the voice of the customer" from outside to inside the organization to guide decisions on what aspects of internal processes and product quality to improve. While CSM provides important learning about customers, it is only a first step toward fulfilling TQM's customer focus initiative. CSM's largely survey methodology yields insights into *what* customers perceive as good and bad about a supplier's product and supporting services, but too often does not reveal enough about *why*. The "why" is crucial because quality initiatives must address these reasons in order to attain improvements that lead to stronger customer-determined performance.

Purpose of the chapter

TQM's promise cannot be fulfilled until organizations understand how to link internal processes to external customer value (for now, think of customer value as what customers want as a consequence of buying and/or using a supplier's product/service). In short, internal quality improvements only affect an organization's performance to the extent that they deliver superior value, compared to competitive alternatives, to customers. It is that superior value that influences customers to buy from one supplier over another, engage in positive word of mouth with others about a supplier's worth, and become more loyal to a supplier over time. In this chapter, we discuss ways to overcome TQM's missing link. Organizations must learn how to learn about customers, and CSM is only part of the answer. In the next section, we argue that current CSM practice can be improved substantially by broadening the "voice of the customer" to including learning about customer value.

The subsequent section offers a new way to think about customer value. It encourages suppliers to better understand how its products and services are helping customers accomplish what they want to have happen in their world. To compete on superior customer value delivery means becoming an expert in the customer's language, what is happening in their product-use situations, and their requirements for achieving their goals. Finally, the chapter ends by discussing ways that a supplier can better manage to compete on superior customer value delivery. Only by translating external customer learning into internal quality initiatives will the full promise of TQM be realized.

Is Current Practice the Best Practice ?

How organizations think about customer value

Perhaps in response to a growing realization that CSM is not the total answer to bringing the "voice of the customer" into organizations, more and more treatises tout the next new idea – manage toward customer value. The popular business press presents persuasive arguments for the merits of competing by creating customer value (e.g., Brand 1991; Gale 1994; Naumann 1995; Slywotsky 1996). Similarly, discussions in academic literature reach the same conclusions (e.g., Day 1990). But, what exactly is customer value, and is it really a different idea than customer satisfaction? Further, do advocates of managing toward customer value offer anything new about how organizations should learn about customers? Let's start with the first question.

Everyone seems to know, intuitively, what customer value is, but the definitions that appear in print suggest otherwise. Think about the following statements (Woodruff 1997, p. 141):

> Value is the consumer's overall assessment of the utility of a product based on perceptions of what is received and what is given. (Zeithaml 1988, p. 14)

> Value in business markets (is) the perceived worth in monetary units of the set of economic, technical, service and social benefits received by a customer firm in exchange for the price paid for a product, taking into consideration the available suppliers' offerings and prices. (Anderson, Jain, and Chintagunta 1993, p. 5)

> Customer value is market perceived quality adjusted for the relative price of your product. (Gale 1994, p. xiv)

> By customer value, we mean the *emotional bond* established between a customer and a producer after the customer has used a salient product or service produced by that supplier and found the product to provide an added value. (Butz and Goodstein 1996, p. 63)

Customer value apparently is a lot of things – utility, monetary worth, quality adjusted for relative price, and even an emotional bond. These definitions are at best confusing, and at worst inconsistent. For example, perceived monetary worth and emotional bond do not seem to refer to the same phenomenon at all. It may be better to look beyond what people say customer value is to how organizations go about measuring customer value in practice. In other words, to find out what customer value really means to managers, look at an organization's research. It is the analysis of these data that influence how customer value gets translated into a supplier's value delivery decisions.

As mentioned above, many organizations have turned to customer satisfaction research to solicit the voice of the customer. Interestingly, these tools assume a particular way of looking at customer value consistent with multi-attribute theory. Essentially, this theory says that customers see products as bundles of attributes, which are the tangible, observable characteristics of products and supporting services. For example, a customer may look at a sport cruiser boat and notice such characteristics as sleek hull design, number of engines, location of instruments and controls, and layout of the cockpit. A boat supplier's services have attributes, too, such as number of days to deliver the boat, terms of a warranty, and video tapes explaining procedures for operating the boat. Importantly, attributes reside in the product and supporting services, and CSM assumes that certain of these attributes are more likely to influence customers' purchase decisions than others.

Attributes offer one way of operationalizing customer value. This view assumes that customers see value in a supplier's product and supporting services to the extent that they possess desired attributes. These desired attributes are the so-called purchase drivers or key buying criteria, and they encourage suppliers to focus internal operations and external market strategy on creating, delivering, and communicating these attributes to customers. Typically, CSM research based on this value concept follows a three-step process. Step one identifies targeted customers. Step two finds out their desired attributes (e.g., Dutka 1994; Gale 1994; Hayes 1992). Then, step 3 relies on satisfaction surveys to measure how well (poorly) customers feel that a supplier delivers these attributes.

Do the advocates of managing toward customer value offer new ways for suppliers to learn about the value that their customers desire? For the most part, the answer is no. They suggest following standard CSM research procedures (e.g., Gale 1994). On the positive side, there are reasons for the popularity of this research. Clearly, CSM is a significant improvement over assuming that the supplier already knows what key buying criteria are.

Further, most suppliers like to know what it is about what they offer (i.e., their attributes) that customers like and do not like. While there are problems of translating from the customers' language (how they describe attributes) into the supplier's language (how it thinks about corresponding characteristics of internal processes and products), suppliers readily recognize that attribute data describe those things that they manage. For example, if customers want faster delivery time or a smaller size package, managers can improve these aspects of its offer. Finally, attributes are easy to measure with customer research. Because attributes are relatively concrete features, customers can readily talk about them, and suppliers can work toward building them into product and service designs and improvements.

Why an attribute view of value is not adequate

With these important advantages, one might think that the attribute way of conceiving of customer value is good enough for driving superior customer value delivery strategies. Unfortunately, that is not the case. It has several weaknesses. First, attribute research can only measure what customers know about. So, the results are likely to reveal only attributes that are already built into competitive offerings. That is, customers will talk about what they have seen and like (dislike) about products and services with which they are familiar. That raises two concerns. One is that competitors in an industry, if they all use attribute research, are likely to have similar understanding about customer value. Over time it will become increasingly difficult for any one competitor to gain advantage over the others through superior value delivery. Perhaps that is why we hear more and more about the parity among products and quality that exists in many of our industries.

One can argue that attribute research is better suited to helping managers make improvement decisions than to encouraging true innovation (Woodruff 1997). Since customers can only talk about existing attributes, the results are most likely going to steer a supplier toward improving selected characteristics already a part of their products and services. Customers are not likely to come up with new and innovative attributes for the supplier. At first, existing attribute improvements are likely to have significant effect on a supplier's performance. But, after a while the opportunities for the most important improvements are exhausted and diminishing returns sets in as suppliers turn to work on less important ones.

Second, attribute research offers little insight into *why* some attributes are preferred over others. This fact is a major impediment to innovation. If customers cannot tell you about new attributes, then the only way to innovate is to look elsewhere for new attributes that offer superior ways to meet customers needs. But where do ideas for new attributes originate? One source, of course, is technology innovation. If a supplier discovers how to do something new, then it can find out if customers see any value to it. However, another source is to use customer research to look behind customers current desired attributes to better understand the reasons for these desires. If you know why customers desire a particular attribute, you may be able to come up with an even better way, based on new attributes, to meet their needs, and that is what innovation is about.

Third, customers are becoming inundated with satisfaction surveys, and they are largely alike. Questionnaires ask customers to rate the performance of a supplier on the several attributes that the supplier thinks customers value. Lots of similar questionnaires asking about the same attributes become tedious to complete. Especially when the incentive for completing the surveys is not clear, customers become more and more reluctant to respond. As a result, there is a growing backlash, both by customers and in supplier organizations, about the wisdom of devoting so much resources to CSM.

For all of these reasons, the attribute way of looking at customer value may have outlived its usefulness. It was a good start toward bringing the voice of the customer into TQM practice, but the time is ripe for finding improved approaches for learning about customers. A new way of looking at customer value may stimulate the search for such new approaches. In the next section, we offer a more complete conceptual understanding as to how customers look at value. Importantly, this view of customer value is based on a deeper understanding of why customers look for certain attributes in products.

A DIFFERENT WAY TO LOOK AT CUSTOMER VALUE

Based on the above discussion, we need a different way to look at customer value; one which can overcome limitations of the commonly used attribute-based value concept. More specifically, this new way must provide two benefits. First, it must clearly capture value from the customer's perspective, not the supplier's perspective. There is no question that these two often differ, and it is imperative to make sure that value delivery initiatives are tied to what the customer wants, not what managers *think* customers want. Second, a new value concept must be one which is capable of providing strategic direction for managers. It must not only provide customer understanding, but also must help managers to prioritize initiatives and direct value delivery decisions.

The customer value hierarchy

Such a concept does exist in the form of the customer value hierarchy (see figure 1.1) (Woodruff and Gardial 1996). This hierarchy provides a

Figure 1.1   Customer value hierarchy

framework for considering the *relationship* which exists between a customer and a product/service. More specifically, it helps explain why certain product attributes or features are valued through understanding the ultimate purposes and outcomes which customers wish to experience. The hierarchy is based upon means-end theory (Gutman 1982), which was originally developed to understand how product information is stored in memory. This theory has been adapted to provide insight into value as perceived by customers.

Beginning at the bottom of the hierarchy and reading upwards, note that the hierarchy is rooted in product attributes. In fact, the hierarchy acknowledges that, at a basic level, customers do think about product and services as bundles of attributes. These are the most tangible and objective characteristics of the product. As discussed earlier, attributes are typically familiar to the supplier because they correspond to aspects of its product offered to customers. In addition, customers often can easily articulate attributes. For instance, when asked to talk about a car-buying experience, the consumer might typically mention, "anti-lock brakes" or "four-wheel drive" or "good gas mileage."

However, the customer value hierarchy tells us that these attributes aren't inherently valued in and of themselves. In fact, they are only important to the customers as means for providing "higher order" ends which they seek. In the middle of the hierarchy are consequences. These are the positive and negative experiences which happen to the customer as a result of product/service consumption. For instance, product use often results in beneficial experiences (e.g., able to stop my car in an emergency without losing control). In contrast, product use can also simultaneously result in sacrifices, represented by costs and undesired experiences (e.g., spending more than I want to spend on gas for my car).

Two characteristics clearly distinguish consequences from attributes. First, while attributes are elements of the product which the supplier creates and delivers, customers experience consequences in specific situations. Since product attributes are in the product, they are independent of use and consumption. However, consequences can only be experienced by a customer as the result of the consumption process. Second, while attributes are often relatively objective in nature (rendering them rather easy to describe, measure, and communicate), consequences are by nature more subjective. They are the user's perceptions and evaluations of experiences derived from product use and, as such, are often more difficult to describe, measure and communicate.

The distinction between attributes and consequences is significant. Managers often believe that customers desire specific product attributes. In fact, which exact attributes are bundled into a product may be irrelevant to the customer, so long as those attributes provide the benefits which are desired (or eliminate the undesired sacrifices). For instance, a diner who desires "a relaxed and comfortable experience" (a consequence) is probably not interested in the specific service attributes by which the restaurant attempts to deliver this experience, such as staff training, management policies, timing of food preparation processes in the kitchen, and the like. Similarly, consumers probably do not care whether a fast food manager adds more staff or simplifies the cash register system (attributes), so long as they do not have to wait in line very long (a consequence). In fact, consumers may not even care to evaluate these attributes, even if they could. In short, the consequences are ultimately more important and more germane to a customer's perception of value than are attributes.

At the top of the hierarchy are desired end states. Just as consequences are the outcomes facilitated by the attribute "means," in turn consequences become the "means" by which customers achieve desired ends states, the highest order "ends" which are desired and experienced by a customer. It may be helpful to think of desired end states as the customer's more long-term, abiding goals and purposes. These are commonly referred to as core *values*. Desired end states represent the core set of underlying motivations which guide the customer through a variety of situations, product decisions, and experiences. As such, they may be more indirectly linked to the consumption of any one particular product/service than are consequences. For example, a customer may want "peace of mind" when driving his or her car. In addition, peace of mind may be a key motivation for the purchase and use of other products as well.

In sum, the customer value hierarchy identifies three levels at which customers evaluate and experience products (attributes, consequences, and desired end states). As such it offers a more complete way of thinking about customer value. In essence, customer value is "a customer's perceived preference for and evaluation of those product attributes, attribute performances, and consequences arising from use that facilitate (or block) achieving the customer's goals and purposes in use situations" (Woodruff 1997, p. 142).

How customer value relates to customer satisfaction

Having defined customer value in terms of the hierarchy, a question often raised is, "What is the difference between customer value and customer satisfaction?" This question is driven by the fact that managers and organizations typically have CSM processes in place. While managers are familiar with CSM, they may not understand how it differs from customer value and its measurement. To answer this question, one must explore how customer satisfaction is defined and how it has been traditionally measured.

Satisfaction may be considered as a customer's evaluative reaction to how a particular product performed when compared to how he or she anticipated that it would perform. This view is consistent with a disconfirmation model (Oliver 1980; Woodruff, Cadotte and Jenkins 1983) which says that customers use comparison standards (e.g., expectations, performance of a competitor's product, ideal) against which to judge their product experiences. When the comparison standard is met, customers typically

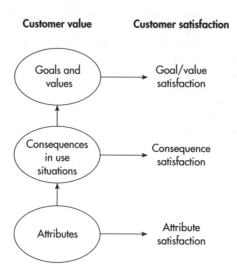

Customer value   Customer satisfaction

Figure 1.2   Customer value drives customer satisfaction

report that they are "satisfied," i.e., they got what they thought they would. Likewise, performance which is below the comparison standard results in varying degrees of dissatisfaction, while performance which exceeds the comparison standard results in increasingly satisfied or delighted customers.

Another way of looking at satisfaction is that it is *the customer's feelings about the value that they received from a particular product experience.* In contrast, customer value hierarchies exist independent of particular products or product use experiences. They *reveal what the customer desires (or doesn't desire) relative to a particular product category.* This distinction suggests that customer value tells an organization what it *should* be delivering to its customers, while customer satisfaction provides feedback which tells organizations how well customers feel that their existing offers *are* performing relative to that goal. The two are complementary and organizations should measure both. Unfortunately, most organizations only measure satisfaction and do not actively pursue information about customer value hierarchies beyond identifying attribute-based buying criteria.

Organizations traditionally measure customer satisfaction by asking customers to judge their perceived satisfaction with a list of product attributes. However, the value hierarchy clearly indicates that customers can be satisfied with a particular product at all three levels; they can evaluate their satisfaction with attributes, they can evaluate their satisfaction with the consequences which they experienced, and they can evaluate satisfaction with the extent to which the product helped them to achieve desired end states (see figure 1.2). Attribute level satisfaction alone will provide only a limited perspective on an organization's performance.

Figure 1.2 also suggests that customer value measurement (CVM) should precede and guide subsequent CSM. You have to first fully understand the way customers see value as reflected in their value hierarchies. Then, you can learn how satisfied they are with your delivery of attributes and consequences. In this way, learning about customer value drives CSM.

Customer value resides in use situations

The more one works with the customer value hierarchy, the more it becomes apparent that organizations must clearly understand the various use situations in which their product is being consumed. The benefits and costs (consequences) which accrue from a particular product are, in turn, dictated by the customer's particular use situation. In fact, the requirements of the use situation help to determine which value dimensions are important to targeted customers.

Consider the purchase of a bottle of wine. The specific value dimensions which a customer desires may vary considerably across consumption situations. In purchasing a bottle of wine for use at a family meal, the consequences which are of highest concern might be "fits within my budget," "I get a pleasant taste experience," "enjoyed by my spouse," and "convenient for me to pick up on my way home." On the other hand, purchasing a bottle of wine as a gift for one's best friend might elicit a very different set of desired consequences. In this case, "what my friend thinks of the winery," as well as "what he or she thinks of the wine's prestige, image, and rarity," might be most important. Further, this customer might have much less concern about the sacrifices associated with cost and availability. Indeed, the "costs" dominating in this situation might be associated with the risk of embarrassment or disappointment if the best friend does not like the wine.

Because the value hierarchy can be highly influenced by use situations, there may be more than one value hierarchy for a particular product, each one corresponding to a different situation. Consequently, the supplier must understand as much as possible about the various situations in which consumers are using its products to learn about these differences. Indeed, understanding use situation requirements may provide additional opportunity and insights to improve on existing value delivery strategies or even create new ones.

Customer value change

Another characteristic of customer value is that it is not static; rather, it is highly dynamic. As customers use products over time, as they experience new and possibly changing use situation requirements, and as their experience and knowledge about the product expands, it stands to reason that their value hierarchies also will evolve to accommodate and reflect these experiences and knowledge. In turn, this means that the perceived value

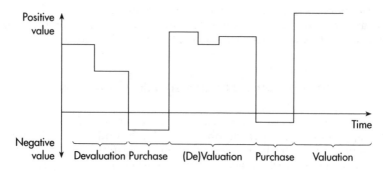

Figure 1.3 Customer value changes over time

which is delivered by a particular product may well fluctuate over time (see figure 1.3).

Changing perceptions of value, due to new use situations and occasions or other events, puts a premium on suppliers staying informed about their customers. Managers must accept that learning about customer value should be a continuous process. The objective should not be just to react to these changes as they occur, but hopefully to anticipate them so that value delivery strategies can be adjusted to meet these changing value dimensions.

While not everything will impact customers' value hierarchies, there probably are specific events or occurrences which do "trigger" some sort of significant change in the value desired by customers. Learning about when these "triggers" occur, as well as how they alter use situation requirements, should become an important managerial objective, for therein lies the key to anticipating value change (Flint, Woodruff, and Gardial 1997). For example, most auto dealers understand that a new car owner's first visit to their service department is an important "trigger" event. Not only is it the customer's first opportunity to experience the service offering, but more importantly, it is likely to elicit a different set of value dimensions than were considered during prior purchase activities. Therefore, regardless of how well value was delivered previously, the dealership is now faced with a critical opportunity to deliver (or not deliver) value in a different situation. Understanding how this new situation may trigger a different set of value requirements is critical, as the dealer may not get a second opportunity to retain their customer's maintenance business, a potentially profitable department for dealers.

Overcoming the "product constraint"

One final word about the hierarchy relates to an earlier stated objective; that the approach should provide "actionable" information for managers.

In the day-to-day chaos and urgency within which most managers live, one of the most pressing issues is often articulated as "what should I do next?" This question concerns which customer initiatives to support versus which ones to abandon. How does the customer value hierarchy help here?

We might first ask how this question gets answered when a supplier does not have an adequate understanding of customer value. In this case, managers quite likely will focus on product attributes, not just which to provide, but also how to potentially improve some and even eliminate others. When managers concentrate at this lowest level in customers' value hierarchies, they are, in effect, committing to a product-oriented approach to decisions and strategies. Often this way of thinking leads to marginal improvements in a product offer and/or to adding "bells and whistles" which may not mean much to customers. Of course, product improvements may be desirable or even necessary at times. However, such improvements are often easily matched by competitors, and in the absence of exceptional circumstances (e.g., a patent), may provide only narrow and short-lived windows of opportunity.

In contrast, when one begins to truly understand value through the customers eyes, most especially at the consequence level and above in a value hierarchy, it become clear that one of the biggest opportunities for value creation is through pursuing a relationship with your customers. Except for the relatively small percentage who are solely price driven, customers ultimately look for a supplier who they trust, who will meet their needs, who will stand by them through good and bad times, and who understands them well enough to help them achieve their ultimate goals. These are things which are provided by a relationship, not a product. Relationships require understanding the total value requirements of the customer. Ultimately, it is through such relationships that a supplier truly bonds with its customers and, in turn, retains them over time. Customer retention must be a high priority goal for any organization which is competing in today's increasingly competitive markets.

IMPROVING CAPABILITY TO COMPETE ON CUSTOMER VALUE

Competing on superior customer value delivery requires bringing the "full voice of the customer" into organization value delivery decisions. But what does that entail? Figure 1.4 describes a process with three major activities. First, an organization should adopt a shared concept of customer value. How managers conceive of customer value influences the entire rest of the process. In previous sections, for example, we showed how the customer value hierarchy concept leads to different learning about customers than does the attribute-based concept.

The second step, customer value learning, requires committing time, effort, and resources to understanding how targeted customers see value.

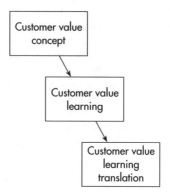

Figure 1.4   Applying customer value learning

Using the customer value hierarchy concept, that means learning about the consequences that customers desire, their linkages to product attributes and to goals and values that these customers want to achieve. For instance, a boat manufacturer should not be content with knowing that users think the location of the steering wheel, controls, and instruments is important when driving the boat. It must learn about what happens during actual driving experiences to understand how the location influences the ease with which the user controls the boat and his/her confidence in being able to handle specific situations, such as docking the boat in a wind. Such enhanced customer learning facilitates finding both improvement and innovation opportunities.

The third step, translating customer value learning into actions, involves identifying those internal processes that are essential to delivering the value that these customers desire. In addition, translation means determining the requirements for these processes so that the resulting value delivery satisfies customers. Suppose a supplier's targeted customers, as a condition for building a long-term relationship, want the supplier to "make them look good with their customers." Further, the supplier discovers that "making them look good" can be done by assisting them in finding new product opportunities for their customers downstream. To deliver this value, the supplier must identify internal processes capable of searching for new opportunities with downstream customers, which may involve both market opportunity analysis and new product design capabilities. Then implementation requires actually reorienting the supplier's internal market opportunity analysis and new product design processes to find specific new opportunities.

In the next sections, we suggest ways that an organization may implement this process. We consider both research requirements and organizational acceptance needed to enhance customer value learning and translation capabilities.

Allocating time and resources to customer value learning

An organization's capability to learn about customer value, itself, can be a source of competitive advantage (Burns and Woodruff 1992). With too many organizations today concentrating on the multi-attribute notion of customer value, parity on this capability prevails. However, by adopting new and more complete views of customer value, such as the customer value hierarchy, some organizations will break away from the status quo and expand their customer-learning capabilities. As we argued earlier, for example, learning about consequences desired by customers may lead to more innovation.

Every organization has some process in place for learning about their customers. You could not stay in business for long without some understanding of what customers want. So, start by reviewing and evaluating this existing process. One critical characteristic to consider is use of research. Past experience suggests that for most organizations, research should play an important role. As we argued earlier, evidence indicates that managers who rely primarily on experience are not good at knowing their customers. But what kinds of customer research are needed?

Need for balance between qualitative and quantitative research

CSM, as a way to bring the voice of the customer into the organization, places considerable emphasis on quantitative measurement. Consequently, research tends to be allocated to conducting periodic surveys of customers to find out what they feel about the supplier's performance. These surveys provide quantitative data that allow computing scores which can then be compared to each other and over time. For example, a multi-store automobile dealer may use satisfaction surveys to compare customer-perceived performance across its stores. Management may also look for trends in satisfaction scores across different seasons of the year and across successive years. Such analyses may be very helpful in picking out the high and low performing stores for further attention.

The ability of a CSM survey to capture those customer perceptions and feelings that drive their behavior depends heavily on whether satisfaction scores correspond to the key customer value dimensions. Too often, organizations do not allocate enough resources to learning what these dimensions are prior to designing their satisfaction questionnaires. As we argued earlier, learning about key buying criteria in the form of desired attributes does not go far enough in understanding what customers value. The customer value hierarchy suggests that more up front research is needed to learn about the consequences, goals and values that customers desire from using a supplier's products and supporting services. Further, this expanded learning should be reflected in satisfaction questionnaires (recall figure 1.2). For example, at least some items in a satisfaction questionnaire should be devoted to asking customers to rate supplier performance in delivering consequence value (e.g., trust, confidence, etc.).

The issue is one of balance. How much of an organization's customer value learning should come from qualitative research that explores customer value versus the amount coming from quantitative research such as CSM? To address this question, an organization must evaluate its own information processes for learning about customers, and then benchmark it against a standard. But, what should that standard be?

Woodruff and Gardial (1996) lay out a customer value determination process that can assist in this evaluation. Importantly, their process incorporates both qualitative research to learn about customer value and quantitative research to learn about customers' satisfaction with a supplier's value delivery. More specifically, the first customer value determination activity, identifying customer value dimensions (i.e., the attributes, consequences and goals and values), depends entirely on qualitative research. The next activity of determining strategically important value dimensions relies in part on qualitative research from the previous activity. It may also use quantitative importance scaling techniques. The third activity, which is customer satisfaction measurement, uses quantitative research to find out what customers feel are a supplier's strengths (i.e., those value dimensions on which the supplier performs very high, particularly relative to competitors) and weaknesses (i.e., those value dimensions where the suppliers performs poorly). Finally, the process shifts back to follow-up qualitative research (after satisfaction survey research) to find out why customers perceive the suppliers strengths and weaknesses as they do. Benchmarking current customer satisfaction measurement practice against the customer value determination process indicates that many organizations ought to rethink the balance of their qualitative versus quantitative customer research in favor of shifting more resources to the former.

Committing to customer value learning

Balancing kinds of research raises a much larger issue, and that concerns an organization's level of commitment to customer value learning in general. Probably most organizations expect managers to *know* about customers, but are they rewarded for and given the time to *learn* about customers? We often hear managers say something like, "I don't have time for all that research," or "just tell me what customers want in a one-page memo, and let me get on with my work." These kinds of comments indicate lack of commitment to customer value learning. You cannot fully understand your customer's world without spending time and effort in a learning mode.

How can organizations build commitment to customer value learning? Becoming a learning organization usually involves changing organizational culture. Managers have to believe that customer value learning leads to improved performance, and they have to be rewarded for that learning. While discussing all that may be involved in changing organizational culture is beyond the scope of this chapter, we offer two observations. First, build some success stories where customer value learning led to improved or innovative actions. Early successes get attention and encourage others to try the same thing. For example, in one company a division implemented the customer value determination process for one product, and gained important new insights into customer value. The results influenced subsequent strategic planning. Later, another division in the same company, upon hearing of the first division's success, requested similar research to assist in their planning. We have seen this same pattern in other companies as well. You can make the old saying, "success breeds success," work for your organization.

Second, customer value learning does not just happen naturally. Rather, it happens as the result of implementing a well-designed learning process, such as the customer value determination process (Woodruff and Gardial 1996). People need training to do that. Some of that training should be devoted to ensuring an organization-wide adoption of a common concept of customer value. As we said before, how you think about customer value definitely influences what you look for when learning about customers. For example, we have already seen how a multi-attribute view of customer value leads to different kinds of learning than does a customer value hierarchy concept. We advocate the latter concept, but that means training those in the organization to understand what the customer value hierarchy says about customers and why it drives superior learning capability.

Once people become intrigued with the potential for new insights into customers offered by the customer value hierarchy, they likely will want to know more about how to acquire those insights. That opens the door for training to use such tools as interviewing customers, analyzing customer transcripts, designing satisfaction surveys, and conducting follow-up focus groups. While it may seem that such training should be reserved for research personnel, often that is not the case. Those who are expected to use the information from a customer value learning process are more likely to do so if they understand where that information is coming from. Also, some organizations want to involve all customer contact persons in the process, not just researchers. For instance, one organization wants to explore using its sales persons to do customer value interviewing in order to both save on cost and to get more frequent feedback from customers.

Finally, the language of customers, such as how they describe consequences and use situations, quite likely is not close to the language of the supplier, which is concerned with its internal operations. Consequently, training is needed to help managers become better at translating customer value learning, based on the language of the customer, into customer value delivery actions. There are some translation tools available, such as brainstorming, customer scenario analysis, quality function deployment, and market research tests of alternative actions. They help to facilitate the largely creative process of finding ways to improve and innovate on current customer value delivery processes and offerings.

Managing the pace of change

It takes time to reorient managers from a primary focus on internal processes to a more balanced orientation toward both external customers and the internal value delivery processes needed to satisfy them. Change must begin with customer value learning. We advocate starting by inventorying what your organizational unit knows about its customers. What do you know for sure? What evidence supports what you know? Equally importantly, ask what you do not know. For example, if your organization has been surveying customers for satisfaction, you may know a lot about how they feel about performance on selected attributes. But, do you understand what consequences your customers are trying to achieve by using your products and services in their use situations? The customer value hierarchy concept can help you frame the right questions to ask. Early successes are most likely to come by focusing on these questions.

Sometimes new insights into customers may come from using new techniques to re-analyze data that you already have. For example, suppose an organization has used focus group research in the past to learn about attributes that drive customers' purchases. Often the transcripts of these interviews will contain data about consequences as well. Customers talk about what is going on in their world even when asked about attributes they look for in a product and seller. You can re-examine these transcripts, using techniques guided by the customer value hierarchy concept, to look beyond attributes to the consequences that customers seek. Similarly, other data, such as customer complaints and salesperson call reports, may be reanalyzed for insights into customer value.

In general, you do not have to scrap your organization's old ways of learning about customer value entirely in order to become better. Change can come gradually as new ways to learn are overlaid on what the organization considers accepted practice. Incremental improvement based on learning new insights may be more feasible than trying to do it all at once.

SUMMARY

Events usually drive change in organizations, and the shift to competing on superior customer value delivery is no exception. More demanding customers, more global competition, and slower growth economies and industries provide more than enough incentive for today's organizations to focus more strategic attention outward on customers. We see less questioning by managers as to whether or not to compete this way, and much more concern for how to do it. In this chapter, we offered three major guidelines for improving an organization's ability to consistently compete on superior customer value delivery. First, re-examine how your organization conceives of customer value. Current practice of looking for attribute-based purchase drivers or buying criteria is not adequate. The customer value hierarchy provides a more complete and customer-oriented view of how customers see value. They want to experience consequences that help them achieve their goals and purposes. Suppliers must learn how to help provide those experiences, not just offer attributes.

Second, build your capability to learn about customer value through training in the tools suggested by the customer value hierarchy. We advocate adopting the customer value determination process and its techniques and procedures. Training should extend beyond research personnel to include the intended users of the customer value learning.

Finally, develop managers' ability to translate that learning, stemming from the language of the customer, into improvement and innovation in internal processes and products that deliver the value that customers seek. In part, managers must become fluent in the language of the customer. Only then will they become more comfortable engaging in the customer value learning process. Next, managers can focus on acquiring expertise in using translation tools to convert that language into actions leading to superior customer value delivery. It is these actions that create improved performance.

References

Anderson, James C., Diput C. Jain, Arol Pradeepk K. Chintagunta (1993), "Customer Value Assessment in Business Markets: A State-of-Practice Study," *Journal of Business to Business Marketing*, 1 (No. 1), 3–30.

Brand, William A. (1991), *Creating Value for Customers*. New York: John Wiley & Sons.

Burns, Mary Jane and Robert B. Woodruff (1992), "Delivering Value to Consumers: Implications for Strategy Development and Implementation," in Chris T. Allen et al., eds, *Marketing Theory and Applications*. Chicago: American Marketing Association, 209–16.

Butz, Howard E., Jr. and Leonard D. Goodstein (1996), "Measuring Customer Value: Gaining the Strategic Advantage," *Organizational Dynamics*, 24 (Winter), 63–77.

Day, George S. (1990), *Market Driven Strategy: Processes for Creating Value*. New York: The Free Press.

Dutka, Alan (1994), *AMA Handbook for Customer Satisfaction*. Lincolnwood, IL: NTC Business Books.

Flint, Daniel J., Robert B. Woodruff, and Sarah Fisher Gardial (1997), "Customer Value Change in Industrial Marketing Relationships: A Call for New Strategies and Research," *Industrial Marketing Management*, 26 (March), 163–75.

Gale, Bradley T. (1994), *Managing Customer Value*. New York: The Free Press.

Gutman, Jonathan (1982), "A Means-End Chain Model Based on Consumer Categorization Processes," *Journal of Marketing*, 46 (Spring), 66–72.

Hayes, Bob E. (1992), *Measuring Customer Satisfaction*. Milwaukee, WI: ASQC Quality Press.

Naumann, Earl (1995), *Creating Customer Value*. Cincinnati, OH: Thompson Executive Press.

Parasuraman, A., Leonard A. Berry, and Valarie Ziethaml (1985), "A Conceptual Model of Service Quality and Its Implications for Future Research," *Journal of Marketing*, 49 (Fall), 41–50.

Oliver, Richard L. (1980), "A Cognitive Model of the Antecedents and Consequences of Satisfaction Decisions," *Journal of Marketing Research*, 17 (November),
pp. 460–9.

Sharma, Arun and Douglas M. Lambert (1994), "How Accurate Are Salespersons'
Perceptions of their Customers?" *Industrial Marketing Management*, 23, 357–65.

Slywotzky, Adrian J. (1996), *Value Migration*. Boston, MA: Harvard Business School
Press.

Woodruff, Robert B. (1997), "Customer Value: The Next Source for Competitive
Advantage," *Journal of the Academy of Marketing Science*, 25 (Spring), 139–53.

——, Ernest R. Cadotte, and Roger L. Jenkins (1983), "Model Consumer Satisfaction Processes Using Experience-Based Norms," *Journal of Marketing Research*,
20 (August), 296–304.

—— and Sarah Fisher Gardial (1996), *Know Your Customer: New Approaches to
Customer Value and Satisfaction*. Cambridge, MA: Blackwell Publishers.

Zeithaml, Valarie A. (1988), "Consumer Perceptions of Price, Quality, and Value:
A Means-End Model and Synthesis of Evidence," *Journal of Marketing*, 52 (July),
2–22.

2

The Emerging Academic Research on the Link between Total Quality Management and Corporate Financial Performance: A Critical Review

George S. Easton and Sherry L. Jarrell

Abstract

This chapter reviews the emerging research on the link between Total Quality Management (TQM) and corporate financial performance. While there are an increasing number of academic studies on TQM, few studies focus on empirical assessment of TOM's impact using externally available financial data. We discuss some of the key research issues involved in developing credible evidence about the financial impact of TQM and provide in-depth review of nine academic studies in the context of these issues. Three other studies are also briefly reviewed. Overall, the vast majority of the studies show positive impact associated with TQM. However, many of the studies have potentially serious methodological limitations.

INTRODUCTION

Total Quality Management (TQM) has been one of the most significant management "movements" in the US during the past 15 years and perhaps one of the most significant management movements since "management" became an identified professional activity. The TQM movement began in the US in the early 1980s, primarily in manufacturing companies that were facing severe competitive pressure, most notably from Japan. TQM, in fact, began largely as an attempt by US companies to implement quality- and customer-focused management systems comparable in character to Japanese Total Quality Control (TQC).[1] TQM has been called a fad by many (e.g., see Jacob 1993). However, if TQM is a fad, it is one of the longest and most significant fads ever.

While the term TQM appears to be falling somewhat out of fashion, quality management continues to evolve and is spawning related approaches and sub-movements. For example, certification with respect to the ISO 9000 standards currently represents a major movement in US industry. Other approaches that are related to TQM, typically emphasizing one or more of its aspects, include "time-based competition," "high performance work practices," "supply-chain management," "world-class manufacturing," and "reengineering." It should be noted that proponents of related approaches (especially consultants) frequently attempt to distinguish the approaches they advocate by denying their origins in the quality management movement of the 1980s and by misdefining and discrediting TQM. For example, Hammer and Champy (1993) devote a chapter to describing how reengineering is different from and vastly superior to TQM. At the same time, however, most of the examples of reengineering provided in the book are from companies that were actively involved in either TQM or Japanese TQC at the time (Gadd and Oakland 1996) and, in fact, these reengineering efforts occurred as a part of these companies' overall improvement efforts under the umbrella of their quality management systems. In an interview conducted in conjunction with the study by Easton and Jarrell (1998) discussed below, the senior quality executive of one of the companies frequently cited by reengineering proponents said: "Process reengineering is just process management. Nothing new."

As the above discussion implies, it is useful to briefly discuss the key characteristics of TQM. While a complete definition of TQM is clearly beyond the scope of this Chapter, some of the most important characteristics include (Jarrell and Easton 1997; Easton and Jarrell 1998):

- Emphasis on the concept of "process" as a fundamental building block of the organization with a resulting emphasis on process definition, process management, and process improvement.
- Widespread organizational focus on quality improvement, cycle-time reduction, and waste (cost) reduction. Adoption of a prevention focus.
- Efforts to apply the process concept and focus on improvement (quality improvement, cycle-time reduction, and waste reduction) throughout the company, including to areas outside of production such as product development and business support processes.
- Emphasis on customer focus, including: (1) emphasis on customer requirements and customer satisfaction to define product and service quality ("customer-defined quality"); (2) emphasis on customer service (lead-time reduction, on-time delivery, field support, technical support, etc.); (3) integration of customer information into the management and improvement systems – particularly into the new product development process and the production and service quality control and improvement processes; (4) efforts to become integrated with customers as appropriate (often called "partnering"), such as joint improvement teams, participation in the customer's new product development processes, or involving customers in the company's own internal processes, such as planning, new product development, R&D, or technology forecasting.
- Emphasis on the deployment of systematic fact-based decision making driven by objective data and information ("management-by-fact").

- Widespread employee involvement in improvement (quality, cycle-time, and waste), usually through teams. Emphasis on employee development through training.
- Explicit emphasis on cross-functional management, including cross-functional improvement as well as cross-functional involvement in key processes, such as new product development.
- Emphasis on supplier quality and service, supplier improvement, and supplier involvement and integration (supplier partnerships), such as joint quality improvement, and participation in new product development.
- Recognition of TQM as a critical competitive strategy and, thus, as a primary concern of all levels of management, including senior management. The role of senior management in providing leadership for the development and deployment of TQM is a natural consequence of recognition of TQM as a (perhaps the) critical competitive strategy.

These characteristics of TQM are not independent. Much of the power of TQM results from synergies that occur from the integration of multiple principles and approaches. This has been long recognized in Japanese TQC and among thoughtful quality management pioneers and practitioners in the US. For example, the employee involvement approaches of Japanese TQC, specifically QC Circles, were developed and became an integral part of Japanese TQC because of their synergistic relationship to the technical issues of process control and improvement. The importance of such synergy appears to be a recently emerging theme in the academic literature. For example, one of the key findings in Lawler, Mohrman, and Ledford (1995) is "[o]verall, the more organizations use TQM practices, the more positive results they get from their EI [Employee Involvement] efforts." This synergy with employee participation was pointed out in Cole, Bacdayan, and White (1993), which discusses evidence in an unpublished study by Levine and Kruse (1990) that found that a focus on quality improvement was the most consistent correlate with the success of employee involvement programs. Snell and Dean (1992) argue that changes in human resource practices are necessary in order for "integrated manufacturing" (defined to be an integration of advanced manufacturing technology, TQM, and just-in-time) to realize its full potential. The potential importance of such interactions has research implications, as further discussed below.

There is considerable controversy concerning whether or not TQM has any tangible impact on firm performance. While there has been much discussion, particularly in the popular business press, there has been very little actual research which adequately addresses this question. Most of the existing research focuses primarily on the impact of TQM practices on internal performance measures or on manager perceptions of TQM's overall impact. There is considerably less research that focuses on the impact of TQM on corporate financial performance. In this chapter, we review the emerging literature on the link between TQM and financial performance.

RESEARCH ISSUES

Research into the impact of management practices on financial performance, particularly the impact of complex management practices, is generally a difficult undertaking. This is particularly true in the case of TQM,
for the reasons discussed below, but it is also true of other management
practices (for similar reasons). For example, there has been some discussion
in the strategic planning literature concerning both the research issues involved in assessing the financial impact of strategic planning and limitations
in existing studies that has been helpful in framing the research issues
described below (e.g., Armstrong 1982; Pearce, Freeman, and Robinson 1987).
    Assessment of the impact of TQM on corporate performance requires
assessment of whether or not (or at least the extent to which) a firm has
implemented TQM as well as an assessment of its impact on financial performance. Evidence concerning the impact of TQM is then developed by
correlating implementation with financial performance. Thus, the research
issues fall into two major categories: (1) issues involving the assessment of
the extent to which TQM has been implemented and (2) issues involving
the measurement of financial impact. We discuss the research issues in
each of these areas below.

Issues relating to assessing the extent of
TQM implementation

Accurate assessment of whether or not a firm has implemented TQM or
the extent to which TQM has been deployed is very important in any study
which claims to assess the impact of TQM on corporate performance. It is
absolutely critical that firms in a sample of TQM firms under study have
actually implemented TQM and have deployed management system changes
of sufficient scope that they can plausibly affect overall corporate performance. When studies are based on samples that include a large percentage
of firms that have not really deployed TQM systems, the impact of TQM is
obviously obscured. The non-TQM firms may "dilute" the effects of TQM
so that no significant associations are observed. Even if statistically significant
positive associations are observed, when the link between the sample selection approaches and actual deployment of TQM is weak, there is increased
plausibility that such results are actually due to correlation of the sample
selection approach with other (non-TQM) factors that are associated with
improved financial performance. Furthermore, in observational studies it
is always difficult to develop credible evidence concerning both existence
of causal relationships and the possible direction of causation; therefore, a
weak link between the sample selection approach and the deployment of
TQM makes development of credible evidence of causal associations even
more difficult.

As discussed above, we believe that the potential for TQM to impact corporate performance depends on the interactions or synergies between the various dimensions of TQM. We conjecture that in order for TQM to plausibly have major impact on corporate performance, a TQM system must reach a "critical mass" in terms of deployment of the various TQM dimensions (e.g., employee involvement, process control, customer focus, metrics and measurement, leadership, etc.) and in terms of the overall level of coherence and integration of the management system. If this conjecture is true, it has some important implications concerning selection of samples of TQM firms and for studies based on such samples.

In particular, in part because the effects of the components of TQM are not additive, firms that are really implementing TQM are sparse. Thus, the typical sample of firms consists largely of firms that are not seriously implementing TQM, are only in the very early stages of deployment, or have only developed one or two approaches (e.g., statistical process control (SPC) or participative management). There would be far fewer firms that have achieved the synergy between approaches necessary for the effects of TQM to "kick in" than it would appear by examining the prevalence of specific practices one at a time. The recent recognition in the literature of an apparent interaction between employee involvement and quality improvement systems discussed above provides an example of such synergy and its impact on results. Neither employee involvement approaches nor technical quality approaches (e.g., SPC) appear to be particularly effective by themselves. Consequently, studies based on samples largely consisting of firms that are immature on both dimensions or have achieved some level of maturity on only one dimension are unlikely to provide evidence concerning the real impact of the integration of quality improvement, technical quality approaches (e.g., basic statistical methods and SPC), and quality-focused employee involvement.

To somewhat overstate the point, we cannot examine the impact of TQM by studying variation in firms that are not really doing TQM. This becomes particularly problematic in terms of constructing a sample if, as we believe, the population of firms that have seriously implemented TQM, as opposed to merely providing it with lip service and limited experimentation with some of its dimensions, is sparse. If there are relatively few such firms, then samples drawn from particular regions or industries are likely to contain few real TQM firms.

Sample selection approaches

There are basically four approaches taken in the literature to assess deployment of TQM. They are:

1 Accept the company's public "announcements" of TQM (e.g., in press releases or newspaper articles) as evidence that the company has implemented TQM.

2 Use of survey instruments with extent of deployment determined by
   an index calculated from manager perceptions of the use of specific
   practices or based on overall manager perceptions of the extent of
   deployment.
3 Use of third-party assessment (such as quality awards) to indicate
   implementation of TQM.
4 Use of in-depth interview approaches with assessment of the extent
   of TQM deployment based on critical evaluation of the interview
   data by the researchers.

Public announcements. Sample selection based largely on public announcements concerning TQM are unlikely to provide credible samples because
of the inaccuracy of the statements and the potential for other biases.
Interview and case-based research (e.g., Easton 1993; Jarrell and Easton
1997; Easton and Jarrell 1998) indicate that many firms claiming to have
implemented TQM actually have made either no substantive changes in
their management practices or have implemented only one or two of the
broad set of practices that comprise TQM. This may occur because the
large amount of attention given to TQM by the business press, particularly
in the years around 1990, encouraged some managers to exaggerate their
involvement in TQM. Further, there was, and continues to be, much confusion about what TQM actually is and many managers legitimately
misperceive their quality-related activities. For example, many managers
believe that the ISO 9002 standard defines a TQM system when, in fact, it
defines a product or service production level quality assurance system
which is only a small portion of a full TQM system as defined, for example,
by the Baldrige Award Criteria (Reimann and Hertz 1996). In addition,
there is a natural tendency for the managers of companies that are ex-
periencing financial success to believe that this success is evidence of the
advanced state of their management systems ("It is just good management. We have always been focused on quality"). These kinds of issues
have been pointed out by many authors (e.g., Jarrell and Easton 1997;
Easton and Jarrell 1998; Anderson, Daly, and Johnson 1995; Reed, Lemak,
and Montgomery 1996).

Surveys. A growing number of studies use surveys of managers to assess
the deployment of TQM. There are numerous issues with respect to conducting high quality survey-based research (e.g., pre-testing, validity, reliability, etc.) that will not be addressed here. The issues we address have to do
with the ability of survey-based research to reliably assess the extent of
deployment of TQM.

In many survey-based studies, the firms to which surveys are sent are
either a random sample or a complete population within a region or
industry. From a methodological point of view, this type of sampling is
positive because it eliminates any potential bias due to self-announcement.
However, since most of these studies have relatively low response rates
(around 25 percent), there remains the possibility of bias due to non-
response associated with a lack of results or poor financial performance.

Further, if the total percentage of firms that are really doing TQM is small, such an approach to sampling can be problematic because of the small number of real TQM firms that are expected to be selected into the sample. The results of such studies, therefore, would have little to do with the impact of TQM.

Another problem with typical survey approaches is that they are based on manager perceptions and are generally undertaken without a significant effort to assess the basis for those perceptions. In-depth interview research and case study and audit experience indicate that manager perceptions frequently do not align with reality (Easton 1993; Easton and Jarrell 1997). That this is a frequent occurrence with respect to TQM is not particularly surprising since, as is well documented in the trade press, deploying more mature TQM systems requires changing many of the managers' fundamental assumptions concerning management and decision-making. Many managers do not have a "benchmark" for what a well-developed TQM system is, but rather rely on often limited exposure to the popular business press' writing about TQM. What survey-based research tends to uncover are patterns and relationships in the *perceptions* of the managers surveyed. We argue that it is not clear that this is an adequate basis for assessing the deployment of TQM in an organization. Specifically, much survey-based research implicitly assumes that the expertise necessary to assess the extent, deployment, and development of TQM exists widely among managers in industry and, in particular, widely among the managers surveyed. There is considerable (non-rigorous) evidence against this assumption. For example, the reported difficulty many managers have understanding the Baldrige Award Criteria is a criticism that has been leveled against the award. Many companies have had considerable difficulty deploying internal TQM system assessment (most commonly based on the Baldrige Award Criteria) and typically rely on trained and experienced assessors.

In addition, most surveys, even very lengthy ones, are superficial and generally lack operational definition of the terms used in the surveys.[2] For example, in Lawler, Mohrman, and Ledford (1995), questions used to assess adoption of TQM include:

- "About what percentage of employees in your corporation are covered by a Total Quality Control (TQC), Total Quality Management (TQM), or similar effort?"
- "In what year did TQM begin in your corporation?"
- "The following practices are often thought to improve quality levels. About how many employees work in units that use the following practices?" The question is followed by a list of 13 practices that are rated on a seven-point scale corresponding to 0 percent, 1–20 percent, 21–40 percent, 41–60 percent, 61–80 percent, 81–99 percent, and 100 percent. Practices listed include "quality improvement teams," "quality councils," "customer satisfaction monitoring," and "just-in-time deliveries."

All of these questions are superficial and have great ambiguity with respect to their operational definitions. The first presumes knowledge of and a reasonable degree of consensus about what constitutes a TQM system. Lawler, Mohrman, and Ledford (1995) report that, in 1993, 76 percent of the 279 firms that responded to the questionnaire sent to 985 of the Fortune 1,000 firms indicated that they had a TQM program and the average percent of employees covered was 50 percent. In our view, such high survey results are not credible. Rather than provide evidence of serious efforts to deploy TQM, these survey results are more likely to indicate over-optimism, mis-understanding about what constitutes a TQM system, or response bias due to a desire to give the "right" answers to the questions.

The second question listed above presumes that the start date of deployment of a TQM system is unambiguous. As is discussed by Easton and Jarrell (1997, 1998), the start date of deployment of TQM is far from unambiguous, frequently occurring after a period of several years of limited and uncoordinated experimentation with various specific approaches (e.g., quality improvement teams). In large companies, TQM often develops in only one division, frequently because of pressure from a key customer. If the start of TQM corresponds to the first use of any TQM-related approach (e.g., teams or SPC), then, especially for large companies, the start date is virtually meaningless as one or more of these methods typically has been used in one or more areas of the company for many years.

Similar ambiguities apply to the rating of the specific practices. For example, what constitutes a "quality improvement team" or a "quality council?" It is virtually impossible to find an organization where multiple groups of people are not actively working on some sort of quality improve-ment activities (e.g., trouble shooting in response to a complaint by a major customer). This kind of activity is quite different from the widespread deployment of systematic and fact-based improvement efforts that are a key component of TQM. Further, what is "customer satisfaction monitor-ing?" Non-TQM firms typically make great effort to keep major customers happy and often have a lot of management and workforce resources devoted to responding to those customers' requirements or complaints and in "fighting fires" associated with delivering product or service to those customers.

The tremendous variation in the meaning ascribed to common termino-logy in different companies makes it very difficult to write non-superficial questionnaires that are effective in multiple organizations. For example, Easton and Jarrell (1998) found that, among companies that indicated that JIT was an important part of their TQM system, the term was used to mean only just-in-time deliveries by the company's suppliers, only just-in-time deliveries to customers ("we built a warehouse near our biggest cus-tomer"), only just-in-time production methods, such as work cells and set-up time reduction, or any combination of the three. Thus, how the practice "just-in-time deliveries" listed in the Lawler, Mohrman, and Ledford (1995) survey is generally interpreted (from suppliers or to customers) and its relationship to deployment of real TQM is unclear. Finally, it should be noted that most companies do not have (readily available, and frequently not at all) the data required for objective answers to questions about percent of involvement in the various practices listed. Thus, at best the responses represent intuitive assessment by the respondent.

The tendency to try to give the "right answers" to questionnaires and interviewers is well known. Since the "good" responses are often obvious in questionnaires, this represents another source of bias. Note that the "set-up" question to the list of practices quoted above clearly indicates that these practices are generally thought to be "good" and this is likely to contribute to bias in the responses.

In the interviews conducted in conjunction with the study by Easton and Jarrell (1998), a tendency for many managers to exaggerate their TQM programs was repeatedly observed. This tendency did not appear to be based on any intent to deceive. Rather, it appeared to be a result of enthusiasm, optimism, and a focus on the future. Specifically, many managers reported practices that were deployed in only a small part of the company as though they were widely deployed, practices that had only just been deployed as though they had been deployed for a considerable period, and practices that were only planned as though deployment had already begun. These exaggerations generally appeared to be almost totally inadvertent and were uncovered through specific questions about the deployment of the approaches and the factual (as versus interpretive) basis for the statements made. In addition, it appears that the rhetoric changes in organizations before the reality changes (e.g., see Zbaracki 1994) and that this may well be a normal (or even required) part of a significant cultural change. It is reasonable to assume that this phenomenon also causes differences between reality and questionnaire or interview responses.

In summary, then, we believe that it is difficult to explore management issues of any subtlety using typical questionnaire-based approaches and that, as a result, most questionnaire-based research examines comparatively superficial issues. This appears to us to be particularly true when studying a phenomenon such as TQM. We believe that few companies are actually seriously implementing TQM. Thus, we expect that the samples on which much of the survey-based research about TQM is based actually contain few firms that are really implementing TQM. Thus, the results of these studies primarily reflect characteristics and results of non-TQM firms.

Third-party assessments. The third approach to sample selection is to rely on evidence from third-party assessment, such as the winning of quality awards. This approach is appealing because of its apparent objectivity. It is a useful approach, as is discussed in the review of the research based on quality awards below. This approach would be particularly appealing when: (1) what is rated is the extent of deployment of TQM (rather than just quality control); (2) the rating organization is independent and does not otherwise influence the outcomes of the evaluated organization; (3) the basis for rating does not include financial performance; (4) the evaluation methodology is uniform and thorough; (5) the evaluation is either of the whole company or at least the majority of the company, so that the possibility of impact on overall financial performance is plausible; and (6) evaluation has occurred for a large enough number of companies spanning a reasonable number of industries.

Unfortunately, no third-party evaluations exist that meet all of these criteria. Most awards (i.e., supplier awards and ISO 9000 registration) focus primarily or, in many cases, exclusively on quality control issues. Most awards are also based on specific sites or even on single production lines. Thus, the awards represent evaluation of only a small part of the company and its operations. In contrast, the data used to evaluate the impact on financial performance are usually available only at the level of the entire firm. There is also tremendous variation in the criteria of different awards, particularly awards given to suppliers by customers. Lack of variation in the criteria and the large number of companies that have been evaluated is a strength of ISO 9000 registration. Overall, the Malcolm Baldrige Award meets the criteria the best. Specifically, the Malcolm Baldrige Award evaluates a broad set of issues, spanning seven major categories that range from leadership to customer satisfaction. The uniformity of the evaluation is exceptionally high. And, in most cases, a large part of the company is evaluated. However, the Baldrige Award is frequently given at the division level of the company and has increasingly emphasized financial results. In addition, during the period of most of the research papers reviewed below, there were an insufficient number of Baldrige Award companies to develop a large enough sample for credible research conclusions. The problem of a lack of numbers is diminishing as more Baldrige Awards are given and it may also be possible to combine samples with winners of the increasing number of state awards, virtually all of which are based on the Baldrige Award Criteria. The potential for bias due to increasing emphasis on financial performance and due to self-selection into the award processes, however, presents serious research problems for samples based on these awards.

In-depth interviews. The fourth sample selection approach listed above is based on the researchers' critical assessment of the firms' deployment of TQM determined via in-depth interviews. This approach has the advantage that the basis for information given during the interview can immediately be explored in considerable depth so that the interview subject's understanding of TQM can be assessed and the information given interpreted in that context. In addition, the extent of actual deployment of specific methods can, to a large extent, be assessed, provided that the manager interviewed has had direct experience with the approach examined. This is because there is a rich "story" that surrounds the actual deployment of a specific approach that can be elicited through questions such as: "What barriers were encountered during deployment?" "What had to be changed during deployment?" "What was learned during the first year after initial deployment and what was subsequently changed based on those learnings?" "What types of employees were resistant to or responded well to the approach?" "If you had to do it again, what would you do differently?" Approaches that have not been deployed or are in early deployment are easily uncovered by a knowledgeable interviewer using this type of approach.

The key disadvantages of the in-depth interview-based approach are that it relies heavily on the knowledge and expertise of the interviewer, the data obtained are largely qualitative, and the interpretation of the information depends on the judgment of the researchers. In addition, it is labor intensive, so it is difficult to use multiple assessors or to conduct multiple in-depth interviews of knowledgeable managers and still obtain a large enough sample to statistically detect a financial impact or to perform in-sample statistical analysis. In contrast, the ability to survey many people within an organization relatively easily is an advantage of survey-based methods (which, unfortunately, most studies do not exploit). It should also be noted that interview-based approaches typically use a search method for identifying potential sample firms, and that possible bias in the financial results due to the interview candidate selection process can potentially survive the interview process.

Research issues relating to the assessment of financial impact

The issues relating to assessment of the impact of TQM on firm financial performance are as important as, and possibly more difficult than, the issues relating to sample selection and the assessment of the extent of TQM implementation. In this review, we focus only on studies that measure TQM's financial impact using publicly available stock return and accounting data. It should be re-emphasized that the majority of studies examining the "performance impact" of TQM are based on surveys and rely only on subjective assessment of the financial performance outcomes by the responding manager. The reason that we limit our review to studies based on actual financial results is the objectivity of the data. As important, however, it is reasonable to believe that subjective assessment of financial performance is systematically biased. For example, if financial results have been positive, then the manager is more likely to interpret this (at least to some extent) as evidence that the quality approaches are better developed, attributing, at least in part, the positive performance to the quality system. The reverse may also be true. If improved results are not observed (within the period of time that the managers believe that results should have occurred), the manager will likely interpret this as evidence that the quality approaches are not working and are not well deployed. This type of bias is particularly likely when the managers sampled are directly involved in the quality management system. These managers are likely to believe a priori in the impact of quality management methods on performance and are not likely to believe that all of their hard work in implementing the quality management system has not yielded positive results.

External accounting and stock return data suitable for research are generally available only at the level of the whole firm. This means that in order for results concerning the impact of TQM on financial performance to be plausible, the scope of the TQM intervention must be large enough so that a company-wide financial effect could be observed. It is simply not plausible that implementation of one or two quality-related approaches in only a small fraction of a company is systematically causally related to significant improvement in overall firm financial results. Thus, in evaluating the credibility of research on the impact of TQM on corporate performance, one factor we consider is whether or not the scope of the intervention examined is sufficient to have causally influenced overall company performance.

Most studies on the impact of management approaches, such as TQM, are based on simple cross-sectional correlation that essentially examines the association between financial measures of performance and the extent or presence of TQM deployment. There are generally two approaches. In the first, multiple regression or structural equations models are used to examine the relationship between deployment of TQM practices or an overall TQM index (e.g., as assessed by a survey) and financial performance, while controlling for other variables such as industry or firm size. In the second approach, the performance of the TQM firms is compared to a non-TQM control sample that is selected in an effort to control for factors such as industry and size.

There are three fundamental problems with such cross-sectional approaches. First, firms that implement TQM are virtually certain to be systematically different from firms that do not implement TQM in ways that are related to performance. The approaches used by most studies do not adequately control for such factors. For example, it is very possible that firms are driven to aggressive implementation of TQM because of competitive pressure and poor financial results. On the other hand, some firms may be willing to experiment with TQM practices when financial performance is good because resources are more easily available. There are also likely to be systematic differences between the types of markets and customers of TQM and non-TQM firms. All of these factors render the performance of non-TQM firms unlike that of TQM firms for reasons that have less to do with the implementation of TQM than with their systematic differences.

The second problem with cross-sectional studies is that the performance differences observed represent a "snapshot" in time and are not closely associated (in time) with changes in the management system. This greatly increases the possibility of confounding factors influencing the results (e.g., fluctuations in the comparative growth of domestic and foreign markets). Studies that examine performance changes associated in time with the actual management systems changes reduce the possibility of confounding by restricting the time period during which such influences are able to affect the results.

The third problem is that, for most studies, direction of causation cannot be plausibly established in cross-sectional research. For example, as mentioned above, good financial performance may enable adoption or experimentation with TQM techniques and may influence the managers' perceptions concerning the state of development of the company's management systems and how much credit it deserves for the current financial health of the firm. In observational studies, causation can virtually never be proved. However, the evidence for causation is more persuasive when the results are associated in time with and follow the management changes. A longitudinal approach similar to the event study methodology of empirical finance (where the implementation periods are aligned cross-sectionally for the purpose of analysis of the impact of the management changes) provides much better evidence of causation.

Another potentially very important research issue is that the decision to implement TQM is an endogenous choice. In theory, the managers of the TQM firms will have chosen to implement TQM only if they have reasons to believe that TQM will improve the firm's performance. Similarly, firms that choose not to implement TQM do so because the managers have reasons to believe that implementing TQM would not improve performance. The choice of whether or not a firm implements TQM represents a self-sorting of the sample based on factors that are correlated with the future financial impact of TQM. Thus, cross-sectional differences in performance may be primarily due to differences in firm characteristics, fit between TQM and firm culture, and firm opportunities rather than causally resulting from implementing TQM. Taken to a logical extreme, if we assume that all firms' managers always choose exactly (and immediately) the optimal strategy for maximizing firm performance based on the available information set, then the decision to implement TQM will always be deterministically driven by the information set. In this case, if we are able to fully control for exogenous variables in the information set, there will be no observable effect of TQM.

These assumptions are, of course, unrealistically strong. Managers do not always make perfectly optimal decisions and certainly do not always do so immediately or even quickly. In particular, firms that decide to implement TQM are not fully optimized, but rather are attempting to move towards an optimal management system. Examination of the performance impact of TQM is an examination of the transient performance effects due to deviation from the theoretical setting described above. Theoretically, such deviations should be transient, as competitive pressure drives the economic system towards optimality, an optimality that is dynamic and continually changing as the circumstances change (e.g. technology). This has important implications for cross-sectional studies, because observable competitive advantages due to TQM should be reduced over time. If TQM really does represent a competitive advantage in an industry, then competitive pressure will, over time, drive TQM adoption throughout the industry. Further, any firms that do not adopt TQM will nevertheless have equivalent competitive advantage due to non-TQM means, or they would not survive in the long term.

Ideally, then, in studying the performance impact of TQM, what is desired is comparison of the performance of each TQM firm with what the performance would have been had the firm not implemented TQM (i.e., a perfect clone but with no TQM). While this ideal is obviously not attainable, what is required is the careful construction of a performance benchmark for each firm that incorporates expectation of future firm performance (that is, the expected performance effects of the firm's characteristics prior to the implementation of TQM) as well as adjusts for subsequent exogenous economic events (e.g., a recession).

Finally, in long-term studies of the impact of TQM on corporate performance, making an effective case for impact requires examination of both accounting variables and stock returns. The reason is that, over the long term, neither stock returns nor accounting variables give a complete picture of performance. Accounting variables provide information on what actually happened during the period under study, but they do not provide information about the value of expected future cash flows. In addition, at least several accounting variables must be examined as no one variable captures all relevant dimensions of performance. While the stock returns provide an overall assessment of the market's consensus view of performance, they are based on expected future performance and, thus, do not provide a clear snap shot of what happened year-by-year during the period under study. Their interpretation also depends on assumptions of strict market efficiency. Thus, the most effective case for the impact of TQM is made when both accounting variables and stock return data are examined and when the results based on analysis of all of the variables present a consistent overall picture.

In summary, then, there are at least five key themes that underlie our assessment of the research approaches used to measure the financial impact of TQM on corporate performance:

1 The scope of the changes in the management system examined should be large enough so that an impact on overall firm performance is plausible;
2 The approach to assessing financial impact should focus on changes in performance associated in time with implementation of the management changes;
3 The control portfolios or other control methodologies should adequately match TQM and non-TQM firms;
4 The performance benchmark should incorporate anticipated performance due to both factors unrelated to TQM and factors associated with the endogenous choice to implement TQM; and
5 For studies of long-term TQM impact, results for both accounting and stock return performance variables should be examined.

LITERATURE REVIEW

In this section, we review the academic studies of the impact of TQM on corporate performance. The literature review is based on review of 394 studies relating to TQM identified through searches using ABI/INFORM together with examination of previous related literature reviews and our own knowledge of work that has occurred in this area. Three previous review papers were examined. The first, Hiam (1993), analyzes 20 survey-based studies, only three of which represent academic studies. None of these three (or the other 17) empirically examine the impact of TQM on corporate performance. The other two review papers are US Department of Labor reports that review the literature on "high performance work practices" (United States Department of Labor 1993) and "innovative work practices" (Mavrinac, Jones, and Meyer 1995). The first of these two reviews contains no studies of the impact of quality management approaches on firm financial performance. The second provides brief summaries of several of the papers discussed here.

We have organized our discussion below by the method of assessment of TQM practices. In particular, we discuss studies based on surveys, quality awards or quality certifications, self-announcements, and interview methods. First, however, we briefly discuss two non-academic studies that are of such prominence in the trade literature that they deserve more than just citation here.

Non-academic studies

The United States General Accounting Office (1991) study of the effects of total quality management is one of the most cited studies on the impact of TQM, especially in the trade literature. The study was based on 18 firms that had been site visited in 1988 and 1989 as a part of the Malcolm Baldrige National Quality Award evaluation process. The site-visited companies represent the highest scoring companies in their categories (manufacturing, service, or small business) based on evaluations of written descriptions of their quality management systems.

The study examines a variety of performance indicators (employee satisfaction, customer satisfaction, etc.), including three measures of financial performance (sales per employee, return on assets, and return on sales). Financial performance data were made available for these three measures by 12, 9, and 8 companies respectively. Twelve of twelve companies reported an increase in sales per employee, 7 of 9 companies reported an increase in return on assets, and 6 of 8 companies reported an increase in return on sales.

The GAO report was not intended to and does not represent valid academic research. The report is very accurate and candid in its own assessment in this regard. In particular, because of the small sample sizes, no statistical assessment of the results is made. Against the standards of academic research, there are a variety of other serious problems with the study. For example, there is no attempt to compare performance to appropriate controls; non-TQM firms in the industries represented by the firms in the GAO sample might also have experienced improving results for the three financial measures discussed above.

The International Quality Study (American Quality Foundation and Ernst & Young 1993a and 1993b) is another frequently cited study, possibly because it touts itself as "The Definitive Study of the Best International Quality Management Practices." This study is a large-scale cross-sectional survey and interview-based study of 584 firms in the US, Canada, Japan, and Europe focusing on four industries. Against academic standards, the study is seriously deficient. In particular, the research methods and sampling procedures are only vaguely described and no statistical analysis of the results is reported. The sample also does not appear to have been selected based on implementation of TQM.

Much of the analysis presented in the International Quality Study is based on comparisons of reported use of quality-related methods by firms that are categorized by relative performance within their industries. Since only a small percentage of the firms in the sample are likely to have been seriously or successfully implementing TQM, the results of such an analysis are likely to driven by spurious correlations between superficial use of various specific TQM-related methods and the financial performance of the sample companies. The study also is likely to suffer from the other limitations of cross-sectional studies described above. One of the key conclusions of the study is that many quality improvement initiatives fail and that many of the key methods and approaches associated with TQM have been effectively deployed by only a small percentage of the firms. This is consistent with the observation that the sample largely consists of firms that are not seriously implementing TQM.

Studies based on surveys

There are a fairly large number of survey-based studies of quality management. We have uncovered only one academic study, however, that directly examines financial performance (Lawler, Mohrman, and Ledford 1992, 1995). This study is part of an ongoing sequence of surveys that evolved out of a 1987 survey conducted by the GAO. Surveys have been subsequently conducted in 1990 (Lawler, Mohrman, and Ledford 1992) and 1993 (Lawler, Mohrman, and Ledford 1995). The surveys are sent to the CEOs of the Fortune 1,000 firms (987 firms in 1990 and 985 firms in 1993) and primarily focus on employee involvement and its relationship to TQM. The number of companies responding were 313 in 1990 and 279 in 1993.

Lawler, Mohrman, and Ledford (1995) examine the relationship between financial performance and employee involvement and TQM via cross-sectional regressions of accounting and stock return variables for the year 1993 on employee involvement and TQM variables derived from the 1993 survey. The seven dependent variables examined included total factor productivity, sales per employee, return on sales, return on investment, return on assets, return on equity, and total return to investors. The regressions used data from all of the Fortune 1000 firms (whether or not they returned a survey) to estimate and control for financial effects due to industry and capital intensity. The financial impact of employee involvement and TQM practices was examined separately for each of the seven financial measures and was assessed as the statistical significance in the regression of the group of employee involvement and TQM variables taken together (presumably using a partial F-test). Although the regression based on stock returns (total return to investors) does not show a significant relationship, significant positive associations (at the 5 percent significance level) are found for five of the seven other financial variables, with a marginally significant result (at the 10 percent level) for sales per employee.

The study goes on to examine the relationship between the results of the 1987 survey and firm financial performance for the period 1989–91. TQM practices were not assessed in the 1987 survey, so only possible effects of employee involvement could be examined. These "lagged" survey results are examined because employee involvement and TQM approaches may take several years to affect financial performance and because the ability of the earlier survey to predict future financial performance is interpreted as much stronger evidence of a causal effect. Three years of financial performance data were used "to reduce the impact of anomalies such as large write-offs that may result in non-representative one-year performance." The results of the lagged regressions show significant positive results (at the 5 percent level) for all of the variables except total return to investors and sales per employee.

Most of the limitations of this study in terms of the evidence it provides concerning the impact of TQM on corporate performance are acknowledged by the authors. In particular, the cross-sectional nature of the regression of the 1993 financial performance variables on the 1993 survey results provides little evidence of causation and the reliance of the results on financial performance in only one year (1993) makes the results subject to the specific characteristics of that year, weakening generalizability to other time periods. From the point of view of assessing the impact of TQM, the lagged results are problematic, as the earlier survey did not assess TQM practices.

In addition, the absence of any relationship between the employee involvement and TQM variables and stock price performance seriously limits the possibility of interpreting the results as evidence of a positive impact of TQM and greatly increases the likelihood that the observed relationships with the accounting variables are due to other factors. We believe that the authors over-interpret the evidence of causation provided by the lagged analysis. The reason is that these accounting variables are correlated over time, so that a contemporaneous association in the cross-sectional regression in 1993 would predict similar associations with the earlier surveys. The stock return variables should be uncorrelated over time, so that lagged association for these variables could more readily be interpreted as indication of causation. However, these associations are not significantly different from zero.

Finally, the study has several of the other limitations discussed above, including the possibility of performance-related non-response bias, the superficiality of the assessment of TQM deployment, and the fact that the sample probably contains only a small number of firms that have made serious efforts to implement TQM. It should be noted that this study was not specifically designed to determine the impact of TQM on corporate financial performance, so the criticisms of the study discussed here involve a tangential part of the research. However, for the purpose of this review, the evidence provided by the study relating to the impact of TQM on financial performance is inconclusive.

While we uncovered only one survey-based study that examined actual firm financial performance, there are an increasing number of survey-based studies that examine manager perceptions of TQM impact on performance. Several of these studies use very careful survey-based research methodology and provide some interesting results. As studies of manager perceptions, they have the limitations discussed above in terms of their evidence concerning the financial impact of TQM. It is nevertheless appropriate to reference some of the key studies, even though we do not review this literature here. They include: Saraph, Benson, and Schroeder (1989); Benson, Saraph, and Schroeder (1991); Flynn, Schroeder, and Sakakibara (1994); Flynn, Sakakibara, and Schroeder (1995); Flynn, Schroeder, and Sakakibara (1995); Powell (1995); Black and Porter (1996); and Dean and Snell (1996).

Studies based on quality awards or quality certification

In this section, we review four papers based on firms that have won quality awards, and one paper based on firms that have received ISO 9000 registration. Three of the four papers on quality awards are by Hendricks and Singhal (1995, 1996, 1997), and the fourth is by Christensen and Lee (1994). Anderson, Daly, and Johnson (1995) examine the impact of ISO 9000 registration. These five papers focus on an examination of the impact on either stock returns or accounting data.

Stock price event study: quality awards

The earliest of the papers by Hendricks and Singhal (1996) uses the event study methodology to examine the stock market reaction to the announcement of winners of quality awards. Sample firms were identified by doing a key word search of the Trade and Industry Index (TRND) and the Dow Jones News Service (DJNS). Firms were eliminated from the sample if they were not traded on the New York Stock Exchange, the American Stock Exchange, or NASDAQ, if the required stock return information was not available, if the announcements were made during the week of the October 1987 market crash, or if the firms had one or more articles or announcements about them in the Wall Street Journal during the five trading days centered on the day of the announcement. The resulting sample consists of 91 award announcements that occurred for 76 different companies between 1985 and 1991. The sample firms, event dates, and names of the awards each firm received are not provided in the paper.

The study focuses on the abnormal return on the day of the quality award announcement (day 0). The analysis in the paper includes adjustment for size and risk, and includes examination of changes in the risk of the firms in the year before and after the event.

The results of the study show a significantly positive abnormal return for day 0 for the full sample (mean abnormal return of 0.587 percent). Examination of the changes in the (equity and asset) betas of the firms shows a statistically significant decrease in the betas in (approximately) the year following the award announcement in comparison to the year prior to the award announcement. The authors interpret this result as evidence that the observed positive abnormal return is not a result of the transfer of wealth from debtholders to stockholders as a result of changes in risk.

The sample is also analyzed separately for large and small firms (those above and below the full sample's median size as measured by total assets) and for awards given by customers and by "independent" organizations. The abnormal return is significantly positive for the small firms and insignificant for the large firms. The abnormal return is also significantly positive for the subsample of 26 firms that received awards from independent organizations and is not significantly different from zero for the firms that won awards from their customers (although the significant positive performance of the small firms persists in the subsample of 14 small firms that won awards from their customers).

We believe that the Hendricks and Singhal paper on stock price reaction to quality award announcements is a careful study with interesting results. The analysis of the changes in risk is useful and adds to the credibility of the main results. The analysis by debt ratio, firm size, and type of award ("independent" or customer) is also interesting. The overall results of the study appear credible, particularly when interpreted narrowly in terms of the stock market reaction to the announcement of a quality award.

We have four reservations about this paper. First, we believe that the focus of the paper on the stock price reaction on the day of the award announcement is too narrow, particularly given the reversal in results (i.e., negative returns) observed on day +1. We would prefer to have seen additional results for multiple-day cumulated abnormal returns around the announcement (e.g., −1 to +1, −10 to +1, and −10 to +5), as is customary in studies using the event-study technique. Multiple-day event windows, particularly those within plus or minus one day of event day 0, are customary because it is easy for the researcher to miss the "real" event day zero by one day because of delays between newswire reports and actual publication dates and because of other potential sources for leaks about the award from such sources as press releases from the firm.[3] Hendricks and Singhal (1996) argue that increasing the event window decreases the power of the statistical tests. This argument may be valid under the assumption that market consensus stock price reaction is virtually immediate. However, we believe that the paper would be more convincing if the analysis over multiple-day windows were presented and the reader allowed to assess the result in the light of the arguments and interpretation presented.

Second, we are concerned about the possible impact of the filtering that results from the sample selection criteria. For example, while the issue of confounding events is clearly an important one, the elimination of firms that are mentioned in the *Wall Street Journal* during the five-day period centered on the event day virtually assures a higher rate of elimination of certain large firms which are mentioned virtually every day. In addition, only 76 firms are used in the study during a period of time when hundreds, and perhaps thousands, of quality awards were being given. For example, while Christensen and Lee (1994) report that there were over 4,000 Ford Q1 designated suppliers between 1983 and 1989 and that, of these, 110 have continuously available data on the COMPUSTAT database, Hendricks and Singhal include only 15 Ford Q1 designated suppliers in their sample. Christiansen and Lee further indicate that the Q1 designation dates for these 110 firms are reported in *Wall Street Journal* announcements (advertisements) that are sponsored by Ford. Only one company that won an award from Texas Instruments (TI) is included in the sample although TI gave many awards during this period. Of the seven publicly-traded Baldrige Award winners during the years 1988 to 1991, only three are included in the sample. Thus, the percentage of the (unknown) population of publicly traded award winners represented by their sample appears small, although how small is not clear. The concern, of course, is that sample selection bias prohibits generalizing the results to the population of firms winning quality awards. Issues relating to the small number of event firms are not addressed in the paper and the apparently small percentage of firms from the target population that made it into the sample raises the level of uncertainty about the overall results.

A third issue has to do with the sub-sample of "independent" awards. The intent of this category appears to be awards for which there is no customer/supplier relationship. While some of the awards listed (e.g., the Malcolm Baldrige National Quality Award – three firms) do not involve a customer/supplier relationship and do have a high degree of independence, this is not the case for the other "independent" awards listed. For example, three NASA awards are for suppliers to NASA and it is not clear that the relationship between NASA and its suppliers is substantively different (with regard to the issues in this study) from the customer/supplier relationships for the awards categorized as "customer to supplier" awards. In addition, six other "independent" awards are from governmental agencies and it is unclear how many of these were given to the agencies' suppliers. Finally, the Philip Crosby Quality Award is an award that, during the period addressed in the study, was given to clients of Crosby's Quality College that were implementing Crosby's approaches to quality management. This award was based on nominations from the clients' customers.

Thus, the extent to which this award can be termed independent is unclear. As a result, it is not clear (to us), in contrast to the implications in the paper, that the significant performance of the subsample of firms winning "independent" awards is likely due to a more accurate assessment of the company's management system provided by unbiased third-party assessment. A real worry is that the results in this subsample primarily reflect market reaction to the information contained in the awards about government/supplier relationships.

Our fourth concern has to do with the interpretation of the results. The results clearly have implications about how the market values announcements of quality awards, which is interesting in its own right and is made even more interesting by the rigor of the research methods that can be used to address this question. Hendricks and Singhal (1996, p. 415), however, interpret the results as providing "a lower bound for the impact of implementing an effective quality improvement program." This presumes that the awards contain substantial information about the implementation of quality improvement methodologies. While this is true for some of the awards given by customers to suppliers, it is probably not true for most of them, especially during the period prior to 1990 (most of the period examined in this study). There is enormous variation in both the formal criteria used by such award givers and in the actual criteria applied to the suppliers. First, many awards are based only on customer metrics (e.g., incoming inspection, on-time delivery, defects identified in the customer's process) and do not examine any aspect of the supplier's improvement approaches. There are many examples of firms winning quality awards from a major customer based entirely on aggressive inspection and on giving this important customer top priority in every way possible. Such awards obviously do not indicate advanced quality systems. Second, many other awards (the 1984 revision of the Ford Q–101 Standard is an example) focus virtually exclusively on quality control, not quality improvement. Third, the awards are frequently given to only one plant or even one production line. Thus, receiving an award frequently does not indicate widespread adoption of quality control and improvement approaches across the entire company or even a major portion of it. As discussed above, widespread adoption of a quality methodology is necessary in order for measurable impact on the firm's overall financial position, as is assumed in studies of stock prices, to be plausible. Finally, the customer-to-supplier quality awards frequently are not entirely free of factors unrelated to the quality management systems. For example, awards often include screening of the supplier for financial stability and are likely to signal information about the security of the supplier's position with the customer (which is frequently based on factors unrelated to the development of their quality control and improvement systems, e.g., low cost and the expense of quality). Thus, it is difficult to link, with any certainty, quality awards with widespread deployment of excellent quality control or quality improvement systems, much less with comprehensive deployment of TQM.

Stock price event study: quality certification

Anderson, Daly, and Johnson (1995) examine the impact of ISO 9000 registration on stock returns surrounding the effective date of registration. It should be noted at the outset that the ISO 9000 standards are standards for a quality assurance system at the plant level. During the period of the study, the ISO 9000 standards focused virtually entirely on quality control issues and not on continuous improvement. The ISO 9000 standards in no way represent a comprehensive TQM system.

The sample of firms were identified from an exhaustive database of sites of US and Canadian firms that were ISO 9000 registered between January 1, 1990 and December 31, 1993. The 4,096 sites listed in the database correspond to a total of 221 firms with the required COMPUSTAT data that own these sites. For this sample of 221 firms, the abnormal returns are examined for a seven-day period beginning four days prior to the effective date of the registration and ending two days after the effective date, and are computed as market model residuals using the value-weighted market index, with a 200-day estimation period ending 10 days before the event date. The results show no significant evidence of any impact due to achieving ISO 9000 registration. The authors, however, report a significant shift in the variance on days – 3 to –1 prior to the event which they interpret as indication of "a wealth effect associated with ISO 9000 certification."

The paper then analyzes variables that are associated with the decision to seek ISO 9000 registration and which might then influence the investors' assessments of the likelihood that a company will seek ISO 9000 registration, as well as their assessment of the value of achieving such registration. The approach taken is to develop a probit model for the probability of ISO 9000 registration, using the population of all firms in the primary four-digit SIC codes of at least one firm that attained certification during the 1990 to 1993 period. The significant variables in the probit model include: (1) the presence of existing sales in Europe; (2) the presence of other international sales; (3) the extent to which the firm sells to other manufacturers (intended to capture exposure to other quality audits); (4) advertising intensity; (5) R&D intensity; (6) whether the firm was identified by Easton and Jarrell (1998) as having made serious efforts to implement TQM; and (7) whether the firm had won an external quality award. Anderson, Daly, and Johnson (1995) then analyze the relationship between the cumulative abnormal returns for days –1 and 0 and the variables that predict ISO 9000 registration with a non-linear regression equation which specifically models the endogenous nature of the decision to seek ISO 9000 registration. The model is based on the idea that managers will not choose to seek ISO 9000 registration unless the predicted benefits exceed a certain level. The results of this analysis show a significant and similar association between the variables that predict the probability of seeking ISO 9000 registration and the abnormal returns. In particular, the co-efficients for all of the variables are significantly positive except for R&D intensity and advertising intensity, which are significantly negative.

This study is a very interesting study that uses a sophisticated analysis method to uncover the associations between stock return performance and the variables that predict ISO 9000 certification. The analysis is interesting in that it indicates that, while ISO 9000 registration in general has no apparent positive impact on stock returns immediately around the effective date of the registration, it does have a significantly positive impact for certain types of firms, namely those that sell to international manufacturing firms, have implemented TQM, or have won another external quality award.

While the associations with the variables are significant, it should be noted that the overall R^2 of the model is small. We also have some concerns about the small windows used as the basis for the event study and the analysis of the abnormal returns. One key reason is that the effective date of the registrations is not an "announced event" in the usual sense in financial studies. Unless announced via press release by the company, it appears that official announcement occurs in a monthly update to the directory of registered companies. Thus, it is unclear how, or how reliably, the information gets to the market before the next month's registry update (which would not typically occur during the event window). The authors appear to assume that it does. It should be noted that press releases are examined in the study to ensure that the announcement did not occur prior to the effective date. However, it is not clear to us that the information reliably reaches the market and market consensus occurs during the short event windows examined in the paper. The paper would be strengthened by reporting results for a variety of windows around the event.

We are also concerned about the scope of the intervention that ISO 9000 registration represents and the plausibility that such an event would have a detectable impact on the firm's company-level financial performance. This issue is also raised by Anderson, Daly, and Johnson (1995). As they point out, ISO 9000 registration is awarded to specific sites, not to companies. While some firms have many registrations (e.g., DuPont has over 75 registered sites), most of the firms in the sample have only one registered site. Thus, for many of the companies, the scope of the potential impact of registration is small. The weaker the plausible link between deployment of the ISO 9000 system at a site and overall financial performance, the more plausible it becomes that the reported results are due to unidentified confounding factors.

Accounting data studies: quality awards

The two quality award papers by Hendricks and Singhal (1995 and 1997) that analyze accounting variable performance examine a 10-year period containing the quality award date. These two papers are very similar, differing only in firm categories for which results are presented. The papers are based on a sample of 394 firms, although, according to the sample sizes listed in their results tables, only about 200 firms apparently had the

required data during the period from one year prior to three years following the award announcement (the exact number of firms depends on the
variable reported). Firms for this sample were identified by searching PR
Newswire and Businesswire for the key words "quality" and "award" and
by directly contacting a number of firms that give quality awards. The
accounting data were obtained from COMPUSTAT.

The accounting performance measures are based on the difference
between the event firm and a control firm that is matched on the basis of
two-digit SIC industry code, a similar fiscal year, is closest in size as measured by the book value of assets in the year prior to the event, and has the
same country of incorporation. These requirements were met by 335 firms.
Because this selection procedure would have eliminated very large firms
(due to difficulty finding an appropriate match), potentially introducing a
size bias into the sample, large firms were matched instead based on one-
digit SIC code and the requirement of similar fiscal years was relaxed. This
resulted in inclusion of an additional 59 firms to bring the total number
of firms in the sample to 394. The difference in the sample size from the
76 firms used in the Hendricks and Singhal (1996) paper on stock price
reaction to the quality award announcements is due to: (1) differences
in the searches performed – the studies using the accounting variables
searched different databases and included identification of firms based on
the inclusion of additional years of events (1992 and 1993); (2) differing
requirements for the availability of the financial data; and (3) the need to
identify a control firm for each event.

The variables examined include operating income, operating margin
(operating income/sales), operating income/assets, operating income per
employee, and sales, among others. Overall, relative to the controls, the
results show no significant difference in the winning firms' performance
in the "implementation" period[4] and strong improvement in the "post-
implementation" period for the percent change in operating income, the
percent change in operating margin, the percent change in operating
income/assets, and the percent change in operating income per employee.
The percent change in sales, percent change in sales/assets, and percent
change in sales/employee show a similar lack of significance in the implementation period. Of the variables based on sales, only the percent change
in sales is significantly positive in the post-implementation period, however, while the percent change in sales/assets and percent change in sales
per employee are not significantly different from the controls.

Hendricks and Singhal (1995) also present comparisons between smaller
and larger firms, lower and higher capital-intensity firms, more and less
diversified firms, earlier and later implementers (first quality award won
before and after 1986), "independent" awards and awards from customers, and multiple and single award winners. Based on Hendricks and
Singhal's analysis of the means for each of the groupings, lower capital-
intensity firms perform better in comparison to the controls than higher
capital-intensity firms, and companies receiving "independent" awards perform better in comparison to the controls than companies receiving awards

from customers. There is no statistically compelling difference[5] between smaller and larger firms, less and more diversified firms, earlier and later implementers, and multiple or single award winners.

We have several concerns about the two Hendricks and Singhal papers based on the accounting variables. First, while the number of event firms identified for the sample is much larger in this study (463 that had the required COMPUSTAT data with 394 event firms remaining after the selection of the control portfolios), the results are primarily based on about 200 to 220 firms. This is less than half of the 463 that had the required data and less than 60 percent of the firms for which there were also controls. It is not clear from the paper exactly why these other firms were eliminated, although it clearly must be due to data availability. Nevertheless, in comparison to the 110 firms identified by Christensen and Lee (1994) based only on consideration of one award giver, namely Ford, the overall number of events appears small. Thus, concerns about possible effects of the selection process remain.

There are also several technical issues. First, the matching of the control firms based on two-digit SIC codes (with 56 firms matched on only one-digit SIC codes) does not ensure that the control firms are very like the event firms since the two-digit SIC classification is very broad. For example, the two-digit SIC code 36 includes "household appliances" (SIC code 3630), "semiconductor related device" (SIC code 3674), "electric lighting, wiring equipment" (SIC code 3640), "magnetic, optic recording media" (SIC code 3695), and "phono record, audio tape, disk" (SIC code 3652). As a second example, the two-digit SIC code 37 includes "aircraft" (SIC code 3721), "motor vehicles and car bodies" (SIC code 3711), "railroad equipment" (SIC code 3743), and "ship and boat building and repairing" (SIC code 3730). Thus, it is not likely that companies in the same two-digit SIC codes are in similar industries, which is critically important when the control firm is used as the only performance benchmark. Issues relating to the sensitivity of measured financial results to the choice of industrial classifications are discussed in detail in Kahle and Walking (1996).

As discussed below, an appropriate benchmark for assessing accounting variable performance must also include some method which proxies for expected performance and adjusts for potential pre-event differences between the firms in the sample and the firms in the control that predict later performance. For example, firms that give quality awards are almost certainly not evenly distributed across the industries represented by two-digit SIC codes. Instead, the companies that give quality awards are very likely to be concentrated in industries that either have suffered severe foreign competitive pressure or compete internationally. Firms that do not receive quality awards are more likely to be in markets where quality awards are not given, especially given the broad definition of two-digit SIC codes, and these markets are likely to be fundamentally different than those in which there are high concentrations of quality award givers. Thus, within the "industry" defined by a two-digit SIC code, there are likely to be systematic differences between the companies that receive (or have an opportunity to receive) quality awards and companies that do not for reasons that have nothing to do with the firm's quality management systems – for example, because of differences in their customer bases and, ultimately, the markets their products serve.

The sample of quality-award-winning firms is also likely to be different from typical firms within a two-digit SIC code in two other ways. First, it is likely that quality-award-winning firms are more likely to have large customers (since large customers are more likely than small ones to develop supplier quality award processes) than typical firms within a two-digit SIC. Second, for similar reasons, it is plausible that quality-award-winning firms are much less likely to sell directly to either distributors or consumers, since distributors and consumers do not give quality awards. Thus, there is likely to also be a systematic difference in the position of the quality-award-winning firms in the value chain. Failure to use a methodology that attempts to adjust for systematic differences between the event and control firms that are unrelated to the development of their quality systems, but are likely to influence future performance, seriously weakens the credibility of the results.

The over-interpretation of the actual meaning of winning a quality award is also more exaggerated in these two papers than in the Hendricks and Singhal (1996) paper examining stock price reaction to quality award announcements. In these papers, the period from six years to one year before winning a quality award is interpreted as the "TQM implementation period." The period from one year before the quality award to three years after is interpreted as representing a post-implementation period. The papers do acknowledge that these periods are arbitrarily selected. But, as discussed above, there is scant basis for interpreting the winning of a typical quality award as indicative of implementation of a TQM system. Many awards are based on delivered quality and timeliness results. Far fewer directly evaluate the systems that produced the results (e.g., through on-site audits) and most of these, especially during the 1980s, focus only on manufacturing quality control systems. The vast majority of the awards examine only one site (e.g., plant) or even one product line and thus do not indicate widespread use of quality methodologies throughout a sufficient fraction of the company that it is reasonable to expect an observable impact on the overall financial results at the firm level. Obviously, looking at a sample of firms that have won quality awards should include a higher-than-average concentration of firms that really have seriously implemented a TQM system than a sample of firms that have not won a quality award. Virtually all companies that do seriously implement TQM receive quality awards, and usually multiple quality awards. However, the increased representation of such firms in a sample selected on the basis of winning a quality award is likely to be slight because quality awards are common and many are easy to obtain. This fact contrasts with the very strong accounting variable performance reported in the paper. These strong positive results could only result from changes in the event firm management systems if such changes were major and widespread. It is possible that the sample of roughly 200 firms that are the basis for these results do represent firms that have successfully implemented largely complete TQM systems in the majority of their businesses. However, if this were the case, it must be due to some other aspect of the overall sample selection process, not just the fact that the firms are quality award winners.

Another study based on quality awards that examines performance using accounting data is by Christensen and Lee (1994). This study uses a sample of 110 publicly-traded firms that received the Ford Q1 Preferred Supplier designation between 1983 and 1989. The study examines the differences in seven accounting variables between firms that have obtained the Q1 designation and firms with the same SIC codes that are not Q1-designated suppliers. Analysis is presented for each of the years between 1984 and 1989 and by each of the two-digit SIC codes represented by the Q1-designated companies. The results of the comparisons show consistently stronger accounting performance for operating income/sales and operating income/assets for the Ford Q1-designated suppliers than for the control groups. The results are consistent both across years and across the represented SIC codes. The overall positive results are less certain for operating income per employee.

This study's reliance on two-digit SIC code for matching the control portfolios is subject to the methodological problems and possible biases discussed above. The study is longitudinal and does not attempt to examine changes in performance associated with the deployment of the quality management approaches, which weakens possible causal interpretation of an association between deployment of the quality management approaches and improvement in performance. The controls are also not individually matched to the Ford Q1 sample firms; thus, unlike the Hendricks and Singhal (1995 and 1997) papers, there is no attempt to match on characteristics, such as size, as is standard practice in financial research.

Christensen and Lee also attempt to interpret the Ford Q1 Preferred Supplier designation as indicative of the deployment of TQM within the company. The 1984 revision of the Ford Q101 Quality Systems Standard and the deployment of the on-site audits that determine the Ford Q1 Preferred Supplier designation had a major positive impact on the quality movement in the US beginning in the mid-1980s; it was the starting point for development of a comprehensive TQM system for many companies. Nevertheless, the Q1 audit focuses primarily on quality control and product qualification issues and not on comprehensive deployment of TQM. In addition, Ford Q1 audits are at the plant level and focus only on products supplied to Ford. Thus, these audits do not indicate deployment of quality methodologies throughout the company. Most importantly, however, the results of this study are confounded by differences in performance between Ford suppliers and non-Ford suppliers. This is particularly important since the period of the study is during the same period of the turnaround of the financial performance of Ford, so it is plausible, particularly with the trend towards longer-term relationships and reduction of the number of suppliers, that any apparent quality-award-related result is instead driven by the performance of Ford.

Studies based on self-announcement

This section examines two studies that base sample selection on the companies' self-announcements of their TQM implementations. The first, by Holder and Pace (1994), examines both accounting and stock return performance for a sample of 632 firms that had identified themselves as either having implemented TQM or being in the process of implementing TQM. These firms were identified by searching the COMPUSTAT PC Plus Corporate Text database which contains 10Ks, 10Qs, 20Fs, and Proxy Statements for companies listed on the New York and American Stock Exchanges since July 1987 and National Market System filings since January 1989. The search phrases used were "Total Quality Management," "TQM," and "Continuous Improvement." The sample firms also had to have the required financial data in the COMPUSTAT PC Plus database. The documents identified by the firms were read to ensure that the firms had indicated that they were indeed adopting or had adopted TQM and to identify start dates. If a start date was not specifically mentioned, then the document date was used.

A control group for the sample firms was identified by selecting all firms with the same four-digit SIC code. This resulted in a control population of 5,232 firms. Seven accounting variables were analyzed, including inventory turnover, receivables turnover, asset turnover (sales/assets), net profit margin (net income/sales), return on assets (net income/assets), return on equity, and stock returns. The impact of TQM on each of these performance measures was examined by regressing the performance variable for either 1991 or 1988 on a TQM indicator variable and the firm's stock beta and size as measured by the log of the total value of the firm's outstanding shares.

Overall, the results of this study are mixed. The coefficient of the TQM indicator variable is significantly positive for asset turnover. It is significantly negative, however, for inventory turnover and receivables turnover, which, Holder and Pace suggest, indicates that the TQM firms are less efficient at managing working capital. In addition, stock return performance is also significantly negative.

The Holder and Pace study, however, has some significant limitations. First, the sample is selected based on self-announcements by the firms. As the authors acknowledge, "it is clear that firms claiming to use TQM may, in reality, not be doing so, particularly since TQM has become a 'trendy' term." Second, the study tries to infer the actual TQM implementation date from the documents identified by the searches, with the document date being used as the implementation date when such a date is not explicitly given. Third, the analysis is essentially cross-sectional, with financial performance analyzed only for 1991 and 1988. Because of these limitations, we believe that the results of this study contain little evidence concerning the actual financial performance of TQM firms.

The second study, by Lemak, Reed, and Satish (1996), examines the stock return and profit margin (operating income/sales) performance of a sample of 60 firms selected on the basis of self-announcement of their TQM approaches in the president's letter of the firms' annual reports. The sample selection approach is particularly interesting because the authors seek a sample of firms that show sustained commitment to implementation of TQM. Candidate firms for the sample were first identified through a search of the Compact Disclosure annual report database for "quality" in the president's letters. Firms that appear to have sustained commitment were then identified through independent review of the president's letters by two assessors for mention of at least one aspect of TQM content and one aspect of TQM process (see Reed, Lemak, and Montgomery 1996) for five consecutive years. The repeated mention of TQM in the president's letters is taken to demonstrate sustained commitment to TQM.

For most of the firms in the sample (70 percent), the starting date of the TQM program was taken to be one month before the first occurrence of reference to both TQM content and process. For the remaining 30 percent of the firms, the text of the president's letter indicated the starting year. For the stock returns, firm cumulative excess return was analyzed for 6-month intervals beginning 6 months before the start date to two years after the start date. The excess returns were calculated based on the market model estimated using daily returns for years 2 and 3 before the start date and for years 2 and 3 after the start date.

The stock return results indicate significant positive excess returns for two six-month periods, between 0 and 6 months after the start date and between 12 and 18 months after the start date. The cumulative abnormal returns are negative, but not significant, for the periods between 6 and 12 months following the start date and for the period between 18 and 24 months following the start date. The cumulative abnormal returns are also not statistically different from 0 (it is slightly positive) for the period between 6 and 0 months before the start date, which is interpreted as some indication that the research design is valid.

Lemak, Reed, and Satish (1996) interpret the stock return results as evidence that "[f]irms that implement TQM will experience a significant increase in their stock value on a market- and risk-adjusted basis during and after the period that the information about the adoption of TQM is made public." They go on to conclude that the results are evidence that "the market sees TQM as a value-creating process and it appears to factor in much of the potential gains earlier rather than later." These conclusions appear to be based primarily on the significance of the positive performance in the six-month period between 0 and 6 months following the start date and, to a lesser extent, also on the significance of the positive performance for the period between 12 and 18 months following the start date. The negative performance for the period between 6 and 12 months following the start date is explained as possibly due to the October, 1987 market crash. About 30 percent of the firms in the sample had a start date of 1987, so the crash would have occurred during this six-month period for these firms. In addition, the negative performance for this period and for the period from 18 to 24 after the start date are both not statistically different from 0.

We do not believe that the evidence presented in the paper justifies the conclusions drawn. Specifically, the interpretation of the positive performance in the period from 0 to 6 months after the start date critically depends on having an accurate start date. It does not appear that the approaches used to determine the start date in the paper would provide this degree of accuracy. First, the actual start date of deployment of a company's TQM system is often not defined in an obvious way. Interviews conducted in conjunction with Easton and Jarrell (1998) indicate that many companies spend two or more years involved in some type of limited TQM-related activity before any company-wide initiatives occur (see Easton and Jarrell 1997). The dates of TQM announcements in companies' annual reports can range anywhere from a year or more prior to the actual deployment of a company-wide initiative to three or more years following the deployment of such an intiative. Thus, the relationship of the annual report announcement to the actual activities within the company is not clear, and the variation is on the order of years, not months. This variation obviously affects certainty about the event date with respect to when information about the firm's TQM programs becomes "known" to the market.

The sample of firms in Lemak, Reed, and Satish also contains a mix of start dates identified in two different ways. For about 30 percent of the firms, the start date is given in the text of the president's letter, but for the remainder, it is inferred from the first date that TQM is discussed. It is unclear that these two approaches result in roughly equivalent start dates. No analysis or discussion is given in the paper concerning the relationship between the announcement dates and the actual start dates. The start dates also appear to be used for two different purposes – as the date that TQM implementation began (in the analysis of the firms' operating margins) and as the date that the market became aware of the implementation of TQM (in the stock return analysis) – and we believe that these two dates might be substantially different.

Lemak, Reed, and Satish recognize in the paper this ambiguity with respect to the start dates, arguing that the start date is not accurate for a variety of reasons including that the annual reports are "usually in preparation for weeks or months" and that "some information is revealed to the analysts before it is revealed in the annual reports." They go on to use this inaccuracy in the event date to justify examination of the stock returns over a two-year period rather than over a window of just a few days surrounding the announcement, as would be the case in a typical event study in the financial literature. While we agree with this argument, it is inconsistent with the subsequent strong interpretation of the significance of the results for the period from 0 to 6 months after the start date. The start dates are simply too uncertain to attribute the market response to this period rather than expecting it to be "blurred" throughout the two-year post-event period.

The argument given in the paper that the negative results observed in the period from 6 to 12 months after the event are due to approximately one third of the sample being affected by the October 1987 crash may very well be correct. However, essentially no analysis is provided to support this conclusion such as analysis that either removes these firms from the sample or that eliminates or "corrects" the returns that occurred around the time of the crash. The paper also does not present cumulated returns for the entire two-year period. However, rough calculations that can be made based on the data provided in the paper suggest that the cumulated returns for the entire two-year period would not be significantly positive.[6] This appears to be true even when the negative cumulative returns for the post-event period from 6 to 12 months are removed. However, these calculation are approximate as the required information for exact calculations is not given in the paper. The apparent lack of significance of the stock returns over the two-year period draws into question the paper's conclusions.

Lemak, Reed, and Satish also examine changes in operating margin associated with the start dates. This is done by first adjusting each firm's operating income and sales by subtracting the average operating income and sales for the firm's industry. The operating income variable is then regressed on sales, a "TQM" indicator variable that takes on the value of 1 in the post-start-date period and 0 in the pre-start-date period, and a sales*TQM interaction variable (several other models are also examined). The coefficients are estimated using a pooled cross-section time series model. The slope coefficient on sales can be approximately interpreted as the profit margin in the pre-event period, while the coefficient on the interaction term sales*TQM can be interpreted as the change in the profit margin between the pre and post periods, the key variable of interest. The results indicate that the profit margin increases by about 2 percent between the per- and post-event periods and this increase is strongly significant. Lemak, Reed, and Satish interpret this as evidence of a positive impact of TQM on profit margin.

Exactly how the model is constructed and estimated is not particularly clear in the paper. It does not appear to us, however, that this model controls for industry effects on the slope coefficient of sales*TQM (i.e., industry effects on the pre-post change in profit margin). Thus, the results could be driven by industry effects rather than as a specific result of implementation of TQM. This is particularly true because the start dates for 75 percent of the firms are the years 1987 and 1988. Because of this event-year clustering, event-relative time is substantially confounded with calendar time. Thus, the TQM indicator variable is also confounded with calendar time, so that changes in the slope coefficient of sales*TQM may capture widespread changes or trends in profit margin occurring in the period around 1987–8. It is also not clear to us the extent to which the key variables in the regressions (firm operating income – industry operating income, and firm sales – industry sales) are confounded with firm size so that the coefficient on sales captures differences in profit margin between small and large firms.

Lemak, Reed, and Satish (1996) also potentially suffers from bias due to self-announcement discussed above. While the approach to selecting firms that are committed to TQM based on repeated consecutive announcements in the annual reports is very interesting, it may exacerbate possible bias due to a correlation between financial performance and willingness to "announce" TQM. While financial performance might have little influence on the existence of a single announcement of TQM for a firm, it seems likely that the willingness of the president of a firm to repeatedly discuss TQM year after year might well be influenced by "success." Perception of "success" may very likely be influenced by financial performance.

In summary, the approach taken by Lemak, Reed, and Satish for identifying companies committed to TQM is very interesting, although it may exacerbate problems associated with self-announcement. The stock return results in the paper, however, do not provide statistical evidence of a positive effect (notwithstanding the interpretation of the authors) and there appear to be several methodological problems with the identification of the start dates of the companies' TQM initiatives and with the analysis of the profit margin data.

Studies based on in-depth interviews

We are aware of only one study (Easton and Jarrell 1998) that uses in-depth interviews to select the sample of TQM firms. This study uses a sample of 108 firms that were judged, based on interviews with a senior quality executive at each firm, to have made serious efforts to deploy TQM. Candidate firms for this study were selected through searches of several publicly available sources. The primary sources were the ARS full-text database of on-line annual reports from Nexus/Lexus, the Businesswire full-text database of press releases, Standard and Poor's Corporate Register of Directors (1993), the GAO report's list of Baldrige Award site-visited companies (United States General Accounting Office 1991), and lists of the institutional affiliations of Baldrige Award examiners. The ARS Annual Report and Businesswire Press Release databases were searched for quality-related terms, such as "total quality management," "just-in-time," "Baldrige," "Deming," "Juran," "Crosby," and "quality award." The Standard and Poor's Corporate Register of Directors was searched for such titles as Vice President or Director of Quality, Continuous Improvement, or Customer Satisfaction.

The documents identified by the Annual Report and Press Release searches were reviewed for indication that at least one quality-management-related approach (e.g., statistical process control, just-in-time manufacturing, quality training, and problem-solving teams.) either had been deployed or was currently under deployment. Information on more than 500 firms was reviewed and candidate firms for interviews were identified based on the evidence of deployment of TQM-related approaches.

A total of 207 firms were approached for interviews with a senior quality executive or other executive familiar with the development of the company's quality management system. In the process of trying to identify the appropriate executive and set up the interview, 17 firms were determined not to have a TQM system. Fourteen of the remaining 190 firms declined to participate in the study. Thus, a total of 176 firms were actually interviewed for a response rate among the potential TQM firms of 93 percent (176/190).

The executives interviewed were typically a Vice President or Director of Quality. The interviews were conducted by George S. Easton, a former Examiner and Senior Examiner with the Malcolm Baldrige National Quality Award between 1989 and 1992. The interviews generally lasted about 45 minutes. The objective of the interview process was to develop a time line of the development of the company's TQM systems, to determine what key approaches were used and, through in-depth probing in a few areas, to determine the actual extent of deployment of the company's approaches. The interviews were conducted using a semi-structured approach, which allowed flexibility in the specific topics discussed. The managers were promised complete confidentiality concerning the content of the interviews. It should be noted that the volume of information conveyed in a 45-minute interview far exceeds that captured by even the most lengthy questionnaires.

The interview process occurred in two phases. The objective of the first phase was to elicit from the manager, with minimal prompting, the major milestones in the development of the company's TQM approaches as they came to the manager's mind. Questions were asked, as necessary, to establish the level of detail required and to determine, as specifically as possible, the dates of the events surrounding the beginning of the TQM approaches. Questions about approaches or methods not mentioned by the manager, however, were avoided in order to avoid influencing the description. The managers' impromptu descriptions are very revealing concerning what aspects of the development of the TQM system the manager believes are important and what the key drivers of the system actually are.

The second phase of the interview process was intended to fill in any important gaps in the description of approaches used and to probe in-depth some key areas in order to assess actual levels of deployment. This phase was guided by a list of possible topics. The objective was to discuss in detail a few areas that were appropriate for the company's approaches and the expertise and experience of the manager interviewed. If not adequately addressed by the manager's initial description of the time line, four areas were always covered: production, customer satisfaction measurement, supplier management, and new product development and design. In general, the extent of deployment of the approaches mentioned was assessed by asking specific questions concerning the number of employees involved, the training they had received, and the dates of the various events mentioned. Deployment was also assessed by asking questions, such as those described above, that were intended to elicit the "rich story" surrounding actual deployment.

Companies were included in the sample if, based on the interviews, they appear to have made serious efforts to implement TQM approaches in the majority of their business (as measured by sales). The standard of "serious efforts" for inclusion in the sample is quite low; it is not a requirement that the company's efforts resulted in a comprehensive and well-integrated approach. Companies were eliminated from the sample for several reasons. The most common was that their TQM efforts were deployed in only a small fraction of the company. Other reasons ranged from a lack of any significant deployment efforts to confusion of TQM with other approaches. Fifty-three firms (30 percent) were eliminated from the sample based on the interviews, and an additional 15 firms of those surviving the interviews were eliminated because the required accounting and stock return data were not available.

For the remaining 108 companies that were included in the sample, the start date for deployment of their TQM systems was selected to be approximately six months after the beginning of the first major initiative. In most of the companies, this major initiative was the deployment of wide-spread quality training. This start date was chosen because most of the initiatives take a substantial period of time to roll out. For example, it is not uncommon for large-scale training initiatives to take over a year to complete.

The sample was divided into 44 firms judged on the basis of the interviews to have more advanced TQM systems and 64 firms with less advanced TQM systems. This separation was made by making a rough estimate, based solely on the interviews, of what the firm's score would be in terms of the approach and deployment aspects of the Baldrige Criteria. It should be noted that the interviews focused only on the approaches taken and the extent of their deployment and not on the operational or financial results that were achieved.

In this study, the impact of TQM on corporate performance was assessed using both accounting and stock return variables by examining performance for a five-year period following the start date of the deployment of the companies' TQM systems, as determined by the interviews. The method used is adapted from the approach developed by Jarrell (1991) to study the long-term impact of takeovers. For each TQM firm, a control portfolio of three firms not known to us to have implemented TQM was selected by matching on the basis of industry, calendar time, projected performance (the Value Line timeliness rank) and, to the extent possible, market size, debt to equity ratios, and a market risk factor (the Value Line "safety" rank). Matching on the basis of industry and calendar time is designed to control for economic, political, and regulatory influences impacting both the TQM and non-TQM control firms. The industry classifications are defined by the Value Line Investment Survey and verified with the SIC code. The matching included a detailed review of the companies' product lines as described by Value line, so the matching is far better than would be provided by the Value Line industry classifications or SIC codes alone. Matching based on projected performance helps to ensure that the control portfolio is as similar as possible to the TQM firm in the post-event period.

For the accounting-based variables, the approach to constructing the performance measure consists of two main components. First, the firm's *unexpected performance* is measured by the difference between the firm's actual performance and an analyst's forecast (provided by Value Line) of the expected future performance made just prior to the event. Second, the event firm's unexpected performance is compared to the average unexpected performance of the matched control portfolio. The performance impact is then measured by the *excess unexpected performance*, the difference between the unexpected performance of the event firm and the unexpected performance of its control portfolio. Where analysts' forecasts are not available (e.g., inventory levels), excess actual performance is used (the difference between the actual performance of the event firm and the actual performance of its control portfolio).

The use of analysts' forecasts in constructing the benchmark for the accounting variables and in matching the control portfolios on the basis of projected performance are unique features of the approach developed by Jarrell (1991). Use of such forecasts is important because they incorporate an expert's evaluation of the future impact of the firm's particular circumstances prior to deployment of TQM. Such factors may be associated with the firm's (endogenous) decision to implement TQM. The failure to control for such exogenous factors can introduce potentially significant bias into the results, as discussed above. Such factors may also not be apparent in the firm's historical financial data (e.g., impending foreign competition, the expiration of a patent, developing labor issues, and pending changes in regulations or tax rates). We believe that the use of analysts' forecasts to adjust for anticipated future performance is an important strength of the methodology used in this study.

For the stock return variable, performance is assessed by the *excess actual cumulative returns*, the difference between the cumulative with-dividend continuously compounded daily stock returns for the TQM firm and its control portfolio. Unlike accounting variables, stock prices inherently include a forecast of the future performance of the firm, so the use of analysts' forecasts is neither necessary nor appropriate when examining stock returns. It is, however, important that the control portfolios are well-matched to the TQM firms in terms of their non-diversifiable risk, since the expected stock return is a function of non-diversifiable risk. For the firms in this study, analysis of the stock betas indicated that the matching procedure used to select the control portfolios resulted in control portfolios that are very well matched to the event firms in terms of non-diversifiable risk.

The accounting variables examined in the study include variables based on net income and operating income scaled by sales, assets, and number of employees. Inventory-based variables and the percent change in sales, assets, and number of employees are also examined. The analysis is also performed separately for the subsamples of less and more advanced TQM firms. Overall, the results show a strong statistical association between deployment of TQM systems and improved financial performance in the period 3–5 years following initial deployment. The results are consistent across both the accounting-based variables and the stock returns. The results are much stronger for the subsample of companies judged to have implemented more advanced TQM systems. For example, the mean excess stock return in year five following the beginning of TQM implementation is 24 percent for the full sample and 32 percent for the subsample of more advanced firms. It should be noted that evidence of improvement is weak for the subsample of less advanced TQM firms, suggesting that the real benefits of TQM require determined and relatively complete implementation.

The paper also assesses the possible effects of downsizing by examining separately firms with negative and positive percent change in the number of employees relative to the matched control portfolio. This was examined because downsizing that occurred in conjunction with implementation of TQM was thought to be a possible confounding factor that might explain the improved performance associated with TQM. The results, however, do not support this hypothesis. The results indicate that there is improved performance associated with the implementation of TQM whether or not there was a comparative decrease in the number of employees.

Before turning to the limitations of this study, we would like to remind the reader that we are the authors of the study and, thus, are likely to be biased about its methodology. We will, however, attempt to report the most important concerns that have been raised.

The key concern that has been raised about this study is the reliance on qualitative approaches for assessing whether or not firms have made serious efforts to deploy TQM and whether or not they have achieved more advanced TQM systems. The interview-based approach makes the study difficult to replicate and highly dependent on the skill and expertise of the interviewer. However, at the same time, this is also one of the study's strengths since, as argued above, the approach (1) does not rely on subjective self-assessment of the extent of TQM implementation by the respondents and (2) allows assessment of actual deployment via in-depth questions in a few areas. A related concern is the use of only one rater in assessing the extent of TQM deployment. This is a valid concern that is offset somewhat by the extensive training and experience of the interviewer in assessing TQM systems, both through written documents and on-site examination, using the Malcolm Baldrige National Quality Award Criteria, the de facto standard for TQM assessment instruments. As a practical issue, it would also be difficult to obtain multiple lengthy interviews from the appropriate executives within the companies, which would likely reduce the response rate. However, it is certainly possible that multiple expert rating based on multiple interviews (or ideally even on-site audits) would be an improvement.

Another concern that has been raised is the potential for bias having been introduced into the sample through the screening methods used to initially identify firms and for this bias to have survived the interview process. This concern has been primarily focused on the use of quality awards as one method for identifying interview candidates. To a lesser extent, there has been concern about possible bias due to self-announcement that could occur as a result of the document searches used to identify candidate TQM firms (i.e., annual reports and press releases). The concern is that both self-announcement and the winning of quality awards might be influenced by financial performance so that samples selected based on such criteria may have a bias towards positive financial performance that is not a result of implementation of TQM.

The possibility of a non-quality-related bias associated with quality awards clearly affects the research reviewed above that is specifically based on quality awards. Examples of such biases include potential differences in customer size, markets (domestic or international), or the fact that suppliers to companies that give supplier awards are frequently screened for financial stability as a part of supplier base reduction efforts. The Easton and Jarrell (1998) study was actually conducted in two phases, and quality awards were not a basis for selection in the first phase of the study. The results are consistent for both phases of the study. In addition, the final sample was re-analyzed by omitting all firms for which winning a quality award was a factor in their selection.[7] The results of this analysis show that the positive association with TQM implementation persists in the sample of firms not identified via a quality award.

It should also be noted that, because of the use of both stock returns and analysts' forecasts for the accounting variables, bias associated with either self-announcement or winning a quality award would have to be due to factors that are not incorporated into the forecasts by the market and the analysts. This makes the possibility of such a bias much less likely. In interpreting the results of this study, it is important to keep in mind that the real performance benchmark is the forecasts, not the performance of the control portfolio. The control portfolio serves to "control" the forecast errors not the actual performance, and thus to correct for the effects of subsequent economic events and analyst bias. Further, the control portfolios are matched (in addition to industry classification and market value) based on analyst assessment of projected performance. Finally, even if bias does result from the initial screening methods, it does not explain the observed difference between the more advanced and less advanced firms, since both of these groups experienced the same screening procedure. Thus, the more and less advanced comparison is an important intra-sample validation of the overall method.

A third concern raised about the study is that there is no verification that firms in the control sample have not made serious efforts to implement TQM. We argue that this is unlikely to be a problem, for two reasons. First, an assumption that impacts the overall research design is that the percentage of firms that are actually seriously implementing TQM in the majority of their businesses is small. Thus, without any screening, the degree of contamination of the control portfolios with firms that have made serious efforts to implement TQM will be small, especially during the examined five-year implementation period of the event firms.[8] Second, we interpret the absence of evidence of TQM implementation uncovered by the initial document searches as evidence that the control firms have not implemented TQM.

The final concern raised about this study involves technical issues surrounding the use of analysts' forecasts in the construction of the performance measures for the accounting variables, especially the possibility of systematic bias in the analysts' forecasts. These issues do not affect the stock return results. Further, the forecast-generating processes should be the same for both the TQM and non-TQM firms, so the control method would correct for systematic bias provided that it affects both the TQM and control firms in the same way. In addition, the performance of the analysts' forecasts in comparison to time series forecasts is examined in the paper. Finally, an extensive literature exists (which is cited in the paper) examining the performance of analysts' forecasts which concludes that such forecasts are effective proxies for market expectations.

An additional study

We mention one additional study because of its different and interesting approach. Eskildson (1995) attempts to assess the impact of TQM by examining general patterns in over 150 successful corporate turnarounds. This approach is potentially of interest because TQM has frequently been positioned as a key strategy for organizational turnaround and competitive renewal. In the sample of successful turnarounds, high costs are listed as a key reason for the downturn in about 130 companies while poor quality is listed for only about 40 companies. The most common approach used in achieving turnarounds was cost reduction followed by approaches to immediately resolve cash flow problems, such as debt restructuring. The study reports that only one or two of 52 TQM-like improvement programs in the sample of turnaround firms were successful in restoring financial performance.

The approach of this study is interesting, but there are many problems with the methodology and conclusions; we believe that the study does not meet academic research standards. First, the study ignores the relationship between cost and quality. To say that a company has a cost problem is to say that it cannot deliver adequate quality at sufficiently low cost. Second, the paper erroneously states that cost control is not an integral part of TQM. Cost control through aggressive waste and cycle-time reduction is a key part of any serious TQM approach. While the study concludes that only one or two of the 52 TQM-like programs were successful in driving the turnaround, no objective basis for this assessment is given. Finally, if as argued above, the percentage of firms that actually do make a serious attempt to implement TQM is small then the number of such firms in the sample would also be small, perhaps only one or two. Nevertheless, the focus on turnarounds used in this article is interesting, and it might be possible to develop rigorous and interesting research based on this type of approach.

CONCLUSION

While there is an increasing number of academic studies concerning TQM, there are still very few papers that examine the impact of TQM on corporate performance using externally available financial data. In this Chapter we reviewed in detail nine studies that have examined this issue. In addition, we have provided brief reviews of two non-academic studies that are widely cited and an additional study based on a novel approach. Of the nine studies reviewed in detail, only one (Easton and Jarrell, 1998) directly focuses on a sample of firms specifically screened for implementation of TQM. Five of the studies (Christensen and Lee 1994; Anderson, Daly, and Johnson 1995; and three by Hendricks and Singhal (1995, 1996 and 1997) focus only indirectly on TQM through the use of quality awards or certification, most of which are given for quality control activities. Two studies are based on self-announcement of the firms' TQM initiatives (Holder and Pace 1994, and Lemak, Reed, and Satish 1996). The final study (Lawler, Mohrman, and Ledford 1995) focuses on the population of Fortune 500 firms, and assesses employee involvement and TQM deployment via a survey instrument. Of these nine studies, eight report positive performance associated with quality (i.e., TQM or winning a quality award). Only one, which examines stock price reaction to ISO 9000 registration (Anderson, Daly, and Johnson 1995), fails to detect an overall effect. However, Anderson, Daly, and Johnson (1995) go on to analyze the association between stock price reaction and firm characteristics that might reasonably be expected to influence the value of ISO 9000 registration. Significant association with firm characteristics are found. The results are interpreted by the authors first as evidence of "wealth effects" associated with ISO 9000 certification and second as evidence that, for some types of firms, ISO 9000 has a positive impact, while for other types, it has a negative effect.

We also describe in some detail what we believe are the most critical research issues involved in addressing questions concerning the impact of TQM. In particular, we argue that, since financial performance is assessed at the firm level, it is critical that the intervention examined in the research study be sufficiently large so that there is a credible mechanism that could effect overall firm performance; that is, TQM must be implemented in a majority of the firm. We also argue that it is critical that studies on the impact of TQM must (1) be based on samples that contain a large enough number of firms that are making serious efforts to deploy TQM (as opposed to those that are "dabbling" in TQM or only seriously making efforts to deploy one or two of TQM's broad scope of approaches) and (2) be able to identify the TQM firms. We also argue that the assessment of long-term impact must be made using both accounting and stock return variables, should focus on the TQM implementation period, and must be based on a credible control methodology that captures, to the extent possible, what the TQM firm's performance would have been had it not implemented TQM. Such a control methodology requires controlling for systematic differences between TQM and non-TQM firms that affect firm performance, but are not a result of the TQM implementation. In particular, this means controlling for the fact that implementation of TQM is an endogenous choice. The factors that influence the decision to implement TQM almost certainly would affect future performance of the firm had it not implemented TQM.

While it is reassuring for TQM advocates that the vast majority of these studies show improved performance associated with TQM (or quality awards), there is substantial variation in the credibility of the evidence presented by the studies when examined in the context of the research issues we describe. In our opinion, only three of the nine studies that are reviewed in detail above, those by Easton and Jarrell (1998), Hendricks and Singhal (1996), and Anderson, Daly, and Johnson (1995), are based on credible research methods. The results of two of these three studies (Easton and Jarrell; Hendricks and Singhal) show positive financial impact associated TQM implementation. The third study, that on ISO 9000 registration by Anderson, Daly, and Johnson, finds no overall effect. None of the additional three studies reviewed briefly (two non-academic studies, and the study by Eskildson (1995)) are based on credible research approaches.

Finally, we believe ultimately that the case for the impact of TQM will be made by both studies of overall financial impact at the firm level and studies of the impact within the plant, site, or business unit. Studies of operational impact within companies are difficult, because available performance measures are different in different companies and variables with a common name often have very different meanings. This makes analysis of the data and development of adequate controls problematic. It is important to note that improvement in the operating variables per se is not evidence of the effectiveness of the management techniques examined, as virtually all firms that remain in business must improve. At the operational level, the competitive advantages provided by TQM that lead to above-market rates of return are a result of the rate of improvement, the ability to maintain a gap in comparison to competitors ("early improvement adoption or discovery"), firm-specific improvements that are not available to competitors, more rigorous control, and distributed learning throughout the workforce.

One line of research we have not mentioned here that we feel is particularly promising for making the internal operational impact aspect of the case for TQM is based on in-depth field studies within specific industries that examine objective performance data. This research is promising because of the objectivity of the metrics (as opposed to the use of manager perceptions) and because the focus on specific industries (and the industry-specific expertise the researchers develop) allows development of comparable measures across firms. The study by Ichniowski, Shaw, and Prennushi (1993), which focuses on the steel industry, is an example of this type of research (also see Ichniowski, Shaw, and Crandall 1995).

It is also important, however, that the impact of TQM on internal performance be studied for key processes outside of production, such as new product development. As is heavily emphasized in both TQM practice in advanced companies and in the TQM trade literature, much to most of the improvement due to TQM occurs because of integration of true customer focus into the product development process, cross-functional integration of new product development with other areas (particularly with operations), and new product development cycle-time reduction. TQM's impact on operations is only a part of the overall impact. In addition, TQM's impact on other key processes, such as technology adoption into both products and manufacturing, also should be studied.

Acknowledgments

We would like to thank George Benston and four anonymous referees for comments that substantially improved the manuscript. This research was partially supported by NSF grants numbers SBR–9523962 (Easton) and SBR–9523003 (Jarrell).

Notes

1   TQC is also referred to as Company-Wide Quality Control (CWQC). The term TQC was adopted from Feigenbaum (1961). Japanese TQC, however, is substantially different from the approach described by Feigenbaum.
2   In many studies, little information is reported about the actual questionnaire.
3   For example, Hendricks and Singhal (1996) use the stock return for the day of the announcement if the announcement occurs before the stock market closes at 4:00 PM Eastern time. Otherwise the next trading day is used. This means that is it possible in their study for the market to have only a very short time (possibly only minutes) to react to the announcement. It is not clear that market consensus concerning the impact of such an announcement occurs in such a short a period of time.
4   Hendricks and Singhal argue that the announcement date of a firm's quality award can be used to approximately determine the time period of development of a firm's TQM system. In particular, in the second paper (Hendricks and Singhal 1995), they name the pre-event period from −6 to −1 years before the event the "implementation period" of the firm's TQM approach and the period from −1 to +3 as the "post-implementation period."
5   We operationalized "statistically compelling" in this context to be statistically significant at the 0.05 level (one-tailed) on any two of the following three variables: percentage change in operating income, percent change in operating margin, and percentage change in sales. We did not use the variable percent change in cost per dollar of sales (defined as "selling general and administrative expenses" (SGA) plus cost-of-good-sold (CGS) divided by sales) because we believe it should be almost perfectly correlated with operating margin, since operating income is defined by COMPUSTAT to be sales minus (SGA+CGS).
6   An approximate cumulative abnormal return for the two-year period can be obtained by adding the cumulative returns for each of the six-month periods. The standard deviations for the each period's cumulative returns can be

calculated from the ratio of the cumulative abnormal returns and the Z-statistics for each of the six-month periods that are given in the paper. An approximate standard deviation for the two-year cumulative abnormal return can be obtained as the square root of the sum of the squared standard deviation of each period. The Z-statistics obtained are not significant for either the sum of all four post-event periods or for the sum of the three periods remaining when the period from 0 to 6 months is eliminated. These calculations are rough because they ignore issues such as differences in sample size for the four periods.

7 It would be impossible to omit all firms that had actually won a quality award because essentially all firms in the sample would be omitted. Virtually all firms that make a serious effort to implement TQM win one or more quality awards and it would be virtually impossible to develop an advanced TQM system without winning multiple awards. The key point is that quality awards are common and many awards are not particularly difficult to obtain and can be obtained using traditional management methods (e.g., increased inspection and best efforts).

8 Implementation of TQM by the control firms after the five-year period examined for the TQM sample firm has no effect on the results.

References

American Quality Foundation and Ernst & Young (1993a), *The International Quality Study: The Definitive Study of the Best International Quality Management Practices; Best Practices Report*, Ernst and Young, Cleveland, OH.

American Quality Foundation and Ernst & Young (1993b), *The International Quality Study: The Definitive Study of the Best International Quality Management Practices; Top-Line Findings*, Ernst and Young, Cleveland, OH.

Armstrong, J. S. (1982), "The Value of Formal Planning for Strategic Decisions: Review of Empirical Research," *Strategic Management Journal*, 3, 197–211.

Anderson, S. W., J. Daly, and Marilyn F. Johnson (1995), "The Value of Management Control Systems: Evidence on the Market Reaction to ISO 9000 Quality Assurance Certification," working paper, University of Michigan Business School, Ann Arbor, MI.

Benson, P. G., J. V. Saraph, and R. G. Schroeder (1991), "The Effects of Organizational Context on Quality Management: An Empirical Investigation," *Management Science*, 37, no. 9, 1107–24.

Black, S. A. and L. J. Porter (1996), "Identification of the Critical Factors of TQM," Decision Sciences, 27, no. 1, 1–21.

Cole, R. E., P. Bacdayan, and B. J. White (1993), "Quality, Participation, and Competitiveness," *California Management Review*, 35, no. 3, 32–54.

Christensen, J. S. and W. Y. Lee (1994), "Total Quality Management and Corporate Performance: An Empirical Investigation," working paper, College of Business Administration, Kent State University, Kent State, OH.

Dean, J. W., Jr. and S. A. Snell (1996), "The Strategic Use of Integrated Manufacturing: An Empirical Examination," *Strategic Management Journal*, 17, no. 6, 459–80.

Easton, G. S. (1993), "The 1993 State of U.S. Total Quality Management: A Baldrige Examiner's Perspective," *California Management Review*, 35, no. 3, 33–54.

Easton, G. S. and S. L. Jarrell (1994), "The Effects of Total Quality Management on Corporate Performance: An Empirical Investigation," *Journal of Business*, 71, no. 2, 253–307.

Easton, G. S. and S. L. Jarrell (1997), "Patterns in the Deployment of Total Quality Management: A Analysis of Interviews with Forty-Four Leading Companies," forthcoming in *Integrating Research on Quality into the Social Sciences*, R. Cole and R. Scott, eds, Sage Publications, Thousand Oaks (CA).

Eskildson, L. (1995), "TQM's Role in Corporate Success: Analyzing the Evidence," *National Productivity Review*, 14, no. 4, 25–83.

Feigenbaum, A. V. (1961), *Total Quality Control*, McGraw Hill, New York.

Flynn, B. B., R. G. Schroeder, and S. Sakakibara (1994), "A Framework for Quality Management Research and an Associated Measurement Instrument," *Journal of Operations Management*, 11, 339–66.

Flynn, B. B., S. Sakakibara, and R. G. Schroeder (1995), "Relationship Between JIT and TQM: Practices and Performance," *Academy of Management Journal*, 38, no. 5, 1325–60.

Flynn, B. B., R. G. Schroeder, and S. Sakakibara (1995), "The Impact of Quality Management Practices on Performance and Competitive Advantage," *Decision Sciences*, 26, no. 5, 659–91.

Gadd, K. W. and J. S. Oakland (1996), "Chimera or Culture? Business Process Reengineering for Total Quality Management," *Quality Management Journal*, 3, no. 3.

Hammer, M. and J. Champy (1993), *Reengineering the Corporation: A Manifesto for Business Revolution*, Harper, New York.

Hendricks, K. B. and V. R. Singhal (1995), "Firm Characteristics, Total Quality Management, and Financial Performance: An Empirical Investigation," working paper, Georgia Institute of Technology.

Hendricks, K. B. and V. R. Singhal (1996), "Quality Awards and the Market Value of the Firm: An Empirical Investigation," *Management Science*, 42, no. 3, 415–36.

Hendricks, K. B. and V. R. Singhal (1997), "Does Implementing an Effective TQM Program Actually Improve Operating Performance? Empirical Evidence from Firms that have Won Quality Awards," *Management Science*, 43, no. 9, 1258–74.

Hiam, A. (1993), *Does Quality Work? A Review of Relevant Studies*, The Conference Board, New York.

Holder, M. E. and R. D. Pace (1994), "Total Quality Management and Shareholder Returns," working paper, College of Business Administration, Valparaiso University, Valparaiso, IN.

Ichniowski, C., K. Shaw and R. W. Crandall (1995), "Old Dogs and New Tricks: Determinants of the Adoption of Productivity Enhancing Work Practices," Brookings Papers on Economic Activity, 1–65.

Ichniowski, C., K. Shaw, and G. Prennushi (1993), "The Effects of Human Resources Management Practices on Productivity," working paper, Graduate School of Industrial Administration, Carnegie Mellon University, Pittsburgh, PA.

Jacob, R. (1993), "TQM: More than a dying fad?," *Fortune*, 28, no. 9, 66–72.

Jarrell, S. L. (1991), "Do Takeovers Generate Value? Non-Stock Price Evidence on the Ability of the Capital Market to Assess Takeovers," unpublished dissertation, Graduate School of Business, The University of Chicago.

Jarrell, S. L. and G. S. Easton (1997), "An Exploratory Empirical Investigation of the Effects of Total Quality Management on Corporate Performance," Chapter 2 in *The Practice of Quality Management*, U. Karmarkar and P. Lederer, eds, Kluwer Academic Publishers, Boston.

Kahle, K. M. and R. A. Walking (1996), "The Impact of Industry Classification on Financial Research," *Journal of Financial and Quantitative Analysis*, 31, no. 3, 309–35.

Lawler, E. E., S. A. Mohrman, and G. E. Ledford, Jr. (1992), *Employee Involvement and Total Quality Management: Practices and Results in Fortune 1000 Companies*, Jossey-Bass, San Francisco.

Lawler, E. E., S. A. Mohrman, and G. E. Ledford, Jr. (1995), *Creating High Performance Organizations: Practices and Results of Employee Involvement and Total Quality Management in Fortune 1000 Companies*, Jossey-Bass, San Francisco.

Lemak, D. J., R. Reed, and P. K. Satish (1996), "Commitment to Total Quality Management: Is There a Relationship with Firm Performance?," forthcoming in the *Journal of Quality Management.*

Levine, D. and D. Kruse (1990), "Employee Involvement Efforts: Incidence, Correlation, and Effects," working paper, Haas School of Business, University of California, Berkeley, CA.

Mavrinac, S. C., N. R. Jones, and M. W. Meyer (1995), "Competitive Renewal through Workplace Innovation: the Financial and Non-Financial Returns to Innovative Workplace Practices," U.S. Department of Labor Report.

Pearce, J. A.., E. B. Freeman, and R. B. Robinson (1987), "The Tenuous Link Between Formal Strategic Planning and Financial Performance," *Academy of Management Review,* 12, no. 4, 658–75.

Powell, T. C. (1995), "Total Quality Management as Competitive Advantage: A Review and Empirical Study," *Strategic Management Journal,* 16, 15–37.

Reed, R., D. J. Lemak, and J. C. Montgomery (1996), "Beyond Process: TQM Content and Firm Performance," *Academy of Management Review,* 21, no. 1, 173–202.

Reimann, C. W., and H. S. Hertz (1996), "The Baldrige Award and ISO 9000 Registration Compared," *Journal for Quality and Participation,* 19, no. 1, 12–19.

Saraph, J. V., P. G. Benson, and R. G. Schroeder (1989), "An Instrument for Measuring the Critical Factors of Quality Management," *Decision Sciences,* 20, no. 4, 810–29.

Snell, S. A. and J. W. Dean, Jr. (1992), "Integrated Manufacturing and Human Resources Management: A Human Capital Perspective," *Academy of Management Journal,* 35, 467–504.

United States Department of Labor (1993), "High Performance Work Practices and Firm Performance," (Supt. of Docs. no. L 1.2: P 41/1993).

United States General Accounting Office (1991), "Management Practices: U.S. Companies Improve Performance Through Quality Efforts" (GAO/NSIAD–91–190).

Zbaracki, M. J. (1994), "The Rhetoric and Reality of Total Quality Management," working paper, Department of Industrial Engineering and Engineering Management, Stanford University, Stanford, CA.

3 | Academic Culture and the American Quality Movement: Linking Fundamental Research and Quality Practice

Marietta L. Baba

Abstract

Unlike their counterparts in Japan, American academics have not been particularly prominent in this nation's quality movement. Significant cultural barriers separate the mainstream of academic faculty from the mainstream of quality practice. One result of this separation has been the scarcity of research and teaching on quality in American schools of business and management. The Total Quality Leadership Steering Committee (LSC), an independent consortium of major industrial and academic leaders, set about to bridge the distance between academics and quality practitioners by creating a mechanism to stimulate and support rigorous empirical research on quality. Such research is expected to establish a foundation for teaching about quality in colleges and universities which, in turn, will drive the dissemination of quality principles across the public and private sectors. The efforts of the LSC led to the formation of a new research program at the National Science Foundation – the Transformations to Quality Organizations (TQO) program. TQO, which has been supported primarily by industry funds, is designed to address issues that separate academic theorists and industrial practitioners of quality. This chapter on the TQO program has three principal objectives. One is to overview the historical and cultural contexts of the TQO program, with the aim of capturing the critical conditions and developments that gave rise to this ambitious industrial initiative. Another goal is to document the program's unique design features, and its basic operations and activities. The final goal is to discuss TQO's strategy and tactics within an intellectual framework that may enable reinterpretation of the American quality movement, and contribute to its rapprochement with academia.

"I believe that quality management is a survival issue for American business. I believe we need to do a better job of graduating students who believe in total quality, who understand it, and who can apply it to their work on day one. And, perhaps most important, I believe that we need a much larger body of serious research in quality management – methodical, quantitative, value-added, collaborative research that can

be applied across thousands of enterprises to improve competitiveness,
particularly on bottom-line results."

John E. Pepper, Chairman and Chief Executive Officer,
The Procter & Gamble Company, Chairman,
Leadership Steering Committee, 1996

INTRODUCTION

In a series of unprecedented actions, a leading corps of major American
corporations initiated an alliance with the federal government, explicitly for the purpose of influencing the behaviors and beliefs of faculty
in American institutions of higher education. The tangible embodiment of
this corporate effort to change the culture of American academe is a new
research program at the National Science Foundation (NSF), called Transformations to Quality Organizations (or TQO). On the surface, the program does not seem terribly unusual. University faculty are accustomed to
the ubiquitous "program announcements" of the NSF heralding the availability of grant funds, contingent on success in the NSF's well-known system
of peer-review competition. From reading its announcement brochures,
TQO appears to be another one of these programs. Beneath the surface,
however, are unusual circumstances and even more extraordinary objectives.

For the first time in NSF's history, corporations (rather than Congress)
provided most of the funds to support a research program. Nearly 80 percent of $9 million over three years come from annual industry fund-
raising efforts.[1] The significance of this investment lies not so much in its
size, but in the fact that the large proportion of funds supplied by industry
gives corporations a major voice in the program, and carries with it a
commitment to hands-on activism from the corporate community. Industry provides both scores of subject matter experts to review individual
proposals, and about a dozen carefully selected executives who comprise
one-half of TQO's funding recommendation panel. The program is actively
co-managed by a team of program directors from the NSF and industry.
A joint industry-NSF council is responsible for management oversight.
Virtually everything that happens in TQO reflects a government-industry
consensus. Such intensity of interaction with industry is unprecedented at
the NSF.

The most extraordinary feature of the program, however, is its long-
range objective. The TQO program is not an end in itself, but is part of a
larger industry strategy aimed at drawing the faculty of US colleges and
universities into the American quality movement and thereby, hopefully,
enhancing the vigor and power of that movement in strengthening US
industrial competitiveness. Unlike their counterparts in Japan, American
academics have not been particularly prominent in this nation's quality
movement. In fact, significant cultural barriers separate the mainstream of
academic faculty from the mainstream of quality[2] practice. TQO aims to

transcend these barriers, in part by enabling faculty to approach quality on their own terms (e.g., through disciplined empirical inquiry) and in part by transforming the nature of quality itself. Empirical research is expected to build a base of academic literature which fundamentally alters our understanding of quality, and simultaneously removes or reduces some of the cultural barriers to faculty involvement. All of this is directed toward the introduction of quality into the core of academic culture – teaching – meaning both curricular content and pedagogical practice. The teaching process, in turn, will drive the large-scale dissemination and subsequent application of quality principles across the public and private sectors.

This chapter on the TQO program has three principal goals. One is to overview the historical and cultural contexts of the TQO program, with the aim of capturing the critical conditions and developments that gave rise to this ambitious industrial initiative. Another goal is to document the program's unique design features, and its basic operations and activities. The final goal is to discuss TQO's strategy and tactics within an intellectual framework that may enable reinterpretation of the American quality movement, and contribute to its rapprochement with academia.

BACKGROUND: HISTORICAL AND CULTURAL CONTEXTS OF THE TQO PROGRAM

The origins of the TQO program date to the early and middle 1980s. This was the era in which large American manufacturing firms such as Motorola, Xerox, Ford and others engaged in serious, even life-or-death, struggles with Japanese competitors, and in the crucible of battle became convinced that total quality principles and practices were an integral element of the critical skill set needed to survive in the global business arena. A major impediment to the acquisition of this skill set, however, was a lack of knowledge about quality within America's management and workforce. Companies recognized that short-term training could not substitute for an in-depth education in quality. Future managers and employees needed time to study, reflect and practice quality during their formative educational years, and in so doing, to become steeped in the modern quality tradition. Only such an immersion would enable America's corporations to become world leaders in quality.

Unfortunately, the new recruits coming to industry from the academy, including those from elite colleges and universities, also were not knowledgeable about total quality principles and practices.[3] Corporations found that they needed to provide remedial training in quality to new employees after they came on board, rather than hiring knowledgeable young people who would help the company push the quality envelop. As a result of the lack of preparation of new hires, American firms felt that they were at a disadvantage with their international competitors, and might never become global leaders in quality.

The total quality leadership steering committee and its working councils

Believing that executive leadership was needed to introduce quality into academic curricula, David Kearns, then Chief Executive Officer of Xerox Corporation, convened on August 1, 1989 the first of a series of annual meetings between business and academic executives. In these meetings, which became the Total Quality Forums, industry leaders expressed a keen interest in partnering with academia to fulfill several industry expectations, including the delivery of graduates who understand quality issues, and the integration of total quality topics and courses into the curriculum.[4]

Information gathered within the context of the Forums confirmed the scarcity of teaching on quality in American schools of business. A survey by Professor Robert Kaplan at the Harvard Business School showed that in 20 leading business schools in the US, only 20 percent of the introductory operations management courses spent more than three sessions on quality (Robinson et al. 1991).[5] Kaplan's survey of four leading operations management journals further showed that of the 278 articles published over a period of several years, there was virtually no direct coverage of total quality. These surveys suggested a *link between teaching and research* – faculty need a body of valid and reliable academic literature on which to ground their instruction if a subject is to become part of the curriculum. Recognizing that an absence of literature would frustrate efforts to increase the teaching of quality, the 1991 Total Quality Forum recommended the establishment of *a national research agenda* on total quality as one of four key objectives.[6]

Shortly after the 1991 Forum, Edwin Artzt (then Chief Executive of Procter & Gamble), organized the Total Quality Leadership Steering Committee (LSC), primarily to ensure that the four key objectives were realized. This leadership body, in turn, organized a system of Working Councils to pursue the four objectives. One of these – the Total Quality Research Working Council – was charged with the task of developing the national research agenda (Evans 1992). (Appendices A and B provide membership lists for the LSC and the Research Working Council.)

The Research Working Council began by surveying the literature on total quality and confirming Professor Kaplan's findings. Of the 17,000 articles published in English that had quality as a key word, the vast majority were practitioner-oriented works filled with anecdotes and prescriptives, but short on rigorous, systematic empirical data. The working council noted several barriers to faculty research on total quality, including the following:

1   the lack of connectivity between academic researchers and their "organizational customers" – academic researchers are disconnected from potential organizational users of their findings, and often publish more for each other than for external audiences;
2   a shortage of funding for research on total quality;

3   the functional (disciplinary) nature of academic institutions, mean-
    ing that research on quality, which is cross-functional in nature, has
    no academic "home" and may be perceived as high risk with respect
    to tenure and promotion decisions;
4   insufficient publishing opportunities, related primarily to the single
    discipline bias of most research journals, and the lack of value placed
    on problem-oriented vs. theoretical research; and
5   a general lack of recognition among faculty of the importance of
    research on quality, growing out of the conditions noted above, and
    the view held by many faculty that quality is a management fad.
    (Evans 1992)[7]

The national research agenda on quality constructed by the working
council was designed to address these barriers. It was the Research Working
Council that recognized explicitly the critical relationship between research
and teaching, and recommended actions to establish a quality-oriented
research program. In the words of the council:

> If America's top researchers focus their main attention on TQ, they will be
> able to point the way to accelerate the practice of TQ. The expanded faculty
> interest and expertise in TQ will also lead to rapid changes in curricula.
> Future company employees (university graduates) will then be trained at the
> cutting edge, bringing in new and advanced skills and practices in TQ, not
> just core competencies. (Evans 1992, ch. 6, p. 5)

Before going on to examine the council's national research agenda, it is
necessary to pause for a moment to take a second look at the barriers
noted by the working council. While there is little doubt that the barriers
are real and significant, many of them appear to be symptoms rather than
causes. If there is a scarcity of funding, a shortage of publication outlets,
and a general lack of recognition regarding the importance of research
on quality, we may still ask: Why? A lack of faculty connectivity to external
audiences and the single discipline bias of universities do not provide
satisfactory answers to this question. While these structural features obviously create special problems for research on quality, they do not by themselves explain the avoidance of quality by the mainstream of American
academia. Universities in Japan also may be characterized generally by
these structural features, but that did not prevent the emergence of a
significant faculty presence in Japanese quality-oriented research and writing. To understand the reasons why American faculty generally do not sit
at the quality table, further explanation is required.

Culture clash: the total quality movement and American academia

If one considers the local knowledge, shared understandings, and habitual
practices of faculty in American higher education (especially those in

schools of business), it becomes clear that there is a deep divide between the cultural realities of campus life on the one hand, and the assumptions, values, norms and behaviors associated with the quality movement on the other. This divide is not only structural, it is intellectual and epistemological; it grows out of profound differences in the way knowledge has been constructed in different social contexts and the webs of meaning that attach to these different constructions. The following sections discuss some of these differences and their significance to the teaching of quality principles.

Perceived lack of empirical support and theoretical validity

Apart from statistics, which provides the scientific basis for statistical process control, there is a fairly widespread view among academics that total quality principles and practices represent a loose collection of heuristics and methods that have been developed by industrial practitioners, and that these heuristics lack solid empirical evidence or a theoretical framework to give them intellectual integrity. Sidney Winter (1994), for example, defines quality management as a set of heuristics:

> Quality management is the quest for improvement in organizational routines through the application of a particular collection of problem-solving heuristics and techniques . . . A problem-solving heuristic is an approach to problem solving that is useful in spite of limitations deriving in part from vagueness and in part from uncertainty regarding its domain of application . . . Quality management in its present form is largely a body of methods that have emerged from practice. (Winter 1994, pp. 93–4)

Other writers such as Anderson et al. (1994) express the view that quality practices lack theoretical rigor:

> Despite the apparent effect that the Deming management method has had on the practice of management around the world, there is little empirical research for its effectiveness beyond anecdotal evidence. This is in part because no theory describing, explaining, and predicting the impact of the Deming management method has been presented to guide the progress of the empirical researcher; neither its theoretical contribution nor its theoretical base has yet to be articulated. (Anderson, Rungtusanatham, and Schroeder 1994, p. 472)

The lack of academic literature on quality noted earlier corroborates these statements; presumably, an academic literature would present the empirical data and theorizing that should elevate quality concepts and practices to the status of a scientifically-grounded field of study and application. The view of quality as a pragmatic but non-scientific subject area explains the scarcity of teaching on quality – if there is no empirical data and no theory to explain in reliable and valid terms the what, how and why of quality practice, then in academic culture there is little or nothing of value to teach.

The disconnect between quality as a body of practical know-how on the one hand, and the mainstream academic literature in western organizational and management theory on the other, is a subject worth exploring further. It is recognized generally that the principles and practices of the modern total quality movement largely were invented and developed in Japan. Prior to the invention of Japanese quality control circles, traditional "quality control" meant detection of defects via an elaborate system of quality assurance inspections (an approach developed by Frederick Taylor in the US, following the principles of industrial organization outlined by Adam Smith). While the statistical dimension of Japanese quality practice was transferred directly from statistical process control theory originating in Great Britain and the United States, the Japanese rejected the management theory of Frederick Taylor, and created their own unique approaches to quality management. This rejection relates to Japanese beliefs concerning the proper scope and domain of scientific knowledge.

While the Japanese believed that the sciences of physics, chemistry, and mathematics were universal and could be transferred across nations, they did not agree that quality control management could be transferred in the same way (Ishikawa 1985). The Japanese do not agree with their counterparts in the west that management and "control" of people are proper subjects of scientific investigation; generally speaking, management is viewed as beyond the domain of scientific analysis (Lillrank and Kano 1989). This is probably one reason why Japan traditionally has not had schools of business administration. The lack of belief in the possibility of "scientific management" also accounts for the fact that the Japanese adopted western methods of statistical process control, but rejected Taylor's managerial theory of quality control, which they considered to be both wasteful (since the Japanese could not afford armies of specialized quality inspectors) and distasteful (since they did not care for the idea of workers behaving as machines; this Tayloristic view was thought to be dehumanizing; Lillrank and Kano 1989).

When the Japanese created their own approaches to quality management, these were more or less divorced from the American scientific management tradition, and the social and organizational science constructs that accompany it. The Japanese university professors who were involved through the Japanese Union of Scientists and Engineers (JUSE) in supporting the invention and development of quality control circles in Japanese plants were not social or organizational scholars, but "hard" science and engineering professors (Cole 1985; Nonaka 1995). Social, organizational and management science theories were not significant factors in the development of Japanese total quality practice (Lillrank and Kano 1989). When Japanese quality practices diffused to the United States, the two bodies of management knowledge – one western and one eastern – were divorced from each other, both in their epistemological origins, and in their intellectual content.

We will leave aside for the moment the question of whether or not the pragmatic knowhow that emerged from Japanese industrial experience can

be considered part of a scientifically valid body of knowledge, and return
to this question after examining another related issue – the reputed dis-
harmony between western management theory and total quality principles.

Conflicts with existing economic and management theory

Not only do the principles of quality management appear to be disconnected from the mainstream body of western organizational and managerial theory, they often seem to contradict established theory in ways that
are difficult to ignore. A number of writers have discussed these conflicts.[8]
For example:

- Sitkin et al. (1994) points to the incompatibility between contingency theory in mainstream organizational science on the one hand,
  and existing quality literature on the other. While contingency theory
  holds that organizational effectiveness depends on the "goodness of
  fit" between alternative managerial options (e.g., choices regarding
  structure or technology) and external or internal conditions, quality
  proponents often seem to be arguing that there is a universal set of
  best practices or "one best way" to handle virtually every management
  decision.
- Cole and Mogab (1995) provide detailed descriptions of two different conceptions of productivity improvement, one based on orthodox
  economic theory and the other emerging from the logic of quality
  principles. The orthodox approach requires massive one-time capital investments in new technology, long learning curves, and reductions in headcount, versus the other in which investments are made
  in workforce knowledge and empowerment, followed by a process
  in which the workforce makes multiple incremental improvements in
  existing technical processes resulting in significant productivity increases over time, with no significant headcount reductions. Comparative advantages of the quality approach (called *kaizen* in Japan) are
  that it does not require massive capital investment, it does not need
  to be imported from external sources and "integrated" in a way that
  disrupts production, it enables more rapid responses to external
  change, and it creates little or no resistance in the workforce.
- Grant et al. (1994) argues that the traditional economic theory of
  the firm and quality management principles reflect two fundamentally different models of business organization. In the traditional
  economic model, profit maximization and increases in shareholder
  wealth are the primary goals of the enterprise, while the emerging
  quality model holds improvements in customer satisfaction and
  increases in value delivered to multiple stakeholders (including
  employees) as the driving objectives. These authors are convinced
  that the differences between the two models are so profound that

they color virtually every aspect of managerial policy and practice, with quality principles reflecting a bona fide revolution in management theory.

The conflict between existing management theory and total quality principles has led some to argue that quality represents a Kuhnian style paradigm shift – an alteration in the underlying axioms that structure one's view of the world (see for discussion Cole and Mogab 1995). Proponents of this view argue that existing management theory puts a thick lens of biased assumptions over the eyes of managers and faculty alike, and the whole world is perceived through that lens. Until this lens of assumptions is removed, or at least made visible, one cannot appreciate the validity of quality principles.

If this argument has any merit, it is clear to see the dilemma facing faculty. It is difficult for faculty to embrace a set of concepts and principles that contradict the core ideas set forth in basic management textbooks, especially when the textbooks of the "revolution" have yet to be written. Further, there are even more serious difficulties. In a Kuhnian revolution, anomalies build up until existing theory collapses under their weight. New competing theories emerge, and those that explain the anomalies best (while still explaining much of what the old theory covered) gain in favor. While it is true that significant anomalies have gathered around traditional management theory – the serious difficulties faced by American manufacturing in the 1970s and 1980s are a large case in point – it is not so clear that quality principles explain these anomalies while simultaneously covering the old territory. Indeed, quality has its own anomalies, they are significant, and faculty in business schools are acutely aware of them, as discussed in the next three sections.

Results are not replicated in the United States

Although the Japanese experience with quality generally was positive over the course of several decades (Lillrank and Kano 1989), the same cannot be said of US efforts to transfer total quality practices to this country. Spectacular cases of failure, in which successful quality programs in American companies preceded disastrous financial results and even bankruptcy, made business news headlines on more than one occasion (Sterman et al. 1996). Less dramatic studies of large samples of firms implementing total quality programs showed widespread dissatisfaction with bottom-line results, or the lack thereof (see American Society for Quality Control 1990, 1993; Ernst and Young 1991; Taylor 1992). For example, a 1992 Arthur D. Little survey of 500 manufacturing and service firms that implemented quality programs revealed that 64 percent did not achieve a significant competitive improvement as a result. In another 1992 survey by Rath and Strong, more than 50 percent of 95 firms with quality programs gave these programs a grade of D or F for results; only 20 percent got grades of A or B.

More than half of the respondents indicated that the programs did not improve customer satisfaction.

The reasons for these failures seem to be legion. Robert Cole (1995, pp. 3–4) summarizes some of the causes in the following passage:

> early company efforts that simplistically grasped at quality circles to provide the whole solution; over-reliance on statistical methods; under-reliance on statistical methods; the bellowing of top management about quality, without any follow-through; wholesale training of employees without immediate application; unrealistically high expectations for quick results; the bureaucratization of quality efforts; quality zealots who claimed quality to be a costless solution and a cure for whatever ailed a company; the failure to redesign traditional reward structures and organizational objectives to bring them into line with the new quality initiative (business as usual, but let's add quality to what we are doing); the failure to recognize the tight linkage between quality objectives and increased employee participation; the failure to integrate key functions like marketing into quality improvement activities; the unwillingness to adjust quality initiatives to special circumstances related to nation, industry, and firm-level conditions such as length of product cycle and competitive environment; the inability to move away from traditional results-oriented American management style; and the failure to build customer expectations and needs into daily organizational activities. All of these factors contributed to some spectacular failures and a massive waste of resources over the last decade.

This suggests that total quality practitioners lack the knowledge base needed to implement their principles successfully, and throws into doubt the validity of the principles themselves. Even cases of successful bottom-line results in individual firms often were greeted with skepticism by academic economists who asked, "So what?" Usually, published reports of successful quality initiatives do not provide much information about investment costs, or the cost of continuing the program. Thus, from the standpoint of traditional economics, the bottom-line value of the effort cannot be determined (Winter 1994).

If a theoretical revolution is to be supported, academics generally demand dispassionate evidence that an overthrow of the old order will leave them in a better position intellectually (or at least with respect to their careers), otherwise the risk is likely to judged too high. Such evidence has been hard to come by. Indeed, the very passion of the evidence that has been offered exacerbates the skepticism, as discussed below.

Ideological fervor creates suspicion

Given that total quality is not grounded in a base of systematic empirical research (as we define such in the United States), that it conflicts sharply with existing economic and management theory, and that it is basically unproved in this country, skepticism would appear to be in order – at least from an academic perspective. Yet, the behavior of total quality proponents often seems to reflect the opposite intellectual stance. Their passionate prosteletizing and utter conviction that total quality is *the* correct way to manage has the flavor of religious zealotry. One has the sense that total quality is an ideological movement with political overtones (e.g., it is critical of American management and it pushes for worker empowerment), rather than an objective body of knowledge appropriate for teaching to students.

American culture generally is not inclined favorably toward ideological excess – middle class members of this culture tend to respect things, including ideas, that work well. Other kinds of ideas often are greeted with suspicion, distrust, or disinterest. While American academics may embrace ideologies with political implications (remember Marxism?), the total quality movement is tainted by shades of crass commercialism. Thanks to the business press and publishing industry, most management and engineering faculty have heard of consultants and trainers who "cleaned up" financially by playing to the fears of struggling corporations. Could the passionate cries for quality be tied in any way to the economic self-interest of those who claim to know "the truth"? Such speculation did much to fuel the academic turn-off to total quality.

Culturally inappropriate concepts and language

Quality consultants and trainers not only hawk their wares to corporations, but also to institutions of higher education. A small but growing number of American colleges and universities implemented total quality programs during the 1980s and 1990s, largely as the result of central administration efforts to improve the quality of services to students (Roberts 1995). Although the bulk of these efforts have not been aimed at the classroom (faculty, of course, still rule the core of the academic enterprise), professors have obtained some direct experience with quality on campus, and for the most part the taste has not been sweet. Many faculty have been soured by participation in campus quality programs that attempt to force on them concepts and language which reflect an alien environment. Some illustrations follow:

Customer satisfaction. Customer is not an accepted concept on campus. It is a word that comes from the commercial world, and the academy is supposed to be separate from that world. If there is any customer in the "marketplace of ideas", it is your academic colleagues who read your papers and decide if you will get published. Students definitely are not accepted as customers by faculty. There is a large status difference between faculty and students, with students in the lower status. Students are supplicants – they come on bended knee, and they are reminded of their powerlessness constantly.[9] If there is a customer in the faulty-student relationship, it is the professor – the student must please her teacher, otherwise dissatisfaction will result in the student being punished with a poor grade. The cultural logic of academia often makes student satisfaction an oxymoron; if all of the students are satisfied, maybe the course was too easy.

Leadership/employee participation. University administrators often are not viewed as leaders by the faculty – the faculty's leaders are other professors who write important articles and books, and sometimes members of the faculty senate who can express traditional academic values with great eloquence. So called leaders (i.e., administrators) may be viewed with disdain – if they want something, this may be a good reason to ignore it. This sentiment could explain why the efforts of the Leadership Steering Committee to push the teaching of quality from the top down was not fully effective. Academic leaders may lead other academic leaders, but typically they do not lead the faculty. Further, faculty are not "employees" – they are members of a discipline who happen to hold a position at an academic institution; the best faculty are mobile and can readily go elsewhere if they do not like the way they are treated. There is a high degree of professional autonomy, and the sense that the faculty already control their work process. They don't need to be "empowered", they are already there.

Cross-functional cooperation. Academia may be the last stronghold of functional stovepipes, where the stovepipes (i.e., disciplines) are revered and thought to represent a fundamental structural mechanism necessary for gaining and transmitting knowledge. Fighting the stovepipes is hard going. In many academic institutions, faculty positions and budgets are awarded on the basis of student enrollment in courses, counted on a departmental and college basis. There are enormous incentives to devise ingenious ways to entice students into your department, and to prevent them from going to other departments. This builds up your headcount, and your justification for more faculty lines. It is possible that academe represents the only type of organization where the "employees" do everything in their power to keep the "product" in their department for as long as possible. Teaming up with faculty in other departments or colleges means sharing student headcount (and grant overhead funds), practices which may be strongly discouraged or even forbidden by one's "leaders". In some institutions, the natural cross-functionality of total quality may be all but impossible to implement in a teaching context.

Reliability and control. Faculty would be very unhappy and, if unionized, might strike if management tried to impose more structured processes on their work. Faculty have chosen to be academics because they want freedom and creativity. Highly structured work processes cut into their professional autonomy. Indeed, the path to fame for faculty is to increase the variance in one's domain, not decrease it. This may mean developing radical new ideas in one's discipline, teaching concepts in entirely new ways, or cooking up some innovative venture for one's department or professional association. Following Sitkin et al.'s (1994) observation, academia appears to be one of those types of enterprises where "total quality *control*" is inappropriate. On the other hand, if you tell faculty that they should work to develop "total quality *learning*" practices, they will tell you that they do this already (Roberts 1995).

When faculty attend campus-based quality orientation or training sessions held by consultants who have been hired by their president, provost, or dean, they encounter the alien or inappropriate concepts and terms described above. This experience only serves to reinforce their suspicion that total quality cannot possibly work, and that they should get as far away from it as possible.

In summary, American faculty are oriented toward the published knowledge base. They read the mainstream literature, do their own research related to this literature, and create courses that transfer the knowledge that is in the literature. Because quality management did not grow out of the tradition of western management theory, but in fact conflicts with it in many ways, there are fundamental problems related to the teaching of quality. To teach total quality requires a leap of faith without a safety net. Given its controversial nature, committing oneself to total quality research and teaching is a high risk gamble. Ones' colleagues (who make decisions about promotion and tenure) do not view total quality as a serious subject of scientific research, but see it as something commercial, concocted by consultants, with questionable validity. Faculty witness the way in which companies start and stop their quality programs; they see the same thing happen on campus. The faculty note that American management is prone to fads (Cole 1995). They often conclude that, this too, is a passing fad, not a lasting part of the knowledge base. All of this creates an institutional climate where quality has not been admitted to the mainstream of academic thinking.

In the next sections of this chapter, we will consider the role of the NSF's TQO program as a potential catalyst in the reduction of cultural distance between American academe and the quality movement.

Blueprint of a solution: design for a national research agenda

Recognizing a need to bridge the gap between academia and the quality community, the Research Working Council of the Leadership Steering Committee designed many of the core features of what is now the NSF's Transformations to Quality Organizations Program (although at the time, the council did not know that their recommendations ultimately would produce an NSF program). These core features, which aim to reduce barriers to quality-oriented research, are summarized below, together with descriptions of the ways in which the features have been operationalized at the NSF.

Design feature 1   Strengthen connections to customers

Academic researchers often are not aware of high priority research issues in industry[10] due to a lack of connectivity between the researchers and potential customers (i.e., organizational users of research products; Evans 1992). Lines of communication between researchers and customers are not well developed, meaning that potential customers have difficulty articulating their research needs, and that researchers face difficulty obtaining regular feedback on their research from potential users. This lack of connectivity results in a "closed loop" system in which faculty conduct research and publish for each other, and the practical implications of research may not be discovered until years after the research has been published.

In the view of the working council, a national research agenda on quality management should require faculty to be linked closely with the users of research. Stronger linkages would enable users to express their critical research needs to the faculty (thereby convincing faculty of the importance of such inquiry), and would allow faculty to interact with users during the course of the research process (thereby generating research results that address critical user needs).

The working council recommended that research on quality management be conducted by teams of academic–industry partners that include faculty and representatives of companies or other organizations. Such partnerships would provide several benefits to academics, including ease of access to research sites, the possibility for direct and indirect financial support, and opportunities for collaboration with users which would increase the chances that research results would be implemented (academics often cite implementation of results as a valued outcome of research).

The academic–industry partnership concept is reflected in several TQO features. First, TQO guidelines require the gathering and analysis of primary empirical data in one or more organizational entities (public or private sector). This feature promotes an orientation toward potential external users of new knowledge. Second, all research proposals must include signed letters from one or more organizational partners indicating their agreement with the research topic, guaranteeing access to organizational data,[11] and stating their interest in implementing results as appropriate. Third, it is expected that partners will be involved in the research activity. This involvement may range from the inclusion of industry personnel as full-fledged members of the research team, to the establishment of special company advisory bodies to receive periodic reports on research progress and offer regular feedback. Fourth, each proposal must contain an action plan for dissemination of research results to targeted user communities, including both educational and industry users. Dissemination of findings to educators is especially critical, given the ultimate goal of influencing the content and practice of teaching.

Finally, and perhaps most important, formal input from the community of organizational sponsors and partners is obtained by the NSF at all stages in the peer review process. Representatives from the sponsor firms,[12] including the LSC's research director,[13] participate in designing and reviewing drafts of the TQO program announcements. A large group of industry representatives from sponsor firms provide expert technical reviews for each individual proposal (i.e., through the NSF's mail review process). The TQO funding recommendation panel is comprised of approximately half academic members and half industry members. To be funded, a proposal must not only have strong scientific merit, but also must address high priority research issues as defined by potential users; that is, industry panelists. All of these features were recommended by the working council as a means to give industry a voice in the research process, and to increase the chances that research results will return value to key stakeholders.

Design feature 2   Support cross-functional research

Many performance problems in organizations derive from narrow functional perspectives that drive optimization of results in one or a few organizational subsystems without recognizing the detrimental impact of such actions on the system as a whole. Traditional academic research strengthens the tendency toward subsystem optimization by focusing research and teaching on disciplinary specialties – graduates typically learn a great deal about the best ways to optimize finance, engineering or marketing, but generally learn less about approaches that integrate these functions for overall high performance.

A robust understanding of organizational phenomena, one that encourages cross-functional integration, requires that disciplinary research specialists join forces to create cross-disciplinary frameworks for data gathering, analysis and interpretation. As noted previously, cross-disciplinary research is tough to do, given heavy structural constraints in universities and the echoing of these constraints in academic publishing and grantsmanship.

The working council recommended that quality-oriented research involve cross-functional collaboration, both on the research team and in the definition of research problems or questions. TQO encourages such collaboration in several ways. The NSF portion of program funding is shared equally by the Directorate for Social, Behavioral and Economic Sciences (SBE) and the Directorate for Engineering (ENG). The program is co-directed by staff from each directorate, and all major decisions require consensus across the social science and engineering arms of NSF. In this way, two fundamentally different disciplinary domains have an equal share and stake in the program and an equal voice in decision-making, a political economy meant to stimulate cross-disciplinary interaction. Further, TQO guidelines require that the research itself be inter- or multidisciplinary.

In the first year of the program, this latter requirement was interpreted loosely to mean either multiple disciplinary perspectives on the research team, or in the research objectives and design. As it turned out, however, relatively few of the first year awards went to engineering–management teams (i.e., 3 out of 16 projects). This was worrisome, especially when combined with the fact that only three awards went to teams led by engineers.[14] The working council had emphasized that outstanding quality in organizations requires close collaboration and integration of engineering and management perspectives. TQO could be hampered in its ability to deliver new knowledge on such integration if little of the research embedded integration of these disciplines. Generating results that would be valued by both management and engineering faculty required that members of both of these communities contribute to the research process.

Therefore, in its second year, TQO escalated the requirement for cross-functional collaboration. Based on recommendations from an ad hoc advisory group of engineering faculty, a new section was added to the TQO program announcement in year two, emphasizing the importance of engineering involvement in the research. Also, higher priority now was to be given to proposals from research teams that included management and engineering faculty.

The results of this new emphasis were encouraging. More proposals were submitted by principal investigators from colleges of engineering (39 percent compared with 21 percent the previous year), and more were submitted by engineering-management teams (59 percent versus 40 percent previously). Results of peer review also were positive – four of the nine new projects funded in year two were led by engineers, and seven of nine awards went to engineering-management teams. Although data still was limited at this early stage, the integration of engineering and management perspectives in TQO research appeared to be headed in the right direction.

Design feature 3   Establish a research agenda on quality

After surveying the literature on quality, the working council developed a remarkably broad framework for a national research agenda on quality, defined in both functional and cross-functional terms. The functional component of the framework included human resource management, customer-supplier relations, strategic planning, marketing, statistical methods, operations management, financial accounting, and engineering. The cross-functional component was provided by the Baldrige core concepts.[15] To this wide universe were added research interests expressed by industry representatives, and participants from the Baldrige award process. Significantly, topics of interest to engineering faculty did not appear to be especially prominent.

It may seem incredible that so many subject matter areas could be taken seriously as the scope for a national research agenda, but the size and complexity of the domain derive logically from quality principles. Total quality embraces virtually all dimensions of organizational and management policy and practice, so almost nothing is truly out of scope (so long as it links to the quality objective of customer satisfaction). Anything an organization does is fair game.

The difficulty with such a broad definition of the research agenda, and a lack of connectivity between a broad set of quality principles and an explicit theoretical framework, is that there is little or no possibility of concentrating resources in areas that appear to be most promising for future intellectual advancement. Further, the linkage of research findings from separate projects, and the interpretation of ambiguous or conflicting results, is hindered when a theoretical framework is absent. With limited resources and little or no research focus, it is possible that research efforts could be spread too thin and be too diffused to achieve the intellectual breakthroughs needed to produce the next generation of quality knowledge.

Despite these difficulties, the NSF settled on use of the Baldrige core concepts as a means to frame the research scope for TQO.[16] Employment of a cross-functional approach increased the likelihood that research projects would be cross-disciplinary in nature. To the Baldrige core concepts were added several other cross-cutting or integrating research issues emerging from the pre-TQO workshops hosted by the NSF.[17]

Recognizing that lack of a theoretical framework for the definition of program scope presented obstacles to the maturation of TQO as a legitimate field of scientific inquiry, the NSF requested that the National Academy of Science's Commission on Behavioral and Social Science and Education (CBSSE) organize a series of workshops aimed at exploring the linkages between mainstream social science and organizational theory on the one hand, and quality research on the other.[18] The hope was that these workshops would begin to suggest priority areas for TQO research that could simultaneously advance the quality agenda while also stimulating the evolution of mainstream theory, and perhaps enabling the two separate intellectual domains gradually to converge. Results from the workshops were to be reflected in new TQO program announcements to be released in the third and fourth rounds of competition.

Design feature 4   Develop and administer a funding pool

Recognizing that faculty respond well to the carrot of new research dollars, the working council advised that the Leadership Steering Committee establish a multimillion dollar funding pool to support quality-oriented academic research for a period of five years. The administrative entity for handling proposal submission and distribution of funds was to be an already-established granting agency. As it turned out, determination of the administrative agency was not to be an afterthought, but would have a powerful impact on all other considerations. After discussion of various options for fund administration (including placement of the funding pool at the American Society for Quality Control or the Baldrige Office, and the establishment of an independent research entity such as JUSE), it was decided that the LSC should approach the National Science Foundation as a possible partner in the effort.

Selection of NSF as a potential administrator was considered carefully. Some industry representatives wondered if an agency of the federal government would be receptive or responsive to input from the private sector, and would practice total quality in the administration of the research. In the final analysis, industry recognized that NSF already was established as a premiere research agency with legitimacy in academic circles, and that it had a proven method for selecting the most promising scientific research program (Garry Huysse, personal communication, 1995). Placement of the funding pool at the NSF would signal to faculty a turn toward greater rigor and scientific validity in collective knowledge about quality. This shift toward higher quality in quality research ultimately could accelerate the development of better management practices, as data from NSF studies entered mainstream literature and then the classroom, where it would influence future generations of managers.

Following this logic, the LSC's John Pepper (then President of Procter & Gamble) invited the Director of the NSF (Walter Massey) to the November 11–13, 1992 Total Quality Forum in Cincinnati. At a Forum dinner session, Dr Massey joined several corporate CEOs and university presidents to discuss the role of the NSF in America's quality movement. In a follow-up meeting at the NSF, held on December 22, 1992, representatives of the LSC and NSF agreed to explore in detail the creation of an LSC-NSF research partnership.[19]

Over the year that followed, a series of intensive interactions among the LSC, NSF and the American Society for Quality Control (ASQC) resulted in construction of the main elements of what would become TQO. Included in these discussions were questions related to funding contributions and how industry monies would be administered, how the program would be staffed, data confidentiality versus freedom of information, and program guidelines. In the course of these discussions, the NSF explored its existing research activities to determine the extent to which quality research would overlap with current research programs. A review of the data base of all projects funded by the Division of Social, Behavioral and Economic Research revealed that only one currently funded project had the word "quality" in its title.

Ultimately, a memorandum of understanding (MOU) was developed which set forth the funding formula and other requirements for TQO.[20] Although the funding structure was less ambitious than that the $20 million originally recommended by the working council, it still provided a total of $9 million over three years, more than any other source of academic quality research in the United States. Important provisions of the MOU are summarized below:

> *Funding structure*: Over a period of three years, the LSC was to provide $6 million, the NSF would provide $2 million, and the American Society for Quality Control would provide $1 million. Monies from the LSC and ASQC were to be deposited in the NSF Trust Fund, in escalating annual increments.[21]
>
> *Co-management and oversight*: An Executive Council, comprised of 50 percent LSC representatives and 50 percent NSF representatives, was to meet annually to review and advise on all program activities, and report recommendations to NSF management.
>
> *Staffing*: The NSF would recruit and employ a temporary program director (i.e., Intergovernmental Personnel Assignee (IPA) or Visiting Scientist/Engineer to manage selection of awards and coordinate dissemination activities with the LSC.

Timetables. A time schedule and deadlines for activities and events such as proposal due dates, grant awards, and program announcements appear throughout the document, lending an unusual sense of urgency to the program.

Annual conferences. The NSF would organize an annual conference at which grantees would present their findings to industry sponsors.

The ASQC, a major player in the financial arrangements, was not a direct party to the MOU, but was considered an informal partner of the LSC. The ASQC volunteered to take the lead in activities related to broad dissemination of knowledge about TQO, a role facilitated by their technical strength in practitioner publication and other media (and the fact that ASQC has about 140,000 members, most of whom are quality practitioners).

Response to the first TQO program announcement validated much of the thinking of the working council on how to get the attention of American faculty. This program announcement called for concept papers – five-page descriptions of an intended research project – which could be screened by the NSF to determine whether they were in scope, and used as a basis to provide feedback to researchers on whether to proceed with a full proposal. On May 16, 1994 (the concept paper deadline) the NSF was shocked by the arrival of 510 concept papers, a volume that greatly swamped expectations. Clearly, pent-up demand for research support in the area of organizational management had been tapped. It took NSF staff nearly one business week to open all the proposal envelopes. About 90 concept paper authors were encouraged to submit full proposals, with 16 research projects ultimately being recommended by the TQO Panel for funding in year one. The full three-year cost of these projects was approximately $5.5 million. From a second round of 60 proposals in 1995, an additional 9 projects were funded, at a total cost of about $2.25 million. Thus, in its first two years of operation, TQO committed around 85 percent of the total $9 million to 25 projects.[22]

The research content of TQO projects reflects several important goals of the program. Three key goals are illustrated in the following brief project descriptions:

(Goal 1) Build the Base of Scientific Knowledge and Theory. Illustration: Sim Sitkin (Duke) and Kathleen Sutcliffe (Michigan) are testing the hypothesis drawn from contingency theory that work processes characterized by a high degree of uncertainty and non-routineness will require innovative approaches to quality management versus control-oriented approaches which seek to reduce variance.

(Goal 2) Solve Industry Problems Related to Quality. Illustration: John Sterman (MIT) and his colleagues are exploring the unanticipated negative consequences of successful quality programs that at times have yielded negative financial results for certain firms. Their findings will be embedded in "management flight simulators" which will be used to train future managers to anticipate and cope with the systemic consequences of quality improvement.

(Goal 3) Encourage Interdisciplinary Collaboration. Illustration: Don Falkenburg (Wayne State) and his associates are combining qualitative knowledge from ethnographic studies of work organization with quantitative approaches drawn from modeling and simulation to build object oriented models of team interaction dynamics that incorporate both social and technical variables. The models will enable managers to anticipate the quality outcomes of team redesign experiments without actually changing the organization.

These projects and others funded by TQO also support the goals of legitimizing a quality focus in academic research, enabling access to organizations for researchers, and linking new knowledge to education and practice through dissemination of findings. (For a description of all 25 research projects, see ASQC Item B0513, "Research for the Next Generation of Quality".)

A REINTERPRETATION OF QUALITY

Thus far in this chapter we have reviewed some of the structural and cultural barriers to academic involvement in the American quality movement, and examined elements of the TQO program that are intended as a means to surmount those barriers and enable cultural change.[23] The TQO program is largely a structural mechanism to achieve these objectives. The program encourages faculty to work together more closely (a) across disciplines, and (b) across the industry–university boundary. Encouragement is provided in the form of incentives that are meaningful to faculty – research grants, and access to organizational data. These are basically structural solutions – altering relationships among social actors.

Culture change, however, may be catalyzed not only through shifts in structure, but from new understandings or shared reinterpretations of phenomena that can result from a variety of sources, including the introduction of new ideas or gaining access to different vantage points. In this section of the chapter, we pursue this theme of reinterpretation by taking up the thread of an idea introduced earlier in the chapter – namely, that the portrayal of quality practices as atheoretical is a portrait that is culturally constructed (i.e., it is atheoretical from the perspective of western management thought). A shift in our viewpoint, however, may enable us to glimpse the hidden pattern of implicit theory within the body of quality doctrine. This shift in viewpoint is accomplished through the reinterpretation of quality practices as a body of inductive knowledge focused on organizational transformation in a global environment. By making the implicit explicit, we may contribute to the convergence of quality and western management thought, and also to the process of culture change.

Induction and the rise of an implicit conceptualization of the quality organization

We noted earlier the belief of established management scholars that ideas and methods associated with total quality do not represent a coherent theory of organizational systems or management. Despite this belief, there is evidence that quality principles and practices embed an important, if unexpressed, conceptualization of organizational reality and change which is founded on a wealth of inductive knowledge. We argue here that emerging theory in the social sciences is beginning to articulate the nature of this reality, creating the possibility of linkages between social science theory and quality practice. If this argument has merit, then there is the potential for emergent theory to guide future research on quality, and for quality research to contribute to the evolution of theory. A reinterpretation of quality practices as a body of inductively-discovered knowledge also could help to transform such practices from the status of mere practitioner heuristics to that of serious scientific subject matter.

The argument for an implicit conceptualization of organizational systems within quality practice begins from an appreciation of the role of inductive processes in the development of science. As suggested initially by Francis Bacon in the *Novum Organum*,[24] and validated historically in fields as diverse as chemistry, medicine, and anthropology, knowledge of natural phenomena may be gained through careful and systematic observation and experiential engagement with the world of nature.[25] The processes of induction – whereby human understanding of a phenomenon proceeds from the careful study of particulars, then moves toward immediately attainable local axioms, and finally, in a gradual and patient process, develops more general axioms – is an integral dimension of the scientific method[26] (Copleston 1963). Bacon contended that the discovery of natural laws through induction would increase human power, enabling our species to dominate nature through practical applications of knowledge in the process of invention.

The inductive methodology described by Bacon is, in fact, the basic process through which quality principles and heuristics initially were developed in Japan. The human observers in this case were industrial practitioners who gained their experience through decades of experimental intervention on the frontier of a highly stressed industrial system (e.g., Japanese industry after World War II[27]). Inside thousands of individual Japanese firms, managers, engineers, and workers engaged in direct observation and experimentation with newly emerging quality methods and techniques. The learning gained by these individual firms was gathered together, disseminated, and synthesized through activities organized by JUSE. Cole (1989) describes the complex national network of quality circle centers, chapters and conferences organized by JUSE in which groups of workers from individual firms presented the results of their quality circle learnings to audiences of workers from other firms. The best practices surfacing from these presentations were published for broader dissemination. JUSE also published a wide variety of materials that synthesized learnings on key topics from the individual experiences of multiple firms. Japanese university faculty in engineering and the sciences, together with company executives, played a leading role in the JUSE committees that distilled broad lessons from the experiences of thousands of different companies.[28] The body of knowledge generated through this essentially inductive process contained powerful and practical insights which, as Bacon would have predicted, endowed Japanese firms with an innovative competitive advantage (a point which has been well documented in the literature; e.g., see Womack et al. 1990).

The practitioners did not utilize their inductively-generated insights to create an explicit theory of organization, in large part because they were not members of the community of organizational scholars, and they did not have backgrounds or expertise in the social and behavioral sciences.[29] As a result, there is no explicit theoretical model of the quality organization, one which carefully identifies core and secondary concepts, indicates relationships among concepts, or suggests conditions for their application.

Yet, while the early observers did not develop an explicit theory of organization, their process of induction gave birth to a body of knowledge that embeds an implicit model of organizational systems and change processes. This implicit model is at odds with orthodox management theory in several respects, but there are also points of compatibility with new and emerging theory in the social and organizational sciences. This compatibility is not a coincidence, but reflects an emergent objective reality underlying the work of both eastern practitioners and western theorists, a reality that is driven by the necessity of global competition. From different points of view, both of these communities are "modeling" the reality of modern organizational systems engaged in transformation processes within a dynamic, global economic context. This modern reality is quite different from the early industrial world that existed when mainstream organizational and management theories first arose at the beginning and middle of the twentieth century. The tumultuous economic changes that have rocked our world in recent years may go a long way toward explaining why so much of the quality movement appears to contradict older and more orthodox theories of management and the firm.

From implicit to explicit theory

While limitations of space do not permit a comprehensive discussion of the linkages between quality principles and emerging theory in the social and organizational sciences, it is possible to suggest the nature of these linkages with a small sample of illustrations.

■ Sidney Winter (1994) first recognized a relationship between quality practices and evolutionary economic theory, especially with respect to the way in which a firm's capabilities are conceptualized. Evolutionary economics views a firm's capabilities as fragmented, distributed across, and embedded within multiple sets of routines (Nelson and Winter 1982). These routines constitute the most important form of storage for an organization's operational knowledge, much of which is tacit. The routines result from an historical learning process that is unique to each firm. Change in a firm's capabilities requires change in one or more sets of routines, which in turn requires a process of organizational learning that captures and stores new knowledge within the routines. Viewed from the perspective of evolutionary economics, quality practices represent a significant basic invention (a "mutation") in the set of search routines that enable innovation in other routines (i.e., it is a "meta-innovation"; Winter 1994, p. 100). This invention involves a repetitive sequence of activities (i.e., quality practices) which, if performed successfully, can systematically generate improvements in any of a firm's other multiple types of routines.

- Quality practices emphasize the importance of organizational linkages, and the need for partnerships between internal and external suppliers and customers to enable problem-solving across processes. Spencer (1994) argues that, implicit within this emphasis on process, linkages and partnerships is a systems-theoretic conceptualization of the firm that parallels, in many respects, the systems theory approach to organizations of the 1950s and 1960s. The systems approach largely was abandoned in favor of contingency theory, however, in part because of difficulties experienced in translating systems concepts into practical guidance for managers – a problem that quality practitioners have surmounted. Both systems theory and quality principles are compatible with an emerging *philosophy of interdependency* among social actors and units, contrasting with the individualistic world view underpinning neoclassical economics and modern management theory (see Alter and Hage 1993).

- Ethnographic research in work organizations has documented the important role of local knowledge in the effective operation of technical processes (see Baba 1990). Local knowledge is defined as an informal (i.e., not symbolically encoded) system of information, distinctive to a localized setting, that is created or possessed by operations-level employees. This information system develops in response to unforeseen problems emerging from the work process, and is required to operate technical systems effectively. Employees in US firms often hold such knowledge closely, using it for their own purposes (e.g., get the work out the door, enhance status and prestige in the work group, take shortcuts). This knowledge rarely is shared with or codified by management, and indeed, may embed actions that are contrary to firm policy. The quality movement recognizes the value of such local knowledge, and utilizes various mechanisms to encourage its transformation from informal and tactic to formal or explicit. One important type of mechanism involves an alteration in the psychological contract between employees and the firm so that employees are willing to "give up" something that the firm has not explicitly contracted with them to provide (for example, giving employees the authority to redesign their own work processes; Adler 1993). This latter mechanism recognizes employees as the owners of specific forms of knowledge that are already active in the production process, and offers them something of value (e.g., participation in decision-making) in exchange for the transfer of this asset to management.

The intent of these illustrations is to point toward emerging theoretical frameworks across several intellectual traditions that potentially can explain the pragmatic potency of the quality movement. They represent an argument in favor of developing an explicitly articulated network of concepts and hypotheses concerning quality principles and practices that can be tested under the canons of deductive scientific logic. A robust scientific method should link inductive and deductive processes in ways that capture the unique insights gained through experiential learning, and enable distillation of these insights through the rigor of systematic, empirical observation and measurement.

Inductive knowledge generated by practitioners should not be expected to possess the complexity and sophistication of modern organizational theory. The inductive model of organizational systems embedded in quality practices is in its early stages of development, and thus it is not surprising that it displays characteristics similar to those of early organizational theory (e.g., generic or undifferentiated models, a focus on micro-level phenomena; see Scott 1991). Over time, however, deductive research strategies such as those supported by the NSF's Transformations to Quality Organizations program should contribute to the maturation of these models and their intellectual sophistication.

CONCLUSION

This chapter has described the formation and operation of a culture change catalyst, one conceived by American corporations and targeted initially at the educational practices of American faculty. Whether or not this catalyst will successfully accomplish the hoped for change cannot be determined at this point; it is simply too early to tell. Ultimately, however, we will need to look not only on campuses, but inside the American quality movement itself, to find evidence of culture change. This is so because the initial conceptualization of the scope of change – faculty teaching – proved to be too limited, and did not describe the full domain of practice that must be altered if quality in America is to achieve global leadership. In fact, the domain of practice that needs to be changed includes the behavior of industrial practitioners themselves. They must become dissatisfied with the current state of expert advice on quality (i.e., consultant-driven) and demand a knowledge-based expertise that rests upon systematic empirical inquiry. This demand from the customers will fundamentally alter the American quality movement by pulling academics in and elevating the intellectual integrity of quality practice.

In some ways, we already have evidence that this latter kind of culture change in taking place. The industrial originators of TQO came to the NSF to change faculty teaching, but by the second year of the program's operation they were hooked on the research itself. After seeing the results of the first annual report out, industrial sponsors said that the quality, rigor and relevance of the work "exceeded expectations". Suddenly, company representatives were asking: "How can I get these researchers into my company to help us solve similar problems?" Suddenly, industry leaders were talking about the value added by the research itself, and asking for breakthroughs – new knowledge to solve quality problems became a goal co-equal to that of training students. This shift in the behaviors, expectations, and discourse of the companies suggests that their culture change program in fact is changing them, perhaps as much or more as it is changing the faculty.

In thinking further about the cultural barriers to academic participation in the quality movement, it is important to remember that quality is just that – a social movement. It certainly was a full-fledged, mass social movement in Japan (Cole 1989), and it probably is an incipient social movement in the United States. Like all social movements, the quality movement mobilizes people and resources in response to perceived societal problems (Mauss 1975). Because movements respond to problems, they often invite social criticism and controversy about existing policy and practice, carry political implications, and generate zealous emotional responses pro and con.

It may be that the political and emotional dimensions of the quality movement have alienated academics, some of whom prefer a more dispassionate approach to new ideas. Yet, where there is heat there may also be light. The social movement through which science itself emerged centuries ago had huge political and emotional consequences, but it also unleashed vast reservoirs of new knowledge. It is faulty reasoning to assume that passion automatically signals a lack of intellectual integrity. A better understanding of quality as a social movement, and its role in the revitalization of modern societies, could help to alleviate one of the persistent cultural barriers to academic participation, and perhaps could contribute to the maturation process of the movement itself.

APPENDIX A: LEADERSHIP STEERING COMMITTEE MEMBERSHIP – 1992

John F. Akers
　　Chairman of the Board, IBM

Paul A. Allaire
  Chairman and Chief Executive Office, Xerox Corporation
Edwin L. Artzt
  Chairman of the Board and Chief Executive Officer
  The Procter & Gamble Company
John V. Byrne
  President, Oregon State University
Livio D. DeSimone
  Chairman of the Board and Chief Executive Officer, 3M
Meyer Feldberg
  Dean, Graduate School of Business, Columbia University
Christopher B. Galvin
  Senior Executive Vice President and Assistant Chief Operating Officer
  Motorola, Inc.
Roger Milliken
  Chairman and Chief Executive Officer
  Milliken & Company
C. Warren Neel
  Dean, College of Business Administration, University of Tennessee at
  Knoxville
John E. Pepper
  President, The Procter & Gamble Company
Frank H. T. Rhodes
  President, Cornell University
James D. Robinson III
  Chairman and Chief Executive Officer
  American Express Company
William R. Showalter
  Dean, School of Engineering, University of Illinois
Donna E. Shalala
  Chancellor, University of Wisconsin at Madison
Robert C. Stempel
  Chairman, General Motors Corporation
Charles M. Vest
  President, Massachusetts Institute of Technology
John A. White
  Dean of Engineering, Georgia Institute of Technology
B. Joseph White
  Dean, School of Business Administration, University of Michigan

APPENDIX B: TOTAL QUALITY RESEARCH WORKING COUNCIL

Co-Chairs

Mark P. Finster
  Professor, Grainger School of Business, University of Wisconsin at Madison

Stephen B. Schwartz
Senior Vice President, Market Driven Quality, IBM

Members

Robert Cole
Professor, Haas School of Business, University of California at Berkeley
Stephen L. Graves
Deputy Dean, Sloan School of Management
Massachusetts Institute of Technology
Robert King
Executive Director, GOAL/QPC
Peter J. Kolesar
Professor, Graduate School of Business, Columbia University
Mary Kowalski
Senior Partner, 3M
Lucy Morse
National Science Foundation
Howard D. Wilson
Director, Market-Driven Quality, IBM

Notes

1 Corporate research partners provided additional in-kind support estimated at $4–$6 million during this period.

2 Quality is a multidimensional construct with a multitude of definitions (Reeves and Bednar 1994). Here, the term "quality" or "total quality" represents a set of management principles and practices directed toward improvements in customer satisfaction. The term "total quality management" is avoided, due to its association with various management "fads."

3 This comment does not apply to statistical training in schools of engineering, where many students are exposed to courses in statistical process control. It was primarily the management aspects of quality, also referred to as total quality, that were not represented in the curricula of most business or engineering schools.

4 At this point in time, industry did not appear to be particularly interested in research that the faculty might conduct. Teaching was the target.

5 In the author's own experience as an MBA student at a major university, her cohort was exposed to one week on total quality in the operations management course, and one weekend program on total quality, with no exams at the end of the weekend. The weekend program did not teach fundamental principles and methods, but instead served up "dog and pony shows" in which company representatives talked about their firms' experiences with quality.

6 The four key objectives were: (1) define the core knowledge generic to total quality that will serve as a foundation for the integration of total quality into curricula; (2) propose curricula and materials for teaching total quality in business and engineering schools at the graduate and undergraduate levels; (3) develop strategies to facilitate educators' understanding of and commitment to teach and practice total quality; and (4) and create a national research agenda for total quality. In their 1991 letter to the *Harvard Business Review*, the

Leadership Steering Committee omitted the second objectives, cutting the number to three.

7 Surveys of more than 500 business and engineering school deans conducted by one of the working councils suggested that the majority of faculty did not believe that quality was very or extremely important; according to the deans, most faculty believed the teaching of quality principles was somewhat important, not very important, or not at all important (Evans 1992).

8 Much more infrequent are writers such as Spencer (1994) who review comprehensively the points of consistency, as well as inconsistency, between total quality concepts and mainstream organizational constructs and theory. The points of consistency will become important in later sections of this chapter.

9 This reality was brought home to me in my recent experience of participant observation in an MBA program. While on an international business course study trip to the Far East, several of the students requested a "kaizen meeting" (the students' term) with the faculty to discuss some aspects of the course with which they were not satisfied. This event caused great consternation among the students, many of whom feared that their attendance at the meeting would result in a poor grade for the course. About half of 60 students attended the meeting, at which the senior professor in charge of the MBA program told the students, in angry tones, that it was impossible for them to request a "kaizen" meeting because, as students, they knew nothing about his work process and so they couldn't possibly have any information that would be relevant to course improvement. This professor then stormed from the room, refusing to accept the students' input. A second professor, who was responsible for the study trip, did listen to the students' comments, but it is not clear whether any action was taken to address their concerns.

10 The working council defined industry to include profit and non-profit organizations in the private and public sectors.

11 The opening of industry doors to academic research could be the most significant aspect of the TQO program. The NSF and other scientific organizations have identified limitations of access to company data (i.e., for proprietary reasons) as one of the primary constraints to the further evolution of organizational and management theory.

12 Sponsor firms are those that make annual contributions to the NSF Trust Fund for support of TQO research. The sponsorship concept will be discussed in detail in a later section.

13 While Jean Kinney of Procter & Gamble was the original LSC representative appointed to work with NSF staff member Cathy Hines in the formation and initial launch of the TQO program, it was Garry Huysse (also of P&G) who was the LSC's hands-on research director responsible for collaboration with the author (TQO's first full-time program director) and Pius Egbelu of the NSF's Directorate for Engineering (TQO's co-director).

14 Difficulty in attracting engineering faculty, and engineering-management teams, was foreshadowed in the NSF workshops that preceded formation of the TQO program, as discussed later in the paper.

15 The Baldrige core concepts incorporated in the 1995 TQO Program Announcement were: Continuous Improvement and Learning, Customer-Driven Quality, Design Quality and Prevention, Employee Participation and Development, Fast Response, Leadership, Long-Range View of the Future, Partnership Development, and Results Orientation.

16 Use of the Baldrige concepts to define program scope actually represented a compromise that emerged from a tense moment in one of the pre-program

workshops held at the NSF as part of the process leading up to the formal announcement of the new TQO program. Participants in the workshop could not reach agreement on a definition of quality, with particular disagreement dividing the engineering and management faculty in attendance. The point of crisis was passed when several workshop leaders went into a closed door session in the evening and came out with the Baldrige concepts as the agreed-upon definition. The disagreement on definition was viewed as a reflection of the embryonic state-of-the-art at the time. Even so, there still was concern that the Baldrige concepts were slanted toward management interests, and did not provide appropriate incentives to stimulate engineering research.

17   The cross-cutting research themes were: Integrative Models and Theoretical Frameworks, Culture Change, Diffusion of Ideas or Innovations, and Measures of Effectiveness. Topics of special interest to engineers were not added until year two.

18   The first workshop was held on September 6–7, 1996, and was co-chaired by W. Richard Scott, a member of CBSSE, and Robert Cole, chair of the TQO Advisory Council.

19   John Pepper and Paul Allaire (CEO of Xerox) represented the LSC at this meeting. The NSF was represented by Walter Massey, Cora Marrett (Assistant Director for Social, Behavioral and Economic Sciences), Joseph Bordogna (Assistant Director for Engineering), and Constance McClindon (Director of Information and Human Resources). Initially, Mr Pepper and Mr Allaire were not certain that the NSF would be interested in a partnership. Dr Marret and Dr Bordogna, however, seized upon this opportunity as a means to bring their directorates into a closer working relationship. Dr Marrett thus agreed to take the lead in exploring the partnership concept at the NSF, while Ms McClindon headed up a parallel effort to consult with LSC staff on bringing total quality expertise to the management of the NSF.

20   The MOU was never signed, but an informally accepted version was transmitted from the NSF to the LSC by the NSF's corporate counsel on March 4, 1994. Both parties have abided by this understanding, despite its non-binding legal status.

21   The companies providing financial support to the NSF's Trust Fund for the TQO program include: American Express Company, Amoco Corporation, AT&T, Bell Atlantic Network Services, Inc., Chevron Corporation, Corning, Inc., Deere & Company, Eaton Corporation, Eastman Chemical Company, Eastman Kodak Company, First National Bank of Chicago, Fluor Corporation, Ford Motor Company, General Motors Corporation, GTE Corporation, Honeywell, Inc., Lucent Technologies, McDonnell Douglas Corporation, Milliken and Company, Mobil Corporation, Motorola, Inc., The Procter & Gamble Company, The Quaker Oats Company, Rockwell International Corporation, Texas Instruments, Inc., 3M, TRW, Inc., Union Pacific Railroad Company, Whirlpool Corporation, Xerox Corporation.

22   In 1996, the TQO partners (LSC, NSF and ASQC) agreed to commit an additional $3 million to support the fourth and fifth years of TQO, thus ensuring a third and fourth round of proposal funding.

23   Culture change is defined as the irreversible alteration of a distinctive shared pattern of behavior and belief. Under this definition, the acceptance of quality as a legitimate area of scientific inquiry by mainstream academic leaders, the regular integration of engineering and management perspectives in research on quality, and the routine incorporation of total quality principles into business and engineering school textbooks and core courses, would constitute evidence of culture change in American academe.

24 *The New Organon,* first published in 1620.
25 In fact, Bacon argued that induction was the only method that could produce valid scientific knowledge.
26 Unfortunately, the modern social sciences have been dominated by the hypothetico-deductive approach, meaning that there is little understanding or recognition of the role of induction; see Lincoln and Guba 1985.
27 Evidence exists that Germany also has experienced a similar process, but the focus in this country has been on Japan (Thurow 1992).
28 Robert Cole (1989) notes that JUSE had about 250 technical committees, with about 1,600 volunteers by the mid 1980s. Of these volunteers, about 35 percent were university researchers and educators. There is no organization comparable to JUSE in the US. Here, consultants spread ideas, but they are driven by their commercial interests, which sometimes dilutes the validity and reliability of their practice.
29 In fact, Cole (1989) notes that western behavioral science concepts were introduced after the fact to "make sense" of the Japanese innovations.

References

Adler, P. 1986. New technologies, new skills. *California Management Review,* Fall, 9–28.

Adler, P. 1993. Time-and-motion regained. *Harvard Business Review,* Jan.–Feb., 97–108.

Alter, C. and J. Hage 1993. *Organizations Working Together.* Newbury Park, CA: Sage Publications.

American Society for Quality Control 1990. Quality: Everyone's Job. Summary and Highlights of a Gallup Survey of Employee Attitudes Toward their Jobs and Quality Improvement Activities. Milwaukee, WI: ASQC.

American Society for Quality Control 1993. Teaming Up for Quality: Employee Attitudes on Teamwork, Empowerment and Quality Improvement. Milwaukee, WI: ASQC.

Anderson, J., M. Rungtusanatham, and R. Schroeder 1994. A theory of quality management underlying the Deming management method. *Academy of Management Review,* 19(3), 472–509.

Baba, M. L. 1990. Local knowledge systems in advanced technology organizations. In: *Organizational Issues in High Technology Management.* L. Gomez-Mejia and M. Lawless, eds. JAI Press, pp. 57–76.

Cole, R. E. 1985. The macropolitics of organizational change: a comparative analysis of the spread of small-group activities. *Administrative Science Quarterly,* 30, 560–85.

Cole, R. E. 1989. *Strategies for Learning. Small-Group Activities in American, Japanese, and Swedish Industry.* Berkeley, CA: University of California Press.

Cole, R. E. 1995. *The Death and Life of the American Quality Movement.* New York: Oxford University Press.

Cole, W. and J. Mogab 1995. *The Economics of Total Quality Management.* Cambridge, MA: Blackwell.

Copleston, F. 1963. *A History of Philosophy.* Volume III. New York: Doubleday.

Dean, J. W. and D. Bowen, eds. 1994. A Total Quality Special Issue. *Academy of Management Review,* 19(3).

Ernst and Young 1991. International quality study – top line findings. International quality study – best practices report. (2 reports) Ernst and Young/American Quality Foundation.

Evans, J. 1992. *A Report of the Total Quality Leadership Steering Committee and Working Councils.* November, 1992. Cincinnati, OH: Procter & Gamble.

Grant, R., R. Shani, and R. Krishnan 1994. TQM's challenge to management theory and practice. *Sloan Management Review,* Winter, 25–35.

Ishikawa, K. 1985. *What is Total Quality Control? The Japanese Way.* Englewood Cliffs, NJ: Prentice-Hall.

Lillrank, P. and N. Kano 1989. *Continuous improvement: quality control circles in Japanese industry.* Center for Japanese Studies. University of Michigan. Ann Arbor, MI.

Lincoln, Y. and E. Guba 1985. *Naturalistic Inquiry.* Beverly Hills, CA: Sage.

Mauss, A. 1975. *Social Problems as Social Movements.* Philadelphia: J. B. Lippincott.

Nelson, R. and S. Winter 1982. *An Evolutionary Theory of Economic Change.* Cambridge, MA: The Belknap Press of Harvard University Press.

Nonaka, I. 1995. The recent history of managing for quality in Japan. In: *A History of Managing for Quality.* J. M. Juran, ed. Milwaukee, WI: ASQC Quality Press.

Reeves, C. A. and D. A. Bednar 1994. Defining quality: alternatives and implications. *Academy of Management Review,* 19(30), 419–45.

Roberts, H., ed. 1995. *Academic Initiatives in Total Quality for Higher Education.* Milwaukee, WI: ASQC Quality Press.

Robinson, J., H. Poling, J. Akers, R. Galvin, E. Artzt, and P. Allaire 1991. An open letter: TQM on the campus. *Harvard Business Review,* November/December, 94–5.

Scott, W. R. 1991. The evolution of organization theory. In: *Studies in Organizational Sociology: Essays in Honor of Charles K. Warriner.* Gale Miller, ed. London: JAI Press.

Sitkin, S., K. Sutcliffe, and R. Schroeder 1994. Distinguishing control from learning in total quality management: a contingency perspective. *Academy of Management Review,* 19(3), 537–64.

Spencer, B. 1994. Models of organization and total quality management: a comparison and critical evaluation. *Academy of Management Review,* 19(3), 446–71.

Sterman, J., N. Repenning, and F. Kofman 1996. Unanticipated side effects of successful quality programs: exploring a paradox of organizational improvement. Forthcoming in *Management Science.*

Taylor. P. 1992. Such an elusive quality. *Financial Times.* 14 February, 9.

Thurow, L. 1992. *Head to Head: The Coming Economic Battle Among Japan, Europe, and America.* New York: William Morrow.

Winter, S. 1994. Organizing for Continuous Improvement: Evolutionary Theory Meets the Quality Movement. In: *Evolutionary Dynamics of Organizations.* Joel A. C. Baum and Jitendra V. Singh, eds. New York: Oxford University Press.

Womack, J., D. Jones, and D. Roos 1990. *The Machine that Changed the World.* New York: Macmillan.

PART
II

 Systems

4 | High Performing Organizations

Garry J. Huysse and Sheron Kennedy

Abstract

The term "High Performing Organizations" is used to describe an environment which has been designed such that every person brings out their best resulting in an organization capable of consistetly delivering outstanding business results.

This chapter reviews the evolution and theory, describes the foundations, addresses the issue of organizational results and highlights an implementation approach used in the manufacturing arm of Lucent Technologies.

The ultimate reason for changing to a High Performing Organization is to generate improved business results – above and beyond what could otherwise be delivered. Organizations moving to a high performing organization should consider all the impacting business and behavioral elements of this changed environment. The time and resources for this journey demand commitment from both leadership and all associates and must be measured against the defined business mission, planned investment and business goals over time.

INTRODUCTION

Today, many organizations in the public and private sectors are developing and implementing approaches to optimally link the organization's work and employees for improved business results. A number of factors account for this direction including competitive challenge, the rate of technological innovation and change, increased knowledge and capability of the workforce, research and writings of leading social scientists, quality management resources and business consultants, and institutionalized processes such as the Baldrige National Quality Award Criteria for Excellence. While specific approaches vary widely, and numerous names (such as Team Based Management, Participative Management, and Work Systems) are used, we will use the term "High Performing Organizations" to describe an environment designed to bring out the best in every person resulting in an organization capable of delivering outstanding business results.

The purpose of this chapter is to describe High Performing Organizations – a key element of effective quality management. This will be done by reviewing the evolution and theory, describing the foundations, discussing some organizational results and highlighting implementation considerations.

The proper implementation of High Performing Organization principles and approaches offers the potential for substantially improved business results when used in conjunction with other aspects of quality discussed in this handbook.

EVOLUTION AND THEORY

Evolution

The first recognized discussion of production economics was by the economist, Adam Smith, at the time the factory system was emerging. Smith observed the division of labor in the factory system and included a description and the economic advantages of an extreme division of labor in *The Wealth of Nations* in 1776. Smith cited three advantages: (1) development of skill or dexterity; (2) saving of time normally lost in changing over from one activity to the next; and (3) invention of machines when man specialized effort on tasks of restricted scope. Although Smith's observations were not deduced in a theoretical way, it is likely that recognition of the factory system by a great scholar accelerated the division of labor (Buffa 1965, p. 3).

Another Englishman, Charles Babbage, wrote *The Economy of Machinery and Manufacturers* (1832) in which he supported the observations of Smith. Babbage pointed out that if a factory were reorganized so that each person performed the entire sequence of operations, the wage paid would be dictated by the most difficult or rarest skill required. With division of labor, just the amount of skill needed could be purchased. In addition to the productivity advantages cited by Adam Smith, Babbage recognized the principle of limiting skills as a basis for pay (Buffa 1965, p. 5). The division of labor accelerated during the first half of the twentieth century with the automobile assembly lines representing one of the most extreme applications.

Frederick Winslow Taylor's work in the late 1800s and early 1900s established a philosophy that was the basis for organization for most of the twentieth century. Taylor advanced from the ranks of workers; understood the production system of the day; and challenged the current norms by producing as much as he possibly could. With this approach, he quickly rose through the ranks to a position of authority where he could try some of his own ideas about the production system. Taylor believed that the scientific method could be applied to all managerial problems, and that the methods by which work was accomplished should be determined by management through scientific investigation (Buffa 1965, p. 6).

Taylor suggested development of a spirit of cooperation between workers and management to insure work would be carried out in accordance with the scientifically devised procedures. The key attributes of his system are: (1) work sub-divided into small components with individual workers assigned to each specialized role; (2) responsibility associated with each job limited to a minimum to provide better managerial control; (3) pay based upon individual performance; (4) scientific selection, training, and development of workers by supervisors; and (5) quality control as a separate function (McGregor 1967, p. 84).

While Taylor's writings about division of labor placed emphasis on cooperation between workers and management, most employers used his scientific management approach simply to get more out of employees. In those cases, it was quite likely that quality and productivity declined instead of rising. A careful reading of his work suggests that he placed the workers' interest as high as the employers' and some modern management theorists, such as W. Edwards Deming, credit Taylor with generating the principles upon which they acted (Eldred: Internet).

The classic investigations of informal work groups in industry are represented by the pioneering experiments at the Hawthorne Plant of the Western Electric Company (Costello and Zalkind 1963, p. 90). In this study, lighting levels were increased for an experimental work group and performance went up. Similarly, when lighting levels were decreased, performance went down. Performance increased again when employees were told light intensity was increased, when actually it had been lowered (Buffa 1965, p. 300). These studies demonstrated that informal work groups establish norms which guide the behavior of workers on the job which allow management problems to be dealt with through manipulation of work groups and supervisory behavior.

Systems theory was proposed in the 1940s by the biologist Ludwig von Bertalanffy and furthered by Ross Ashby (Introduction to Cybernetics 1956). von Bertalanffy emphasized that real systems are open to, and interact with, their environments, and that they can acquire qualitatively new properties through emergence, resulting in continual evolution. Systems theory focuses on the arrangement of the relations between the parts which connect them into a whole. This particular organization determines a system, which is independent of the concrete substance of the elements (e.g., particles, cells transistors, people, etc.). Thus, the same concepts and principles of organization underlie the different disciplines (physics, biology, technology, sociology, etc.), providing a basis for their unification (Heighlein and Joslyn 1992).

The development of Socio-Technical Systems theory began in the 1940s and 1950s. Earliest work was done at the Tavistock Institute in Great Britain by researchers Fred Emery, Eric Trist, and their colleagues (Hinckley 1995, p. 2). They discovered improved results were occurring versus normal coal industry norms with the use of semi-autonomous work groups in the South Yorkshire coal fields. These work groups interchanged roles and shifts, regulated work group activities and participated in decisions concerning their work arrangements (Trist 1981, p. 8). Up until this time, the traditional work organization in the coal fields had been highly mechanistic, dividing workers functionally into individualized jobs, and integrating them through a vertical hierarchy (Baba and Mejabi 1996, p. 4). The results of this different organization approach were lower absenteeism, fewer accidents, higher productivity and greater personal commitment.

The informal organization structure that emerged in the coal fields most likely came about because workers' basic needs were largely being met and they became interested in satisfying higher level needs in an environment where previous experiences could be taken into account.

This is consistent with the work of Abraham Maslow and Frederick Herzberg during the 1950s and 1960s which links directly to the thinking of proponents of the Socio-Technical System of work. Maslow theorized that an individual's behavior is a response to a hierarchy of needs beginning with fulfillment of basic needs and progressing upwards to self-actualization.

Herzberg described factors that satisfy (motivate) and dissatisfy (hygiene) workers' needs. He believed that emphasis on removing dissatisfiers would provide interim relief while a focus on motivators would generate long-term benefit. For example, if an employee who is dissatisfied with pay gets a pay raise, how long will it be before dissatisfaction again sets in? Herzberg's motivators included work itself, achievement, recognition, responsibility, growth and opportunity. Dissatisfiers are company policy, administration, supervisors, working conditions, interpersonal relations, and salary.

One can conclude from Maslow and Herzberg that employees will be driven to satisfy higher level needs (such as a desire to excel, a desire to display individual competence, and individual self actualization) once their more basic needs were met. This research tended to see the causes of action or behaviors in terms of needs which was consistent with Maslow's statement that "Man is a wanting animal" (Haasen and Shea 1997, p. 33). Other research on how the human mind stored, processed and analyzed information before acting (cognitive psychology) and how a situation or environment shaped people's behavior was also underway in the 1950s.

The discovery of semi-autonomous work groups and the related study of Maslow, Herzberg and others, caused a gradual shifting of thinking about the nature of work away from the prevailing thoughts of Taylor. In this new thinking, organizations were viewed as systems in which *people and equipment were equally important.* The level of business results and job satisfaction were dependent upon the quality of the relationships in this Socio-Technical system (Trist 1981, p. 10). Douglas McGregor's description of underlying beliefs about the nature of man (Theory X and Theory Y) helped generations of managers understand and adopt the managerial strategy that was most consistent with their beliefs.

Current quality management models, such as the Baldrige Quality Award and related state quality awards in the United States, the Deming Prize in Japan, and the European Quality Award have aspects of the Socio-Technical Systems theory built into their evaluation criteria. This recognizes the interrelationship between the technological, interpersonal and individual systems within an organization. For example, the 1997 Baldrige Award Criteria for Performance Excellence identify seven categories that are key for organizational success. These categories are all important for High Performing Organizations and category 5 (Human Resource Development and Management) links directly to High Performing Organizations.

Figure 4.1 The functioning of the organization as a system

Theory

Socio-Technical Systems Theory provides a conceptual framework and methodology for the identification and management of human factors in dynamic technical environments, and for the redesign of work organizations to enable more effective integration of human and technological resources (Baba and Mejabi 1996, p. 3). Katz states that the theoretical model for the understanding of organizations is that of an energetic input-output system in which the energetic return from the output reactivates the system. Social organizations are flagrantly open systems in that the input of energies and the conversion of output into further energetic input consist of transactions between the organization and its environment. Systems theory is concerned with problems of relationships, of structure, and of interdependence (Katz and Kahn 1966, p. 14).

A model of a Socio-Technical or open system can be represented as in figure 4.1.

The model displays the repeated cycles of input, output, feedback, and the functioning of the organization as a system (transformation process), which comprises the organizational pattern. This model reveals the need to identify and understand the inputs to the organization, transformation resulting from the effort of the organization, and outputs and feedback (renewed input) to gain maximum results. It points out that outputs (such as organization results) are the products of the transformation of inputs. This model is taken from the open system theory as promulgated by von Bertalanffy (1956).

An example of this in industry is producing and marketing a product. The firm utilizes all types of inputs including customer needs, government regulation, raw materials, capital, etc. to develop the desired product. Within the firm, resources in all areas including Manufacturing, Sales, Advertising, Product Assurance, Finance, Human Resources, Information Systems, Product Development, Environmental, etc., seek to add value while producing and selling the product. The output of this is a product that is used as a finished product (i.e., peanut butter) or as an input to another transformation (i.e., sheet steel). Feedback comes primarily in the form of customer comment, repurchase, and profit, all of which are inputs to the next cycle.

For this model to achieve optimal results, transformation must effectively and efficiently link the technological, individual and social core processes within an organization. This requires understanding of the technology and social interactions of people in the work force as well as knowledge of what motivates individuals. The Socio-Technical Systems model is the basis for High Performance Organization design and implementation which will be discussed later in this chapter.

Since the 1960s many companies in the United States and around the world have utilized this theory or its resultant models, principles, and approaches to substantially improve their organizational capability. Some of the major organizations applying High Performance Organization approaches include Motorola, Xerox, Texas Instruments, Procter & Gamble, Lucent Technologies, Milliken, Federal Express, Levi Strauss, Herman Miller, AES Corporation, and some firms in the concrete pipe and steel industries. These approaches are also being applied in the public sector in universities, and in government (i.e., North West Missouri State and the City of Madison, WI).

FOUNDATIONS OF HIGH PERFORMING ORGANIZATIONS

Overview

The discovery of a different way of getting work done with better results by coal miners in England by the Tavistock Institute began a gradual transition from Taylor's scientific management to the Socio-Technical Systems approach. The researchers discovered that productivity was nearly 30 percent higher in the new system (McGregor 1967, p. 86). Key characteristics of this new approach included self-selected teams of miners with responsibility for the total task of coal extraction; acquisition of all the skills required for all tasks by team members; and team shared wages. Clearly this approach was different from the scientific management approach described below by Frederick Winslow Taylor:

> The work of every worker is fully planned out by the management at least one day in advance, and each person receives in most cases written instructions, describing in detail the task which is to be accomplished, as well as the means to be used in doing the work. This task specifies not only what is to be done but how it is to be done and the exact time for doing it.
>
> The task is always so regulated that the person who is well suited to the job will thrive while working at this rate during a long term of years and grow happier and more prosperous, instead of being overworked.

The Socio-Technical System approach required a framework to replace the fundamental beliefs, assumptions, structures and systems of scientific management which were no longer optimal. As discussed earlier, scientific management (Taylor's system) became less popular not because of intention, but because of overzealous application; misunderstanding of the role of the worker; and the increased desire for involvement by the workers.

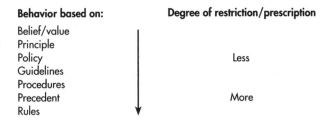

Figure 4.2 Leveraging the higher level capability of workers

Several fundamental beliefs and assumptions have emerged as the foundation for application of high performance work systems in the public and private sectors.

Fundamental beliefs are particularly important in this system because it is a principle-based management approach versus a rule-based approach. A principle-based approach consists of a set of core values; principles of operation; and motivated employees who develop the specific actions to achieve desired outcomes. This approach reduces the need for audit and middle level "approvers," instead counting on employee behaviors to produce results.

In considering construction of the structure, systems and style of High Performing Organizations, care should be taken to avoid becoming overly prescriptive and restrictive. This is essential if an organization is to fully leverage the higher level capability of workers. Figure 4.2 may be helpful when considering the approach and degree of prescription/restriction to be built into organizational structures, systems, and style.

The fundamental beliefs and the foundations of most High Performance Organizations are:

1 Focus foremost on adding value for the costomer.
2 Utilize values and principles versus rules.
3 Lead by example.
4 Respect and expect everyone to contribute.
5 Collaborate and work in teams to deliver results.
6 Continuously improve.
7 Achieve data driven business results.

We believe that these fundamental beliefs described below are virtually the same for organizations which are striving to become total quality organizations, learning organizations, or high performing organizations.

Focus foremost on adding value for the customer

Business success depends on satisfying *external* customers. In some organizations, particularly in public and service industries, the term stakeholders is used in place of customer. Therefore, it is essential that the organization understand who these customers are, what their requirements are, and how well the needs are being met today. Focusing on the customer means not only satisfying the needs and reasonable expectations of customers, but also having an attitude that puts the needs of the customer first. Meeting these needs should be viewed as the work of the organization – not an interruption from internal work. To be successful over long periods of time, organizations must provide recognized customer value (quality, cost, and speed) that results in market leadership. This is discussed further in this book by Woodruff and Gardial.

Many organizations use this customer focus to emphasize the importance of considering all external aspects (such as competition, community, etc.) as well as the internal capabilities of the organization. In focusing on external customers, internal relationships can be thought of as a series of value added customer-supplier chains between employees and/or work groups.

The Socio-Technical Systems model accounts for external factors including the customer in the input and feedback sections. These are considered resources and feedback to the internal process of the organization. This outward look is key to changing the current technologies, capabilities, attitudes and approaches of those working within the organization. Once this customer focused mind set is in place in an organization, the way work gets done will inevitably change. Individuals and teams who internalize this foundation will begin to think about how their work adds value. There will be a desire to eliminate work that is viewed as rework or that is not related directly to satisfying the customer. Therefore, focus on the customer is an essential element in a dynamic High Performance Organization.

Utilize values and principles versus rules

In High Performing Organizations, values and principles – not rules or procedures – are used as the basis for problem solving and decision making. Values in successful organizations do not normally change significantly over time, thereby providing a constancy of purpose for the organization.

Principles are developed from the values and become the basis upon which specific actions and behaviors are taken to run the operation. They help create the culture of an organization when used to: (1) communicate; (2) develop broad understanding; and (3) expect adherence. An example of a principle may be helpful at this point. The principle of decision making can be described as problem solving and decision making led by those who have the data, knowledge and skills and involving those who are impacted.

In utilizing values and principles versus rules or procedures, freedom is given to individuals and teams to apply their unique capabilities to deal with business issues and opportunities. Additional benefits include the reallocation of most "policy writers" to more customer valued work, simplified decision making and increased involvement of associates in the business. Instead of measuring compliance to rules, the effectiveness of the system can be evaluated by the actions and behaviors developed to meet customer needs.

Lead by example

Transition to a High Performing Organization requires leaders to rethink how work gets done in the organization, in their own roles and in their behaviors. Many leaders conceptually understand and support High Performing Organization approaches. Often, however, systems, procedures, practices, and leadership behaviors do not energize the organization to become High Performing.

Adoption of the foundations of High Performing Organizations must be followed by development of leadership actions and behaviors that will drive the transition from the top. Dr Warren Bennis states that "Leadership is influence. The capability to translate intention into reality and sustain it." Entrepreneurs see change as healthy. They search for change, respond to it, and turn it into an opportunity (Drucker 1980, pp. 225–31). By their personal example, leaders at all levels of the organization should become role models for the transition. Two key areas of leadership are development of customer focused business strategies that achieve long-lasting breakthrough results and use of data-based decision making.

Respect and expect everyone to contribute

McGregor identified two extreme sets of management beliefs that can be described as Theory X and Theory Y. Proponents of Scientific Management subscribe to Theory X assumptions that the average human being has an inherent dislike for work and will avoid it if it is possible. Because of this dislike for work, most people must be coerced, controlled, directed, or threatened to get them to exert effort toward the achievement of organizational objectives.

In contrast, proponents of Socio-Technical Systems Theory are closer to Theory Y and believe that everyone can and wants to contribute to his or her fullest capacity. Key elements of this include beliefs that expenditure of physical and mental effort in work is natural; external threat and control are not the only means for bringing about effort toward organizational objectives; commitment to objectives is dependent on rewards associated with achievement – the most important being those that satisfy needs for self-respect and personal improvement; the capacity to exercise a high degree of imagination, ingenuity, and creativity in the solution of problems is widely distributed; humans learn under the proper conditions to seek responsibility; and intellectual potential of most humans is only partially utilized.

Everyone has something to contribute if given a chance. A key way to *respect and expect* capability is to treat associates as business owners. To make this work, it is important to pay particular attention to selection, training, development, communication of business situation, involvement in decision making, participation in development of business metrics, assessment of contribution against business results, and sharing in the financial success of the organization.

While much is written about ways to respect the capability of individuals, the important topic of expecting high quality performance is not often emphasized. The best leaders in any field link higher level individual performance to the business product or result. This is because leaders with a true respect for capability understand that long-term motivation and contribution comes from delivering top notch results.

Collaborate and work in teams to deliver results

The world we live in is changing rapidly. Over the past 50 to 100 years, organization characteristics have changed from essentially a manufacturing and sales focus within a specific geography to a business focus on a regional or global basis. Today and in the future, increased emphasis is being placed on the service industry and knowledge work; less emphasis is placed on manufacturing. There are many factors for this shift including population changes, free trade legislation, information explosion, emergence of global companies, stagnation of growth in current markets and opportunities in emerging markets.

To compete in this new environment, organizations need to continually add increased value at an ever increasing rate. How can firms do this? One solution is to continually seek out and develop the very brightest and most capable employees. By developing personal mastery, each individual will have the potential to contribute fully to business results (Snell and Dean 1992).

It must be recognized, however, that today's customer needs for ever increasing speed and value are more complex and often require solutions beyond the knowledge or capability of any one person. Solutions are more interdependent than ever. In these situations, be they in physical work or knowledge work, individuals must be able to communicate, collaborate, and work together to solve one-time problems and in on-going teams within their function and across the organization. Full integration of the knowledge and experience ultimately results in the best possible solution being developed and fully implemented.

This foundation recognizes that the importance of acquiring and transferring knowledge and developing effective solutions to customer needs is greatly enhanced when employees are able to communicate and collaborate effectively. This must happen across the organization and at its interfaces with other organizations. In support of this foundation, attention should be placed on selection of employees who understand and have displayed the ability to communicate effectively and work in teams.

High Performing Organizations have learned over time that the best business solutions are developed when teams have a rich diversity in experience, capability, and cultural experience. When considering how to get the best solutions, keep in mind that there is always a sound business rationale for inclusion of experienced and newer hires, managers and line workers, minorities, women and men in collaborative work.

Continuously improve

Continuous Improvement is an essential element of Total Quality as described by Flynn and Flynn on page 6 of their chapter of this book entitled *Product Development Speed and Quality: A New Set of Synergies?*. The foundation philosophy is that no process, no product, and no person is perfect and can, therefore, be improved using the Deming Wheel of Plan-Do-Check-Act. The payoff for continuous improvement is continually increased value of product or service to the customer.

For long-term business success, it is important to think in terms of both day to day improvement efforts (daily management) and discontinuous (breakthrough) improvements. Both are necessary for sustaining value added products or services. In quality terms, PDCA is necessary to plan and implement change and SDCA is required to stabilize the operation after change. In High Performing Organizations, experience (both positive and negative), benchmarking, reapplication and innovation are reviewed to determine opportunities for continuous improvement of results.

With regard to the organization itself, it is recognized that advanced work systems, or High Performing Organizations, never have a clear end point and it is essential for them to undergo continual assessment and improvement. It is important to be alert for work system "drift" from original intentions. Drift will invariably occur unless the entire system (management as well as non-management) is designed comprehensively and assessed periodically.

Achieve data driven business results

The ultimate reason for moving to a High Performing Organization is to improve the capability of the organization to achieve increased business results. In order to do this, it is important to focus on delivering critical business results as well as those key internal measures that are early predictors of success. Therefore, organizations must develop relevant business metrics for their long-term success. Once the business metrics (quality indicators) are determined and the overall work process are understood, internal early indicators (process indicators) can be used to track progress. Establishing the right metrics is the first key step. Continuous utilization of the gathered data is the key to objective decision making leading to long-term success.

There are a number of measures of business results a firm should consider before locking in on the appropriate ones. Some of these are: return on assets, return on sales, net income, inventory, sales per employee, volume, and stock price. Easton and Jarrell discuss this topic in more detail in their chapter *The Emerging Academic Research on the Link Between Total Quality Management and Corporate Financial Performance: A Critical Review.*

An example of one set of growth goals is spelled out in the 1996 Procter & Gamble Annual Report. John Pepper, CEO, and Durk Jager, COO, discuss three growth goals for the company. These are: (1) double unit volume in ten years; (2) achieve share growth in the majority of P&G categories; and (3) deliver total shareholder return (TSR) that ranks P&G over time among the top third of its peer group.

Examples

As discussed earlier in this section, foundations are particularly important in High Performing Organizations. This is because these organizations are principle-based versus rule-based. In considering construction of the structure, systems and style of High Performing Organizations, care should be taken to avoid becoming overly prescriptive and restrictive. This is essential if an organization is to fully leverage the higher level capability of all employees.

It may be helpful to have several examples of the contrast in practices and systems used in High Performing Organizations and more traditional organizations. First, let's consider the area of *job design* and *work design*.

The 1997 Baldrige Award Criteria for Performance Excellence defines work design and job design as follows:

> *Work Design* refers to how employees are organized and/or organize themselves in formal and informal units. This includes work teams, problem solving teams, functional units, cross functional teams and departments.
>
> *Job Design* refers to responsibilities, authorities, and tasks assigned to individuals. (1997 Baldrige Criteria, p. 12)

In the area of *job design* and *work design*, traditional organizations tend to think of a fixed job definition, individual performance of and accountability for work, and separation of work into doing and planning. High Performing Organizations address job design and work design by considering work as flexible and dynamic, combine doing and planning and, where appropriate, expect individuals and teams to perform and be accountable for work.

Compensation policies in High Performing Organizations address group achievement and equity, equality of sacrifice, and pay linked to skills and mastery. In a business downturn, High Performing Organizations are likely to look for solutions that productively employ all employees whereas traditional organizations tend to treat hourly employees as a variable cost. Traditional controlling organizations think about individual incentives, pay geared to job evaluation and a "fair day's pay."

A final contrast is made in the area of *management structure, systems and style*. Traditional organizations have layered structures and control top down. Coordination is usually done via rules and procedures. Hierarchical status is reinforced by emphasis placed on prerogatives (such as title, parking space, office size and location, etc.) and position. High Performing Organizations utilize resources to problem solve based on expertise and access to information. In these organizations, there is a flatter structure where coordination is done across work processes via shared goals, values and traditions.

BUSINESS RESULTS

Walton et al. state that the ultimate reason for moving to a High Performing Organization is to improve the capability of the organization to generate increased business results. Leaders must have a clear business rationale for changing to a High Performing Organization or they will not commit the resources to this effort. This is because change requires time for education, understanding, application and behavior change in leaders and everyone in the organization. If there is no business rationale to change to a High Performing Organization, resources will be distracted from delivering business results.

One way to articulate the business rationale is to incorporate it into the organization's goals and strategies and measure its contribution to bottom line results. This is important because it makes the important connection to bottom line results and building organization capability.

There is much manufacturing and anecdotal evidence of improvement, but little *organization level* business results improvement data available at this time. The work of Easton and Jarrell described in their chapter of this book addresses this issue and provides important insights in this area. An important review of organization level results is that of Robert Levering, author of *100 Best Places to Work in America*, who reports that the Great Place to Work Institute has gathered considerable research indicating the positive correlation between best work place practices and superior financial performance. Independent financial analysts found that the "100 Best" firms consistently outperformed their competitors in total return (BARRA 1993).

Since Baldrige Award criteria incorporate many elements of High Performing Organizations, we can look at Baldrige Award winning companies to determine how well they have done at the organization level since achieving the Baldrige. The Commerce Department's National Institute of Standards and Technology (NIST) reported that investing in quality management can result in an impressive payoff. NIST reported the success of investment of a hypothetical sum of money in Baldrige winning firms from the first business day in April of the year they won the award to August 1, 1995. As a group, the 14 companies soundly outperformed the S&P 500 by greater than 4 to 1 achieving a 248.7 percent return on investment compared to 58.5 percent for S&P 500 firms. NIST found that five whole company winners did even better outperforming the S&P 500 by greater than 5 to 1, a 279.8 percent return on investment compared to a 55.7 percent return for the S&P 500 (NIST 1996).

Some may describe the correlation between the Baldrige Award and High Performing Organizations as weak because: (1) the High Performing Organization approach is only one aspect of the award which might play a small part in achieving the award, and (2) some Baldrige recipients are no longer as successful or competitive due to market place changes or internal changes from the approaches that earned Baldrige recognition.

This skepticism is good! However, before discounting this comparison, one should thoroughly analyze those Baldrige winners who have achieved longer term success. This analysis may help generate a business rationale for High Performing Organizations within an organization.

Examples of improved results in manufacturing include the work of Ichniowski and Shaw who compared performance in four dominant combinations of Human Resource Management (HRM) practices in the US and Japanese Steel Industry. They found that the High Performance HRM system stimulates significantly higher productivity than any other HRM systems. A conservative estimate of the productivity advantage of the high performance work system over the traditional system is about 7 percent. The High Performance HRM system generates not only the highest levels of productivity, it also produces the highest product quality (prime yield rates). The results of the analysis are clear. The full complement of progressive, participative priorities stimulates the highest levels of both productivity and quality performance (Ichniowski and Shaw 1997).

Further data is available from the original Socio-Technical Systems work in the Yorkshire coal fields where it was reported that the results of this different organization approach were lower absenteeism, fewer accidents, higher productivity and greater personal commitment. Productivity as a percentage of estimated potential of the coal face increased nearly 30 percent (Trist: 1963). A before and after study in another mine indicated a gross improvement of 20 percent.

Is this data sufficient to convince organizations to transform themselves from current approaches? The answer is not simple and is a function of the situation, leaders' preference and application of organization science. While the data is incomplete, many organizations have started the transition. In his book *What America Does Right: Lessons from Today's Most Admired Corporate Role Models*, Robert Waterman describes some examples of success and discusses ways to evaluate that success at Applied Energy Services Corporation, Federal Express, Levi Strauss & Company, Merck, Motorola, Procter & Gamble and Rubbermaid.

IMPLEMENTATION THROUGH PEOPLE ENGAGEMENT

To this point, we have described background, theory and foundation of a high performing organization. This section describes an approach and example of a High Performing Organization implementation framework recognized in the Manufacturing areas of Lucent Technologies.

Successful businesses in today's global environment must have high performing organizations and that means high performing people. People who understand what drives their businesses and are dedicated to a mindset of sustained growth year over year. Without question, they know what customers value. They know their competition and where they stand in relation to their company's performance to that competition. They are constantly focused on the delivery of quality products and services that are planned and managed through real-time communication matching just-in-time customers' requests.

This concept of people engagement was reinforced for the employees of the newly established Lucent Technologies (*New Jersey Star-Ledger,* September 15, 1996), with the restatement of the beliefs of Henry Schacht, Chairman and Chief Executive Officer of Lucent Technologies. Schacht explained in the chapter that he wrote for the 1986 book "*What Works For Me: 16 CEOs Talk About Their Careers and Commitments*":

> We want every person in the company to have the same degree of knowledge as the senior management, even if it's painful and scary as hell.

People in high performing organizations clearly understand their value to the organization as individuals or team contributors. People are engaged in managing the business with clear accountability and authority to act within the boundaries of their responsibilities. The business operating environment encourages spirit of innovation and creativity where people are continuously provided the opportunity to develop their skills and talents to maximize their contribution to business. High performing organizations timely recognize and reward performance measurements and behavior values that have been clearly defined as the goals of the organization by their leadership.

This organizational behavior is reinforced by Lucent Technologies' Values Statement:

- An obsession with serving our customers
- A commitment to business excellence
  - Speed
  - Innovation
  - Quality
- A deep respect for the contributions of each person to the success of the team
  - Integrity and candor
  - Mutual respect and teamwork
  - Personal accountability
- A strong sense of social responsibility

High performing people have leaders who are focused strategically and act decisively to allow knowledgeable people to manage their segments of the business. Leaders of high performing organizations have a clear vision and direction for the company and can articulately communicate that mission and know that it is understood by the people. They know that it is understood because they listen and learn through their continuous, proactive people feedback processes. Leaders set the tone for an open and sharing environment where information flows to the right people at the right time utilizing the most appropriate and effective communication medium.

In the May, 1997 issue of *Lucent Magazine,* Henry Schacht identified specific behaviors that are needed in Lucent's culture to create a high performance operating environment:

> Like Rich (McGinn, Lucent's President and Chief Operating Officer), first and foremost, I want us to have a culture where everyone is obsessed with meeting and exceeding customer expectations. Also, I think it's important that we have an open and supportive environment at Lucent, a culture marked by candor and widespread sharing of information. I would like everyone, at every level and from every organization, to feel they are part of the overall team, working on and contributing to common goals.
>
> We all want a culture marked by clear and constant communication, one where leadership teams hold regular town meetings in a setting where everyone is free to speak their minds and where positive debate is encouraged.
>
> An environment that supports risk-taking also is important. There are valuable lessons to be learned from making mistakes if they are communicated up, down and across the organization through a 360-degree feedback approach.

Leaders in high performing organizations select members of their own leadership team who clearly understand their roles in achieving the mission and living the values (honesty, trust, openness, respect for others) of the company. They reflect commitment, agility, decisiveness and ability to translate a shared vision into action.

Leaders allow their people, who on a daily basis are the closest to the products and services, and know better than anyone, to manage the day to day segments of the business. People know the impact of their work on business results which are periodically shared. Individual and team contributions to the business are recognized and rewarded. People understand their own linkage and contribution to the business.

High performing people know their boundaries of their accountabilities and responsibilities and possess the authority to act. They have a clear understanding of the path for approval escalation and why it is required. They are continuously skilled and educated to enhance and improve their performance. They understand that no longer does a person in an organization have just a single task but rather multiple skills and talents including both technical and interpersonal performed by multiple people working together in teams. People understand and accept that change is and will be constant. They know that proficiency at change – agility or resiliency – is what makes high performing individuals, teams, organizations and businesses.

High performance work teams or systems provide an avenue for engaging people in the day-to-day operations of the business. Globally, businesses are introducing the concepts of high performance work teams into segments of their operations. Generally, this movement to teams is

Figure 4.3 Framework for transition to high performance teams

initiated from the operating or line organizations where the benefits of engaging the people directly involved with the production and delivery of the product and services in managing their segments of the organization are immediately observed with improved operating results.

Organizations or companies moving to a high performing organization with high performance teams, whether transitioning from an established organization or creating this operating management structure anew, should consider all the impacting business and behavioral elements of this changed environment *before its introduction.* The time and resources (financial and human) for this journey demand commitment from both leadership and all associates and must be measured against the defined business mission, planned investment and business goals over a period of a minimum of three years to a maximum of eight to ten years in an established location.

A framework for introduction of high performance teams is defined in fourteen key elements (figure 4.3) for organizational transition and implementation.

Linkage to customer focused business strategies

The concept of high performance teams is a design structure for organizing people and processes to manage the business operations. High performance team members are multi-talented and fully engaged associates who know their boundaries of responsibilities and have the authority to act – to speedily provide products and services to customers.

All associates clearly understand their individual and team contributions and linkages to their organization's customer-focused business goals. All team members are knowledgeable of:

- The business and its customers.
- The strategic business direction.
- The company's integrated operations.
- Their industry competitive position.

Leadership commitment, shared vision and values, and continuity of champions

Initiatives to transition to a more customer-focused, competitive business management structure found in a high performance team environment are most often led by line or operations leaders. Most critical for success, however, is that the commitment to support these change initiatives required for high performance teams must be recognized and sustained by organization and company leadership. Until high performance teams have become the accepted structure for managing the business, a change in leadership without a continuous commitment for the team concept will create a pause or complete breakdown in the implementation process. To sustain progress, new leadership must share the same vision and values and be as committed as their predecessors to encourage team concepts.

Leadership commitment must be reinforced through clear communication of the business vision and values as well as the leadership's actual behavior. It is the leaders who create the environment that is accepting of change and that encourages the engagement – empowerment – of the people in the organization. This transition is dependent upon energetic creativity, openness and a dedicated spirit of business entity partnering that is embraced by the leadership team.

Transition structure

Establishment of participative oversight, planning and work teams including union partners are essential for structure formation and include the following:

Steering committee

An ongoing leadership team providing vision, commitment, guidance and parameters for team member engagement and accountability for high performance team implementation including:

- Selection of Design Team members and financial budget time frame for initial pilots and plans for full workforce implementation with an evaluation process.
- Selection of an Education/Training Team to provide planning for the development, delivery and verification of an education and training curriculum.
- Determination of an individual and team-based recognition and compensation/reward system.

Design team

A group of cross-functional representatives (6–10 members) engaged for a specific period of time to draft the plan and processes for implementation of teams. This includes defining and understanding of:

- An assessment of work redesign with improved work flow.
- Boundaries of work including customer and supplier partnerships, financial and business accountabilities of team members and their authority to act.
- Team size and structures (natural work groups or cross-functional teams) focused on attainment of performance results.
- Integrated customer, business and team/individual metrics.
- Communication plans: within the Design Team and between the Steering Committee, business leadership team and all associates.
- Skills and knowledge requirements of team members.
- Selection and promotion system(s).
- Proposed allocation of time and resources.
- Anticipation of internal corporate and business linkages/partnerships as well as external influences such as governmental compliances and Labor laws impacting the establishment of teams.
- High performance team coordinator(s) who will act as advisor(s) with ongoing responsibilities for development of high performance teams for the organization.

High performance teams

A participative group of team members who manage and operate a portion of the business. An interactive group of people with complimentary skills who are committed to a common purpose and performance goals. They operate and manage a segment of the business holding themselves mutually accountable for results.

Effective high performance team implementation relies on the energetic creativeness and openness of the shared learning among all three interfaces.

Creative funding resources

High performance team members are engaged in continuous learning, much of which is education and training demanding planned financial support.

In a high performance team environment, learning can be shared beyond traditional classroom and "on-the-job" training through *team teaching* where:

- Operation team members with both desire and capabilities rotate into the Education and Training Group for a period of time.
- Leadership (management, professionals and engineers) and team members facilitate or provide instruction to others as a segment of their work responsibilities.

Course development and delivery costs can be reduced through a "bartering" process between internal/external company sources. Course delivery through distance learning technology should be maximized when available. To supplement internal company resources, there are outside collaborative considerations:

- Direct governmental programs (both federal and state)
- Indirect governmental assistance through coalitions including industry where research and work projects beneficial to high performance organizations are shared with involved companies:
  - AEA (American Electronics Association)
  - Agility Forum
  - NAM (National Association of Manufacturers)
  - NCMS (National Center for Manufacturing Sciences)

Organization gap assessment and work redesign

The key role of the Design Team is to assess the current work flow and individual and leadership responsibilities and to recommend an operation redesign where necessary for a high performance team environment. The business redesign will cover two work aspects:

Technical

- Work flow and process activities: know the operation's output. (product(s)/service(s)), customer and supplier requirements.

- Quality controls methods.
- Physical layout.
- Equipment and tooling.

Social

- Organization structure: how people are grouped and supporting relationships.
- Skills and knowledge requirements: current and future.
- Supervisor's role shift.
- Roles and engagement: boundaries of responsibilities and authority to act.
- Information systems: internal/external date to manage work, goals, measurements and feedback processes.
- Communication processes.
- Education and training plan: individual and team competencies needed for effective teamwork and operations management.
- Team member selection, recognition and reward systems.

Changing roles of leadership

A key transition role for high performance teams is that of the first line supervisor/manager. The role moves from directing to consultative based on the team's development and engagement. The coach/advisor sets the tone by allowing team members with their known/learned expertise to make decisions for their responsible portion of the operations.

Coaches/advisors become more strategic and less tactical in their work. They are focused on and aware of the total company business directions impacting both the products/services and processes of the entire organization.

They are teachers. Central to their added value is to encourage team members to take risks for growth and development. They continue to be liaisons for communication between the organization's leadership and team members, but not the only means as team members have direct interfaces with other operations, support groups, customers and suppliers.

Defined team member boundaries of accountability with authority to act

The success of the high performance team structure for organizing and managing an operation begins with a clear definition of the boundaries of accountability and responsibilities with designated authority to act for all team members. High performance teams require a shift in structure, systems, roles and behavior that can be dramatic change for some organizations.

Maximization of knowledgeable talent in both depth (primary expertise) and breadth (cross-functional skills) must be realized or developed for:

- Company leaders and team members: permanent full-time or part-time exempt and non-exempt workers
- Contingent workforce members: contract or temporary workers

In concert with the Design Team, team members and leaders must determine the level of expertise required and the number (all or a portion) of team members needed to possess those complimentary skills/knowledge necessary to achieve the goals of the operation.

Skills/knowledge requirements are determined by the product/service and processes' *current and future* demands with input from technical designers and business developers and planners.

With current and future expertise known, an assessment of the *current talent of team members and leaders* is made against *targeted skills/knowledge requirements* for a high performance organization. That skills/knowledge gap is filled by the education and training curricula.

Education and training curricula development and verification

Organization leadership creates an environment for learning and skills attainment that supports the company's business values and mission. The education and training curricula provides the "bridge for learning" to close the gap between the targeted skills/knowledge requirements and the assessment of the workforce's current skills/knowledge base.

Course development and delivery is dependent on-going communication of both product/service developers/engineers and curricula developers to assure both current and future knowledge/skills are identified and possessed by the workforce to support business execution.

The education and training curricula planning is dependent on the organization's working principles for learning and skills attainment in three areas:

- *Individual*: Development of each associate's primary area(s) of expertise
- *Team*: Specific skills/knowledge for team members in each area of work
- *Total Workforce*: Core skills/competencies desired for all associates in the company

Curricula course content for a workforce operating in a high performance team environment must include the following:

- *Technical:* Products/services design and development, materials management, logistics, manufacturing and information systems.
- *Business:* Company's customers, vision and mission, short term and long term goals, individual and team performance linkage to company's performance and financial results and company's competitive position.
- *Human:* Interpersonal relationships, leadership, reasoning, decision-making and problem solving.

Timely planning for the continuous learning – education and training – of the workforce is critical for business success and cost effectiveness. Whenever possible, select team members and leaders already possessing the behavior and talents required before joining the organization.

Take advantage of courses already developed and certified. Be aware of other internal/external sources, course content and costs. A central resource can prepare and make available a source document easily accessible that provides courses already developed and certified (figure 4.4).

Organizations transitioning to high performance work teams must understand that education and training costs extend beyond the development, delivery and verification/certification of team members. In addition to costs for trainers' salaries and operating expenses for an Education and Training group within or external to the organization, the cost of education and training also includes the team members' time off work for this learning. Whenever possible, utilize in-house leadership or team member skills/knowledge for "team teaching."

Communication and accessible/easily understood information

In a high performance team environment, there are fewer management messengers to filter communications and more direct sharing of information from leadership to teams, among team members and between teams. The emphasis is on continuous, real-time communication with people internal and external to the organization who impact a project or product/service deliverable. To be effective, this communication must be precise, clearly stated and easily understood.

In the spirit of openness, timely accessibility to information impacting the segment of the operations supported by team members is required for planning and timely, effective decisions.

With the advanced technological capabilities for communication and information sharing, personal one-on-one interaction should not be underestimated in creating a climate for acceptance of change for improved performance. Leaders still lead in a high performance team environment and must demonstrate their continuous commitment to this organizational management structure.

Sources

Business unit location/contact	Internal and/or affiliate					External		Courses	Hrs
	Local ed/trn	Bu ed/trn	School of bus.	Alliance ETOP	/WPOF/ Rutgers	College/Univ./Tech. school	Consultant/company		
(Location A)									
(Name)									
(Phone)					X			WPOF workshop	25.0+
(Fax)							Productivity development systems	Changing role of supervisor	40.0
(E-mail)							PDS	Team concepts	25.0
(Location B)									
(Name)					X			WPOF orientation training	8.0
(Phone)							Zenger Miller	Team effectiveness	11.0
(Fax)							Edge Learning Institute	Changing role of supervisors	24.0
(E-mail)	X							WPOF teambuilding (Power sys. training)	8.0
							Pritchett & Associates	Employee workshop for organizational change	4.0
	X							Skilled empowered team – effectiveness training	8.0
	X							Team leader workshop	16.0

Figure 4.4 Lucent Technologies high performance team implementation education and training curricula

A new work relationship: a mutual investment

Leadership can partner effectively with high performance teams by clarifying expectations of their responsibilities and boundaries of accountabilities. *Both team members and leaders* must be committed to a mutual working relationship as *business owners. Both* company leadership and individual team members must commit to invest their time and resources for success.

Given clear expectations of responsibilities with authority to act, education and training to solve problems and make decisions, and time to learn from both success and failures, team members and their leadership can partner together effectively in a high performance team environment. Transferrable skills – cross-functional knowledge and competencies gained through an engaged/empowered working environment – are assets beneficial for both team member and leadership personal growth, development and mobility as well as organizational success.

Alignment of support systems

Continuous competitive demands require reduced cycle time of the entire operation from design, development, marketing, sales, procurement, manufacturing, delivery and on-going customer support.

High performance team members with their leaner leadership team must work together within an organizational behavioral climate, focused on the customer, that knows the value of an integrated operating and functional supporting group structure.

Both operations and support groups (information systems, human resources, financial, materials management, procurement, etc.) must work proactively together to provide integrated policies, practices and systems that are aligned in both planning and delivery.

Business valued measurements

High performance team leaders and members who are truly engaged as *business owners* have the desire and commitment to delight customers with their effectiveness and quality and speed of service. Every team member and leader knows how their values and work – both as individuals and team members – link directly to their organization's business vision, values, mission and objectives.

Team members are active partners with their leaders in setting goals for their segments of the business operations. Team members understand the business measurements and their performance impact on each metric. Leaders provide team members with on-going periodic reviews of business results that include:

- Customer satisfaction of company's quality, delivery and communication.
- Individual and team/unit and company performance.
- Personal and team development.

A competitive reward mix of linked incentives

High performance team recognition and rewards systems must at the same time incent both individual team member and leadership growth and development as well as promote an interdependency of complementary skills, competencies and values to achieve team goals for organizational effectiveness.

There must be a linkage of individual, team, unit and company reward incentives that are a competitive mix of pay, benefits and added value programs that attract, motivate and retain the talent required for business success.

Organizations supporting high performance teams encourage and reward behavior in people who at the same time continuously contribute to business performance success and actively invest in their own personal and team development. Reward systems reinforce a culture of business ownership with recognition to significant individual and team performance and contribution to business results.

Implementation effectiveness evaluation

The transition and/or implementation of high performance teams can be realized through the company's or organization's achieved results and sustained business growth. The culture of the organization clearly recognizes team members manage the operations with leadership strategically focused on the vision and mission of the business.

The achieved and sustained business performance reflects:

- The entire workforce has an obsession with serving customers.
- Customers and suppliers are recognized as committed business partners.
- Both individual and team skills and competencies are maximized.
- Continuous learning, innovation, sharing of information and trust are core drivers of workforce behavior.
- Communication is constant.
- Leaders create the climate for change and live it.
- Leaders and team members are the owners of business results and are recognized for their individual and team performance in achieving those results.
- People understand that proficiency at change must be operationalized as an accepted organization cultural behavior.
- It is recognized that leaders and team members in high performing organizations who embrace change thrive in global competition.

SUMMARY

The intent of this chapter was to describe High Performing Organizations by reviewing the evolution and theory, describing the foundations, addressing the issue of organizational results and defining key elements for transition and implementation of high performance teams.

The discovery of semi-autonomous work groups in the South Yorkshire coal fields by the Tavistock Institute led to the development of Socio-Technical System theory in the 1940s and 1950s. This work coupled with the study of Maslow, Herzberg and others caused a gradual shift in thinking about the nature of work from the prevailing thoughts of Frederick Winslow Taylor.

Socio-Technical Systems theory provides a conceptual framework for management of human factors in dynamic organizations. It also provides a model for use in the redesign of organizations to enable more effective integration of human and business systems and approaches.

The conceptual framework is taken from the open system theory which identifies relationships between inputs, transformations, outputs and feedback. The model describes continuous: (1) identify the inputs to the organization (such as customer need, raw materials, or government regulation), (2) understand the change that occurs to the inputs within the organization, (3) deliver the outputs (products or services) from the transformation and (4) incorporate feedback as an input.

The foundations of High Performing Organizations are:

1 Focus foremost on adding value for the customer.
2 Utilize values and principles versus rules.
3 Lead by example.
4 Respect and expect everyone to contribute.
5 Collaborate and work in teams to deliver results.
6 Continuously Improve.
7 Achieve data driven business results.

The ultimate reason for changing to a High Performing Organization is to generate improved business results – above and beyond what could otherwise be delivered. We believe that implementation of High Performing Organization principles and approaches at all levels of an organization offers the potential for substantially improved business results.

Leaders must have a clear business rationale for changing to a High Performing Organization. This is because change requires time for education, understanding, application and behavior change in leaders and everyone in the organization. If there is no business rationale to change to a High Performing Organization, assigned resources will be distracted from delivering business results.

There is much manufacturing and anecdotal evidence of improvement, but little *organization level* business results improvement data available at this time. The work of Easton and Jarrell described in their chapter of this book addresses this issue and provides important insights in this area. An important review of organization level results is that of Robert Levering, author of *100 Best Places to Work in America*, who reports that the Great Place to Work Institute has gathered considerable research indicating the positive correlation between best work place practices and superior financial performance. Independent financial analysts found that the "100 Best" firms consistently outperformed their competitors in total return (BARRA 1993). Ichniowski and Shaw found in the steel industry that the High Performance Human Resources System stimulates significantly higher productivity than any other Human Resource Management system as well as the highest product quality. Before rejecting High Performing Organizations because of the lack of data, consider available information and whether it could provide a business rationale for helping meet the strategic needs of your organization.

Organizations moving to a high performing organization, whether transitioning from an established organization or creating this operating management structure anew, should consider all the impacting business and behavioral elements of this changed environment *before its introduction.* The time and resources for this journey demand commitment from both leadership and all associates and must be measured against the defined business mission, planned investment and business goals over a period of a minimum of three years to a maximum of eight to ten years in an established location.

The value and worth of the journey will be realized and measured by delivering sustained business results and growth. People in a high performing organization will be energized by the open and supportive environment where they understand that they are recognized and rewarded as business partners performing at their highest level with an obsession of serving customers.

References

Ashby, R., 1965, *Introduction to Cybernetics.*

Baba, M. and Mejabi, B., 1996, Advances in Socio-Technical Systems Integration, Special Issue of *International Journal of Human Factors in Manufacturing.*

Babbage, C., 1832, On The Economy of Machinery and Manufacturers, Knight, London.

Buffa, E., 1965, *Modern Production Management,* John Wiley & Sons, New York.

Costello, T. and Zalkind, S., 1963, *Psychology in Administration: A Research Orientation,* Prentice-Hall, Englewood Cliffs, New Jersey.

Dean J. and Goodman, Toward a Theory of TQ Integration, Academy of Management Presentation Paper, 1994.

Drucker, P., 1980, *Managing in Turbulent Times,* Harper and Row, New York.

Eldred, Frederick Winslow Taylor, 1856–1915, http://www.tiac.net/users/eldred/fwt/taylor.htm/,internet.

Haasen A. and Shea, G., 1997, A Better Place to Work: A New Sense of Motivation Leading to Higher Productivity, AMA Management Briefing.

Heighlein, F. and Joslyn, C., 1992, *Cambridge Dictionary of Philosophy,* Cambridge University Press.

Hinckley, S., 1995, *A Perspective on Reengineering.*
Ichniowski, C. and Shaw, C., 1996, Human Resources Practices and The Productivity and Quality Performance of U.S. and Japanese Businesses, Presentation for TQO Research Sharing Session.
Ichinowski, C. and Shaw, C., 1997, Human Resource Management and Competitive Performance in the Steel Industry.
Katz, D. and Kahn, R., 1996, *The Social Psychology of Organizations,* John Wiley and Sons, New York.
Levering, R. and Moskowitz M., 1996, 100 Best Places to Work in America, Great Place to Work Institute, San Francisco, California.
Lucent Magazine, May 1997.
Malcom Baldrige National Quality Award, 1997 Criteria for Performance Excellence, U.S. Department of Commerce, Gaithersburg, MD.
McGregor, D., 1967, *The Professional Manager,* McGraw Hill, New York.
NIST Stock Study, 1995, NIST Update, Feb. 5, 1996.
Procter and Gamble Annual Report 1996.
Smith, A., 1776, *The Wealth of Nations.*
Snell and Dean, J., 1992.
Taylor, F., 1919, *Principles of Scientific Management,* Harper and Brothers, New York.
Trist, E., 1963, *Organizational Choice,* Tavistock, London.
Trist, E., 1981, The Evolution of Socio-Technical Systems, Occasional Paper 2, Ontario, Quality of Work Life Center, Ontario, Canada.
von Bertalanffy, 1968, anthology: General Systems Theory.
von Bertalanffy, 1956, General Systems Theory, Yearbook of the Society of General Systems Theory, Volume 1.
Waterman, R. H., 1995, *What America Does Right: Lessons from Today's Most Admired Corporate Role Models,* Plume/Penguin, New York.

5 | Organizational Culture and the Total Quality Organization

Kyle M. Lundby, Jacquelyn S. DeMatteo, and Michael C. Rush

Abstract

This chapter discusses the relationship between organizational culture and Total Quality Management. Traditionally, researchers have characterized organizations as having a single overarching culture. A strategically differentiated culture is presented as a more accurate depiction of large multi-unit firms. It is argued that a strategically differentiated culture, one that is aligned with the nature of the business and the needs of the customers, is the preferred form of culture for firms hoping to capitalize on the potential benefits of Total Quality Management.

INTRODUCTION

The last few decades have witnessed a major transformation in how business is conducted. Organizations – large and small, public and private – continue to strive for high productivity; but, quality, innovation and value are replacing the drive for short-term efficiency. In essence, Total Quality Management (TQM) has become the mantra of many reform-minded business leaders hoping to capitalize on the sources of competitive advantage embodied in the principles and practices of TQM. Like many other approaches to organizational change, however, Total Quality Management often fails to live up to the expectations of its proponents (Beer, Eisenstat, and Spector 1990). Critics of TQM point to reports of failed quality initiatives and argue that it is nothing more than another management fad (Jacob 1993). For example, in a recent survey of 500 companies using Total Quality Management, only 36 percent felt that TQM had contributed in any meaningful way to their competitiveness. Similarly, Business Week (1992) reported another study in which only 26 percent of the organizations surveyed believed that Total Quality Management had helped them meet such goals as increased market share and customer satisfaction. There have also been reports that a lack of positive outcomes derived from Total Quality Management has led to the demise of as many as two-thirds of the programs less than two years old (Day 1994).

Unfortunately, the tangible and intangible losses associated with failed Total Quality Management programs can be significant (Kotter 1996).

Substantial financial and human resources are required to indoctrinate employees and managers in the TQM philosophy, and to train them in the proper application of TQM's practices and tools. In addition to these tangible losses are a number of intangible losses that are not easily recovered. For example, damage to employee morale, commitment, and satisfaction, while not readily quantifiable, are clearly significant. Moreover, these intangible losses may have both immediate and long term consequences, particularly if they create a climate of cynicism among employees (Dean and Goodman 1994). In order to avoid some of these problems in future applications of the TQM approach, quality proponents have sought to identify the factors that contribute significantly to the successful implementation and long-term viability of Total Quality Management.

As we will show in this chapter, successful application of Total Quality Management depends on more than refined technology and appropriate application of quantitative techniques. Probably the most critical factors have to do with people and the extent to which the philosophies and purposes embodied in TQM permeate the norms and values of an organization's culture. Organizational culture is important not only because it provides normative standards of what is deemed appropriate action, it also creates a shared sense of purpose or meaning among employees that guides their behavior. Traditionally, researchers have discussed culture as if organizations could be best characterized by a single overarching or TQM culture. In this chapter, however, we propose that a strategically differentiated culture – one that is characterized by the presence of an overarching or suparaordinate set of norms and values (e.g., providing customer value) while allowing for unit-level or subordinate norms and values – is the ideal culture to support an organization's Total Quality Management efforts and long term competitive advantage. In the following section, we discuss the importance of total quality's integration into organizational culture and the implications for TQM viability. We then explore culture's role in shaping behavior and present several perspectives on culture. These different perspectives supply the foundation upon which the notion of a strategically differentiated culture is developed. The concept of market orientation is then presented as a framework for understanding strategically differentiated culture. Finally, the chapter ends by discussing some of the ways that organizations can achieve Total Quality Management integration.

TOTAL QUALITY INTEGRATION

The issue of *total quality integration* is receiving increasing attention as an important factor in facilitating Total Quality Management's long-term viability. Total quality integration refers to the extent to which the principles and philosophy of Total Quality Management are fully integrated into the organization's culture. Often, the practices of TQM are easily incorporated into the organization's technical system (i.e., its standard operating procedures), and its administrative systems (i.e., its process and information technology), but the social system – the norms and values that comprise the organizations' culture – remain unchanged. As a result, TQM merely exists as a *collateral structure* – one that functions parallel to the normal organizational structure without being fully integrated into the organization's culture (Dean and Goodman 1994). In essence, the organization continues to function as always but engages in Total Quality Management activities as well. As a collateral structure, TQM's fate is tenuous and this lack of integration often contributes to the rapid demise of TQM programs in many contemporary organizations. To avoid this outcome, organizations must strive to achieve a level of integration such that the organization's culture and Total Quality Management are virtually indistinguishable. That is, the Total Quality Management approach should become the norm for conducting business and meeting the needs of customers. Consequently, Total Quality Management will take on a life of its own.

In order to achieve Total Quality Management integration, researchers and practitioners must have a clear understanding the role of organizational culture. However, organizational culture has typically been treated in a manner that does not fully capture its multidimensional and complex nature.

Historically, researchers have written about organizational culture as if organizations were comprised of one overarching or supraordinate culture. In actuality, organizations are likely to exhibit multiple cultures with different norms and values existing concurrently at different levels and across organizational boundaries. That is, in addition to the norms and values that comprise an overarching or supraordinate culture, organizations are also likely to exhibit lower-level or subordinate cultures corresponding, for example, to different functional business units or product lines. Different cultural norms and values may also exist for dealing with internal issues (e.g., operational excellence) and external issues (e.g., customer satisfaction). Thus, instead of exhibiting one single overarching culture, as culture has typically been presented in the literature, organizations are more likely to exhibit multiple cultures. To appreciate these points further, the following section discusses organizational culture, the function it serves in the work place, and the various types of culture that have been discussed in the literature. Later, we introduce the notion of a "strategically differentiated culture" and discuss market orientation as an example of a strategically differentiated culture. Finally, we return to the issue of TQM integration and institutionalization for the long-term viability of an organization's Total Quality Management efforts.

ORGANIZATIONAL CULTURE

Organizational culture has been identified as an important factor in explaining differences in organizational effectiveness and performance that cannot be accounted for by differences in structural characteristics of organizations (Pascale and Athos 1981). As Ouchi and Wilkins (1985) note, interest in culture and its relation to organizational functioning grew out of the realization that traditional models of organizations could not always explain the observed disparities between organizational goals and outcomes, and between strategy and implementation. Masters (1996) identified organizational culture as one of the most common barriers to Total Quality Management. Specifically, the inability to change an organization's culture to be more supportive of TQM principles and practices has been cited as a factor that thwarts the successful implementation of TQM. Consequently, understanding how organizational culture contributes to the success or failure of organizational interventions, such as Total Quality Management, is an important endeavor.

While there has been a great deal of interest in the topic of organizational culture, researchers have yet to arrive at a comprehensive definition (Barney 1986; Martin 1992). Instead, organizational culture has been defined in a variety of ways by different authors. Nevertheless, commonalities can be found among these various definitions which give meaning to organizational culture. One common way of describing organizational culture is in terms of consensus. That is, culture can be thought of as consensus regarding how to conduct business, embodied in the organization's norms and values (Kotter and Heskett 1992). For example, employees of IBM and Apple Computers have often been cited for their stereotypical dress. IBM employees are known for their blue suits while employees of Apple Computers are known for their casual attire. In both organizations, there appeared to be a high degree of consensus among employees regarding appropriate dress and this consensus was no doubt a function of their respective norms and values. Norms and values also suggest appropriate employee behavior. A firm's production employees, for example, are likely to respond in kind when asked for an appropriate number of widgets to produce in a given span of time.

Organizational culture has also been defined in terms of patterns of configurations of interpretations. Martin (1992), for example, describes organizational culture as the individual interpretations of behavioral and physical manifestations unique to a particular organization. In particular, Martin emphasizes three manifestations of culture: forms, practices, and content themes. Forms include rituals, stories, jargon, humor, and physical layout. These are relatively tangible characteristics of culture and are often encountered when one comes into contact with an organization. Practices, on the other hand, are not as tangible, and refer to formalized aspects of culture, such as organizational structure, job descriptions, policies and procedures, and financial controls. Content themes are the least tangible manifestations of culture and reflect shared concerns or underlying assumptions of right and wrong, such as pursuing quality or valuing employee input. According to Martin, these cultural manifestations (forms, practices, and content themes) are experienced by employees and customers when they interact with firms and their representatives. These individuals then interpret the cultural manifestations and their interpretation, not the manifestations per se, are what constitute organizational culture. Unlike Kotter and Heskett's (1992) consensus view of culture, Martin's cultural manifestations approach suggests that organizational culture resides in the meaning that organizational members and nonmembers attach to forms, practices, and content themes. Thus, when asked to explain his behavior, the employee who responds, "We do it this way because . . .", is revealing an aspect of the organization's culture. In Martin's view, culture is the *why* of behavior.

Culture has also been defined in terms of levels. Like Martin, Schein (1990) describes culture as occurring at three levels ranging from tangible to intangible. Artifacts are considered the most tangible elements of culture and are synonymous with Martin's forms (rituals, stories, jargon, humor, and physical layout). According to Schein, artifacts include the easily observable items one might encounter when entering an organization, such as company logos, awards, and physical layout. A visitor to a large manufacturing organization, for instance, may enter the establishment and be immediately drawn to its display of quality awards. Similarly, an individual may be impressed by an organization's dramatic facade, modern interior, or grand mission statement displayed prominently in the lobby. A more telling representation of culture can be found in an organization's norms and values. Norms and values evolve over time and represent a deeper level of culture. Consequently, they are more likely to influence individual behavior than artifacts. For example, Nordstrom is widely cited for its high quality customer service. Underlying the high quality service that Nordstrom customers receive, regardless of where they shop, is a shared value for providing a high level of service. At Nordstrom, service quality is the norm. Finally, at the deepest level of culture are the organization's underlying assumptions. Similar to Martin's shared meaning, Schein's assumptions are the taken-for-granted reasons that underlie members' perceptions and behaviors.

Taken together, these authors offer several different perspectives on culture and how it operates. Kotter and Heskett (1992), for example, view culture in terms of consensus regarding appropriate behavior. Appropriate behaviors, according to Kotter and Heskett, are embodied in the organization's norms and values. Martin, in contrast, views culture in terms of the shared meaning that organizational members and non-members attach to various manifestations (e.g., forms, practices, and content themes). Finally, Schein views organizational culture in terms of levels of abstraction (e.g., artifacts, norms and values, and underlying assumptions). While all of these authors conceptualize culture slightly differently, they generally agree on the importance of norms and values regarding appropriate behavior and shared meaning. As we will see in the next section, these aspects of culture are important elements in culture's ability to shape employee behavior.

ORGANIZATIONAL CULTURE'S
BEHAVIORAL INFLUENCE

Traditionally, organizations have relied almost exclusively on manager led, bureaucratic control. In a bureaucratically-controlled organization, a hierarchy of authority exists that is supported by a complex set of rules and regulations guiding employee behavior. The governance and power over employees stems from the system itself. That is, power is derived from adherence to the rules, regulations, and authority inherent in a hierarchy. By contrast, organizations who succeed in their TQM efforts tend to rely more on *concertive control* (Barker 1993). Concertive control is value-based; that is, behavior stems from shared meaning or consensus regarding which behaviors are appropriate and which are to be reinforced. For example, Barker found that the concertive control among self-managing teams in a large organization developed over time among team members as their "value consensus" regarding the meaning of quality and customer service evolved into a system of normative rules. The locus of control in a concertively controlled organization shifts from managers controlling employees, to employees who work collaboratively to develop their own form of behavioral control regulated by internalized values (Kelman 1958). Among Total Quality organizations, shifting the source of control from rules and regulations to norms and values allows members to achieve this type of negotiated or concertive control.

The norms and values inherent in a concertively controlled Total Quality Management organization guide members by serving two important functions: internal integration and external adaptation (Schermerhorn, Hunt, and Osborn 1995). Internal integration refers to the manner in which members resolve issues associated with living and working together. By facilitating internal integration, culture fosters the creation of a unique and shared identity, answers such questions as who is or is not a member, and clarifies whether certain behaviors are acceptable or unacceptable (Schermerhorn et al. 1995). Internal integration can be seen at the organizational level, such as when all employees share a common vision or allegiance to an organization. Internal integration can also be seen at the unit level, such as when business unit employees share a common identity. Thus, internal integration facilitates both unit-level and organization-level coordination.

The second function, external adaptation, concerns the way in which organizational members deal with outsiders (Schermerhorn et al. 1995). By facilitating external adaptation, culture helps clarify a number of important questions such as, "What is the real mission? How do we contribute? What are our goals? How do we reach our goals? What external forces are important? How do we measure results? What do we do if specific targets are not met? How do we tell others how good we are? When do we quit?" (Schermerhorn et al. 1995, p. 258). External adaptation also addresses the question of what is important, customer information or competitor information? Thus, shared norms and values enable individuals throughout the organization (e.g., across function, product, or unit boundaries) to respond to external issues in a similar fashion and create a shared perception of the firm's competitive advantage.

Thus, Total Quality Management organizations, characterized by concertive control, rely on norms and values to serve important internal integration and external adaptation roles. Internal integration and external adaptation help organizational members make sense of their environment and guide their behavior. This sense-making and controlling function helps employees successfully navigate their daily activities as they communicate with coworkers and interact with their internal and external environment to achieve high levels of quality and customer service. Consequently, internal integration and external adaptation facilitate smooth organizational operations and lead employees to act in a manner consistent with organization level and business unit level norms and values supportive of TQM initiatives.

DIFFERENT PERSPECTIVES ON ORGANIZATIONAL CULTURE

As evident from earlier sections of this chapter, organizational culture has been defined in many ways. Similarly, different *types* of culture have been described in the academic and applied literature. The next section reviews two qualitatively different views of culture widely accepted in the business literature: Kotter and Heskett's (1992) strong, strategic, and adaptive culture types, and Martin's (1992) integrated and differentiated culture types. As described below, TQM organizations seeking to achieve long term competitive advantage will benefit from a culture that synthesizes elements of both Martin's and Kotter and Heskett's culture types to create a *strategically differentiated* culture.

Kotter and Heskett (1992) describe three types of culture which they refer to as strong, strategic, and adaptive. Strong cultures, according to Kotter and Heskett, are those whose norms and values are clearly understood and exert a significant influence on managers and employees. Wal-Mart, Home Depot, and Microsoft are three organizations that are commonly noted for their strong cultures. Clearly communicated norms and values inherent in strong cultures enable their members to engage in rapid and coordinated action, for example, in response to threats from competitors or to aid their customers. Unfortunately, culture strength isn't always synonymous with superior organizational performance. As Kotter and Heskett (1992) note, strong cultures can lead otherwise intelligent people to walk in concert off of a cliff, such as when organizations hold firm to outdated or inappropriate procedures. To avoid such problems, Kotter and Heskett suggest that strong cultures must also be aligned with important organizational objectives. That is, strategic cultures have sufficient strength to clearly communicate important organizational norms and values to members while simultaneously aligning these norms and values with the organization's strategy. Thus, strategic cultures combine both strength and fit. Kotter and Heskett's third type of culture is the adaptive culture. Like the strategic culture, adaptive cultures also fit their context. In addition, adaptive cultures are malleable and change over time to fit their context. According to Kotter and Heskett, only cultures that allow organizations to adapt to changing environmental conditions will enable them to achieve superior performance over time. Thus, Kotter and Heskett proposed several different types of organizational culture. Like much of the extant culture literature, however, Kotter and Heskett propose that organizations have single overarching organizational cultures.

Offering a different perspective, Martin (1992) proposes two types of culture: integrated and differentiated. According to Martin, integrated cultures are those with similar norms and values across functional, product, or unit boundaries. For example, a corporation comprised of multiple business organizations all exhibiting similar norms and values would be described as having an integrated culture. In other words, norms and values embraced by any one unit would be representative of the whole organization. In contrast, differentiated cultures are those whose norms and values vary across functional, product, or unit boundaries. Thus, the same corporation with norms and values unique to each function, product, or unit would be classified as having a differentiated culture. In the latter example, any one unit's norms and values would not necessarily be an accurate representation of the overall organizational culture. Rather, the organization's culture is defined by the presence of multiple, sub-unit cultures.

In reality, organizational cultures are likely to exhibit a combination of these characteristics. That is, they may combine elements of the strong, strategic, adaptive, integrated, and differentiated culture types. Total Quality Management organizations, in particular, are likely to benefit from a *strategically differentiated* culture – one that exhibits characteristics of Kotter and Heskett's (1992) strategic and adaptive cultures as well as characteristics of Martin's (1992) differentiated culture. A strategically differentiated culture is one characterized by the presence of an overarching or supraordinate set of norms and values while allowing for unit-level or subordinate norms and values that are consistent with the strategies of those units. In other words, individual units may be aligned with an organization's overarching culture (e.g., to provide customer value) while also exhibiting unit-level norms that are consistent with their strategy (e.g., provide customer value via quality products versus providing customer value via low prices). For example, in a recent survey of Eastman Chemical Company's business unit managers, there was wide agreement and support for the organization's overarching or supraordinate objectives (e.g., maintaining superior competitive advantage). At the same time, however, managers of commodity and specialized units differed in their view of the way they pursued the corporation's overarching objectives. Commodity unit managers viewed pursuing long term competitive advantage as focusing on reliable product delivery and competitive pricing. In contrast, specialized unit managers viewed pursuing long term competitive advantage as developing and delivering new and innovative products to their customers. Thus, while commodity and specialty units were focused on a similar overarching goal (e.g., long-term competitive advantage), the business-unit cultures differed as a function of the nature of their businesses. Specifically, norms in the commodity units supported reliable deliveries and competitive pricing while norms in the specialty units supported providing new and innovative products.

The concept of market orientation provides a particularly useful framework for understanding a strategically differentiated culture as it relates to TQM. Market-oriented organizations are known for their focus on customers and competitors through superior market-sensing techniques (Day 1994). Market-sensing involves the systematic gathering and interpretation of market information. It enables organizations to understand their environment and utilize that information to adapt to local market conditions. As a result, market-oriented firms create shared understanding among members through their systematic market-sensing and are better able to provide valued goods and services to their customers and maintain a competitive advantage (e.g., Deshpande, Farley, and Webster 1993; Jaworski and Kohli 1993; Narver and Slater 1990; Ruekert 1992).

MARKET ORIENTATION

It has long been noted that achieving above average market performance over time requires the creation of sustainable, superior value for customers (Narver and Slater 1990). Value, as a concept, can be thought of as the difference between a customer's perceptions of the expected benefit of a product or service and its expected cost (Zeithaml 1988). Consequently, firms can create value through two different avenues: increasing customer benefits and decreasing customer costs (Forbis and Mehta 1981). Desire on the part of organizational members to create superior customer value and sustainable competitive advantage, should drive a business to create and maintain a culture that will produce the behaviors necessary to achieve these high levels of performance (Narver and Slater 1990).

Market orientation has been described as the "organizational culture that most effectively and efficiently creates the necessary behaviors for the creation of superior value for buyers and, thus, continuous superior performance for the business" (Narver and Slater 1990, p. 21). Market-oriented firms identify how they can most effectively create sustainable superior value for existing and future customers by routinely examining alternative sources of competitive advantage (Narver and Slater 1990). A market-oriented culture enables firms to provide sustainable, superior value for customers and, thus, maintain a competitive advantage in the market place. According to Day (1994), the objective of a market-oriented culture is to "demonstrate a pervasive commitment to a set of processes, beliefs, and values, reflecting the philosophy that all decisions start with the customer and are guided by a deep and shared understanding of the customer's needs and behavior and competitors' capabilities and intentions, for the purpose of realizing superior performance by satisfying customers better than competitors" (p. 45). A market orientation involves the acquisition of the skills necessary to understand and satisfy customers (Day 1990) and is comprised of a set of beliefs that puts the customer's interests first (Deshpande, Farley, and Webster 1993), the ability of the organization to generate, disseminate, and use superior information about customers and competitors (Kohli and Jaworski 1990), and the coordinated application of interfunctional resources to the creation of superior customer value (Narver and Slater 1990).

A market-oriented culture consists of three components: *customer orientation, competitor orientation,* and *interfunctional coordination* – as well as a long-term focus and an emphasis on profitability. Customer orientation and competitor orientation include all of the activities involved in acquiring information about the customers and competitors in the target market and disseminating it throughout the business. Specifically, a customer orientation involves obtaining sufficient understanding of one's customers to be able to create superior value for them over time. This requires an understanding of a customer's entire "value chain" (Day and Wensley 1988) as it evolves over time and adapts to internal and external market dynamics. A competitor orientation is characterized by an understanding of the short-term strengths and weaknesses, and long-term capabilities and strategies, of current and potential competitors (Aaker 1988; Day and Wensley 1988). The third component of a market orientation, interfunctional coordination, involves the business's coordinated efforts to create superior value for buyers. Value creation is believed to require the integrated effort of all human and other capital resources (Narver and Slater 1990). A market-oriented culture is characterized by the valuing of and shared commitment to these components (customer orientation, competitor orientation, and interfunctional coordination) by organizational members. As such, a market oriented culture involves a uniform or shared interpretation by organizational members of the behaviors necessary to provide superior customer performance.

Market-oriented culture resides in the mental models or cognitive representations of competitive advantage that managers use to guide their behavior. Day and Nedungadi (1994), for example, recently found that the mental models managers used to represent the competitive advantage of their firms helped the managers search for incoming information, select information relevant to their situation, and, on the basis of that information, determine whether or not competitive advantage had been achieved. These mental models or cognitive portrayals of competitive advantage help managers adapt to their environments in the sense that they contain decision rules for filtering information and heuristics for strategic decision making. In their research, Day and Nedungadi (1994) identified four qualitatively different mental models or cognitive representations of

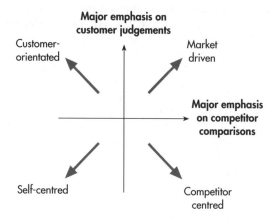

**Major emphasis on
customer judgements**

Customer-
orientated

Market
driven

**Major emphasis
on competitor
comparisons**

Self-centred

Competitor
centred

Source: Adapted from G.S. Day, and P. Nedungadi (1994).
Managerial representations of competitive advantage.
Journal of Marketing, 58, 31–44

Figure 5.1   Representational modes

competitive advantage, each varying in terms of the emphasis placed
on customer versus management judgments about where and how competitors differ.

As shown in figure 5.1, these judgments correspond to the relative
emphasis placed on a customer-orientation versus a competitor-orientation.
For example, businesses that focus on competitors are apt to hold mental
representations of competitive advantage that emphasize competitor comparisons. They are likely to base strategic decisions on comparisons with
competitors and relative performance is determined by comparing their
own costs and profits with those of competitors. Conversely, businesses that
focus on customers are likely to hold mental representations in terms of
their customers. Consequently, decisions are based on customer needs and
performance is evaluated on the basis of customer judgments regarding
relative product utility and satisfaction. Consistent with previous research,
market-oriented firms were found to exhibit an external, rather than an
internal, focus. That is, they focused on both customers and competitors.
In contrast, self-centered firms were low on these same dimensions and
inwardly focused. According to Day and Nedungadi, self-centered firms pay
little attention to their competitors or to the needs of their customers.
Not surprisingly, self-centered firms also exhibit unstable competitive strategies, characterized by a lack of agreement among their members.

Managers' shared representations of competitive advantage are a function of environmental factors and organizational strategy. Taken together,
environmental factors and organizational strategy comprise the broader
organizational context and influence the type of information that businesses use to determine whether a competitive advantage exists. Specifically,

managers form representations of competitive advantage by scanning the environment for information, conducting directed inquiries, imitating successful practices, or reflecting on past experiences. This information is then communicated, interpreted, and compiled into organizational memory. The resulting knowledge is encoded in the form of normative decision rules for accepting or rejecting information, shared cognitive models for deriving meaning from that information, and routines for responding to the information. Thus the content of learning is both the shared pattern of cognitive associations developed by members and the behavioral outcomes that reflect these associations (Fiol and Lyles 1985). These patterns of shared cognitive meaning which in turn give rise to behaviors, are consistent with Martin's (1992) view of culture. That is, culture can be viewed as the shared interpretation and meaning of behaviors and purpose that are unique to a particular organization.

A growing body of literature has examined market orientation for its role in enabling a firm to achieve a competitive advantage in the market place (e.g., Deshpande, Farley and Webster 1993; Jaworski and Kohli 1993; Narver and Slater 1990; Ruekert 1992). For example, Day and Nedungadi (1994) found evidence that firms with a market orientation, in which the focus is on both customers and competitors, outperform those that are oriented toward either customers, competitors, or themselves. Specifically, self-reports of financial performance were more strongly related to market orientation than either a pure customer orientation, competitor orientation, or self-centered orientation. Narver and Slater (1990) also found that firms with a high degree of market orientation exhibited a high level of profitability. Similarly, Jaworski and Kohli (1993) found that a market orientation was related to judgments of overall business performance, organizational commitment, and esprit de corps. Taken together, these findings suggest that a market-oriented culture can play a critical role in firm performance.

Though the literature suggests that both dimensions of market orientation, a customer and a competitor focus, are needed for success, there are reasons to believe that the *relative* emphasis on customer orientation versus competitor orientation may depend on factors in the competitive environment, the business's strategy, and the nature of the business (Day and Wensley 1988). This is an important point because the concept of value and, thus, perceived sources of competitive advantage, may differ across businesses as a function of these important elements. That is, characteristics of the competitive environment such as the structure of competition, customer buying power, cost and investment structure, and the rate of market growth may influence the extent to which a relative emphasis on customer or competitor orientation is most appropriate (Day and Nedungadi 1994). For example, early in a product's life cycle, environmental uncertainty regarding market demand and customer requirements may be more salient, necessitating a customer orientation. Later as growth slows and uncertainty regarding customer needs declines, the emphasis is likely to shift to concerns over market share, which increases the focus on competitor moves. In essence, elements of the organization's culture (e.g., its relative emphasis on customer needs and competitor moves) adapt and change over time as the competitive environment changes. The ability to adapt and change in response to local conditions exemplifies one aspect of the strategically differentiated culture.

The type of business strategy adopted by a firm may also influence the extent to which a relative emphasis on customer-versus competitor-orientation is appropriate. For example, a cost leadership strategy requires an aggressive approach to producing products more efficiently than competitors through cost-cutting techniques (Porter 1980). As such, adopting a low cost position in the market place demands constant comparisons with direct competitors to ensure one's own competitive advantage. As a result, managerial representations of competitive advantage by firms pursuing a cost leadership strategy are inevitably dominated by competitor comparisons. Conversely, strategies of differentiation through superior quality and service or through faster responsiveness require more customer-oriented representations because the success of these strategies depend on satisfying customer requirements (Day and Nedungadi 1994). Again, this variation in strategies in response to local conditions exemplifies the strategically differentiated culture.

The extent to which a firm emphasizes customer versus competitor concerns may also be influenced by the nature of the firm's business. For example, specialized businesses seek to dominate target market segments by exceeding the capabilities of competitors. Success comes from identifying and meeting the needs of their customers. To do so, specialized businesses must be responsive to information about their competitive positions as judged by their customers. In contrast, commodity businesses sell products which are essentially identical in quality and performance to those of competitors. In trying to create superior value for customers, commodity businesses must add customer benefits to their generic products which exceed the benefits of their competitors and/or they must reduce costs (Narver and Slater 1990).

To summarize, factors in the competitive environment, business strategy, and the nature of a firm's business may influence the relative importance of a competitor or customer focus among market-oriented firms in their attempt to achieve a competitive advantage. Accordingly, the organization's culture should be aligned with the strategic goals of the business to increase the probability that organizational members will act in accordance with those strategic goals. Moreover, a firm with multiple agendas (i.e., a firm like Eastman Chemical which has both specialized and commodity businesses) may be best served by adopting a differentiated culture to more closely align the culture at the business unit level with the requirements of it's environment, strategy, and business. Thus, a firm pursuing Total Quality Management objectives may benefit from a culture that is both strategic and adaptive as well as differentiated.

Taken together, a strategically differentiated culture should facilitate the long term viability of an organizations' Total Quality Management initiative as well as its competitive advantage. As noted, strategically differentiated cultures are those that exhibit both company-wide supraordinate norms and values (e.g., maintaining competitive advantage) while allowing for variation at the unit or subordinate level (e.g., customer orientation versus competitor orientation). In our study of Eastman Chemical Company, evidence was found for such practices. Throughout Eastman, managers agreed on the importance of service, quality, and customer value for Eastman's long term competitive advantage. However, at the business unit level, managers pursued these overarching goals in ways that were appropriate to their context. For example, the culture in specialized business organizations emphasized high quality customer service while the culture in commodity business organizations emphasized product pricing and availability. Thus, both groups exhibit norms that contribute to Eastman's overarching goals of customer service, quality, and value, but in ways specific to the nature of their business.

BUILDING CULTURES

In this chapter we have attempted to highlight the importance of a strategically differentiated culture for the viability of a Total Quality Management initiative and for sustained firm performance. Previous research has revealed a number of important factors in the development of organizational culture. Organizational founders and leaders play a critical role in shaping culture. Organizational founders, in particular, are often credited with instilling organizations with their core set of norms and values. Henry Ford of Ford Motor Company and Sam Walton of Wal-Mart, for example, are often credited for instilling in their organizations many of the norms and values that are still evident today. However, leaders must also be wary of outdated, inappropriate, or ineffective norms and values that may have evolved over time into "sacred" practices or traditions that resist change and undermine an organization's adaptability (Kotter and Heskett 1992). Moreover, they must work to maintain a balance between those core organizational norms and values that are timeless (e.g., valuing customers, stockholders, and employees) and those that must vary to fit the needs of an organization's context and current business environment (e.g., focusing on competitive pricing versus customer service) (Kotter and Heskett 1992). In so doing, organizations can remain true to their core norms and values – those deemed appropriate by the firm's founder and maintained by subsequent leaders – while remaining sufficiently flexible to adapt to changing conditions.

In the same fashion, leaders play a critical role in ensuring the long term viability of a Total Quality Management program. From their positions of authority, leaders in TQM firms have the ability to see that Total Quality Management progresses beyond the point of a collateral structure to something that is highly ingrained by instilling the principles, practices, and techniques underlying TQM into the firm's administrative (the set of processes for accomplishing work), technical (the firm's process and information technologies), and social systems (its culture). According to Dean and Goodman (1994), successful integration greatly increases the long-term viability of a TQM effort and ultimately determines if the program will be self-sustaining.

As noted earlier, Total Quality Management integration refers to the assimilation of TQM principles and practices into all aspects of an organization, particularly the culture (Dean and Goodman 1994). Integration requires learning, commitment, problem-solving, and institutionalization. First and foremost, organizational members must acquire the skills necessary to apply TQM's practices in an appropriate manner. Second, they must be committed or "morally involved" in the program. That is, they must accept and internalize the principles underlying Total Quality Management. Commitment to these principles increases the probability that individuals will continue to pursue TQM efforts in spite of difficult or challenging conditions. Organizational members must also posses the problem-solving skills that will enable them to remove obstacles to performance and apply TQM principles and practices in situations or areas where their application may not be readily apparent. Finally, the principles of TQM must be institutionalized. Institutionalization concerns organizational culture and the extent to which Total Quality Management is embedded in the organization's norms and values. Institutionalized principles will be evident across organizational members, accepted as fact, and persist over time (Goodman and Dean 1982).

There are five facets of institutionalization: knowledge of behavior, performance, preferences for behavior, normative consensus, and values (Dean and Goodman 1994). The extent to which each of these are present or absent is indicative of the degree of institutionalization. Knowledge of behavior refers to whether or not organizational members understand which behaviors are appropriate and inappropriate in a TQM organization. Thus, institutionalization is indicated by the extent to which organizational members are aware of the principles, practices, and techniques that underlie the Total Quality Management approach. Institutionalization is also indicated by the degree to which organizational members engage in Total Quality Management practices and have shared perceptions of the source of their competitive advantage. That is, institutionalization involves understanding TQM and applying it's principles and practices. The third facet of institutionalization concerns individuals' preferences for engaging in the behaviors. Total Quality Management is institutionalized to the extent that organizational members' choose to engage in TQM practices. The fourth facet of institutionalization involves members' awareness that others are performing TQM behaviors and their consensus regarding the appropriateness of those behaviors. Institutionalization is indicated when organizational members are aware that others engage in Total Quality Management practices and agree that those TQM practices are appropriate and valuable. Finally, shared values comprise the fifth facet of Total Quality Management's institutionalization. In a Total Quality Management organization, institutionalization would be indicated to the degree that organizational members share the values underlying TQM.

Institutionalization occurs over time as the facets of institutionalization (knowledge of behavior, performance, preferences for behavior, normative consensus, and values) interact with one another as described by Goodman and Dean (1982):

> People probably have some cognitive representations of a behavior before it is performed. Performance of a behavior generates experiences, as well as rewards and punishments that affect people's disposition toward that behavior. As many people perform the behavior, they become aware of others' performance, which leads to consensus about the appropriateness of the behavior. If there is normative consensus about a class of behaviors that reflects a particular value, over time we expect some consensus on that value among organizational participants. Or, stating the obverse, if a new value consensus emerges over time, we would expect that value to be derived from a set of normative behaviors. The normative consensus in turn depends on the private acceptance of that behavior, which in turn reflects experiences from the performance of that behavior. (p. 233)

For Total Quality integration to occur, however, all of the above elements (e.g., learning, commitment, problem-solving, and institutionalization) must be communicated in some fashion. Socialization and diffusion play a critical role in that process (Goodman and Dean 1982). Specifically, socialization and diffusion refer to the process whereby important aspects of Total Quality Management (e.g., its policies, practices, and procedures) are transmitted to individual organizational members and throughout the organization. For example, in a strategically differentiated culture, the socialization and diffusion process helps create a sense of shared meaning both within and across unit boundaries by clarifying unit-level as well as organization-level norms and values. Socialization and diffusion, while critical for Total Quality integration, do not occur automatically.

Integration is initiated and maintained by organizational change practices. Change practices are the specific programs or steps that are taken to increase integration. There are a number of change practices available to organizations.[1] At a minimum, firms implementing Total Quality Management must incorporate training in order to demonstrate the principles and practices associated with Total Quality Management. Organizational leaders also play a critical role in TQM integration. They must demonstrate their commitment to the principles and practices of Total Quality Management through their actions as well as their words. Change practices, such as these, will facilitate Total Quality Management's assimilation into all aspects of an organization and help ensure its long term viability (Dean and Goodman 1994).

SUMMARY

The last few decades have witnessed major changes in how organizations conduct their business. Total Quality Management, in particular, has played a significant role in those changes. Unfortunately, Total Quality Management efforts often fail to live up to the expectations of their proponents

(Beer, Eisenstat and Spector 1990). Recall that in a study of nearly 500 companies, only one-third of the respondents felt that Total Quality Management had contributed to their competitive advantage. Similar results were discussed in Business Week where only 26 percent of the organizations surveyed indicated that Total Quality Management had helped them increase market share or customer satisfaction. Failure to achieve significant gains has prompted a number of researchers and practitioners to take a closer look at TQM and the reasons underlying those instances in which it fails.

Subsequent research and speculation has focused attention on organizational culture and its role in Total Quality Management's success (or failure) and firm performance. Organizational culture is thought to significantly impact organizational performance indirectly through several means. First, culture plays an important coordinating role in the sense that it clarifies who the firm's important stakeholders (e.g., its employees and customers) and competitors are, and, via organizational culture's norms and values, guides organizational members in their interactions with customers and one another (Barney 1986). Organizational culture also serves an important integration role by blurring the distinction between the administrative (the set of processes for accomplishing work), technical (the firm's process and information technologies), and social systems (its culture). Thus, culture coordinates and integrates a variety of important organizational elements.

Kotter and Heskett (1992) defined organizational culture in terms of value consensus. Specifically, they define culture as consensus regarding how to conduct business. Underlying the consensus inherent in culture are the organization's norms and values. However, to facilitate a firm's competitive advantage, the norms and values must be relevant to the business at hand. In the case of Eastman Chemical, specialty units pursued objectives that were similar to those of commodity units (e.g., long term competitive advantage). Nevertheless, the culture in these business-units differed as a function of their businesses. In this chapter, we introduced strategically differentiated culture as the ideal culture to support this type of organizational structure. A strategically differentiated culture is one that is aligned with the organization's overall objectives (e.g., providing customer value), while allowing for unit differences in how they achieve those objectives (e.g., pursuing customer value through a customer orientation; pursuing customer value through a competitor orientation). The common or overarching objectives embedded in a strategically differentiated culture enable organizational members to confront obstacles and pursue opportunities that are unique to their particular situations in a manner that is nevertheless consistent with the organization's supraordinate objectives. In other words, a strategically differentiated culture allows individual units to capitalize on their own sources of competitive advantage while remaining true to the organization's primary mission.

To capitalize on the potential benefit of a strategically differentiated culture, individuals must be cognizant of the firms' supraordinate and subordinate norms and values. They must be sufficiently aware of the organization's supraordinate norms, values, and goals to engage in behaviors that are consistent with the firm's higher level overarching objectives. At the same time, individuals must be cognizant of their unit level norms and values. Long-term competitive advantage is more likely to be achieved by organizations whose members are able to recognize these differences and capitalize on them in a way that maximizes the competitive advantage of their units and the organization as a whole. Consequently, organizational leaders should attempt to assess the extent to which managers' representations of competitive advantage are appropriately strategically differentiated for the product-customer interface.

Note

1   Specific change techniques are beyond the scope of this chapter. However, interested readers may choose from numerous texts that are available to facilitate organizational change and development efforts. For example, issues surrounding culture changing are discussed in P. Atkinson (ed.), *Creating Culture Change: The Key to Successful Total Quality Management*, London: Pfeffer and Company, 1990. Also see Goodman and Associates (eds), *Change in Organizations: New Perspectives on Theory, Research, and Practice*, San Francisco: Jossey-Bass, 1982.

References

Aaker, D. A. (ed.) (1988). *Strategic market management.* New York: John Wiley & Sons, Inc.

Barker, J. R. (1993). Tightening the iron cage: Concertive control in self-managing teams. *Administrative Science Quarterly*, 38, 408–37.

Barney, J. B. (1986). Organizational culture: Can it be a source of competitive advantage? *Academy of Management Review*, 11, 656–65.

Beer, M., Eisenstat, R. A. and Spector, B. (1990). Why change programs don't produce change. *Harvard Business Review*, Nov.–Dec., 158–66.

Business Week (1992). *Quality: Small and midsize companies seize the challenge – not a moment too soon.* November, 66–75.

Cameron, K. S. and Freeman, S. J. (1991). Cultural congruence, strength and type: Relationships to effectiveness. *Research in Organizational Change and Development*, 5, 23–58.

Day, G. S. (1994). The capabilities of market-driven organizations. *Journal of Marketing*, 58, 37–52.

Day, G. S. and Nedungadi, P. (1994). Managerial representations of competitive advantage. *Journal of Marketing*, 58, 31–44.

Day, G. S. and Wensley, R. (1988). Assessing advantage: A framework for diagnosing competitive superiority. *Journal of Marketing*, 52, 1–20.

Day, G. S. (1990). *Market-driven Strategy. Processes for Creating Value.* New York, NY: The Free Press.

Dean, J. W. and Goodman, P. S. (1994). *Toward a theory of total quality integration.* Paper presented at the Academy of Management National Meeting.

Deshpande, R., Farley, J. U. and Webster, F. E. (1993). Corporate culture, customer orientation, and innovativeness in Japanese firms: A quadrad analysis. *Journal of Marketing*, 57, 23–37.

Deshpande, R. and Webster, F. E. (1989). Organizational culture and marketing: Defining the research agenda. *Journal of Marketing*, 53, 3–15.

Fiol, C. M. and Lyles, M. A. (1985). Organizational learning. *Academy of Management Review*, 10, 803–13.

Forbis, J. L. and Mehta, N. T. (1981). Value-based strategies for industrial products. *Business Horizons*, 24, 32–42.

Goodman, P. S. and Dean, J. W. (1982). In Goodman and Associates (eds). *Change in organizations*. San Francisco: Jossey-Bass.

Jacob, R. (1993). TQM: More than a dying fad? *Fortune*, 28, 66–72.

Jaworski, B. J. and Kohli, A. K. (1993). Market orientation: Antecedents and consequences. *Journal of Marketing*, 57, 53–70.

Kelman, H. C. (1958). Compliance, identification, and internalization: Three processes of attitude change. *Journal of Conflict Resolution*, 2, 51–60.

Kohli, A. K. and Jaworski, B. J. (1990). Market orientation: The construct, research propositions, and managerial implications. *Journal of Marketing*, 54, 1–18.

Kotter, J. P. (1996). Kill complacency. *Fortune*, August, 168–70.

Kotter, J. P. and Heskett, J. L. (1992). *Corporate culture and performance*. New York: The Free Press.

Masters, R. J. (1996). Overcoming barriers to TQM's success. *Quality Progress*, May, 53–5.

Martin, J. (1992). *Cultures in organizations: Three perspectives*. New York: Oxford University Press.

Narver, J. C. and Slater, S. F. (1990). The effect of a market orientation on business profitability. *Journal of Marketing*, October, 20–34.

Pascale, R. T. and Athos, A. (1981). *The Art of Japanese Management*. New York: Simon and Schuster.

Porter, M. E. (1980). *Competitive strategy*. New York: Free Press.

Ouchi, W. G., Wilkins, A. L. (1985). Organizational culture. *Annual Review of Sociology*, 11, 457–83.

Rousseau, D. M. (1990). In Schneider, B. (ed.). *Organizational climate and culture*. San Francisco: Jossey-Bass.

Ruekert, R. W. (1992). Developing a market orientation: An organizational strategy perspective. *Journal of Research in Marketing*, 9, 225–45.

Schermerhorn, J. R., Hunt, J. G. and Osborn, R. N. (eds). (1995). *Basic organizational behavior*. New York: John Wiley and Sons, Inc.

Schein, E. H. (1990). Organizational culture. *American Psychologist*, 45, 109–19.

Stone, D. L. and Eddy, E. R. (1996). A model of individual and organizational factors affecting quality-related outcomes. *Journal of Quality Management*, 1, 21–48.

Zeithaml, V. A. (1988). Consumer perceptions of price, quality, and value: A means-end model and synthesis of evidence. *Journal of Marketing*, 52, 2–22.

6 | An Organizational Model For Implementing A Total Quality Management System

Andrew G. Kemeny

Abstract

Improving performance is a mandate common to all organizations. Institutions in education, commerce, industry, government, and health care are all striving to become better and more competitive in what they do. The concept commonly known as Total Quality Management (TQM) has been embraced by many organizations in various walks of life as the means to achieve performance improvements.

At times the plans for improvement may take place over many years, other times the need is immediate. Dramatic changes may be followed by periods of continuous improvement, or vice versa. In any case, the moment of truth arrives when it is time to implement. I believe that the exact plan for designing and implementing a system for total quality must be custom engineered to the needs and circumstances of each specific organization. What I offer in this chapter is a *model.* The centerpiece of this model is the organizational approach to quality system design and implementation. Issues of leadership, process management and the role of information technology are also addressed. Please study the model, evaluate its applicability to your circumstances and proceed to create your own plan for success.

INTRODUCTION

This chapter is about bringing to life a quality system in your enterprise. The "quality system" may be referred to as Total Quality Management (TQM) or by other labels essentially representing the same concept. The "enterprise" may be an institution in the field of commerce, education, government or any other grouping you feel comfortable to be included. Importantly, this chapter is not about defining the precise meaning of Quality, or about achieving acceptance of the idea of quality as the means to competitive advantage, or an imperative for just plain survival. It is assumed that those issues have been settled within your enterprise, and now you are faced with the task of making "it" real.

Chances are that there was considerable effort expended in your enterprise in reaching the decision of moving ahead with implementation of a quality management system. There were supporters and skeptics. The supporters won the battle. Now it is time to win the war and to sustain the victory. What follows will provide you with a framework that, when adapted to your own environment, will give you a good chance for success. This will require a strategic plan for implementation, a structure for governance of the entire initiative, and processes for ongoing management and operations.

To ensure a precise and shared understanding of the key elements, four brief definitions follow.

> *Strategic Plan*: The output of strategic planning; a documented set of coherent, unified and integrated decisions that determine and communicate the intent of the enterprise concerning a critical issue, in terms of objectives, action programs and resource allocation priorities.
>
> *Governance*: A properly authorized and communicated structure specifically established for management, control and coordination.
>
> *Process*: A set of interrelated work activities that are characterized by a set of specific inputs and value-added task that produce a set of specific outputs for customers.
>
> *Quality Management System*: All activities of the management function that determine the quality policy, objectives and responsibilities and implement them by means of a system consisting of organizational structure, procedures, processes and resources.

The need for a strategic plan is paramount. The very essence of quality demands planning. The scope of the quality initiative will surely include all aspects of the enterprise. Eventually, enterprise strategy, structure, processes and culture will be transformed. The change will require significant resources, and will often place conflicting demands on the best people in the organization. Both the enormous change and the resource intensity dimension of the quality transformation initiative mandate a strong and well-defined structure of governance to drive the implementation of the strategic plan. And, once the momentum is established, a set of well-designed processes must be put in place with the objective of managing and improving the operations of the enterprise. As the organization matures, these processes become the way we work. Quality management becomes an integral part of the overall enterprise management approach. The quality initiative, a separate and distinct subject at the start of the journey will blend in the everyday way of doing business.

The "quality management system" is a subject of countless articles and books. The definition provided above is a synthesis of many views. When prefaced by the word "total," the implication is that the quality management system is all pervasive in the enterprise. There is no other formal system for management and operations, customer focus is paramount, suppliers are treated as partners, and employee involvement is in evidence everywhere.

What I aim to accomplish in the balance of this chapter is to present a pragmatic scenario that encompasses the most significant aspects of implementing quality management as the way of improving enterprise performance. For illustrative purposes I will provide examples borrowed from a fictional entity and use fictional people. Let us start by painting a picture of this hypothetical enterprise.

OUR ENTERPRISE

Arguably, the attributes of the enterprise may have significant implications on the way we go about implementing a quality system. I contend, however, that the differences among various enterprises do not alter the fundamentals of the model offered in this chapter. For example, what is our line of business? Or, does it matter? Yes, it does matter, but primarily in the details of execution. The model that will be recommended works equally well for manufacturers, service providers, universities or government agencies. So, from here on we shall simply refer to our fictional enterprise as the *"Institution."* The important thing is that the *Institution* has recognized the need for performance improvement, and elected to install a quality management system to achieve that objective.

What is the size of our fictional *Institution*? Or, does it matter? Yes, it does matter, because size influences the complexity of the model. So does geography. However, the model accommodates these kinds of variations. For the purposes of our hypothetical *Institution* assume that it has about 13,000 associates (employees, if you will), operates in seven locations, and has five Divisions that are present at most locations. By the way, what kind of associates do we have? Are they engineers, production workers, teachers? Are they represented by a Union? Or does it matter? Yes, it does matter, but primarily in the details of execution, and our model does take care of the variations. Our fictional *Institution* has Union represented workers and non-union professional and managerial associates, both.

What is our position in the marketplace? Are we the leaders, the followers or the also-runs? Are we in a crisis, a turnaround situation, facing a hostile take-over or bankruptcy. Or, are we growing, gaining reputation, market share and value? Are our funding sources drying up, or are we well endowed to carry out our mission? Do we need ISO 9000 certification to compete successfully? Naturally, the answers to these questions will influence the specific application of our model, primarily as far as the urgency of implementation is concerned and the prioritization and focus of our plan. Fortunately, our hypothetical *Institution* is currently well positioned, but faces increasing challenges in the marketplace.

Naturally, there are many other attributes that could further define our fictional *Institution*. To make the picture somewhat more complete, assume that our *Institution* is publicly owned, has a Chief Executive Officer (CEO), a Management Executive Committee (MEC), and a Board. It serves a very large number of customers. Sporadically held past surveys have shown moderately favorable overall customer satisfaction. Employees consider the *Institution* a good place to work. The main proponent of introducing the quality management approach is the head of one of the divisions, a Senior Vice President. Her name is Susan Blount.

ALTERNATIVE STYLES OF QUALITY
MANAGEMENT SYSTEM IMPLEMENTATION

Susan Blount studied the ways by which other enterprises brought quality systems into existence. She observed three basic styles of approaches:

"Let a thousand flowers bloom" is one approach to implementation followed by many, especially in the early days of the quality movement. The fundamental belief of the proponents of this approach is that once all people in the organization have been trained in the basic philosophy of quality and in the use of some of its popular tools, they are in the best position to target improvement opportunities. "Empowerment" becomes the key buzz-word. Typically, management provides large-scale training to all, and encourages the formation of quality improvement teams. The teams then select the problems they wish to solve, following one of the several well proven problem solving methodologies. Ms Blount observed that generally, in the organizations electing this style emphasis is placed on adherence to the methodology and on team independence, rather than on results. While initial employee excitement and participation may be high, they tend to decrease substantially along with support from management, as management fails to realize the anticipated performance improvements in key operating results.

"Quality by decree" is another style that Susan Blount noted when visiting with organizations. Frequently, a highly-placed official of the enterprise becomes the disciple of one of the well-known quality "gurus." The chief then launches a quality initiative by forcing ideas through the hierarchical channels of the organization under his/her control. "Quality driven" becomes the buzz-word. In these situations some initial progress may appear rather quickly, motivated by fear rather than by conviction. Success is typically measured by the "numbers," such as the number of Quality Circles, number of projects, number of employees participating, number of awards given and the like. Depending on the strength of the leader, some good things are accomplished, but more often than not, the quality movement quickly evaporates once the sponsoring official moves on to another position.

In contrast to these two styles, and variations thereof that create the image of quality as the "fad of the day," Susan Blount found several organizations where the leadership *fosters a participative and inclusive way of implementing quality management* in the enterprise. "Empowerment" is replaced by "trust." In these situations all constituencies of the organization have a voice in both the strategic and tactical aspects of implementation, measures of success are gaued by improvements in operational results, and customer and employee satisfaction. The quality effort is sustained, and in the long term becomes totally integrated in the fabric of the enterprise. It is this style that Susan suggested to the Executive Management Council of her *Institution.*

RECOMMENDED QUALITY SYSTEM IMPLEMENTATION MODEL

The top leaders of the *Institution* have spent significant time on deciding the means by which enterprise performance can drastically improve both in the near term and the long term. After due deliberation, the leadership team choose to pursue the implementation of a total quality management system, utilizing the style of approach recommended by Susan Blount. The decision was clearly communicated to the entire organization, and discussed in detail with the Union representing many of the workers. Susan Blount was asked to head up a sub-group of the Management Executive Committee (MEC) to create a high level Strategic Plan for the effort. This plan consisted of the following sections:

1. Purpose
   Why is the quality system approach the strategic direction of the *Institution*? How is it expected to improve performance across the organization? What is the alignment between the quality system and the *Institution's* overall vision, mission and values?

2. Desired End State Goals
   What will the *Institution* look like when the quality system is fully operational, in terms of customer experience, market position, employee behavior, benefits to employees and financial measures? What kind of improvement is anticipated over the present situation?

3. The Quality Management System of the *Institution*
   What is the quality system? Why was it chosen? What is "Process Management and Improvement"? How is it different from present operations?

4. Structure
   What is the governance structure? How will the *Institution* organize its resources to implement and operate the quality system? What are the roles and responsibilities?

5. Implementation Methodology
   How will the *Institution* develop and implement the quality system? Specifically, how will the constituents of the *Institution* be involved in decision making and implementation?

6. Implementation Schedule
   What are the key milestones? When are they expected to be reached? What type of training and education will be provided, when and how?

7. Key Leadership Assignments
   Whom are the individuals appointed to key leadership assignments? Are they full time, or is the appointment an additional duty? If full time, who is to fill the vacancy, if any?

8 Resource Commitments
   What resources are needed to design, implement and operate
   the quality system? How are they to be funded? Where do they
   come from? What cost benefits will the *Institution* realize, how,
   when and where?
9 Information Technology
   How will Information Technology be utilized in the design, implementation and operation of the quality system?
10 Communication
   How will the *Institution* communicate with all of its constituents
   about the quality initiative?
11 Critical Success Indicators
   What are the key factors for achieving progress? How will these
   be measured and reported?

The task group headed by Susan developed the plan within a month.
During their work they utilized input from several focus groups, and had
one-on-one interviews with all top executives as well as a representative
sample of senior managers of the *Institution*. The task group enlisted the
help of their colleagues, for example the CEO provided a briefing to
the Board, and the VP of Human Resources discussed the initiative with the
Union. They also visited with several of the Malcolm Baldrige Award winning
enterprises. The group then presented the Plan to the MEC for approval,
which was enthusiastically granted. The MEC thanked the "Blount" task
force for their outstanding contribution, and began to put in place the structure recommended in the Plan in order to continue the quality initiative.

As you consider bringing quality management into your enterprise, I
highly recommend that you consider adopting an approach similar to the
one utilized by our fictional *Institution*. Your success will be immensely
enhanced by initially involving the top management team as well as other
key constituencies, and by gaining their endorsement. Their support needs
to be far more than playing lip service to quality. Having a strategic plan,
and having it understood, accepted, funded and enunciated by the leadership team provides the rest of the organization with purpose and direction.
Most importantly, it signals the priorities by identifying the implementation of the quality system not merely as just one of many projects in the
enterprise, but as the single focus of performance improvement necessary
for the sustained success of the enterprise.

Keeping in mind that this chapter focuses on the organizational
aspects of implementation, I will begin with the structure, which is an
output of the strategic planning process. Other subjects of discussions will
include the concept and practice of Process Management, the roles of
teams and leadership, and the application of the power of information
technology.

The implementation of a total quality system involves the leadership,
structure, processes and culture of the organization, in integrated and iterative ways. In our fictional *Institution* the Management Executive Committee

(MEC) is composed of the CEO and the most senior executives. This powerful management body is typically present in almost all enterprises in one form or another, and traditionally operates at the policy-making level. Now it must assume the top leadership role in the quality implementation effort. To facilitate design, deployment and operations of the quality system, the MEC authorized an organizational framework (see figure 6.1) that serves three purposes:

1   Provides governance.
2   Accomplishes enterprise wide implementation.
3   Assumes responsibility for ongoing process management and improvement.

The components of the structure designed to fulfill these purposes will now be discussed in some detail. These components are:

The Executive Quality Council (EQC).
The Institution Quality Office (QO).
The Steering Committee (SC).
Process Owners (PO).
Process Management and Improvement Teams (PM&IT).
Quality Improvement Teams (QIT).
Local Implementation Management Teams (LIMT).

Depending on the size and complexity of the enterprise, a single structure or several parallel structures may be deployed. For example, in a very large enterprise, each division may deploy the entire structure. In a multi-national company, each country unit may replicate the entire structure. In some situations parts of the structure may exist only at the enterprise level, while other parts are cascaded throughout the enterprise. Regardless the way it is deployed, the intent of the structure is to enable the establishment of a cohesive and comprehensive quality management system.

The Executive Quality Council (EQC)

From an organizational perspective, the MEC provides initial focus to the quality implementation effort by actually functioning under a new identity, the Executive Quality Council (EQC) while dealing with quality management issues. I emphasize the word *initially*, because as the effort matures, the work of the EQC becomes the way the MEC works normally, and the distinction disappears. The activities of the EQC will be described in three phases: (1) Preparation Phase, (2) Implementation Phase, and (3) Operational Phase.

At the start, the preparation phase may overlap with the initial conceptual planning time frame of the formulation of the quality systems idea. Formally, it begins with the birth of the EQC, marked by the point in time

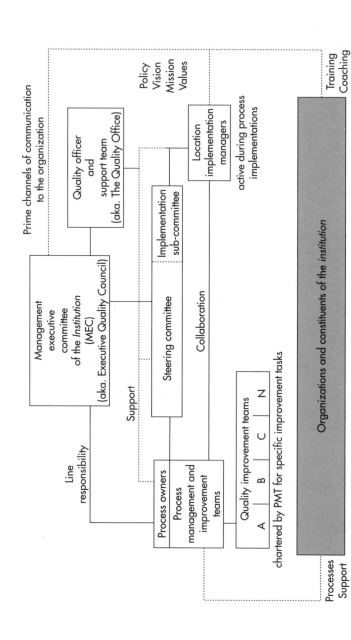

Prime channels of communication
to the organization

Policy
Vision
Mission
Values

Quality officer
and
support team
(aka. The Quality Office)

Location
implementation
managers

active during process
implementations

Management
executive
committee
of the *Institution*
(MEC)
(aka. Executive Quality Council)

Implementation
sub-committee

Steering committee

Collaboration

Support

Line
responsibility

Process owners

Process
management and
improvement
teams

Quality improvement teams

A   B   C   N

chartered by PMT for specific improvement tasks

Organizations and constituents of the *institution*

Training
Coaching

Processes
Support

Source: Kemeny Consulting, Montclair, NJ.

Figure 6.1 Organizational model for quality management system implementation

when the MEC decides to embark on a formal quality management system implementation journey. Correspondingly, the CEO performs the role of the chair-person of the EQC. During the preparation phase the EQC gains the knowledge and fundamental skills needed to make informed decisions and to provide leadership to a quality organization. This requires dedicated time commitment on the part of already busy senior executives. Securing their time and implanting the necessary learning is the first major challenge faced by the champions of the cause. It is safe to say that without the personal active involvement of the CEO the chances for success are minimal. The good news is that right at the start we should know whether or not it pays to continue. The key success factor during this stage is the education activity. It must be at the strategic level, not in tools and methods. It must be delivered effectively and efficiently, respecting the scarce availability of senior executive time. It must be presented by someone of unquestioned integrity and wide range of experience. It must be delivered with total understanding and sensitivity to the political climate of the institution.

In addition to gaining knowledge, the major output of the preparatory phase is the high level Strategic Plan described previously. By high level I mean that it focuses on the specifics of the "What." What is the Purpose? What is the look and feel of the desired end state? What are the major milestones of the journey? Answers to "Who?", "When?", "How" is also addressed, but at a lesser level of detail. These details will be provided during the implementation phase by the many people and teams that become involved with the effort. Also, it is during the preparatory phase that initial consensus of all key constituencies is sought and hopefully secured, at least in an ideal situation. In most cases, a "wait and see" attitude is the probable outcome. This is fine, the important thing is that the seeds of dialogue, inclusion and participation are planted. The preparatory phase ends with the approved and funded Strategic Plan, and with the communication of the institution's strategic intent to all constituents. The issuance of the Enterprise Quality Policy document could be the culminating event in this phase.

The implementation phase starts with the identification of the key leaders and team members of the elements of the structure depicted in figure 6.1. One of the first appointments made by the EQC of our hypothetical *Institution* was that of a Quality Officer, Mr Elmer Glue, previously Director of Institutional Planning, and creating the Quality Office (QO). The Quality Officer also assumes the role of Secretary of the EQC. Additionally, the Steering Committee (SC) is established, with the Quality Officer serving as the chair-person. The EQC also appoints Process Owners and Local Implementation managers during the initial part of the implementation phase. We will cover the roles and responsibilities of each a bit later.

During the course of the implementation of the quality system throughout the enterprise, the primary role of the EQC is to coach, support and monitor the teams involved in the various activities. Progress versus plans is systematically reported by the QO, SC and POs, and the EQC authorizes adjustments as required to stay on course or change the course. The EQC members also spend a great deal of time personally visiting with field organizations and maintain an ongoing dialogue with all of the Institution's constituents. Major emphasis is placed by the EQC on the customers of the enterprise to ensure that they fully understand and appreciate the changes under way. Customers assured that service is not only maintained, but improves during implementation. The implementation phase ends with full operation of the enterprise's processes at each of its locations.

The operational phase begins with the EQC functioning on an ongoing basis to sustain the initial gains and foster continuous improvement. These aims become totally integrated with the way the institution is managed. All measures of success, including financial, are one and the same as those developed by the Process Owners. Gradually, the EQC terminology distinction may disappear, and the top leadership group continues to function under the MEC label. Quality becomes the business of the business. The operational phase therefore never ends.

The Quality Office (QO)

The Quality Office, headed by the Quality Officer is one of the few additional resources required by the structure. It serves as the nerve center of the entire effort. It is the depository of all plans, schedules and status. It is the only authorized source of communication regarding the quality effort with outside constituencies and the media. It coordinates all in-house communication vehicles and events with the purpose of ensuring the dissemination of accurate, frequent, extensive and timely information about the quality system implementation effort. The QO also arranges for both initial and ongoing education and training for all those involved in the quality initiative. An important aspect is "training the trainers," to infuse knowledge and skills throughout the organization. Internal quality system audits are carried out under the auspices of the QO. In general, the QO constitutes the center of professional excellence in matters of quality management. The size of the QO is typically very small, is at peak during the implementation stage, and can be staffed with individuals temporarily assigned to it. Later, these folks can become the in-house experts in the parent organization.

The Steering Committee (SC)

The evolution of the SC can be viewed in four phases: (1) Formation and Education Phase, (2) Process Management Initialization Phase, (3) Implementation Phase, and (4) Operational Phase. The first phase begins with the establishment of the SC by the EQC. The initial membership of the SC consists of executives designated by each member of the EQC. Thus, the hierarchical view of the organization is represented. Others may also be included to represent key constituents of the enterprise. For example, in our *Institution* a Vice President of the local Union joined the SC. As Process Owners (Level 1, to be explained later) are appointed by the EQC, they also join the SC, thus the process view of the organization also becomes represented. As mentioned before, the Quality Officer is the chair-person of the SC. Having the same person also serving as the Secretary of the EQC provides an excellent linkage on a day to day basis between the two groups. The SC receives the same training as the EQC.

The Process Management Initialization Phase of the SC's work begins with the identification of the major processes of the enterprise. Once this is done, the Process Owners assume ongoing responsibility and further decomposition of their processes. The SC continues to coordinate the design of the Institution's process map, to ensure that all work is covered on one hand, and that no duplication exists on the other. Should the need arise to establish new process, subdivide or combine existing ones, the SC will make that decision. The Process Initialization Phase ends with all Level 1 and Level 2 processes identified, defined and owners appointed.

The Implementation Phase of the SC's work begins with the formation of an implementation sub-committee that consists of the Local Implementation Managers appointed by the EQC. It is the task of this group to refine the overall implementation template contained in the Strategic Plan. At this stage location specific time schedules and resource assignments are created. The overall SC closely supports implementation activities, and monitors adherence to schedules. In the case of our hypothetical *Institution* the implementation strategy was to use Susan Blount's division as the pilot. The quality system was first deployed in this Division, lessons learned were incorporated into the Plan, and then each of the processes was implemented across all locations, one process at a time. The implementation phase ends with all processes implemented at all locations. At that time the implementation sub-committee of the SC goes out of business.

The Operational Phase of the SC's work begins with the entire Institution functioning in a process managed mode. From here on the primary function of the SC is to coordinate the work of the Process Owners as they deal with the impacts of the Institution's strategic direction, changes in its environment, and ongoing improvement activities. The Operational phase never ends.

Process Owners (PO)

The Strategic Plan identified the concept of Process Management as the foundation of the new, quality based enterprise. While the present hierarchical organization structure is well known, the new process based structure is yet to be defined. To start this transformation, as part of the Process Management Initialization phase the members of the SC, working as a group, identify all the high level processes in the Institution. The EQC then appoints a Process Owner (PO) for each process. The PO is the single individual entrusted to coordinate the multiple functions of the process, and is ultimately accountable for the performance of the process in achieving cost-effective customer satisfaction.

Responsibilities and duties of Process Owners typically include:

Establishing and organizing the Process Management and Improvement Team (PM&IT).
Appointing Process Owners for the next layer of processes as necessary.
Communicating roles and responsibilities.
Securing and allocating resources.
Measuring and tracking the teams' progress.
Establishing and maintaining process control.
Resolving or escalating process issues.
Documenting the process.
Instituting process reviews.
Participating as a member of the Steering Committee.

Characteristics of a Process Owner critical for selection demand that the individual:

Has an adequate knowledge of the process, end to end.
Has the authority and ability to effect change.
Is responsible and accountable for results.
Is ready to accept blame as well as credit.
Is willing and able to carry out PO responsibilities.
Has the credibility to obtain needed resources.
Is a role model for quality values and an able catalyst for change.

It is customary to select a well-respected individual of appropriate level/rank from one of the principal organizations currently engaged in the process. In many cases this individual's job is absorbed by others, as a signal that costs will be cut, not increased as the result of the activity. (Team members may be part time or full time, but again, it is desirable to play a "zero sum game".) It is also helpful to provide a new work location for the PO, a signal that the position is not temporary. The authority and resources to both effectively manage and improve the process must accompany the assignment of process ownership.

Process Management and Improvement Teams (PM&IT)

The very first thing one must emphasize that there is a significant, but often overlooked word in PM&I, and that is the "and" word. These teams are entrusted to do two things: (1) to manage the process, and (2) to improve the process. The temptation the teams must overcome is to jump into the more glamorous improvement stage without investing the time to thoroughly understand the process and establish measurements of performance. The work of the PM&ITs can be viewed in four phases: (1) the Formative Phase, (2) the Documentation Phase, (3) the Implementation Phase, and (4) the Operational Phase.

The Formative Phase begins with the establishment of the PM&IT. This includes the identification of the team members, whom are normally representatives of the departments involved in the process. They are expected to bring their respective functional (for example, sales, human resources, etc.) subject matter expertise to the team. They are also expected to serve as the liaison between the PO and their hierarchical organization's management. Others may also be invited to the PM&IT. For example in our *Institution* some teams included representatives of their internal customers. Team appointments are worked out between the PO and the department heads, and approved by the SC. Members then must be trained in several quality management skills, including Process Management, Problem Solving, and Teamwork. This first phase ends with a set of PM&ITs staffed and trained.

The Documentation Phase begins with the teams embarking on the arduous task of defining how the process presently and actually works. The word "presently" needs to be emphasized, because what we need to document is the way the process works now, and not the way it used to be. The word "actually" also needs to be emphasized, because what we need to document is the way work is really being done, and not what we think happens, or what we think should happen. There are several good methodologies available to document processes and many are well supported by computer software. The QO is responsible for selecting and standardizing a suitable methodology for the enterprise, and for establishing a document control schema. The effort involved in this phase can be quite extensive, depending on the complexity of the enterprise, on the state of available documentation, and on the existing degree of process standardization. The last consideration is very important in determining the strategy of process development. It is probably the rule, rather than the exception that processes are not carried out uniformly in an enterprise of any appreciable size. Practices may vary division by division, or location by location. The question then becomes; if we are to document the way things actually work, must we document all existing variations and permutations? The solution here might be for the PM&IT to find and agree on "best practices," and document those as the existing process. Sometimes there is simply no process of any kind in place, work is accomplished in an ad-hoc fashion. So, how can you document chaos? The answer is that you cannot, and therefore the process needs to be designed from scratch. A critical element in the documentation effort is the identification of measurements that describe process performance. The Documentation Phase ends with all processes documented and validated according to the Institution's standards.

The Implementation Phase begins with the finalized and coordinated quality system roll-out plan formulated by the QO and all of the PM&ITs, and approved by the SC. This triggers the establishment of the local implementation teams under the leadership of the Location Implementation

Manager. Once the local teams are ready, the implementations of the standardized processes begin, according to the master plan issued and maintained by the SC. The magnitude of the implementation effort can vary greatly. Factors that come in play include the size of the enterprise, the complexity of the processes, the existing level of standardization and documentation, and the strength of resistance to change. Training can be accomplished by a combination of the PM&IT and location implementation team personnel. The PM&IT should utilize internal quality auditors from the QO to assure that all aspects of the implementation activity are effective and consistent with the plan. The enterprise-wide Implementation Phase ends with all locations operating according to the standard processes.

The Operational Phase begins with the Process Owners and their teams regularly and systematically evaluating the metrics associated with their processes. Their objective is to keep the processes in control within the pre-established performance boundaries. Corrective measures are taken whenever a process fails to stay in control. These measures may include additional training, resource allocation and the like. Typically, processes will undergo constant changes during the Operational Phase. Changes may emanate from many sources, such as the external and the internal business environment, economic factors, competition, technology, customers, regulations, etc. The PM&ITs need to modify the processes in response to these drivers. Most importantly, the teams must continuously and systematically look for improvement opportunities in order to create increased economic value and customer satisfaction. This is the "I" part of PM&I. Whenever the team decides to actively pursue an improvement opportunity, the Process Owner assembles a Quality Improvement Team (QIT) chartered to study the problem and recommend a solution. The Process Owner, assisted by the PM&IT, has the authority to accept the solution and implement the necessary changes in the process. The Operation Phase never ends.

Quality Improvement Team (QIT)

Members of OITs are selected from the PM&IT or the organization at large. In fact, QITs provide an excellent vehicle for engaging everybody in the quality system implementation. Neither is membership an exclusive domain of management. For example, factory workers, engineers, university faculty, computer technicians, nurses, clerical employees, and customer service associates all can make excellent contributions to a particular QIT.

A QIT is formed for a single purpose, that is to solve a specific problem in the process. Criteria for selecting processes to improve include:

A process that directly impacts the customer(s).
A process that causes inefficiencies, waste, or churn.
A frequent or high volume process.

A process that is within the control of the group.
A process that, when improved, will yield a high level of payoff.
A process that can be worked within staff and cost constraints.
A process that is measurable and observable.

Once the problem solution is accepted by the Process Owner and the PM&IT, the QIT is dissolved, following due recognition of their contribution. To be effective, QIT members need training in the fundamentals of quality management and in the specifics of problem solving techniques. It may be necessary to provide a trained and experienced facilitator to help the QITs get on track. However, once employees gain experience by participating on a few teams, the use of facilitators can be cut back.

Local Implementation Management Teams (LIMT)

An important part of the Strategic Plan addressed the method of implementation. This called for the identification, by the EQC, of an executive at each enterprise location to assume responsibility for all facets of the implementation effort. The Local Implementation Manager then assembles a cross functional Local Implementation Team consisting of representatives of all the processes that exist at the particular location. The entire team receives training in Process Management and in Teamwork, in addition to a fundamental overview of the enterprise quality system. The Team establishes the location specific implementation plan in cooperation with the Process Owners, and within the overall framework of the enterprise master plan. Their work is concentrated during the implementation phase. Much of it involves training employees not only in the processes, but also in skills required to interact with customers. The local team is also responsible for documentation dissemination, start-up coaching of all employees and in general, on assuring that the standardized processes function effectively in the location's specific environment. Problems encountered are brought to the attention of the Process Owners, who are responsible for resolving them. At the conclusion of the successful implementation of the quality system, the local team has discharged its responsibility. Process Management and Improvement becomes the way by which the enterprise continues to function and prosper.

PROCESS MANAGEMENT AND IMPROVEMENT

Installing PM&I as the engine of the enterprise involves the re-orientation of the current organization silos into value creating processes. This can be an awesome task, but well worth the effort. Figures 6.2 and 6.3 will help us to explore the issues.

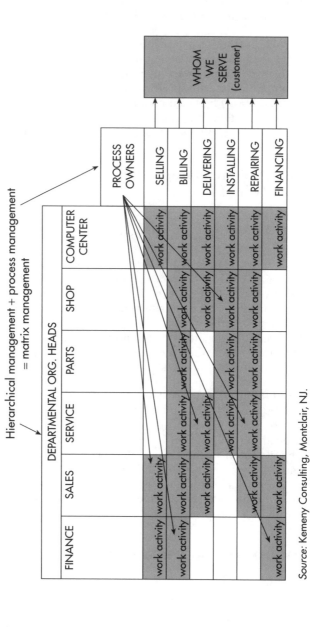

Where the rubber hits the road . . .

Hierarchical management + process management
= matrix management

DEPARTMENTAL ORG. HEADS

	FINANCE	SALES	SERVICE	PARTS	SHOP	COMPUTER CENTER	PROCESS OWNERS
	work activity	work activity					SELLING
	work activity	work activity	work activity	work activity		work activity	BILLING
		work activity	work activity		work activity	work activity	DELIVERING
			work activity	work activity	work activity	work activity	INSTALLING
		work activity	work activity	work activity	work activity	work activity	REPAIRING
	work activity	work activity				work activity	FINANCING

WHOM WE SERVE (customer)

Source: Kemeny Consulting, Montclair, NJ.

Figure 6.2 Matrix management

"The Universe" = the earth moving equipment sales and service division of the *Institution*

Processes		Functional departments					
Level 1 processes	Level 2 processes (a.k.a. sub-processes)	Finance	Sales	Service	Parts	Shop	Comp. ctr.
A Selling		P	O				P
	A1 Advertising		O				
	A2 Prospecting		O				P
	A3 Qualifying, etc.	O	P				P
B Billing		O	P	P			P
	B1 Calculating	O	P	P	P	P	P
	B2 Taxing	O					P
	B3 Rendering, etc.	P	O				P
C Delivering				O	P	P	P
	D1 Receiving			P	P	O	P
	D2 Prepping				P	O	
	D3 Testing, etc.					O	P

O = Process owner, P = PM&I team member

The information needed to define processes includes:

Process name	The process starts with...	Value added process steps (work flow)
Purpose of process	The process ends with...	Measurements of performance
Process owner	Customers	Requirements of performance
PM&I team members	Outputs to customers	Work instruction references
Functional departments	Suppliers	Quality records references
Roles and responsibilities	Input from suppliers	Associated processes

Source: Kemeny Consulting, Montclair, NJ.

Figure 6.3 Process inventory

In our fictional *Institution* the Earth Moving Equipment Sales And Service Division, headed by Susan Blount was used as the organization to pilot the implementation of the quality system. A study of the division's operations revealed that its customers were the recipients of products and services via processes that crossed the lines of several departments. In other words, multiple departments participated in a process that resulted in an inter-action with the customer. The customer experienced the overall performance of the process, not the individual performance of the *Institution's* various departments. Clearly, to improve performance in the eyes of the customer, emphasis must be placed on improving processes. As a first step, Process Owners and Process Management And Improvement Teams were established, based on the matrix shown on figure 6.2. You will note that the SC recommended, and the EQC appointed as POs those department heads who had the major piece of the action in a given process. This is a fairly common practice, but, by no means a rule. The PM&IT members represented the departments performing work activities within the process.

Figure 6.2 depicts what is known as a matrix management structure. Each cell in the diagram has two dimensions. One is the process dimension, the other the hierarchical organization, or functional dimension. And, this is where the rubber hits the road. The subject of matrix management, with its attendant problems and opportunities has been the subject of countless studies, books, articles, etc. It is certainly beyond the scope of this chapter to revisit. However, there are seven principles that I like to suggest you follow to make matrix management, and in turn, process management work.

1   Consider all work foremost as part of a value creating process. If it is not, stop doing it.
2   A process is a set of interrelated work activities that are characterized by a set of specific inputs and value-added tasks that produce a set of specific outputs. A process can be contained within a single functional organization, or it can span several organizations.
3   As a practical consideration, processes should be divided into subprocesses when they appear to be too complicated. Complexity comes about in terms of the number of functional organizations participating, and/or the number of end customers, and/or number of outputs.
4   Process Owners are ultimately responsible for achieving economically feasible customer satisfaction, and thus, for creating value.
5   Functional organizations are justified only by providing economic advantage or as centers of excellence. The heads of these organizations must aim to maximize their departments' contribution to the processes in which they operate.
6   Leadership is responsible for creating an institutional culture that supports teamwork and interdepartmental cooperation with the goal of providing the best value to whom we serve.

7   Leadership is responsible for aligning management and financial reporting systems and reward and recognition systems with the processes of the enterprise. This makes enterprise performance visible along process lines, and compensation can be related to process performance.

The process management oriented structure is similar to a hierarchical structure in one aspect, it may also have layers or levels. The first decision one needs to make is to determine the universe for which to design a process management structure. This universe may be defined as the entire enterprise, or a part of it. The MEC of our fictional *Institution* decided to apply process management throughout the enterprise. However, they also decided to use the Susan Blount division as a pilot, thus the initial "universe' is the Earth Moving Equipment Sales and Service Division. As part of their quality education, the Steering Committee acquired the knowledge and skills necessary to identify all the major groupings of work activities performed in this universe. These are called Level 1 processes. For each of these processes a PO and a PM&IT were appointed. Utilizing their collective expertise, the PM&ITs decomposed each of the Level 1 processes to a set of sub-processes, called Level 2 processes. The SC as a group reviewed the proposed structure to assure that there were no omissions or duplications of any of the work activities that were performed in the "universe." This in turn enabled the creation of an inventory of all the Level 1 and Level 2 processes used in the "universe" represented by Blount's division. Figure 6.3 illustrates the output of this process. Note that the decomposition of processes goes on until the lowest element, called a process step, is reached. The Level 1 PO is responsible to create the structure, utilizing the fewest levels consistent to be effective and efficient in managing and improving the process.

From an organizational perspective, in a process management driven enterprise the POs create the rhythm of management activity. They and their PM&IT translate strategic directions and resultant goals into action programs. Figure 6.4 illustrates this flow. Assume that the *Institution*, utilizing its Strategic Planning Process decides to focus on increasing revenues. A goal of a 15 percent annual increase is targeted for Earth Moving Sales And Service. The Division's EQC charges the POs to create coordinated action plans, utilizing the division's Planning Process. This activity naturally involves the PM&ITs in their triple roles of working team members, subject matter experts, and linkages to their functional departments. Once approved by the EQC, the POs inform the impacted functional organizations of their respective roles and responsibilities in executing the plan. The POs are held accountable for installing measures, monitoring progress, and ultimately to achieve the goal. The functional organization heads are held accountable for accomplishing their specific objectives within the processes.

Naturally, this management approach is not without friction and conflict. For example, a department may disagree with a PO's decision, or some

Institutional strategic direction > goals > action programs enable us to link institutional imperatives to the processes that are impacted so that priorities for improvement can be established in alignment with strategic directions

"The Universe" = the earth moving equipment sales and service division of the *Institution*

Level 1 processes	Level 2 processes (a.k.a. sub-processes)	Functional departments					
		Finance	Sales	Service	Parts	Shop	Comp. ctr.
A Selling		P	O				P
	A1 Advertising		O				P
	A2 Prospecting		O				P
	A3 Qualifying, etc.	O	P				P
B Billing		O	P	P			P
	B1 Calculating	O	P	P	P	P	P
	B2 Taxing	O					P
	B3 Rendering, etc.	P	O	P	P	P	P
C Delivering				O	P	P	P
	D1 Receiving			P	P		P
	D2 Prepping				P	O	P
	D3 Testing, etc.					O	P

Example:
Strategic direction = increased revenue goal = by 15%
Action programs = advertising on TV, increase shop area, etc.

O = Process owner, P = PM&I team member

Source: Kemeny Consulting, Montclair, NJ.

Figure 6.4 Institutional strategic direction

departments may have difficulty coping with the work required by multiple processes in which they participate. It requires a new breed of worker and a new breed of leadership to be successful in a process managed environment.

TEAMS AND LEADERS

Throughout the preceding discussions many references were made to teams. The participative style of quality management system implementation relies heavily on teams and teamwork. The recommended organizational structure and the practice of Process Management both invest trust in teams. There are three kinds of teams:

1. Teams that recommend things.
2. Teams that decide things.
3. Teams that do (produce, service, etc.) things.

Some teams are established to always operate in only one of the above three modes while others may perform in several modes. In either case clarity of purpose is a must. A team should never function but only in one mode at a time. Figure 6.5 depicts how this concept works in our fictional *Institution*. For example, a QIT *does* the investigative work, it *decides* the root causes of the problem, and *recommends* improvement action. It does not select the improvement opportunity, nor does it implement the solution. The PM&IT *decides* the former, and the functional departments *do* the latter. Clarity of team purpose is the most essential factor for their success. It must focus on roles and responsibilities. Clarity can be provided in terms of a mission statement or charter. Leadership can further enhance the success of teams by establishing operating protocols, creating shared values, setting standards for expected behaviors, stating expected results, continuously monitoring progress, and providing moral and material support.

Let us now turn our attention to the predominant characteristics required from our workers and leaders to be successful in the new world of a quality management system. These characteristics go beyond the traditional values of integrity, loyalty, diligence, respect for others, and the like. These traditional values remain very important, but now there is a great deal more that is needed. Fundamentally, our associates must recognize that the enterprise exists only as long as it serves its customers better, faster and smarter than its competition. This philosophy translates to certain specific skills and behaviors required from workers and their leaders.

1. Continuous Learning ... Continuously developing and improving skills and knowledge vital for the success of the enterprise.
2. Strategic Thinking ... Evaluating, synthesizing and interrelating information from internal and external sources when solving problems and making decisions.

Figure 6.5 Illustrative roles and responsibilities of teams in the institution

Team	Recommend	Decide	Do
Executive quality team	Actions requiring board approval	Mission, vision, values, policy Key personnel appointments Priorities, allocation of resources Strategic direction, enterprise goals Reward and recognition programs	Represent *institution* Interact with key constituencies Monitor progress versus plan Communicate, coach, support teams Behave as role model for values
Quality Office and officer	Quality policy to EQC Quality training and education to SC Quality audit plan to SC Quality sys. implementation plan to SC	Quality documentation standards Consultant, trainer, educator selection Quality audit methodology Quality information system requirements	Maintain quality library, records, docu. Deliver training and education Perform quality audits Behave as role model for values
Steering committee	Proc. definitions & owners (Lev. 1) to EQC Overall implementation plan to EQC Resource allocations to EQC Specific goals to EQC Response to major audit findings to EQC	Process definitions and owners (Level 2) Training plans, audit plans PQ&IT members (Level 1) *Institution* wide implementation plan *Institution* action programs	Monitor progress versus plan Review results of quality audits Coordinate PO activities Coordinate implementation activities Behave as role model for values
Process owners (Level 1)	Proc. definitions & owners (Lev. 2) to SC Action programs to SC Process implementation plans to SC Process resources requirements to SC	Process definitions, owners and teams Improvement opportunities and plans Resource allocation within process Process action programs	Monitor process implementation Monitor process performance Collaborate with other POs and LIM&Ts Behave as role model for values
Process management & improvement team	Process performance attributes to PO Improvement opportunities and priorities Resource requirements to PO Performance measurements	QIT membership QIT objectives Process flow and work activities Requirements for supplier partners	Support implementation Serve as liaison to functional departm's Serve as facilitator for QITs Behave as role model for values
Quality improvement team	Specific improvement solutions Resource requirements Schedules and plans	Problem definition Root cause Corrective and preventive measures	Investigate opportunities Collect data Assist in implementation
Location implementation mgr. and team	Overall local implementation plan to SC Resource requirements to SC Training needs to SC	Detailed local implementation plan Local resource allocation Local training and education	Train employees Assist in quality audits Behave as role model for values
Functional departmental teams	Functional operational plan to POs Resource requirements to POs In-process measurements to POs	Specific method of execution Departmental resource allocation Human resources issues	Operate processes Receive training and education Behave as role model for values

Source: Kemeny Consulting, Montclair, NJ.

3   Transforming Strategy Into Results ... Achieving positive results and adding value to the enterprise by translating strategy into action.
4   Inspiring a Shared Purpose ... Engaging all team members in support of a customer focused, shared vision of future outcomes, goals and end states.
5   Creating a Climate of Success ... Generating and sustaining an environment that fosters the stated values of the enterprise.
6   Entrusting People ... Providing individuals and teams with opportunities to learn continuously and with the authority and resources to achieve their best.
7   Seizing Opportunities ... Taking decisive action on emerging opportunities in a rapidly changing, ambiguous environment.
8   Building Partnerships ... Cultivating constructive relationships and alliances across internal, external and geographic boundaries.
9   Leveraging Disagreements ... Constructively using varying views or conflicts between oneself and others, or among team members, to strengthen working relationships and develop customer-focused solutions.
10 Having a Holistic View of the Enterprise ... Assessing situations and taking action with a view towards optimizing enterprise success, and not individual or departmental interests.
11 Focusing on Whom We Serve ... Unwaveringly pursuing the ideal of legendary customer service.
12 Keeping a Balanced Scorecard ... Considering the well-being of the entire constituency of the enterprise, such as customers, owners, employees, and the community at large.

The probability that all your people in senior positions posses or are able to acquire these leadership characteristics is small. Similarly, not all your employees, regardless of their level or rank or function can exist comfortably and productively in a total quality environment. Moving forward with your quality initiative necessitates that you engage all the tools and techniques of change management. You also must be prepared to make some very tough staffing decisions and accept the risk of losing some of your people, should they elect to remain part of the problem, and not part of the solution. Remember that one sure way of failing in a change effort is to try making everybody happy.

While teamwork and leadership are the most important factors for the success of quality system implementation, the troops must also have ammunition and logistical support. Skills and knowledge gained through training and education supply the former, while the use of Information Technology provides the latter.

INFORMATION TECHNOLOGY

Information Technology (IT) plays a pervasive role in the management and the operations of modern enterprises. The term "information highway" conjures only a partial image. IT not only provides the infrastructure for the flow of information, but also stores data, converts data into intelligence, facilitates design, and operates machinery. Furthermore, IT performs work activities with ever increasing speed, efficiency, reliability and accuracy . . . sure sounds like a natural selection for participation in the quality initiative.

The EQC of our fictional *Institution* was keenly aware of the possibilities offered by IT in the implementation and operation of their quality system. The Strategic Plan prepared by the "Blount" task force included high level requirements for IT support. At the recommendation of Quality Officer Elmer Glue, the Chief Information Officer, Ms. Jane Wise was appointed to the SC. Jane and Elmer, working together, created a detailed proposal describing the contribution IT was to make. The SC accepted the proposal, asked and received funding approval from the EQC. The IT Plan addressed six areas:

1   IT Participation.
2   Support for Communications.
3   Support for Quality System Design.
4   Support for Quality System Implementation.
5   Support for Quality System Management.
6   Support for Operations.

We shall take a brief look at each from the perspective of the customer of IT.

IT participation

Aligning enterprise priorities with IT resources has always been difficult at the *Institution*. So was determining the value added component of IT's contribution. The new IT Plan responded to both of these concerns. Alignment was achieved by having the CIO at the decision making table of the SC, and by including IT people on all appropriate PM&ITs. This in turn required the re-orientation of the IT organization from a technical and system based focus to a customer and process based focus. The issue of work priorities and value creation was clarified by including IT action plans and attendant resource requirements in the domain of each Process Owner. This way IT was no longer looked at in isolation, but in the context of the processes it served. The rule that "all work is part of a process" was also applied to IT.

Support for communications

In a customer focused, process management based organization communication is one of the key success factors. IT was recognized by the

Institution as the means to achieving effective and efficient communication. Examples of this included:

- Installation of enterprise wide area and local area networks for voice, data and video, named the "Institunet."
- Implementation of an advanced enterprise electronic mail system with Internet access, replacing several local versions. (The implications of e-mail on the organization culture are profound. In the case of our *Institution* major benefits were realized by creating an opportunity for un-filtered two way communications.)
- Implementation of an "intranet" facility for speedy dissemination of information.
- Initiating a "Questions & Answers" intranet bulletin board to respond to questions and concerns raised by employees about the quality system.
- Conducting instant employee opinion surveys by e-mail.

Support for quality system design

The leaders of the *Institution* recognized that the design of a quality management system involves the best minds of the organization. Most of the people were also continuing to perform their "normal" jobs. IT was used to minimize the impact of the added work load. To accomplish this:

- Non-proprietary software was installed to facilitate word processing and flowcharting.
- Non-proprietary software templates were used for process management and other types of documentation work.
- E-mail was used extensively for communication among team members and among teams.
- Voice and video teleconferencing were utilized as much as possible for meetings.

Support for quality system implementation

The implementation of the *Institution's* quality system throughout all its locations, divisions and processes presented a large project management challenge, and a significant training load. IT helped in several ways:

- Non-proprietary software was installed to assist project management. The package facilitated scheduling, tracking, resource management, status reporting, exception analysis, PERT charting and the like.
- Computer-based training was extensively deployed to provide for self-paced delivery of skills and knowledge. The software package also had the capability to test for training outcomes, and to collect and report this information.

Support for quality system management

A fundamental principle of quality management is fact based decision making, which requires large amounts of data, converted to information and subsequently to intelligence. Another tenet is focus on customer satisfaction, both subjective and measurable. The Process Management component of the quality system relies heavily on information about process performance and on statistical techniques for analysis. At our *Institution* IT was the key to satisfying these needs. The entire results reporting and financial systems portfolio of the *Institution* was revised. Information such as budgets, costs, expenses, assets, employees and so on could now be looked at along process lines in addition to the traditional hierarchical organization view.

- Associates were given access, on a need-to-know basis, to a robust enterprise data warehouse. Using the "Institunet," they could download data to their PCs, perform analysis, generate reports, and create graphs for fact based decision making.
- A number of customer satisfaction data-collecting systems were implemented and a vast data base was continually updated. This enabled the *Institute* to target process improvement activities.
- Measurement systems were implemented for all the *Institution's* processes, giving the PM&ITs the information needed to control process performance.
- A customer complaint system was implemented for the dual purpose of tracking resolution of complaints and serving as an additional source of improvement opportunities.

Support for operations

The ultimate measure of success of any quality system is delighting those whom it serves. To a very large extent the degree of success is determined at the point of inter-action between the enterprise and its customers. Whether inquiring about a tax bill received, registering for courses at a university, buying a plane ticket, or returning goods purchased in a store, the customer and the enterprise jointly experience a "moment of truth." The sum total of these experiences shapes customer satisfaction. The front line employees, represent the enterprise during these encounters. The quality system of the enterprise must support these employees in ways that maximizes their chances for success in creating a positive customer experience during the "moments of truth." Very often the ready availability of timely and accurate information, coupled with the skills to use it provides our associates with the winning combination. At our *Institution* this concept was translated into action by utilizing IT. For example:

- The concept of "case teams" was introduced in customer service operations to simplify and expedite interaction with customers. Case teams include a small group of collocated employees who collectively posses the various types of knowledge and skills required to complete a transaction end to end. The team has access to all the required information systems. Previously, either the work, or the customer was routed from department to department. IT supported this change by modifying, networking and installing the systems used by the teams.

- The case team process eventually evolved to the "case worker" approach. The team was replaced by individuals who were equipped by IT to handle transactions using a single expert system.

- The inbound telecommunications systems of the *Institution* were upgraded with a view towards user friendliness and effectiveness. Many types of transactions that were previously handled manually during business hours could now be accommodated automatically, seven days a week, 24 hours a day.

- Acting on its belief that supplier partners are an extended part of the enterprise, the *Institution* invested in IT to provide electronic linkages with its vendors. Electronic bonding enabled suppliers to reduce the prices charged to the *Institution*, due to improving their ability to plan, and by lowering transaction processing costs.

The spirit of continuous improvement is alive and well in the IT area of the *Institution*. Rapid advances in the IT industry, fast-paced innovation, and steadily improving price/performance characteristics all converge to make IT one of the strongest allies of the quality management system.

SUMMARY

In one's professional life there are few things more exciting and rewarding than helping our enterprise excel and prosper. In the world of intense global competition sustained success mandates a never ending focus on performance improvement. Implementing a comprehensive and well-designed total quality management system is the proven way to achieve and maintain eminence. In the worlds of commerce, education, government and industry not everyone is convinced that this is indeed the way to go. And, many who tried, failed to show the expected results. I hope that this chapter gave you a framework, that when enforced by your own experiences, ideas and innovations will make your enterprise a winner!

EPILOGUE

I had lunch recently with Susan Blount. "How are things going with your quality initiative?", I asked. Susan replied: "Oh, we got off to a great start!

And, we are still making good progress. It is a lot tougher though than we originally thought. We are now running into the 'great expectations' syndrome. People expect that all the problems that existed in the past fifty years in the *Institution* will be solved instantly by PM&ITs, Pareto charts, fishbone diagrams and whatnot . . . The challenge is to keep our focus on mission critical things, things that will make a real difference for our customers, and therefore help our business." Then she added with a smile: "You know that I am an alumna of UTU . . . Utopia Technical University? I just received an invitation from the President to come and visit with him and the University Executive Council. They are beginning to move ahead with a university wide quality initiative . . . the UTU CQI. I am thrilled to talk with them and see if we can work together somehow."

Note

The views expressed in this chapter are based primarily on my real-life experiences with introducing systems for quality in organizations. Naturally, my ideas were shaped greatly by the work of others, obtained from the many outstanding books and other publications in the field of quality management. I have chosen not to include specific references in this chapter, since most of the story told here is a blend of what I read, learned from working with others and created on my own. However, I would like to make one exception, and that is to give credit to my former colleagues who collectively created a wonderful depository of knowledge, known as the "AT&T Quality Library."

PART III

Processes

7 | Process Management and Process Reengineering

William C. Parr

Abstract

Maintaining, improving and reinventing the processes of the organization are vital tasks. Two major streams of work focus on these tasks – process management and process reengineering. We define and illustrate each, and look at how they have been used in modern organizations. We offer lists of patterns discerned which differentiate successful from unsuccessful applications of process management and reengineering.

INTRODUCTION

The author visits with managers from hundreds of organizations every year. All report that they are attempting to be deeply involved in the practice of both Process Management and Process Reengineering. They all view these practices as being essential to their strategies for improving their ability to provide customer value in the future. But, frustratingly for them, few if any report that they are happy with the work they are now doing in this area.

Why is this? Are managers routinely unrealistically optimistic? (Probably so, but this could hardly explain the degree of disappointment routinely reported.) Are Process Management and Process Reengineering such difficult practices that they require a unique set of skills possessed by few and not learnable by the rest? (Not likely – as we see in the sections below on "Major factors differentiating between successful and unsuccessful process management" and "Major factors differentiating between successful and unsuccessful reengineering," the differences are clear, understandable, and the actions to improve success probabilities are clear.)

CONCEPTS OF PROCESS MANAGEMENT – THE CONTINUUM FROM MANAGING WHAT IS TO RADICAL REDESIGN

What is process management? There are as many answerers to this question as there are people answering. Fortunately, most of the answers differ primarily in the fine details, not in the overall conception – or in serious matters of execution.

The AT&T Process Quality Management & Improvement Guidelines define Process Quality Management as "planning and executing the regular activities necessary to sustain process performance and identify opportunities for improving customer satisfaction and reducing costs."[1]

H. James Harrington suggests that that the major objectives of improving business processes are:

- Making processes effective – producing the desired results.
- Making processes efficient – minimizing the resources used.
- Making processes adaptable – being able to adapt to changing customer and business needs.

He further states that "All well-defined and well-managed processes have some common characteristics":

- They have someone who is held accountable for how well the process performs (the process owner).
- They have well-defined boundaries (the process scope).
- They have well-defined internal interfaces and responsibilities.
- They have documented procedures, work tasks, and training requirements.
- They have measurement and feedback controls close to the point at which the activity is being performed.
- They have customer-related measurements and targets.
- They have known cycle times.
- They have formalized change procedures.
- They know how good they can be.[2]

Note that this definition includes everything ranging from: maintaining a process at a current superb level of performance to managing the continual improvement of that process to leading a reengineering effort aimed at a major jump in process improvement. These three activities are in fact NOT opposing or contradictory, but all three fit within the general concept of process management.

PROCESS MANAGEMENT

A key quote illuminates this author's perspective on the need for clearly defined process ownership. An old Thai proverb states "Two masters own a thin horse."

In the absence of a clearly defined owner, the process will not be nurtured. Anyone who has served for long on a committee with vague charge and nobody in the lead can testify – lack of ownership is poisonous. Its natural result is a room full of people, pointing their fingers at one other (while, perhaps not surprisingly, often saying the most politically correct things!) and discussing why progress has not occurred.

MULTI-STEP PROCESSES FOR PROCESS MANAGEMENT

AT&T's Process Quality Management and Improvement Guidelines offer a seven-step process,[3] which is typical of most the author has seen. The Seven Steps of Process Management: AT&T PQMI Guidelines:

1 Establish process management responsibilities.
2 Define process and identify customer requirements.
3 Define and establish measures.
4 Assess conformance to customer requirements.
5 Investigate process to identify improvement opportunities.
6 Rank improvement opportunities and set objectives.
7 Improve process quality.

Detailed discussion of the seven steps of the AT&T Process Quality Management Model

1 Establish process management responsibilities

There must be a process owner. If it is true that "without enthusiasm nothing happens" then it is also true that "without ownership there will soon be nothing to own!"

This fits clearly with our experiences interviewing managers engaged in process management. The relationship between the existence of a strong owner (not merely a sponsor) and success of the process management efforts is clear, and worthy of note by all who intend to practice process management.

Clearly, the owner will be accountable for process performance along all dimensions of outcomes. In addition, the owner must organize the efforts of any required team supporting the effort, lead the efforts at developing and using measurement systems, articulate the customer point of view, develop an understanding of the relationship of the process to the customer and to other organizational processes, marshall resources, and lead the improvement efforts, be they incremental or breakthrough in nature.

2 Define process and identify customer requirements

This step is critical. Without definition of the process (What is its scope? Where does it begin? Where does it end? What is included? What is not included?) those working on the process are likely to drift aimlessly on work of little definition.

Without understanding of customer requirements, there can be no definition of what good performance means. There can be no development of measurements.

3 Define and establish measures

Measurements must be relevant (linked to customer value), timely (obtained often enough to study the process), and focused (not so global that they stare at global hunger, and see nothing).

4 Assess conformance to customer requirements

This step entails using the measures to see how well the process performs against the customer requirements, using the measurements developed in #3.

5 Investigate Process to Identify Improvement Opportunities

and

6 Rank improvement opportunities and set objectives

Considerable creativity can be required on these two steps. Good sources for ideas include the material below on Business Process Reengineering, and the material by Peter Scholtes in the Team Handbook.[4]

7 Improve process quality

Here, the rubber meets the road (if, in fact, the road is not already well-decorated with skid marks). Work proceeds to actual implementation. The manager becomes most concerned with whether the groundwork has been laid for success, leading to worry about factors which make the difference between successful and unsuccessful process management efforts.

Major factors differentiating between successful and unsuccessful process management efforts.

The comments in this section are based on interviews with over 250 managers and executives over the last six years, focused on understanding efforts to improve, both using statistical tools and using more general methods.

The results are presented in tabular format in table 7.1 by naming a dimension, describing the dominant behavior in the unsuccessful attempts at process management, and then describing the dominant behavior pattern in the successful attempts at process management.

Table 7.1   Dimensions on which successful and unsuccessful process
management efforts differ

Dimension of behavior	*Unsuccessful pattern of behavior*	*Successful pattern of behavior*
Link to external customer	Little or no explicit consideration of the external customer	External customer often the topic of discussion ("How will this impact them?") and sometimes even participates in the work on the process
Inclusion of lower levels of organization	Often done to exclusion of higher levels being engaged	Lower levels brought in based on their expertise, likely role in implementation, and the need for inclusion
Extent to which ownership is defined	Low definition of ownership, or ownership broadly shared	Clear definition of ownership, including scope and accountability
Process point of view	Little or none – reactive fire fighting predominates	Strong process focus – "why" questions dominate
Scope of things taken on	Very narrow, usually within a natural work group or department	Moderately broad, often spanning multiple work groups or departments
Provision of regular feedback and measurement points regarding progress of the work	Little or no feedback on impact of the work	Strong feedback and data regarding impact of the work
Measurement	Vague, often done irregularly or using anecdotal information	Customer relevant metrics are regularly reported, studied, and made the focus of concerted improvement efforts

Business process reengineering (radical redesign)

Business process reengineering (BPR), a term coined by Michael Hammer, refers to "the fundamental rethinking and radical redesign of business processes to achieve dramatic improvements in critical, contemporary measures of performance, such as cost, quality, service, and speed."[5]

Several aspects of this definition are worthy of further discussion:

Dramatic improvements: Business process reengineering is not a prescription for a holding action in which the goal is to maintain process performance at a current, either acceptable or even superb level. Neither is it a method for continually, on a day-by-day basis, finding many small improvements to the process which, collectively, add up to major improvement. Instead, BPR is a specific process used to target dramatic improvements – often targeting cycle time improvements of 30–50 percent or more, and comparable improvements in other dimensions.

Fundamental rethinking: BPR often requires that those engaged in BPR view their process in a fundamentally new way. They must ask: Why does this process exist? What must be done? Why should a customer care about this? How could we measure this process' performance? Why do we do the process the current way? Why do we think we must do it that way? What other ways would be much better?

Radical redesign: BPR assumes that the output will be a new process which may have little in common with the old one. As will be discussed later, initial thinking of the first few pioneers engaged in BPR often was that it was a waste of time to spend weeks studying the process as it is – After all, they were going to get rid of all that anyhow!

Business processes: In BPR, the fundamental unit of analysis, and of improvement, is the business process. It is not the department, or the individual. One can't reengineer a department, or a function. The unit of analysis is not "tasks." It is not organizational structure. Instead, the focus of the analysis, the discussion, the improvements, and the implementation strategy are all on the business process – which, after all, is what provides values for the customer.

Measures of performance: BPR is, if anything, a hard-headed, no-nonsense approach. It does not (properly done) brook with "I feel it would be better" or "I like this new way" if such feelings cannot be substantiated with hard, palpable measurement on dimensions of direct relevance to customer and organizational goals.

Neither does BPR tolerate excuses of the form "but we've always done it this way." (This is one of the sources of most of the difficulties encountered by managers attempting to apply BPR without radically rethinking their organization's culture, their own behavior, and their entire perspective on "improvement.") This is in rather stark contrast to the typical approaches carried out under the banner of TQM, in which verbal denunciations of the status quo predominate, but in fact the prime prescription for moving from the status quo to the new future process is by incrementalism – a long, often time consuming, sequence of small improvements.

PRINCIPLES AND METHODOLOGY OF BUSINESS PROCESS REENGINEERING

So much for the definition of Business Process Reengineering. How does it work? To consider this, we break BPR into separate pieces for initial analysis: (i) high level strategies for BPR (the technical strategies), and (ii) organizational strategies for BPR (the "soft side of BPR" – implementation strategies).

HIGH LEVEL STRATEGIES FOR BUSINESS PROCESS REENGINEERING – TOOLS OF PROCESS REDESIGN

Just as most strategies for business process management look about the same at a high level (and hence like the AT&T model discussed in detail above), most strategies for BPR look the same at a high enough level. One strategy often used is:

- Understand the objective of the process in terms of customer value
- Map the process
- Measure the process
- Select a high level strategy for BPR
- Execute the high level strategy for BPR
- Observe improvements via the measurement process
- Install appropriate methods to retain the gains

We now examine each of these steps in turn:

Understand the objective of the process – before improvement is possible, we must know what is required of the process. What are the customer-valued outcomes intended for the process? What are the constraints (things the process must not do)?

Map the process – make a flow diagram of the process, showing both flows of product/service and of information, as the process currently functions. This step is critical. Without knowledge of how the process currently works, the effort could either reinvent the current process as it now works (or in deteriorated version!) or could make uninformed choices.

Measure the process – This step contains much content. It implies that measures (linked to customer-valued process outcomes) must be developed. These measurements must be used to assess process performance against what is required. They must be used to assess process performance against world class processes with similar objectives – that is, they must be measured against relevant benchmarks.

Select a high level strategy – Many ways exist to reinvent a process. Further in this section, we consider a rich set of such ways. One must be chosen, based on organizational situation. (I consider criteria for this choice when we explain these high level strategies.)

Execute the high level strategy – You can't make progress without making progress!

Observe improvements via the measurement process – Improvements which are unobservable are, likely, illusory (and poor illusions at that!). Measurement (in terms of objective hard data, in terms of customer response to the new process and its new outcomes, . . .) is essential in the BPR process, or any other process management method, to ensure the effort remains fact-based.

Install appropriate methods to retain the gains – If appropriate controls are not put in place, the process will likely slide back, over time, to something in between the old version and the new version. This point receives further discussion under the topic of "the soft side of BPR" below.

We now turn to the high-level strategies, and become (thankfully) more specific.

HIGH-LEVEL STRATEGIES FOR BUSINESS PROCESS REENGINEERING – A DETAILED VIEW

Multiple high-level strategies exist for BPR. A partial list follows:

1 Eliminate steps which do not contribute to providing value.
2 Redesign information flows.
3 Holistic redesign.
4 Working with suppliers and internal customers.
5 Work in parallel instead of in series.
6 Standardize – make it easy for all to do, and easy to do in the same way.
7 Organize work around "products/services" or customer groups.
8 Empower front line employees to serve the customer (make decisions and perform work at the lowest appropriate level).
9 Eliminate checks, controls, and reconciliations.
10 Use a case manager for a single point of contact.

For each of these methods, we consider: (i) When the method is likely to be appropriate, (ii) a sketch of the method, (iii) as appropriate, brief cautions regarding the method, and (iv) one or more examples of application of the method.

Method 1: Eliminate steps which do not contribute to providing value

When is the method likely to be appropriate? Typically, this method is most appropriate when a large amount of effort is perceived as being expended on nonessential activities. This method is particularly appropriate for reducing cycle time or cost.

Sketch of the method. The method is straightforward. First, a process map must be constructed. Then, the process components (blocks or lines between blocks) on the process map which do not contribute to providing value must be determined. Then, as many as possible (in principle, all) of these process components must be eliminated.

Cautions regarding the method. A simple caution must be noted regarding this method: Steps which do not aid in providing value for the external customer did not arise of themselves. They are probably there because they do something for somebody – probably an internal stakeholder! If those involved in the BPR effort don't determine why those nonessential pieces exist, they are likely to encounter sabotage from the (unknown to them) constituencies who are served by these (from a customer point of view) nonessential process components.

Example of application of the method. The Internal Revenue Service routinely distributes tax forms to every taxpaying entity (read, taxpayer) in the United States. Typically, they send a standard packet to every taxpayer. To a very limited degree, this packet is customized based on what forms the taxpayer used last year. (We describe in this section the version of the process observed still existing at some sites in 1990.)

If a taxpayer looks at the packet (often on April 14!) and determines more forms are needed to correctly complete the return, that taxpayer has two choices. One is to drive to the Post Office or other appropriate local IRS Forms distribution location. The other is to call/mail in a request for more forms. (If they are doing this close to April 15, this of course probably implies the concomitant need to file a request for automatic extension of time to file.) Presume the taxpayer calls the toll free number. They are greeted by someone who asks how they can be of assistance, and who quickly and competently captures their address and phone number. Then, they also write down, on paper, a complete list of those forms desired, and the quantity of each form.

This list is then given to someone else, who transcribes the list of forms into a more appropriate order (consistent with the layout of the forms in the rather large forms warehouse). This form is then accumulated with others until a large stack exists, when it is then transferred to a third person, who walks through the warehouse selecting the requested forms. The selections are then inserted into an envelope with the printed label, and mailed to the taxpayer.

A quick examination of the process (figure 7.1) makes it clear that we have many steps of the process which add cost and cycle time, but do not

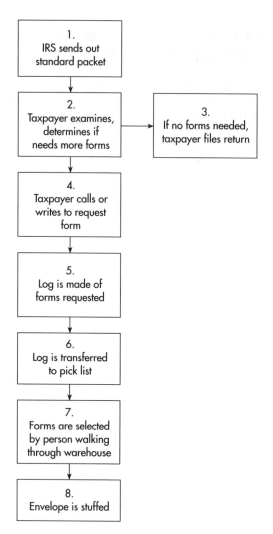

Figure 7.1   IRS forms distribution process (old process)

contribute to providing value to the customer. Some of these include: Writing and then rewriting the list of forms desired, accumulating request lists in large batches, and then walking the line in the warehouse.

A group conceptualized the alternative process, shown in figure 7.2, in a short period, after carefully mapping the existing process and obtaining data to study where the cost and cycle time were in the process.

In the new process, each taxpayer receives a set of forms which corresponds closely to the set they returned the previous year. If the taxpayer, on receipt of the forms, determines they have what they need, they can file immediately. Otherwise, they have the opportunity (if they have World

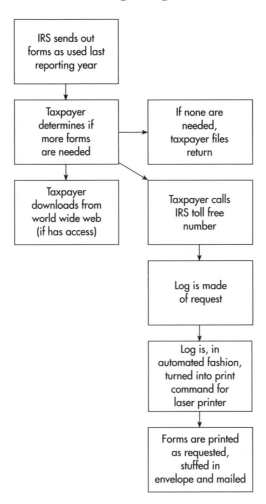

Figure 7.2 IRS forms distribution process (new process)

Wide Web [WWW] access) to directly download and print usable versions of the forms which they require.

Those taxpayers not having WWW access may choose to call the toll free number. There, as the operator takes down their requests, software translates those requests not into a pick sheet, but instead into a print order to have a high speed laser printer print out precisely the needed forms (print on demand), as well as an envelope label. The label is put on the envelope, the forms go in (already being grouped together) and the package goes out.

What is the net impact on performance? The wasteful re-transcription of requests is eliminated (and all the errors, costs and cycle time attendant to that re-transcription). In addition, there is no warehouse required. Nobody walks the warehouse to pick up forms. Only a bank of high-speed printers.

Cycle time has been radically reduced. Only a more detailed analysis than permitted by the length of this discussion could determine the full impact on cost – but it is worthy to note that in many examples, savings such as those hoped for with the old process here (large bulk, and hence presumably cheap, printing) prove to be illusory – canceled out by handling difficulties, spoilage, the cost of managing the inventory, the cost of the warehouse, . . . So, cost, cycle time, and quality (percentage of time the right forms are provided) are all improved.

This last sentence reflects a typical situation worthy of comment: Often, there is no need to choose short cycle time versus low cost. Typically, improvement can be made on multiple fronts at once. Trade-off management is often seen to be a vestige of the past – traditional, within the box, limitations-bound thinking.

Method 2: Redesign information flows

When is the method likely to be appropriate? This method is most often appropriate when a major organizational pipeline process (order fulfillment process, product development process, . . .) is found to suffer from whiplash (continual cycles of oversupply followed by undersupply), or when people working within the process continually find the need to make inquiries to get the information required to perform their work.

Sketch of the method. To carry out this method, first make a map of the process, making especially certain to capture not only flows of products and services, but also those of information, including requests for information.

Then, determine who needs to know what by when, in order to provide customer value.

Lastly, the information flows must be redesigned. Costly and unneeded information flow can be eliminated. More likely, and more typical, more timely or more appropriate information flow must be provided as needs indicate. Typically but not always these improved flows are provided by use of automation. This is not a requirement of the method – but in the current environment of rapidly improving information technology capability, it makes sense and often is the best alternative to explore automation of information flow as an alternative.

Cautions regarding the method. One caution is needed regarding the method. In many traditional autocratic organizations (we repeat ourselves there!) information is a source of power, and redesigns which share information will be viewed as a serious threat by those who have in the past relied on their possession of information as a source of influence and power.

Examples of application of the method. Peter Senge[6] discusses a simulation (the Beer Game) in which the communication of information regarding market demand between retailers and beer producers is very slow – only taking place with multiple delays. The result is great exaggeration of demand fluctuation (including created belief in fluctuation when there is none!) with consequent cycles of major oversupply (10-fold oversupply, or multiple weeks of backlog not being uncommon) and undersupply. Typical valid solutions suggested for this fatally flawed process include radical reexamination of the information flow, in particular getting information direct from the retailer to the producer (brewer) and all others in the supply chain.

Method 3: Holistic redesign

When is the method likely to be appropriate? This method is most likely appropriate when anything even vaguely resembling improvement in place is deemed unlikely to result in improvements of the magnitudes required. It is often pursued when existing internal stakeholders have very strong and diverse opinions, and the only way to go forward seems to be to very clearly and obviously start with a clean sheet of paper. This is the most classic form and best known variety of Business Process Reengineering (some would reserve the term for only this particular high level strategy, or others which stick to some sort of a "clean sheet of paper" theme).

Sketch of the method. The method begins with a careful study of the "as is process." Then, it turns to redrawing a new process, starting with knowledge of customer value requirements plus a clean page. A study is done to determine if the new proposed process will be a major improvement. If the answer is positive, the new process is implemented.

Cautions regarding the method. This method is risky. If those who traditionally have "ownership" in the process either dominate the redesign efforts, the typical result is that the clean sheet of paper redesign looks strikingly similar to the current "as is" process. If these people are kept out of the process, they are likely to sabotage, intentionally or otherwise, the efforts.

Examples of application of the method. The Ford/Mazda accounts payable experience, as reported by Hammer,[7] is a good example of this method. In this case, Ford executives sought to reduce personnel in accounts payable by 20 percent (from about 500 people to 400 people). When they examined Mazda's comparable process, they found only five people doing all the work – not 400. Even after adjusting for company size, the discrepancy between five and 400 was too great to dismiss. They shifted the focus on accounts payable to one on procurement.

Their old process began with a purchase order sent from purchasing to a vendor, accounts payable being copied. When the goods arrived at Ford, a clerk would complete a form stating what was received and send the form to accounts payable. The vendor, in parallel, sent an invoice to accounts payable. If all three documents – the purchase order, the receiving document, and the invoice – matched, the payment was issued. When they did not, reconciliation, lengthy and costly, had to take place.

The new process is fundamentally different. A buyer issues a purchase order, which triggers the order going into an online database. When the

goods arrive, receiving checks a computer terminal for validity of the match
of goods to an outstanding purchase order. If the match is correct, the clerk
accepts the shipment, the receipt is recorded into the database, and the
computer cuts the check to pay the supplier. If the match is incorrect, the
shipment is sent back to the vendor.

The impact: 75 percent reduction in headcount, improved and simpler
material in control, and improved accuracy of financial information.

Method 4: Work with suppliers and internal customers

When is the method likely to be appropriate? This method is most likely to
be appropriate when relationships with internal suppliers and internal
customers are strained, with misaligned expectations and performance.

Sketch of the method. Begin by obtaining clear information about external
customer value, and then work with internal (or external) suppliers, and
internal customers, to determine how to realign expectations and performance to better serve the customer.

Cautions regarding the method. A real danger is the confusion of external
with internal customers here. The expectations of internal customers may
have to changed – the value expectations of external customers are a
different thing altogether.

Examples of application of the method. The Taco Bell K-minus ("Kitchen
minus") experience[8] is a superb example of this method. In the "as is"
model of the process, their suppliers provided stores with raw meat, heads
of lettuce, large blocks of cheese, . . . The result: 70 percent of the space in
a store was devoted to kitchen, only 30 percent to customers. The
reconceptualized process views Taco Bell stores as assembly operations,
with suppliers providing cooked ground meat, chopped lettuce, grated
cheese, . . . The work in the new Taco Bell store is customer interface, plus
assembly of already prepared ingredients. The new store has 30 percent of
its space devoted to kitchen, and 70 percent devoted to paying customers.
Going along with this change was a change in average store revenue
amounting to slightly better than a fourfold increase.

The following article excerpted from the *Wall Street Journal* illustrates
some potent and useful ideas in management of suppliers.

Chrysler's Man of Many Parts Cuts Costs
By Douglas Lavin
Staff Reporter of The Wall Street Journal
Excerpted from Wall Street Journal, March 14, 1993, page B4

Thomas T. Stallkamp, Chrysler Corp. 's vice president, purchasing, wears his
wristwatch on his left hand. He likes French fries. And he is saving millions
of dollars for Chrysler without enraging parts suppliers.

Stallkamp says, "When you start to see your suppliers as the experts, then
they become valuable partners instead of a switchable commodity. You have

to have some technique other than just bludgeoning to get some efficiency out of them."

In short, the slightly pudgy 46-year-old from Pennsylvania is everything that J. Ignacio Lopez de Arriortua isn't.

Mr. Lopez, of course, is the mercurial Spaniard who ran purchasing at General Motors Corp. before jumping to Volkswagen Ag in March. At GM, Mr. Lopez tried to ban fried foods, warned of the end of Western civilization, and had underlings wear their watches on their right wrists to symbolize the need for radical change. More substantively, he sent efficiency teams into supplier factories, tore up contracts with suppliers and demanded double-digit price cuts – all in a crash effort to reduce GM's costs.

Meanwhile, the laid-back Mr. Stallkamp helped Chrysler do something no other US auto maker could do last year: make money. And his methods, while less flamboyant than Mr. Lopez's, are far more radical.

Chrysler has abandoned unilateral price cuts. It has abandoned competitive bidding. It has stopped writing detailed specifications for many parts. Instead, it relies on suppliers to design and build the right parts and to find ways to lower prices. Chrysler and the supplier split the savings, and the supplier gets a long-term relationship. "Chrysler and its suppliers are a virtual enterprise," says Chrysler President Robert A. Lutz. Mr. Stallkamp likens it to a Japanese-style keiritsu system, but without joint ownership.

"At Chrysler, the price doesn't fall until the team gets the cost out," says Timothy D. Leuliette, president of the ITT Automotive Inc. unit of ITT Corp., "as opposed to putting a gun to your head and saying, 'Lower your prices.'"
. . .

In general, says Mr. Stallkamp, the cooperative approach is the quickest route to better, lower-cost parts. Another Magna division, for example, recently developed a proposal for taking out $100 of fabric from each set of seats from Chrysler's low-end minivans.

"Now, do I go back and say, 'Gee if they can save $100 for me, does that mean they are saving $170 internally?'" asks Mr. Stallkamp. "No. I don't care; I really don't care."

Method 5: Work in parallel instead of in series

When is the method likely to be appropriate? This method is often appropriate when cycle time is much longer than appropriate. Often, a study showing that real process time is less than 5–10 percent of total cycle time leads to pursuit of redesign along these lines.

Sketch of the method. This method proceeds by beginning with a clear map of the process, turning to identification of how multiple parts of the process can go on at once, and then redesigning the process as required to make as many as possible of these parts work in parallel.

Cautions regarding the method. Practitioners of this method must beware of unstated requirements. Often internal customers and suppliers may not truly know each others' requirements. The result is that some steps may

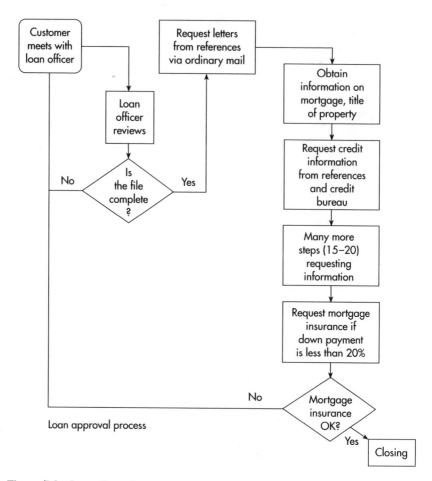

Figure 7.3 Loan flow chart

appear to be doable in parallel, when in fact they are not without other major change. A good corrective to this possible difficulty (which can result in major process failure) is to pilot the new process on a small scale – often a good idea before implementing major process change.

Examples of application of the method. Consider the loan application process depicted in figure 7.3. (The author actually endured a 6-week-long home loan approval process in 1985 which followed this model!)

Note the large number of checks which are done in sequence. Virtually all of these can be done in parallel.

For instance, the various elements of the credit check can be done in parallel – there is no need to do one at a time, waiting on completion of each before beginning the next.

As many banks have made these types of changes, they have begun to deliver commitments on mortgages (sometimes contingent on survey or title search) within 24–168 clock hours – an order of magnitude improvement, for which many customers are willing to pay a slight increase in the interest rate or points.

Method 6: Standardize – Make it easy for all to do, and easy to do in the same (best currently known) way

When is the method likely to be appropriate? This method is often appropriate where many people/shifts/locations do the work differently, and there would be a benefit from having a common process, either in terms of immediate improved performance or more synergistic learning.

Sketch of the method. The method proceeds by first determining the range of ways of doing the work in current practice, then studying and measuring to determine preferable way(s), and then providing the technology, training, or structure and systems to enable all to do work in the preferable way(s).

Cautions regarding the method. The major danger with this method is resentment, as one group perceives that "now we have to do it somebody else's way." It is best to secure a good degree of engagement from all the major groups who currently have to run the process, for the redesign effort.

Examples of application of the method. An example of this method is provided by the registration process for the University of Tennessee at Knoxville Management Development Center (UTK MDC), as described in Parr[9] and shown in figure 7.4. In the old process, customers (executives from industry) called UTK MDC to enquire about a possible short course. Their call was often transferred to a registrar (if the registrar was in), who assessed availability of space. If there were technical questions, the call could be bumped to someone else (if they were in). The result was often a long, protracted game of telephone tag, with the confirmation finally being mailed to the executive, often a week or two later.

In the redesigned process, a set of employees, termed "HUB employees" were equipped with the technology (via online registration information) and the knowledge (via briefings regarding each course, and a HUB notebook kept up to date) to permit any HUB employee to handle all of this work. To get the benefit from this new process structure, a schedule is established for each week on "who is on HUB duty" for each hour during business hours. Whoever is on HUB duty stays at their phone and handles incoming calls (transferred from the receptionist). Virtually all questions are now answered on the first call, within 5–10 minutes, instead of after many calls back and forth, and 5–10 days.

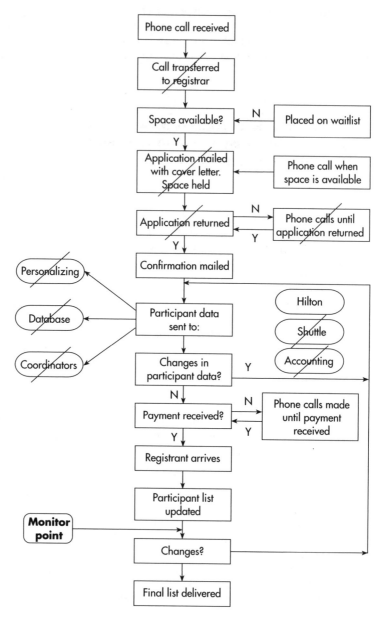

Figure 7.4 Impact on registration process: MDC perspective

Method 7: Organize work around products/ services or customer groups

When is the method likely to be appropriate? This method is often appropriate when employee's lack of ability to focus is caused by a highly diverse customer or product mix, resulting in errors, long cycle times, and higher costs. The method works when smaller groups of employees focused around either products/services or customer groups could perform better and learn more quickly.

Sketch of the method. The first choice in the method is to determine whether it is best to organize the work groups around products/services or around customers. Then, the groups are formed, trained (in group dynamics as well as in technical and customer interface issues) and performance begins (often with initial piloting on one or more large customers or major products/services).

Cautions regarding the method. The major danger of the method is that the groups may not be trained in the group dynamic issues which otherwise can undermine the intra group work.

Examples of application of the method. The company Southern Graphic Systems has a site in Richmond, Virginia. This company takes customer's graphic designs for consumer packaging (food products, tobacco products, . . .) and finalizes that design, and implements it in cylinders which can be used to print packaging with that design.

The site in Richmond has a diverse customer group, and employees were continually having to ask elementary questions ("How does this customer want the traps done?" "Does this customer want proofs?" "How do they like the graphics to be done?" . . .) to do their jobs, due in part to continually switching between doing work for different customers.

The highly successful process redesign involved creating work groups (teams) organized around customers or customer groups. The largest customers had teams assigned to them alone. Slightly smaller customers had their work done by a team which, for instance, might handle work for 5–6 different customers. Very small or new customers had their work handled by a team which handled the rest of the jobs.

The impact: Employees moved up the learning curve with a customer much more quickly, made fewer errors, and were able to reduce cycle time by over 30 percent in the first year of the new process, while also drastically reducing the percent of the time work was not approved by the customer on first pass.

Method 8: Empower front-line employees to serve the customer (Make decisions and perform work at the lowest appropriate level)

When is the method likely to be appropriate? This method is almost always appropriate, but especially impactful when customer service points are geographically separated, communication is difficult, or the need exists for frequent quick decisions to be made.

Sketch of the method. The method begins by an analysis of the decisions which could and should be made at the front line level, and then proceeds to determination of appropriate boundaries for these decisions. Then, appropriate training, empowerment, and education in principles to be used to make the decisions must be provided.

A key aspect of successful applications of this method is the provision of regular opportunities to discuss the tougher decisions being made, particularly in the early stages of the work.

Cautions regarding the method. Not all decisions should be made on the front line. Errors on where the decisions are made can have very serious consequences in terms of customer satisfaction and customer retention.

Example of application of the method. Delta Airlines provides an excellent example of this method. In the author's experience flying Delta (multiple millions of miles, Platinum Medallion Status, typically a hundred or more flight segments per year) they have often had the need to ask for some special assistance of a Delta employee. They have been told yes, and they have been told no. But they have never been told "Please wait a minute. I have to ask my supervisor." And they appreciate it.

A cautionary note: This performance has deteriorated in the last few years (1995 through 1998) as Delta has moved into traditional cost-cutting and other control-focused initiatives. This is an excellent illustration of the difficulty in maintaining empowerment when an organization sends inconsistent signals to its employees.

Method 9: Eliminate checks, controls, and reconciliations

When is the method likely to be appropriate? This method is particularly appropriate in highly bureaucratic organizations, or when many resources are spent reconciling different counts, or carrying out checks, or cycle time is extended beyond that appropriate by bureaucratic controls.

Sketch of the method. The method begins with a process mapping, and an identification of all checks, controls and reconciliations. Assume all these can be eliminated as an initial bias, and test this assumption. Determine a strategy for eliminating all checks, controls, and reconciliations which are not demonstrated to be clearly required. Carry out the strategy.

Cautions regarding the method. Checks, controls, and reconciliations do not come from nothing. They may reflect deep-seated organizational beliefs ("employees cannot be trusted," "Most suppliers are dishonest," "Employees can't manage a budget," . . .) which must be discussed before successful implementation of this type of a strategy.

Examples of application of the method. Examine the (abbreviated) curriculum change process for the University of Tennessee, Knoxville in figure 7.5. Note that there are multiple checks on any proposed curriculum change – the department, the college, the graduate or undergraduate

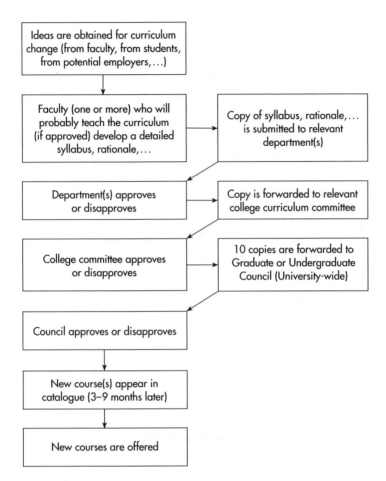

Figure 7.5 Process for curriculum change

curriculum committee, the graduate or undergraduate council, and (finally) the Tennessee Higher Education Committee.

At each successively higher level of approval, less knowledge exists regarding the nature, wisdom and impact of the proposed changes. The result is that many questions must be asked and answered. The entire process takes over 12 months to pursue even a modest curriculum change.

Unfortunately, the strategy has yet to be applied to this process, and figure 7.5 still describes the process as it is today.

Method 10: A case manager provides a single point of contact

When is the method likely to be appropriate? Indicators that this method is appropriate can be provided by consistent and rampant customer confusion about "how to get an answer around here." Alternatively, the lack of any-one with "ownership for getting my problems solved" is a likely indicator.

Sketch of the method. The method is, technically, simplicity itself (but see the soft issues discussed in the next section). Someone has to be given the case manager role, and given the processes appropriate to that role – the authority, and the expectation/accountability, to make things work for the customer. The case of Southern Graphic Systems in Richmond above is a variant of the case manager approach. In addition, the MDC Hub case above is also a variant of the case manager idea – with multiple case managers who can each do the work for a given customer!

Impact of business process reengineering

What has been the impact of Business Process Reengineering? What have been the typical results of application of this method?

From one viewpoint, from the internal stakeholder point of view, the results have sadly often been catastrophic. "BPR" has come to be, in many organizations, a code word for "restructuring and layoffs." One former colleague called the author a couple of years ago, indicating that his rather large and famous company had just begun a major BPR effort in his business unit – and that he had revised his curriculum vitae and wanted to know if the author knew of any suitable places for him to explore future employment – the assumed consequence was an impending major layoff.

He was right about the layoff – though he survived and continues to prosper within the organization.

From the viewpoints of the customer, and of the stockholder, the news has been much better. The table below captures some typical results of BPR.

Examples of business process reengineering

Table 7.2 summarizes some of the most prominent examples of reengineering, listing the organization, the process reengineered (and what was done), and the impact of the reengineering.

Table 7.2 Examples of reengineering

Organization	*Process and what was done*	*Impact*
Taco Bell (fast food restaurant)	Product delivery process – K Minus program turned restaurant into assembly plant (was originally a manufacturing plant).	70% of floor space is devoted to customer seating (formerly 30%) Managers oversee an average of 23 stores each (former average was 5.5). Peak capacity moved from $400 per hour to $1500 per hour. Food prices have fallen by 25%.

Table 7.2   (cont'd)

Organization	Process and what was done	Impact
Engelhard (special chemical and engineered materials company)	Product delivery process and customer Acquisition process	Cost of goods sold was reduced over 20%. Capacity was increased by 45%. Market share was increased by 35% in petroleum catalyst segment, with a significant improvement in profits.
Liberty Mutual (insurance and financial services company)	Customer acquisition and order fulfillment processes	Reduced cycle time by over 50%. Doubled percentage of quotes which turn into business (15% to 30%).
AT&T	Design process for printed wiring boards	Quality moved from 40% correct to over 90% correct. Savings of $4 million in direct costs. Increased sales estimated at $15 million.
American Express	Credit authorization Process	Authorizer's Assistant Expert System led to: (i) $7 million annual reduction in costs due to credit losses; (ii) 25% reduction in average time for an authorization; (iii) 30% reduction in improper credit denials.
Hallmark Greeting Cards (greeting card company)	Concept to market process	Process used to take 2–3 years to introduce new products, now takes less than a year.
Banc One	Loan processing and approval process	Process used to involve 8 departments and take an average of 17 days. Using work cell/team approach and information technology, process was streamlined to take just 2 days. Accuracy of basic customer data has moved from 25% to 50%, and earnings went up 25% in the next year.

The soft side of Business Process Reengineering

All is not well within the BPR community, however. Many independent voices report failure rates of 70–80 percent – that is, they report that 70–80 percent of the reengineering efforts launched fail to deliver what was hoped for, many of them in fact resulting in no substantive change at all.

How can this be? The purpose of the next section is to discuss the resistance to BPR, its sources, and what can be done. We focus in particular on the role which the senior leadership has to play to manage for success.

Resistance, its sources, and its treatment

Resistance to BPR is rampant in corporate America. The author receives calls occasionally from people with the basic message: "I've just updated my resume, and am wondering if you've heard of any openings which might be appropriate. We're into a corporate reengineering effort, and we all know what that means."

What they are referring to, of course, is the fairly common link between Business Process Reengineering, as commonly practiced, and downsizing.

What are some of the prime failures of reengineering efforts which have resulted in these perceptions?

(1) Reengineering has been clearly and persistently linked to downsizing, and as a result an announcement of a reengineering effort typically provokes massive internal resistance.

(2) Reengineering has often been used as a buzzword for more general change efforts – implementing a new computer system, making incremental process improvements, ... The results have been major gaps between expectations and outcomes.

(3) An inappropriate amount of time has been spent studying the "as is" process. Initially, the problem was spending almost no time – all morning was the suggestion of one famous book on the subject – understanding the "as is" process. More recently, the failing has been an overcompensation – spending half a year understanding what is to the second decimal place, when *what is* is so clearly out of touch with *what is required*. Too much analysis can seriously inhibit creative thought.

(4) Reengineering has been attempted without the appropriate leadership. Often, teams, largely divorced from line management, have been chartered to "reengineer the X process." They have attempted this, with little or no participation from those who currently work within the process, or from those who will ultimately make the decisions on whether to go forward with the process redesign. Champy[10] offers, in his first chapter, a fascinating litany of attempts to "reengineer" in which senior leadership has been lacking.

(5) Too often, while the term "reengineering" has been used, the intent has been to "fix a process" via incremental change, instead of transforming à la reengineering.

(6) "Reengineering" has been the term used for work to improve the operations of individual departments. If "reengineer" is a verb, then its proper object is a process – not a department or a function. Nothing but a process – anything else is a profound misunderstanding.

(7) Reengineering has been pursued as a "bottoms up" strategy. It is, by its nature, a top down process. It demands massive buy-in from the top. Without this buy-in, it is best not to begin.

(8) Executives have sometimes hesitated when resistance arises. Such resistance is entirely to be expected in any major change effort.

Ways exist to deal with the resistance:

1 Senior executive engagement, in an operational sense, in the re-design efforts is absolutely essential. Some of those who will have to decide on appropriateness of the redesign must be a part of conceptualizing that redesign.
2 Frankness of speaking about the issue of downsizing is essential. The subject is not pleasant. But ignoring the assumption made in the organization is a sure way to guarantee that those in the organization take the dimmest possible view.
3 Engagement of the current line management with responsibility for the major parts of the involved process cannot be ignored. It should not extend to absolute control, but neither should these line managers be separated from the effort.
4 A clear finite timeline for the efforts is required.
5 A clear commitment to understand the process in its as is state, coupled with understanding the reasons for that process, will equip the management group to deal with the major internal sources of resistance.
6 The external customer should have some degree of involvement. Those within the organization will derive strength from seeing the customer's reaction to the process, and to the anticipated outcomes.

Hall, Rosenthal and Wade[11] looked at 100 companies and their reengineering projects, with a view to determining key factors which drove success versus failure, and impact of the work. Their findings are worthy of review.

One note was that improvements of the redesigned process by 15 percent to 20 percent were common – and were sometimes accompanied by improvement of less than 5 percent in terms of total business performance. This was typically due to processes studied being too small, or measurements being micro-level (departmental costs) instead of macro-level (total cost, total cycle time, . . .).

In a comparison of successful cost reduction, those in the highest 25 percent of breadth of process studied were able to cut costs by an average of 17 percent, while those in the lowest 25 percent of breadth of process studied saved an average of less than 1 percent.

Five elements identified in this work as being key to a successful reengineering project were:

1   Set an aggressive reengineering performance target, spanning the entire business unit and exceeding that achievable without major redesign.
2   Commit 20 percent to 50 percent of the chief executive's time to the project.
3   Conduct a comprehensive review of customer needs, economic leverage points, and market trends.
4   Assign an additional senior executive to be responsible for implementation.
5   Carry out a comprehensive pilot of the new design.

They identified four ways to fail as

1   Assign average performers – not high performers on the fast track.
2   Measure only the plan – not the actual impact of the work.
3   Settle for the status quo – giving up too easy when the politics of the change effort get difficult.
4   Overlook communication – keep things secret.

7-Eleven Japan: Design of the Information System for Improved Customer Service

7-Eleven Japan is an excellent example of strategic use of information systems to provide customer value.[12]

Inside each of 7-Eleven's thousands of stores is a custom NEC computer which captures point of sale data on every transaction in the store. Not only items purchased, but information on customers' sex, age, whether they were alone or accompanied by children, etc. . . . May be captured.

These data are used for:

■   Determining causes for poor sales performance.
■   Determining trends in sales, by stocking unit.
■   Suppliers determining what sandwiches are selling well and need to be supplied as part of their three times daily deliveries.

What is the impact? 7-Eleven charges a premium franchise royalty rate (43 percent for 7-Eleven, 35 percent for its closest rival). 7-Eleven stores in Japan have average daily sales a full 30 percent higher than those of their closest rival. (The per store sales volume is four times as high as United States – based 7-Eleven stores.)

SUMMARY

Process management and reengineering are not transitory phenomena. In fact, the second (reengineering) is a subset of the first. The two are now and will be essential tools for organizations in the decades to come.

What is needed? First, a firm and steady commitment to management presence. Ownership was seen to be an issue in both process management (speaking generally) and in reengineering. It is an obligation which cannot be dodged. Second, a strong reliance on input from the external customer as a source for direction, and a reinforcer for sometime lagging enthusiasm. Third, a commitment to do all this work in the environment of learning about the processes of the organization in order to improve them. It is clear from the organizational track record that without these three things in place, the likelihood of success with process management and process reengineering is minimal. It is equally clear, from the examples offered, that the potential gains in the ability to provide superior customer value while generating handsome returns to this stockholder can be greatly enhanced by process management and process reengineering.

Notes

1 AT&T Quality Steering Committee (1988). *Process Quality Management and Improvement Guidelines.* Indianapolis, Indiana, 5.
2 H. James Harrington (1991). *Business Process Improvement: The Breakthrough Strategy for Total Quality, Productivity, and Competitiveness.* McGraw-Hill, New York, 13.
3 AT&T Quality Steering Committee (1988). Process Quality Management and Improvement Guidelines. Indianapolis, Indiana, 15.
4 Peter Scholtes (1988). *The Team Handbook.* Joiner Associates, Madison, Wisconsin.
5 Michael Hammer (1990). Reengineering Work: Don't Automate, Obliterate. *Harvard Business Review,* July–August 1990, 104–112.
6 Peter Senge (1990). *The Fifth Discipline: The Art and Practice of the Learning Organization.* Currenty/Doubleday, 26–54.
7 Michael Hammer (1990). Reengineering Work: Don't Automate, Obliterate. *Harvard Business Review,* July–August 1990, 104–12.
8 Michael Hammer and James Champy (1993). *Reengineering the Corporation: A Manifesto for Business Revolution.* HarperBusiness, New York, 171–81.
9 William C. Parr (1991). Understanding Cause and Effect Relationships for Suprasystem Improvement: Design of Experiments and Beyond. In Michael J. Stahl and Gregory Bounds (1991), *Competing Globally through Customer* Value: The Management of Strategic Suprasystems, Quorum Books, New York, 275–304.
10 James Champy (1995). *Reengineering Management: The Mandate for New Leadership.* HarperBusiness, New York, 1–8.
11 Gene Hall, Jim Rosenthal, and Judy Wade (1993). How to Make Reengineering Really Work. *Harvard Business Review,* November–December, 119–31.
12 Gale Eisenstadt (1993). Information Power. *Forbes,* June 21, 44–5.

8 | The Role of Process Managers and Understanding Process Variation

Mary G. Leitnaker

Abstract

Since the early 1980s, American businesses and their managers have become increasing concerned with "quality." However, the means by which a business becomes a "quality supplier" to its customers have taken many forms. Consequently, businesses who want to practice "Total Quality Management" have often taken quite different approaches to this objective. It is the judgment of the author of this chapter that, at a minimum, the practice of Total Quality Management must include managers having an informed understanding of system and process variation and knowing how to use and direct the use of this information to achieve improved business operation. This chapter describes the basis on which this judgment is made as well as description of how managers should carry out their responsibilities for managing process operation.

INTRODUCTION – ROLES AND RESPONSIBILITIES OF PROCESS MANAGERS

Significant changes in the roles and responsibilities of engineers and managers charged with process management have occurred in the last ten to fifteen years. These changes in roles and responsibilities have been driven by the ongoing effort of manufacturing organizations to more efficiently provide products which meet the ever increasing expectations of customers. In the early 1980s, the pressure placed on the automotive industry by low-cost, high quality cars produced by off-shore manufacturers was a highly visible example of the need for changing the way in which business processes were managed. Of course, few industries were left unchanged by the demand to continually improve the value provided to customers by products and services. The electronics, pulp and paper, chemical processing, pharmaceutical, and many others have all responded to the need to rethink the way in which business processes are managed to provide customer value. A renewed interest in customer values provided process managers with measurable characteristics against which process performance was to be evaluated. At the process operation level, this implies that a continual evaluation of the process means by which products and services are provided has become a defined role of process managers;

furthermore, this information is used to provide criteria by which to guide changes in processes. Process performance is continually improved in order to more efficiently provide products and services.

AN UPDATED DEFINITION OF PROCESS MANAGEMENT

These changes have dictated that a primary responsibility of managers and engineers is process management. As defined by Leitnaker, Sanders, and Hild (1996) process management is:

- the alignment of process objectives with identified customer values,
- knowledge of the current process configuration and capability to attain process objectives, and
- the selection and direction of needed process improvements.

A past practice for carrying out responsibilities for obtaining process improvements has been to rely on new processing technology or innovations. This practice is insufficient; a dominating responsibility is to take the new technology or innovation and improve what it currently provides and how it is provided. The ability to assume this responsibility requires an in-depth, technical knowledge of process operation. Hopp and Spearman (1996) speak eloquently of the roles and responsibilities of manufacturing managers. It is their belief that "the old concept of a professional manager is bankrupt. In a world of intense global competition, simply setting appropriate guidelines is not enough. Manufacturers need detailed knowledge about their business, knowledge that must include *technical* details. In the future, survival itself is likely to depend on these details."

RESPONSIBILITIES OF PROCESS MANAGERS

The "technical" work that those charged with process management must perform is described by Leitnaker, Sanders, and Hild (1996). The responsibilities of process managers which they have listed are:

1 understanding and disseminating information on what the customers of the organization value;
2 knowing what and how the process contributes value to its customers;
3 developing and deploying practices and methods that provide the intended results and confirming that these methods can be implemented;
4 knowing the past and current performance levels of the process in achieving its objectives;
5 assessing current process performance against requirements; and
6 making appropriate, constructive, and verifiable process changes that enable the process to significantly improve its contribution to creating customer value.

Although, the duties and responsibilities of process managers obviously goes far beyond the use of tools and techniques, statistical techniques for understanding process variation are a critical set of skills for supporting process managers, engineers, and operators in the performance of their respective duties. Knowledge of variation and its effects on process behavior is and will continue to be critical to the effective execution of process management. Statistical techniques for studying variation are used to describe current process behavior, to assess and understand process performance, and to make and evaluate process changes. Knowledge of variation and its effects can be used for more effective and efficient management of processes.

The discussion so far of process management has left the processes to be managed unidentified. Numerous examples of processes at various levels of an organization can be used to illustrate the use of statistical thinking in process management. Processes which encompass the completion of a part assembly or the processing of a chemical batch are better managed using statistical methods. However, one problem which has been observed in the use of these methods is the limitation of statistically based process improvement activities to manufacturing tasks and operations. This delegation of the expectation for "continuous improvement" to the factory floor imposed severe limitations on what issues could be addressed, the magnitude of improvement made, and the ability to maintain realized gains. For example, the process for designing a product is an input to a manufacturing process. The design of the product heavily influences manufacturing quality, cycle time, and manufacturing cost. An evaluation of the effects of the input provided by design is needed in order to provide direction for improving these inputs. Focusing efforts solely on manufacturing means that this type of improvement would go unrealized. Organizations which are working to improve process management will identify the critical process characteristics of design and of manufacturing, how these parameters are managed will be understood, and how change will be undertaken, as required.

Focusing only on lower level manufacturing processes also ignored the interconnections between higher level business processes. For example, a manufacturing process includes vendor-provided items and services; hence, the ordering activity and the checking of incoming materials are both contained within the larger manufacturing process. It is important to remember that large-scale improvements are made by improving the critical processes of the organization and that tasks, activities, and operations only become the focus of improvement efforts after the critical processes are identified and studied.

THE USE OF STATISTICAL METHODS IN PROCESS MANAGEMENT

Any manager or engineer who has been required to report such numbers as weekly line efficiency, overtime hours, shift downtime, machine breakdowns, line stoppages, or yield knows that there is variation exhibited by such numbers. Also understood by managers and engineers is that there exist numerous strategies for affecting such numbers; in other words, some understanding exists about the sources affecting the variation in the numbers. It is the aim of this section to illustrate how the *depth* of understanding of variability can be used to guide process management. Knowledge of the nature of the variation in such numbers, the causes and sources of variation in the numbers, and the effect that different engineering or management practices would have on the numbers will be useful in realizing how improvement in the numbers might be effected. As the depth of understanding about the variation in process outcomes increases, so does the range of viable and effective choices for improving process performance.

Statistical methods for process improvement rely heavily on the Shewhart control chart developed at the Bell Laboratories in the early 1930s. The use of these methods in the context of process management means that:

■ process measurements are consistently taken over time to evaluate a process;

■ data plotted over time are used to convert the numbers into process information; and

■ distinctions between ongoing variations and episodic variations support decisions about the correction or improvement of process operation.

Process results, summarized by control charts, provide a check on process management by focusing on the causes of variation and the reduction or elimination of the effect of those causes.

Statistical control charts are based on a perspective that variability in a series of measurements taken over time is due to common as well as, possibly, special causes of variation. Common causes of variation are those process sources that affect each and every process outcome and are experienced on an ongoing, consistent basis. Special causes of variation are those that occur sporadically and affect only some of the results. This common/special cause model of process behavior provides a valuable way of understanding process behavior. The model ties the variation produced in outputs of a process to the way in which this variation occurs in the process. The separation of variation into these two types, common and special cause, provides a basis for understanding the root sources of variation affecting a process.

An example of the use of control charts for describing process behavior is provided by data collected at the final assembly of a new process for producing electronic components. Every day 100 components are inspected and classified as conforming or nonconforming. The chart below shows a plot of the proportion nonconforming for the past 20 days.

Figure 8.1 indicates that the process for producing the electronic component assemblies is "out-of-control." In other words, the proportion of nonconforming assemblies being produced is not stable or predictable,

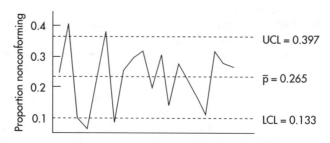

Figure 8.1   Process outcomes: "out of control"

but behaves erratically at some times. Unless the causes for the unstable
behavior are removed, mechanisms to handle the unpredictability must be
put in place. For example, in process inventory may be built up so that the
next process stage will not have to stop because insufficient assemblies are
available. The lack of control in the process also means that costs of the
assembly are difficult to determine. Since the number of good assemblies
which can be made can't be predicted, the cost of the assemblies can also
not be accurately determined.

   Figure 8.1 can be contrasted with figure 8.2. This second chart is from
the same process, but after work to identify and remove special causes of
variation has occurred. Figure 8.2 provides a check that the work on
removing the causes of unpredictable behavior has been successful. All
points lie within the control limits which is taken to mean that the process
is only subject to common cause sources of variation. This knowledge
provides managers and engineers with a powerful advantage. Estimates of
the costs of assemblies can now be reliably forecasted. A schedule for
producing a given number of assemblies can be built since forecasts of the
number of assemblies which can be completed can now be made. Other
benefits from predictability are also had. The effects of work methods,
product and process design changes, and equipment maintenance can be
evaluated when a process is predictable. When process results can not be
predicted, it is difficult to know and verify the effects of a process change.
The erratic behavior would have the effect of obscuring intended results
from process changes. For these reasons, process managers who need to:

- know the past and current performance levels of the process in
  achieving its objectives;
- assess current process performance against requirements; and
- make appropriate, constructive, and verifiable process changes

will want to continually evaluate process outputs over time.

   Additional information about the assembly process is available by comparing the center lines of the two preceding charts. The process which is
described in figure 8.2 is not only stable and predictable, the average
proportion of nonconforming assemblies in this figure ($\bar{p} = 0.115$) is
smaller than the same average was in figure 8.1. However, even though the

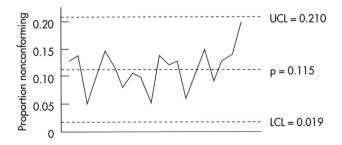

Figure 8.2   Process outcomes: statistical control

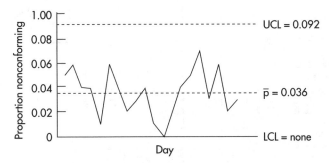

Figure 8.3   Process outcomes: appropriate, constructive, and verifiable process changes

process has been made predictable, the number of non conforming assemblies being produced was considered to be too large. So the responsibility of process managers is to develop the management and engineering knowledge for process redesign or improvement. Before describing the kind of statistical techniques which prove useful in carrying out these responsibilities, the results of this work on the assembly process is described in figure 8.3. Several months after the data collected in figure 8.2 were gathered, additional data on the process were collected to evaluate the work on process improvement. These data are plotted in figure 8.3.

From figure 8.3 it can be seen that the process is still in statistical control, but with a considerably smaller level of nonconforming assemblies being produced. The establishment of a statistical control as seen in figure 8.2 is an inadequate management goal. Although it is important to be able to predict process outcomes, being able to identify *appropriate, constructive, and verifiable process changes* as was done prior to collecting the data for figure 8.3, requires further, technical process work. Possible causal factors affecting process outcomes are identified, and statistical methods are used to confirm, or not, the impact which these factors have on process behavior.

A powerful method for beginning to understand possible factors affecting process outcomes is illustrated by the process map provided in

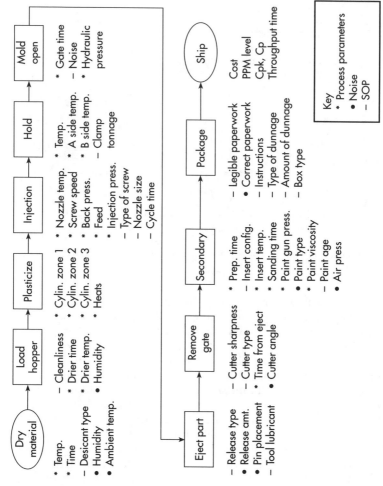

Figure 8.4 Injection molding process flow chart (process parameter classification)
Reproduced by permission of Six Sigma Associates. Copyright Six Sigma Associates.

figure 8.4. This map, developed by Sanders, Cooper, and Ross (n.d.) is a powerful means for beginning to capture what is currently known about *what and how the process contributes value to its customers.*

The example described in the process map of figure 8.4 is for an injection molding process. The map not only describes how material flows through the process, but also begins to identify what the critical sources of variation are in this process. At each stage of the process, important parameters of the process are identified. In addition, information about whether these parameters are controlled or are noise variables is identified.

Possibly more powerful than the process map itself is the intention which is captured by this map. The map is not to be viewed as merely a means of capturing current process knowledge, but rather as a statement of intention about the type of work which must occur in order to improve process operation. In evaluating current process operation, it has been seen to be necessary to plot appropriate outcome measure in order to know process capability. In addition, data on process inputs and process variables must be obtained in order to ensure consistent process operation. This statement implies that critical inputs and parameters are measured and evaluated over time. For example, at the "Load Hopper" stage of the process, data on drier temperature might be collected across time in order to evaluate the consistency at which this temperature is maintained. In addition, knowledge of the relationship between inputs, process variables, and outcome variables will be required. This last need for process knowledge will be aided by further study of process variation.

Collecting data for purposes of evaluating the statistical control of an input, parameter, or output is one important task. However, even more powerful is the further insight into process operation which can be gained from more focused data collection and analysis. Data collection and arrangement can be guided by the need to understand the effects of causes of variation on process outputs. An example of such a data collection plan and its use in understanding process variation is provided by Leitnaker, Sanders, and Hild (1996). This example is used to illustrate how processes which have multiple spindles, heads, molds, cavities, and/or workstations can be evaluated to determine the effects which these differences may have on process outputs. The graph in figure 8.5 is a plot of data which were collected on an output characteristic of a part manufactured on a machine with four different positions. Four parts, from four consecutive cycles of the machine, were collected and a critical dimension measured on each. For each of the positions, the average dimension ($\overline{X}$) of the four parts was calculated. In other words, four averages, one representing each machine position, were calculated. This same procedure was performed repeatedly at fixed time increments until there were 10 averages (and 10 ranges) for each of the four positions available to be examined. These averages are the ones which are plotted in figure 8.5. (The chart of ranges is not included.) It should be noted that the averages for position one have been plotted first, then the 10 averages for position 2, and so forth.

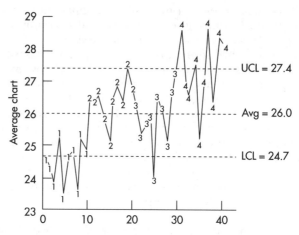

Figure 8.5 Data collection plan example

The chart of subgroup averages indicates that the four positions do not operate at the same average. Position one has considerably smaller dimensions, on average, than does position four. The original intention of understanding the differences which might exist between positions guided a data collection plan and then an analysis which then provided a verification as well as a quantification of this position difference.

Statistical methods, primarily control charts, have been shown to be a means of studying processes with the intent of providing consistent output and then of improving that which is provided and how it is provided. In the example on electronic component assembly, the collection of data from an ongoing process was a passive activity; data were collected at frequent intervals in order to characterize the stability of the assembly process. In the previous example, a more aggressive approach was taken whereby a planned subgrouping strategy led to a better understanding of the effect which a possible source of variation, position, had on an output characteristic. In still other situations, a process parameter may be deliberately changed, data collected after the change, and then the data are analyzed in order to determine what effect, if any, the process change has had. Design of experiments refers to the practice of deliberately changing process variables in specific, patterned ways in order to evaluate the effects which these changes have on one or more output variables. An effect is the average measured change, increase or decrease, in an output variable associated with changes in a process factor. An advantage of using designed experiments is that the effect of many factors can be studied simultaneously. Simultaneous study of factors offers several advantages, two of which are:

1   Time can be saved in investigating the influence of many variables. Designed experiments offer an approach for simultaneously studying the effect of numerous factors, maybe as many as seven or eight,

in order to more rapidly provide information concerning the selection of improved or preferred raw materials and process parameter values.

2   The simultaneous study of the effect of two or more factors allows the investigator to understand complex relationships between factors and the output characteristic of interest. As an example, large variations in incoming density of a raw material might not affect final particle size of a batch process unless the crystallization phase proceeded too rapidly. Consequently, studying the effect of variation in density while holding cycle time constant may not provide adequate process information. Designed experiments can aid the process investigator in sorting out complex relationships among process settings, parameters, and output characteristics.

In the design phase of a product, statistically designed experiments can be used to select raw materials, set specifications, determine machine operating conditions, and recommend parameter settings. However, once a process exists for producing a product, designed experiments take on a very different role. Methods, materials, work practices, machine settings, and a host of other operating conditions for the process are already in place. At issue then is the selection of improved methods, practices, and parameters to improve what is delivered by the process. Consequently, designed experiments for on-line investigations will be most effective when coupled with knowledge of current process behavior. Knowledge of which process output characteristics are critical to providing customer value as well as knowledge of past experience in managing not only these characteristics but the factors which effect them should be in place. Designed experiments then offer an option for rapidly exploring process responses to changes in process parameters, settings, or materials.

CUSTOMER VALUE AND PRIORITIZING WORK EFFORTS

The preceding section on the use of statistical methods in process management focused on how these methods can be used to carry out the second through sixth responsibilities listed earlier. However, the first responsibility of process managers, *understanding and disseminating information on what the customers of the organization value,* may be the more critical activity for ensuring that process improvement benefits the organization by improving the efficiency or effectiveness with which goods or services are provided to customers. It is obvious that which processes and process outputs are selected for study, control, and improvement has a direct impact on long range success. And, those processes which are identified as critical in providing customer value should be the first among those selected for improvement efforts. These processes are typically high-level processes which often provide outcomes to the external customer.

A continued examination of the electronic assembly process illustrates the importance both of identifying and disseminating information on customer value and of working on improving the high level cross-functional processes of an organization. The assembly process examined earlier was one which had been recently introduced at the plant site. At this plant, new designs are common and it is the responsibility of process managers and engineers to introduce the new design into manufacturing. With each new design, problems with assembly are experienced. Managers of the assembly process have consequently become quite expert at finding solutions to these problems. The series of charts in figures 8.1, 8.2, and 8.3 clearly describe the effectiveness of the these problem solving efforts.

Several additional points should be emphasized. First, the customers did not receive nonconforming product. The organization verifies the quality of each assembly before shipment. Secondly, the problem-solving which was so effective with the assembly described, has been repeatedly used with the same success on each new assembly. Consequently, the limitations of this excellent work on improving the assembly process may not be immediately apparent. (Certainly not to the managers of assembly who were being rewarded for their excellent problem-solving skills.)

However, a different perspective on the control chart of figure 8.1 would be that this chart does *not* simply provide information on the assembly process; this chart also reports on the organization's ability to design and hand-over to manufacturing and assembly the newest innovation. The fact that each new device displays similar results to the initial run of figure 8.1, indicates that a critical element of process management is going unattended. Because the ability to initially produce devices is erratic, there will not be accurate knowledge of when devices will be available for the customer and promised delivery dates may not be met. The management group at this site would begin to work on quite different aspects of the assembly and design processes if the focus were on being able to provide customers with the new technology, without the added time and expense of reworking devices.

References

Hopp, Wallace J. and Spearman, Mark L. *Factory Physics, Foundations of Manufacturing Management*, Richard D. Irwin, Chicago, IL, 1996.

Leitnaker, Mary G., Sanders, Richard D., and Hild, Cheryl. *The Power of Statistical Thinking: Improving Industrial Processes*, Addison-Wesley, Reading, MA, 1996.

Sanders, Howard D., Cooper, Antony, and Ross, William. Training materials used by Six Sigma, Associates (n.d.).

9 | Design Quality and New Product Development

Michael E. Kennedy, Carmen J. Trammell, and Clement C. Wilson

Abstract

New products must have high customer value, be robust, and be brought to market in a timely manner. It *is* possible to have product value, product robustness, and process speed simultaneously – but all three attributes must be integrated and balanced to develop the successful product. Product development can be approached as processes that can be defined, controlled, and improved.

A Product Development Process Model, based on lessons learned from case studies of world-class firms, is presented to characterize generally the flow of work in new product development. This process occurs in nine major phases, originating with the Product Ideas phase and concluding with the Product Manufacture, Delivery, and Use phase. Organizations can use a large variety of management and technical methods within the development process, so long as some *essential* elements for success are present.

ROLE OF NEW PRODUCT DEVELOPMENT IN THE TQM ORGANIZATION

Creation of customer value

Products (and services) are the *sine qua non* of a firm; without products and services to offer, a company has no reason to exist. Customers purchase a firm's products only when they find those products to be the most effective for meeting their needs. If a firm is to be successful (or even to stay in business), its products must be more valuable to their customers than other alternatives – they must be more convenient, more productive, easier to use, more easily obtainable, and/or less costly.

New products are truly the lifeblood of a company's long-term economic existence. One survey of executives indicated that over one-half of their firm's revenues derived from sales that came from products that were not in production ten years ago. The 3M Corporation has had a goal to earn at least 40 percent of its annual revenue from products that have been on the market for less than four years (Donaldson 1993). Unfortunately, several comprehensive studies, including those by the MIT Commission on Industrial Productivity (Dertouzos 1989) and the National Research Council (1991), concluded that many US product development efforts are too slow, too expensive, and too often fail to create products with the benefits, performance, and quality that customers want.

Case studies evaluating the development of successful, innovative new products reveal an overarching desire to provide superior customer value. Operations in these firms are not "business as usual"; in some cases, radical changes have been required. In all cases, responding firms have made conscious, focused efforts to improve their product development, design and manufacturing capabilities so as to deliver the superior, innovative products that customers will prefer.

Implementation of strategic focus

There are significant differences in the performance capabilities of successful versus mediocre firms. A 1991 McKinsey study indicated that better firms create 2.5 times more new products on average than laggards (*The Economist*, May 11, 1991, p. 72). Motorola found that "best-in-class" companies have error rates 500 to 1,000 times lower than do "average" firms.

New product development presents multi-faceted challenges. Its aspects cover a tremendously broad scope – from finding the product idea through to sustained manufacturing. Some once-dominant firms have attempted to solve their product development inadequacies through massive organizational restructuring. However, firms which focus strategically on *improving their product development processes* are more likely to be successful in creating high-value, robust, timely products that are successful from technical, marketing, and business standpoints.

Integration of organizational functions

Many good design and manufacturing methodologies have been advanced in recent years to improve product design, manufacturing, and time-to-market. Design-for-Assembly, Design-for-Manufacturing, Quality Function Deployment (QFD), Design of Experiements and Computer-Aided-Design (CAD) are all worthy methods in an ever-growing list of "solutions" for improved product development. *However, these individual methodologies can be executed perfectly, yet products developed using these methodologies can still fail to win customers!*

This is because the ability of individual methodologies to improve new products is limited unless they are used within a coherent *product development process*. The goal cannot be merely to execute the best computer-aided design or fastest assembly, but instead must be to create a product that provides the maximum value, robustness, and quality to customers in the shortest possible time. All activities performed in creating the product must be conducted within the context of an integrated product development process – one that ensures the control of critical product characteristics throughout the entire development and manufacturing effort.

THE PRODUCT DEVELOPMENT PROCESS

Throughout the last eight years, the authors have studied actual case histories involving the successful development of complex, innovative products. Many of these case histories have been from the information products (copiers, printers, transaction recorders, and personal computers) industries, which were among the first US firms to discover that they were not competitive versus their Japanese counterparts. In response, these firms have changed their product development organizations and processes. Their engineering, manufacturing, and purchasing functions have been combined into single teams who value the successful development and production of a high-value product over all other functional objectives. The teams operate as small, vertically-integrated organizations that include all necessary engineering, manufacturing, and other functions.

The common themes arising from these superior product development projects – i.e., the "essential elements" of those projects that contributed most to the product's success – form the basis for the Product Development Process Model presented in figure 9.1.

Development phases and goals

The Product Development Process Model for innovative products is based on lessons learned from case studies of world-class firms. The process occurs in nine major phases, originating with the Product Ideas phase and concluding with the Product Manufacture, Delivery, and Use phase. Each development phase has a "milestone goal" that defines the completion of that phase, as indicated by the numbered "flags" on the phase boxes (see figure 9.1, p. 227). Major management reviews are conducted at the end of these phases to verify attainment of the Milestone Goals. These phase reviews are comprehensive, including engineering, financial, manufacturing, marketing and distribution considerations.

Following is an introduction to the phases contained in the Product Development Process Model. Detailed discussions of each phase can be found in *Superior Product Development* (Wilson, Kennedy, and Trammell 1996).

Product ideas. The milestone goal for the Product Ideas phase is the creation of "high value" product concepts, consistent with the firm's strategic goals. High value ideas provide distinctive customer benefits relative to competition. A successful product will have characteristics that can be identified immediately as making the product superior to other alternatives. Product ideas can be generated from external sources (e.g., customers, advertising agencies, etc.) or internal sources (e.g., marketing staff, R&D staff, etc.). Ideas may arise as unsolicited suggestions or through planned idea generation. Planned ideas can be generated through systematic consideration of possibilities such as addressing customer wishes or complaints, customizing an existing product, and using manufacturing by-products. Product ideas are screened against factors such as internal capabilities, technical feasibility, and financial risk.

Customer future needs projection. The milestone goal for Customer Future Needs Projection is the projection of "high value" product ideas over a future time period. New products must be defined in terms of customers' future requirements, not merely their current ones. Projection of high value ideas means identifying the window of future market opportunity, from product introduction through the end of production. Key activities required to make such a projection are quantifying the customer's definition of product quality, assessing the characteristics of the future market, and analyzing the ability of competitors. A product of high value relative to future customer needs, developed within a defined window of market opportunity, must ultimately be characterized in terms of an optimal combination of the highest product performance, the lowest product cost, and the fastest possible development time.

Product technology selection and development. The milestone goal for Product Technology Selection and Development is selection of appropriate, robust product technologies. Such technologies will meet customers' expectations, work properly in a product environment, and be manufacturable with high yields. They may or may not be the "latest," but will instead be the most appropriate for the product.

Candidate technologies are assessed relative to performance on customer requirements, technical barriers, cost, and relation to the firm's competence. In particular, the controlling variables for each selected technology must be identified and tested over an appropriate range of conditions to confirm adequate function over the full "operating space" (the intersection of relevant performance requirements and operating conditions). Both "current" and "new" technologies may be candidates, depending on the situation.

The specific final result of this phase is a Technology Feasibility Statement which sets forth:

- critical performance parameters, and a description of the technology "operating space";
- any major limitations to design, use, or manufacture;
- special materials or manufacturing processes required; and
- explicit confirmation that a working configuration with needed instrumentation and controls had been successfully tested.

A major management phase review, the Technical Feasibility Phase Review, occurs at the end of this phase. This review also includes the results from the Process Technology Selection and Development Phase.

Process technology selection and development. The milestone goal for Process Technology Selection and Development is the selection of appropriate, robust process technologies. New process technologies are developed simultaneously and in conjunction with new product technologies, since the requirements and limitations of each generally affect design considerations for the other. Process Technology Selection and Development activities parallel the Product Technology and Selection and Development activities described above, and result in a Technology Feasibility Statement for manufacturing process technology.

Final product definition and project targets. The milestone goal for the Final Product Definition and Project Targets phase is the establishment of a set of strategic product and project targets. These targets result from the convergence of marketing, engineering, and manufacturing information and include (1) specifications for the product "family" (i.e., the base product and anticipated derivative products), and (2) the market, financial, schedule, and staffing targets for the project. The Product Concept Phase Review assures that the proposed targets defining the product and project plans are supported appropriately by management.

Product marketing and distribution preparation. The milestone goal for Product Marketing and Distribution Preparation is a product introduction plan. This includes a marketing plan that identifies sales channels, promotional methods, pricing structure and a distribution plan that spells out the logistics of ordering, shipping, and billing.

Product design and evaluation. The milestone goals for Product Design and Evaluation are definition of the product architecture; design, construction, and test of subassemblies; and testing of the integrated system.

A formal Product Design Specification (PDS) is completed before design begins, which comprehensively describes the product's major features, uses, and expected usage conditions. A design readiness review is held after the PDS has been prepared. When the team is satisfied that the PDS is complete, design begins.

The product design is created to be "robust", so that it can accommodate a "worst case" scenario for parts and environment. The critical functional and manufacturing parameters are described in formal product documentation and are well-understood by all team members. The performance of the product is certified through a comprehensive test program. Tests are performed under both routine and nonroutine operating conditions. Deliberate failure evaluation (stress testing) is used to assure that the product will operate under worst case customer usage conditions.

This phase concludes with the Product Release Review, to verify that the new product has indeed been engineered and tested properly and will meet Product Design Specification requirements, the business plan targets, and – of course – the needs of the customer.

Manufacturing system design. The milestone goal for the Manufacturing System Design phase is the selection and implementation of cost-effective, capable manufacturing and assembly processes. Critical process technologies should be controlled internally by the company or controlled *very* closely with preferred suppliers.

Standard, well-understood processes are selected for the manufacturing system. Process feasibility is demonstrated using a manual procedure, with automation introduced only after processes are stable. Criteria for the movement of the product into the manufacturing process are established during the Manufacturing System Design phase. A Manufacturing Readiness Review is held as the final step in the phase to confirm that criteria have been met.

Product manufacture, delivery, and use. The milestone goal for the final phase, Product Manufacture and Delivery, is the ongoing manufacture and delivery of quality products. Processes are controlled through statistical process control, and are continuously improved by the manufacturing team.

The final management review prior to launching the product is the Product Launch Readiness Review. The final review of product performance is the Product Infant Mortality Tracking Program Review, in which early product failures are analyzed to identify root causes of the failures and to prevent their reoccurrence.

Inclusion of product, customer and process orientations

Development time is minimized by utilizing a process consisting of the maximum possible concurrent activity. Marketing (top row of phases in figure 9.1), engineering (middle row), and manufacturing (bottom row) efforts are performed concurrently throughout the entire process shown in figure 9.1.

Carefully planned convergence of marketing, engineering, and manufacturing information is absolutely essential to achieving *effective* concurrency within the development process. While ongoing consultation and feedback occur among activities throughout the process, the explicit, formal convergence of marketing, engineering, and manufacturing information occurs twice in the Product Development Process Model. Formal convergence of what can be described as the "planning" portion of the process occurs at the Final Product Definition and Project Targets phase, and the convergence of the "execution" portion takes place at the Product Manufacturing, Delivery, and Use phase.

Essential elements of superior product development

The Product Development Process Model is a general characterization of the flow of work in new product development. Organizations may use a variety of management and technical methods within the overall development process, as long as the *essential* elements for success are present. While there are also essential elements for each individual phase, the case studies analyzed by the authors also revealed four essential elements that are fundamental to the entire process. These are:

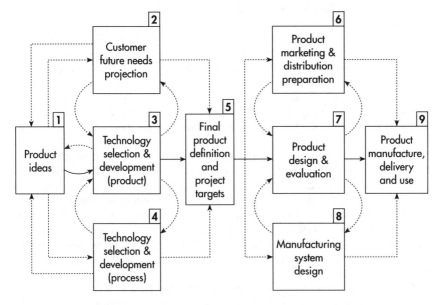

PHASE GOALS

1 Potentially 'high value' product concepts, consistent with future customer needs and the firm's goals/strategies.

2 Definition of target customers and their future needs, understanding of competitive offerings ('benchmarking').

3 Appropriate, timely selection and development (as necessary) of robust product technologies.

4 Appropriate, timely selection and development (as necessary) of robust product technologies.

5 'Frozen' final product definition (of 'base' product plus derivatives); market, business, and resource targets.

6 Development of marketing/sales, customer support, and distribution systems that reflect customers' needs.

7 Development of product design specification that addresses customer needs; 'design-build-test' of product and its subsystems; verification of product's value and 'fitness'.

8 Selection and construction of cost-effective, capable processes for parts manufacture and product assembly.

9 Manufacture and assembly of quality product, consistent with customer demand; process control and improvement.

Figure 9.1 A superior product development process for an innovative product, with milestone goals for each phase

- CONTROL BY A SINGLE TEAM
  - ◆ Team integrates broad skills needed to develop product
  - ◆ Team controls all aspects, from technology selection to manufacturing
- CREATION OF A VISION FOR THE FUTURE PRODUCT
  - ◆ Projection of customers' *future* needs
  - ◆ Team participates directly in future needs projection
  - ◆ Customers provide direct input to team members

- INFORMATION CONVERGENCE AT PRODUCT DEFINITION PHASE
  - Team considers all critical issues early and simultaneously
  - Team establishes common ("consensus") goals and plans
- INFORMATION CONTINUITY FOR CRITICAL PRODUCT CHARACTERISTICS

Sustained market competitiveness requires that a firm create and maintain a superior product development process that utilizes the essential elements for success. This chapter provides one such model.

Control by a single team. First among all the essential elements for successful product development is the selection of a single marketing/engineering/manufacturing team to control the project from technology selection through the first six months of manufacturing. World-class companies have learned that matrix organizations, with their accompanying "turf battles" and lack of responsibility for the product, are not competitive against co-operative, functionally-integrated systems. The single, functionally-integrated product development team is the most essential element for superior product development.

If a single team is to be responsible for the product throughout the development process, its members must contain the proper mix of skills and experience to do the job. Various team members need to have the design, manufacturing, marketing, testing, and other skills necessary to develop the product successfully. The most effective teams have a single leader with the authority to control *all* aspects of the project from the technology selection phase through the first six months of product manufacture. The Xerox Corporation, for example, utilizes a "product delivery team" whose multi-functional members report a "chief engineer."

Studies summarizing the characteristics of effective project teams cite the following important factors:

- co-location of team members,
- mechanisms for informal communication,
- training for team-building,
- leadership based on team facilitation,
- delegation of decision authority to the lowest possible level, and
- performance measurement based on team measures.

Vision of the future product. The second essential element affecting the entire development process is the existence of a product "vision" that sustains the team's momentum throughout the life of the project. A guiding vision of how the product is to meet customers' future needs can create enthusiasm and dedication that contributes immeasureably to achieving the project's goals.

The product vision is created during the Customer Future Needs Projection. It is the team's window to the future throughout the project. The team participates *directly* in the determination of customer needs. Direct participation enhances team members' creative contributions by enabling them to "see" opportunities that they might not see by merely reading reports from distant market analysis groups.

Team interaction with customers continues throughout the development process. One data storage firm has established a Customer Advisory Board to provide direct customer involvement during the design process. This board is composed of technically astute customers, such as data center directors and systems engineers. New product designs are discussed with board members to provide them with advance notice of new products and solicit suggestions for product improvements. Design engineers attend these meetings to answer questions and receive direct feedback from customers.

Direct and ongoing interaction between team members and customers is an essential element in successful development of innovative products. The initial product vision arises from understanding customers' future needs, and the team's momentum is sustained by reinforcing the product vision through continuing customer contact.

Convergence of information from marketing, engineering, and manufacturing. The concurrent and integrative aspects of the development process have already been discussed. Carefully planned convergence of marketing, engineering, and manufacturing information is absolutely essential to successfully completing the development process in the minimum possible time.

Early, simultaneous consideration of marketing, engineering, and manufacturing issues must result in the project leaders' agreement on a common set of product targets. The product market opportunity is to be reflected in the product design specification, and the product design specification in turn must be supported by appropriate manufacturing process technologies. This explicit agreement enables parallel product and process development to occur with minimum conflict. If common targets are not developed at the outset, the concurrent but *divergent* engineering of product and process is likely to result in major product and process rework late in the development process, lengthy project delays, and even project failure.

The final convergence of marketing, engineering, and manufacturing information confirm that plans were executed as intended, that projections are still valid, and that all systems are ready for product launch. Specific confirmation is needed that the product as designed meets the criteria for the product as specified, and that the product as to be manufactured meets the established targets.

Information continuity for critical product characteristics. Quantitative measures for critical product characteristics must be developed at the start of the product development process and used throughout the process for product quality "scorekeeping." Some of the ways in which these measures can be used in the various development phases are illustrated in figure 9.2 (the selected product development phases shown are extracted from figure 9.1).

The selection and development of suitable measures for critical product characteristics is a difficult task, and must be a planned, deliberate activity. Since product characteristics vary widely, measurement criteria and techniques also differ. However, some common elements of superior product characteristic measures clearly distinguish them from other, less effective measures. Superior product measures are:

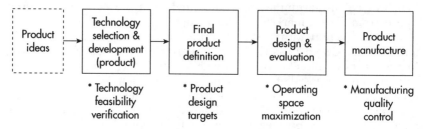

Figure 9.2 Selected phases from figure 9.1, illustrating how measurements of critical product characteristics are used throughout the entire product development process

- Customer oriented:
  - Measures are characteristics that are important to customers;
  - Quantified limits/targets are derived from customer participation;
- Developed at the start of the process through a planned activity;
- Simple and easy to use;
- Measures have multiple uses throughout the development process:
  - Measures are used for product quality scorekeeping;
  - Measures are used to measure and assess the development program.

Even subjective characteristics are measured, as necessary, if those items are important to the customer.

In several major printer development projects, measurements were developed for the important but subjective characteristic of "print quality". Customer surveys were used to establish print quality requirements for the products. The print quality measures were used to verify technology feasibility, to define product design targets and specifications, and to set production quality requirements. In sum, the team used its print quality measures to assess how well they were doing throughout the entire product development process.

The structure of many US organizations makes it difficult to assure that important information related to critical product characteristics is transferred to and understood by the manufacturing organization. The single, functionally-integrated teams utilized in superior projects carry critical product information into the manufacturing phase, since the team is responsible for manufacturing system design and pilot manufacturing.

In one case study involving the development of a computer keyboard, the development team defined a formal method for transferring critical product characteristic information to the manufacturing process. This transfer formally connected development to manufacturing and serves as an outstanding example of how product quality can be improved by ensuring continuity of critical product information throughout the development process. This example is described below and is illustrated in figure 9.3.

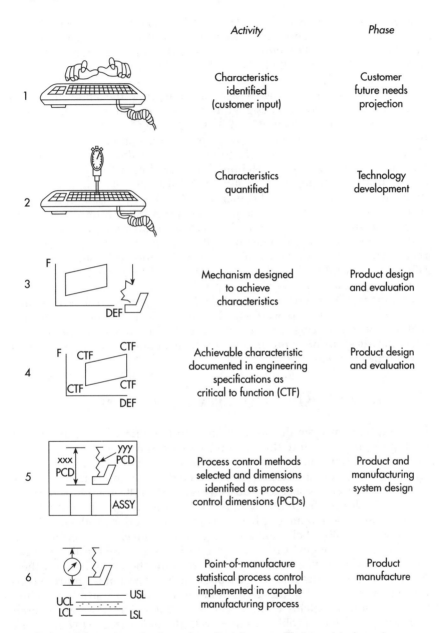

	Activity	Phase
1	Characteristics identified (customer input)	Customer future needs projection
2	Characteristics quantified	Technology development
3	Mechanism designed to achieve characteristics	Product design and evaluation
4	Achievable characteristic documented in engineering specifications as critical to function (CTF)	Product design and evaluation
5	Process control methods selected and dimensions identified as process control dimensions (PCDs)	Product and manufacturing system design
6	Point-of-manufacture statistical process control implemented in capable manufacturing process	Product manufacture

Figure 9.3 Illustration of a formal method for transferring critical product characteristic information into the manufacturing process

Keyboard "touch" is an important product feature for typewriters and personal computers, and can be the deciding factor in a new typewriter or keyboard purchase. Therefore, the force-deflection characteristic for the keys, which determines their "touch," is a critical product characteristic for keyboard design.

Steps 1 through 3 of figure 9.3 illustrate how the characteristic is identified, quantified, and designed in the early development phases. The characteristic is then documented in the product engineering specification as a "Critical-To-Function" (CTF) parameter that must be controlled (step 4). Part dimensions and features that affect the critical-to-function parameter subsequently are identified as CTF dimensions on the engineering drawings. In step 5, some of the Critical-To-Function dimensions are designated as Process Control Dimensions (PCDs) to be used for manufacturing process control. Statistical process control (SPC) is implemented in manufacturing (Step 6) using the PCDs to assure that the process is stable and capable of making a product that will meet all engineering specification requirements. To assure manufacturing adherence to engineering specifications, any off-specification permit for a CTF dimension requires the written, signed approval of a senior program manager.

Converting CTF parameters into PCDs for statistical control of the manufacturing process is a powerful technique. It is a documented, formal method for transferring the necessary information so that critical product characteristics can be controlled properly throughout the entire product development process.

KEY "DESIGN QUALITY" CONCEPTS

It should be clear from the above discussion that efforts to create "design quality" begin well before the "design" has even started. Obviously, a comprehensive discussion of the numerous product development factors affecting design quality cannot be completed within the confines of one chapter. However, a select few can be presented to illustrate how one can leverage both specific methodologies within the design phase itself and those in other development phases to create a superior product.

In the Technology Selection and Development phases, the "critical variables" affecting the performance of the technologies used in the product and the product's manufacturing processes must be identified and their "operating spaces" determined. Throughout the Customer Future Needs Projection and Final Product Definition phases, the team strives to define which customer problems are to be solved, so that design efforts are focused on solving the "right" problems – those with the highest value to customers.

Within the Product Design and Evaluation phase itself, these now-identified customer needs must then be converted into technical requirements that can be embodied in a product design. "Design margin" must be created so that the product is robust in service. A process of "controlled iteration" is used to design and evaluate the critical characteristics of the product throughout the entire range of its potential use environments.

A comprehensive evaluation program is designed and executed to assure that the finished design meets all target objectives.

Identification of critical variables and "operating space"

The primary goal of the Technology Selection and Development phases is to select and develop technologies that perform as intended even when subjected to operational and environmental variations, process tolerances, and other unfavorable conditions. Properly selected product technologies meet customers' value expectations, work properly in the environment surrounding the product, and are manufacturable with high yields. Properly selected process technologies are controllable, stable, and capable of producing high quality products economically. The identification of each technology's critical variables and operating space is not only an essential element of the Technology Selection and Development phase, but also has a direct bearing on the design quality of the product since these two items must be used during design and later controlled during production.

Critical variables. Since the critical variables determine or control the output of a technology, it is imperative that these variables be discovered. This discovery process is especially important when contemplating selection of a "new" technology, since few facts are available initially with which to perform a technology evaluation. Both physical analyses and experimentation are indispensible for determining those factors that are critical to the desired operation of a technology.

For example, three critical variables that determine how well toner is "fixed" to a sheet of paper in the hot roll fuser of a copier or laser printer include temperature, pressure and time. A combination of values for these three variables determine whether satisfactory attachment or fixing of the toner to the paper occurs. The throughput capacity for a product with embedded software may depend on memory and microprocessor speed. In a laser printer, for example, processing time will vary for pages of varying complexity. A page is processed in "chunks," and the upper limit on chunk size is determined by memory. Similarly, the rate at which chunks are moved through processing steps is determined by microprocessor speed. Memory and microprocessor speed, therefore, are critical variables for processing information in laser printers.

Demonstration of "operating space". Once the critical variables are discovered, an adequate "operating space" for the technology must be demonstrated. The operating space for a technology is the range of critical variables over which the output from the technology meets specified requirements. In the hot roll fuser, the range of temperature, pressure and time over which the toner is adequately fixed to the paper creates an operating space of the critical variables for the fuser. The fuser is set to operate in an operating space "box" (figure 9.4), which defines the temperature and residence time boundaries (for a specific pressure) that generate print at or better than a target quality level.

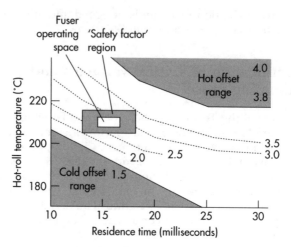

Figure 9.4   An example of an operating space

The team must be able to demonstrate, or at least to predict, that an adequate operating space can be developed *before starting* the product design, otherwise the technology must be rejected as too fragile. Selection of fragile technologies is a key cause of product design failure, since every design using any given technology will have to be capable of controlling its critical variables within each technology's respective operating space.

Maximum product reliability is attained by locating the largest possible operating space regions and/or by minimizing the variability of the controlling variables. The operating space is maximized by finding a range that allows the widest possible variation in the critical variables but still generate the desired output level. The ability to minimize variability of the controlling variables reduces the operating space needed for effective performance. For example, a hot roll fuser technology was enhanced by developing a precise temperature measurement and control system accurate to 1°C, which enabled the fuser to operate well in the copier even though the fuser functioned properly only within a very narrow temperature range (Wilson 1979).

Statistically designed experiments are particularly valuable in quantifying the location and size of operating spaces and in maximizing their usefulness. Indeed, a key goal of multi-variate statistical testing such as "Taguchi[R] methods" is to identify product and process settings that generate acceptable performance with the largest possible variation.

Conversion of customer needs into technical requirements

Even the most brilliant technical design is useless if that design fails to match customer values effectively. Thus, methods for injecting customer needs and perceptions into the product development process, and for using that information to evaluate the progress of the design, are essential elements within a successful effort.

Customer criteria used in technology selection. In the most successful projects, technology selection and evaluation criteria are strongly based on customer needs for performance, quality, reliability, and cost. Technology team members have a significant understanding of the customer needs for which the technology is being developed. The cost of a technology is used only to the extent that target customers are perceived to consider cost as important; quality and reliability of the technology generally are emphasized more than cost. In particular, "product characteristic" measures, such as those discussed earlier, are used to determine which technologies are the most appropriate.

A comprehensive/concise product design specification. The initial step of the Product Design & Evaluation phase is the creation of a comprehensive Product Design Specification (PDS). The PDS describes, in a technical form, all of the customer requirements for the product and the environments in which the product will be required to function. The creation of a complete, concise PDS is one of the most important steps in the entire product development process. Many engineers resist this critical discipline of drafting a written set of product requirements because they are so anxious to start the actual hardware and software design. The process of writing the PDS also appears bureaucratic to some. However, those who begin the design of a complex system without a PDS invariably find that what they have designed is not what others expected them to have designed.

A comprehensive, yet concise PDS provides the development team with a common reference about the full spectrum of product requirements. In his book *Total Design*, Stuart Pugh (1991) characterizes the PDS in great detail, using a "balanced wheel" comprised of around 30 categories. Pugh's numerous PDS topics can be organized within six overall groupings:

- product characteristics (e.g., features, performance, size, weight);
- product life (e.g., competitive life span, shelf life);
- customer use (e.g., installation, maintenance, disposal, documentation);
- product development considerations (e.g., time, environment, materials, safety);
- manufacturing factors (e.g., facilities, processes, quantity, packaging); and
- market definition and plan (e.g., customer identification, competitive assessment, market window).

The PDS categories apply to both the hardware and the software of the product. Many product development groups are not accustomed to developing formal software specifications, but it is essential to do so. Regardless of form, the software portion of a PDS must include (1) all possible user inputs and outputs for both proper and improper use of the product, and (2) the mapping or transition from inputs to outputs.

The following guidelines are helpful in developing and using the contents of a PDS:

- Define target or preferred, quantifiable values for critical variables; if values are not known with certainty, use estimated values. Take advantage of any "critical characteristic" measures developed earlier to define the technical performance for the product.
- Define relative importance or tradeoff criteria for items that might conflict with each other, and resolve specification conflicts immediately, either by adjusting targets or by defining trade-offs.
- Make sure specification priorities agree with the customer benefits defined in the Final Product Definition and Project Targets.
- Create one unified specification; do not split the document into one engineering specification and one marketing specification.

Progress indicators in design. "Product characteristic" measures, such as the fuser print quality indicator shown in figure 9.4, are used repeatedly within the Product Design and Evaluation phase to gauge how well the actual product design replicates the operating spaces for its component technologies.

"Top-down" design

The initial creation of the product configuration sets the stage for all subsequent design activity, for once the configuration is established, the team has to live with all the design limitations inherent to that selected configuration. This design effort is called "Top-Down" to describe the need to design the product first from the system level, then at the subsystem level, and finally to the parts level (figure 9.5).

Both external and internal factors are considered while developing the system configuration. Customer requirements comprise most of the system's

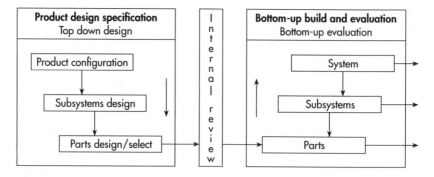

Figure 9.5 The initial product design step of the Product Design and Evaluation phase

external considerations, such as the need to minimize the machine's "footprint" or to provide front access for customer operations. Internal considerations relate to the spacial and functional constraints related to the product's internal functions. These include allocating sufficient space for needed subsystems, providing adequate thermal cooling for heated elements, and a myriad of other issues.

"Paper build" of the product. The top-down design effort process can be illustrated through the drawings that are created as the design is developed. The first drawing is the "zero drawing," which defines only the allowable space for the total system (the "product envelope"), the allocated space for all subsystem modules, the location of a coordinate system from which all critical interfaces are measured, and the dimensions to the critical interfaces between modules. (The location of the coordinate system origin is called the datum, from which all points are measured.) The zero drawing is extended in "design layouts," which illustrate details of and size the product's modules and parts as they are created. There may be design layouts of individual modules and other layouts of multiple modules, as the design dictates. Finally, and lastly, the lowest level of drawing is created, the individual part drawing.

The initial design effort concludes with a full paper or CAD system "build" of the proposed configuration. The building of the product on paper/computer prior to actually building it from ultimate materials is a very important process. This "machine control layout" is constructed by "reassembling" the product from its individual parts geometries and/or drawings (CAD systems make this process much simpler). Many errors and omissions can be caught as parts are placed on the machine control layout to check that they interface to each other as intended. Disciplined engineering teams often require that the machine control layout be completed before prototype parts are ordered.

Engineers at Lexmark International have extended the concept of the geometric layout to one of a functional layout that not only describes the measurement datums and allocation of space, but also describes the "fundamental function" of primary product elements. These functional items include the product's paper path and geometrical properties that affect paper behavior at interfaces, critical forces, velocities, dimensions, etc.

Creation of "design margin" for a robust product

Design "margin" → *robust product design.* Words like "margin," "safety factors," and "safety zone" appear frequently in the design documentation for successful technologies and products. Products with "margin" operate properly with "worst-case" parts and in adverse environments. Margin generally does not occur by accident; rather, it is created by knowledgeable design decisions based on a thorough understanding of the product environment, use, and failure modes.

Derating. "Designing beyond specification" is a common method for providing design margin. For example, the copier hot roll fuser discussed earlier was designed to operate within the operating space shown in figure 9.4, but was also surrounded by a "safety factor region." This built-in margin enabled the copier to operate acceptably even if some unusual event (such as a temperature measurement shift) should cause the fuser to operate outside its normal range. A tape cartridge library design team used the term "derating components" to describe their effort to ensure that their components were significantly "overdesigned" for their tasks. Components were overdesigned from two to 600 times expected life (and even more in a few cases), depending on how well engineers could predict loading conditions and other factors.

Controlled iteration

Controlled iteration during system design. The development of the product "configuration" or "architecture" is an iterative process that requires considerable discipline. Experienced engineers practice a concept known as "controlled iteration" by deliberately creating multiple configurations at this early stage and comparing them over a limited time period. First, PDS requirements are converted into technical system and subsystem requirements. Several configuration concepts are developed, which in turn each are partitioned into subsystem module requirements. The competing configuration concepts are compared using a structured process, such as Pugh's configuration selection process, which provides a structured method for this (Pugh 1991). Finally, the strongest designs are selected for additional development in the next iteration. This controlled iteration continues until the requirements are adequately met and the time limit is reached. The result is that the "winning concept" resulting from this structured configuration selection/improvement method is significantly better than the initial concept.

Controlled iteration of design and evaluation. Many firms organize their product design and evaluation activities in series; that is, they complete the design in its entirety before beginning any evaluation. Government contracts, in particular, are notorious for specifying that design and evaluation be performed separately. Development teams assume significant risks, however, by not performing any significant evaluation until after the design is completely finished. If major product failures occur during the evaluation that require substantial design changes to solve, the time and effort needed to fix the "finished" design will dramatically delay the introduction of the product to market.

Competitive product development processes are managed and controlled through a planned series of cumulative cycles, or "iterations", of design and evaluation. A "minimal" or "baseline" product is built early, during the initial product creation step. Additional functions are added iteratively in controlled steps until all functions have been implemented.

Advantages. Use of controlled iteration throughout the development process offers several advantages:

- Project risk can be managed through choices about what gets the earliest attention. The most novel, complex, highly-used, least well-specified, etc., functions may be planned for early iterations. Other considerations for planning each iteration include decisions on user interface, functional dependencies, and reliability allocation;
- Control of the development process is possible by comparing the performance in each iteration versus quality standards;
- Customer feedback about the evolving product can be a planned part of the development program.

Design reviews

The design review is one evaluation effort that does not necessarily require the construction and testing of an actual prototype. Reviews should generally be held at the conclusion of major milestones throughout the design effort. Engineers from within the organization bring experience from previous projects to bear on this project. The act of defending the chosen product configuration can help clarify the design. If there are glaring weaknesses in technology or configuration choices, they are likely to be caught in the review. Depending on the specific purpose for the review, some key items to be examined include:

- The control or functional layout (paper build).
- The basic configuration for minimum complexity and adequate precision (examined using the Map of Connections) (Wilson and Harrison 1993).
- Parts and subassembly fits.
- A check of critical variables and dimensions to see if they are known and documented for control.
- A design that stays within its operating space for its critical variables.
- A check of critical software and hardware interfaces.
- A check of critical function, tolerances, and manufacturing capability to implement the critical dimensions.
- A check of critical hardware and software timings (functional timing diagram).
- Memory and microprocessor speed calculations for throughput requirements.
- Architecture review of how controlled testing iterations are to be conducted.
- The coordination of software and hardware schedules.

Comprehensive evaluation/testing

At the conclusion of the initial product creation effort, a preliminary evaluation is performed to validate the design as adequate to begin the comprehensive evaluation. The Comprehensive Test Plan is derived from the Product Design Specification and the expected user environment. The product's potential failure modes and conditions are identified using a structured technique such as Failure Mode and Effect Analysis. Testing is performed to provoke these failures, to assure that the failure modes, or at least their harmful effects, are blocked by the product design. Testing usually starts with the most basic functions of the product and is iteratively expanded to include the product's total function.

Preliminary evaluations. The first preliminary evaluation is part verification. Critical dimensions of parts are checked against requirements prior to or concurrent with building prototype assemblies. Part fits are evaluated as the engineer assembles the unit or observes a technician doing the assembly. Any very close fits or interferences call for a detailed tolerance study to ensure parts interchangeability on all subassemblies.

Once assembled, subassemblies are functionally tested, often with the assistance of special test fixtures. Beyond these initial functional tests, extra module-level units are built in parallel and tested in special test rigs for life and wear to obtain this critical information early. Weak areas can then be identified and corrected rather than finding them in later system testing. However, these additional units are not constructed until the initial functional tests indicate that the configuration is stable.

The third phase of the preliminary evaluation is the build and evaluation of the total system. Often this first build is not of the total system, but only of the "main engine." It is important that main engine function be demonstrated to work properly prior to the evaluation of ancillary functions. Thus the preliminary evaluation can proceed in an orderly fashion from the simplest machine to the more complex as the initial problems are uncovered and solved.

Once the preliminary evaluation proves satisfactory (which may require a corrective action cycle of redesign and rebuild to attain), comprehensive testing can be performed, which includes these major areas:

- Tests-to-failure and stress testing, to provoke failures and determine design margin.
- Life testing, to understand and to plan the replacement of any life-limited parts.
- Operating space verification, to ensure that the critical variables are controlled within necessary limits.
- Testing to specification, to assure that everything works right within the operating environment specified.

Testing for failure. Whereas the preliminary testing can be described as "testing for success" since it evaluates whether the product and modules can at least minimally function, the comprehensive evaluation focuses on "testing for failure."

Testing for success is an obvious thing to do – test the product as the customer will use it or submit the product to a Product Test group and solve whatever problems appear. The testing for success approach has merit, but will reveal problems only after a very long test period. When testing for success, one never knows just how close failures lurk just beyond the testing region. Thus a product may be tested successfully in a test laboratory, but may fail in a factory or customer environment that is only slightly out of the lab test range. In testing for failure, the failure modes "hidden" in any machine or system are iteratively revealed by testing at conditions that cause the product to fail.

Stress testing. Stress testing is used selectively to assure that the product will operate as expected when used by actual customers. For example, inkjet resistors were tested at "worst-case" product overpower conditions. When hot roll fuser engineers discovered that solid white and solid black zones caused the worst problems, copiers using the hot roll fuser were tested using both solid white and solid black sheets. Resistive ribbon systems in typewriters were evaluated using a "stress-pak" of papers; twenty types of very "difficult to print on" paper were run through the machine to assure that quality type would be printed on all of the different papers. These tests were designed to attack serious, dominant failure modes that can be stimulated during normal product use.

The results of stress testing requires careful interpretation. When a failure occurs, it must be reported as "the product (or module) failed to meet specific performance requirements under these specific conditions," and not just that "the product failed". In this way the implications of the failure can be interpreted in terms of customer use and an action plan developed to take the appropriate corrective action.

Operating space verification. One key requirement for the test effort is to assure that the product design operating space corresponds to the previously-developed technology operating space. Tests-to-failure and stress testing are imperative in assuring that the product design conforms to the operating space controlling the product's performance. By discovering the limits of the operating space and redesigning to enlarge it, the engineer builds design margin or robustness into the product. This investigation is a partial repeat of the operating space tests made during the Technology Selection and Development phase, but this time the machine hardware is representative of a production process. Mechanical aspects of the product are often configuration sensitive, so when the hardware configuration changes, the operating space must be verified again.

"Bottom-up" approach. The term "bottom-up" testing describes the process of progressing from the "bottom level" of parts testing to the highest level of system testing. It is the evaluation counterpart to the "top-down" methodology for the design effort. Parts, subsystem, and system testing are described briefly in separate topics below.

Parts evaluations. Failure testing for parts primarily provokes wear and breakage modes of failure. Highly stressed areas must be analyzed to quantify the magnitude of the stress, but also must be tested to failure to ascertain the margin of safety that exists. Wear rates are a sensitive function of friction and lubrication conditions and thus may vary an order of magnitude depending upon these conditions. Thus, a large safety margin is necessary to guarantee a robust design that is not sensitive to environmental or machine condition changes. Processes such as case hardening, in which wear resistance and life are a function both of the hardness level and case depth, must be verified as adequate for the part application. The safety margin for critically loaded parts must also be verified by appropriate fatigue tests to assure that the parts will not fail in the field.

Testing of modular subsystems. Modular subsystems make it possible to test specific portions of the product in stressed situations likely to create failure. Electronic circuit boards can be stress tested by exciting the boards mechanically with a random excitation over a comprehensive frequency range while systematically cycling the ambient temperature. As various card failures occur, weak areas are redesigned or process changes made to eliminate those modes of failure. This method creates a margin of safety by solving problems that exist outside the normal operating ranges.

Mechanical subsystems can also be stressed in this manner. For example, mechanical connections are often a source of reliability problems. Fasteners are subject to loosening, and lubrication and strength of elastomer parts are affected by temperature.

Another important use of modular subsystem tests is determining the life of "life-limited" components. Any failures that cannot be "designed out" of the product must be prevented by a parts replacement program at specified intervals so that the product does not fail and interrupt the customer's work.

System testing. While subsystem and parts testing are going on in parallel to answer life-limiting questions, system tests are run to answer certain environment-related and system interaction questions. These tests will also be stress tests to find the operating space relative to the external environment that is to be experienced in the customer application.

Two critical environmental factors are often temperature and humidity. For example, all internal combustion engines intended for automobiles, buses, or trucks must be tested across extremes of temperature and humidity. All paper-handling machines such as copiers, laser printers, and offset presses must also be tested throughout a range of temperature and humidity. Hot and wet conditions (e.g., 90F and 80% RH) cause paper to become very limp and hard to handle. Testing to identify these failure modes has to be done at the system level.

The effects of variation of a moving media such as paper must be tested at the system level if the media moves through several subsystems. Reliability requirements for many products are so high now (for example, 1 paper transport failure per 10,000 sheets fed through a laser printer) that failure analysis must often be done by imagining the mode of failure and then exaggerating it in stress tests to assess what may be redesigned to handle extreme conditions without failure. The interfaces of modules where paper moves from one module to another are the most frequent sources of paper handling problems as a sheet is "handed off" from one set of guides and rolls to another. The guides will often be designed (or redesigned) to handle a sheet with a folded corner or front edge and then tested with sheets with folded corners to see if the paper handling has improved over the previous design.

Electronic boards, particularly those that contain memory devices, must be shielded from electrostatic discharge and electromagnetic fields. These types of tests must be done at the system level even though they may have been done at the board level because the machine itself may generate these environments. Thus temperature, humidity, electrostatic and electromagnetic fields are all examples of environmental conditions that must be tested at the system level.

PRODUCT DEVELOPMENT IN PRACTICE

The Product Design and Evaluation phase is where the major engineering and testing of the product is performed. It starts with the creation of a Product Design Specification and ends with complete drawings, specifications and critical parameter information for manufacture. These work products arise as a result of carefully controlled design iterations and purposeful tests that evaluate product performance over and beyond its range of use and environment. This phase requires a creative and detailed effort to design, build and test prototypes that are representative of the final manufactured product. Inadequate design and/or testing can bring unpleasant surprises when the final product is put into the customer's hands in the customer environment. Unexpected (but avoidable) product failures that arise either in manufacturing or in the hands of the customer are extremely expensive and have even put firms out of business.

Today's superior products must have high customer value, be robust, and be brought to market in a timely manner. Many product development engineers would say that a rapid development cycle attribute is contradictory to the development of a robust product with high customer value simply because more engineering work is usually required to bring forward new customer value features and to guarantee robust performance. However, it *is* possible to have product value, product robustness, and process speed simultaneously – but the product development process must change from one of sequential handoffs from one function to another to make this possible. All three attributes must be integrated and balanced to develop the successful product. For example, it is common for these software and hardware engineering efforts to be the cause of schedule and budget overruns. These need not be the most uncontrollable aspects of product development. Product design and testing can be approached as processes that can be defined, controlled, and improved, as are other aspects of engineering. Factors that speed up the product design and evaluation phase while at the same time delivering product customer value and robustness is shown in this chapter.

Two key challenges pervade the Product Development Process Model. One is customer orientation, and the other is cross-functional integration. Customer orientation can be maintained through two of the essential elements described in this chapter: a vision of a product that will meet the customer's future needs, and customer-oriented measures of product quality that are tracked throughout product development. Cross-functional integration is possible through the other two essential elements in this chapter: control of the project by a single team, and explicit convergence of marketing, engineering, and manufacturing information in the process model.

Clearly, there exist many interrelationships among product development, design quality and other key management and quality approaches presented throughout this book. Leadership, organization and culture all play a role in the effectiveness of the development team. The ability of a firm to innovate quickly and to provide exceptional customer value are directly related to the effectiveness of the firm's product development process. Cycle time, both in terms of how quickly a firm can bring innovations to market and how effectively it can manufacture those products, are the result of a competitive process for developing new products. Process management and principles often can be used to not only improve the manufacture of the product itself, but also of the product development process.

References

Dertouzos, Michael L., et al. and the MIT Commission on Industrial Productivity (1989), Made in America – Regaining the Productive Edge, The MIT Press, Cambridge, MA.

Donaldson, Eric (1993), Notes from Lecture to ME 553, Development of Superior Products and Processes, at the University of Tennessee, Knoxville, Spring Semester 1993.

National Research Council (1991), Improving Engineering Design: Designing for Competitive Advantage, Washington, DC.

Pugh, Stuart (1991), *Total Design: Integrated Methods for Successful Product Engineering.* Workingham: Addison-Wesley.

Stahl, Michael J. and Greg M. Bounds, eds. (1991), *Competing Globally Through Customer Value: The Management of Strategic Suprasystems.* New York: Quorum Books.

Wilson, Clement C., Michael E. Kennedy, and Carmen J. Trammell (1996), *Superior Product Development: Managing the Process for Innovative Products.* Cambridge, MA.: Blackwell Publishers.

Wilson, Clement C. (1979), "A New Fuser Technology for Electro-photographic Printing Machines", *Journal of Applied Photographic Engineering*, Summer 1979, 148–56.

Wilson, Clement C. and Kunlé Harrison (1993), "Comparing Configurations of Complex Machines Using the Map of Mechanical Connections", Proceedings of International Conference on Engineering Design (ICED) 93 (Vol. 1), The Hague (Netherlands), August 1993, 83–92.

"First find your bench," *The Economist*, London, England, May 11, 1991, p. 72.

10 | Product Development Speed and Quality: A New Set of Synergies?

Barbara B. Flynn, E. James Flynn, Susan D. Amundson, and Roger G. Schroeder

Abstract

This chapter proposes that there is a common foundation for both quality and product development speed. It further proposes that this foundation is at the level of organizational culture, in the form of a set of core quality values. An overview of the rationale for combining product development speed with quality, in order to achieve competitive advantage, is provided, as well as a brief discussion of some of the key practices associated with fast product development. Eight detailed case studies of fast and typical product development speed projects are presented, and examples of the core quality values are highlighted within them. It is concluded that there is a substantial degree of overlap between fast product innovation and quality, at the level of organizational culture.

INTRODUCTION

As product development speed increases in importance as a competitive priority, its compatibility with quality comes into question. Conventional wisdom has held that fast product development and high quality represented tradeoffs; increasing the speed of a new product to market necessarily implied taking some shortcuts in terms of quality. However, recent evidence suggests that development speed may be improved through the use of many of the approaches associated with quality management. This suggests that there may be a common set of values which provides the foundation for both quality and fast product development.

This chapter seeks to lay the foundation for study of this important issue. It proposes that a set of core quality values underlies the seemingly disparate approaches to quality management, and that these same values may also provide a foundation for reducing product development speed. Establishment of an organizational culture which is strong in these values should lead to synergies between quality performance and product development speed.

The strategic role of fast product development and strategies used to achieve fast product development will be briefly discussed. Next, a set of core quality management values that have been extracted from the literature will be proposed. These core values embody the essential elements of quality management that underlie many different styles and modes of quality management implementation. Eight in-depth case studies comprised of fast and typical speed product development projects will be presented, extracting from each case a number of lessons learned about fast product development, quality, and their interrelationships. Lastly, key findings that appear generalizable across cases will be presented, discussed in terms of their relationship to quality management.

FAST PRODUCT DEVELOPMENT

Although the practices associated with quality management are well known, research into product development speed is in its infancy. This section provides a brief overview the rationale for fast product development, along with associated practices.

Strategic role of fast product development

Fast product development has the potential for being a powerful competitive weapon. This is particularly critical as more organizations use quality as their primary source of competitive advantage. Thus, the combination of fast product development with quality may offer organizations a unique competitive approach.

Hayes, Wheelwright and Clark (1988) suggest that there are five key dimensions of competitive differentiation: low cost, high quality, dependability, flexibility and innovativeness. Fast product development represents a new competitive priority, which creates a competitive advantage by surprising rival firms with modifications to existing products or by the introduction of new products (Maskill 1991).

When a firm introduces a new or modified product more quickly than a competitor, the competitor is faced with two alternatives, both undesirable (Stalk and Hout 1990). On the one hand, the rival firm can proceed as planned, introducing an innovation to meet a market need which no longer exists. Alternatively, the competitor can stop its development effort and redirect it, causing further delays and risking exposure to additional market and competitive change.

Fast product development offers the innovator potential for a competitive advantage on several fronts, described by Clark and Wheelwright (1993). If an organization is able to develop a new product in, say, six months less time than its competitors, it is faced with several desirable alternatives. First, it can start development efforts at the same time as its competitors and gain a market advantage by releasing the new product to the market six months sooner. Second, it can delay development efforts by six months, in order to obtain more information about market developments, customer requirements and critical technologies. Although it will then release the new product concurrent with its competitors, the product should be more closely aligned with the customers' current needs and may include significant technological advances. Finally, the innovator may use the additional resources freed up by the shortened development time to develop additional new products, during the same time frame.

Strategies for achieving fast product development

There are a number of strategies which are commonly associated with fast product development. They may be grouped into practices which are related to product design (concurrent engineering) and those which are concerned with minimizing ramp-up to full production (design for manufacturability). Each is discussed below.

Concurrent engineering. Design speed is enhanced through concurrent engineering, whereby a design partnership is formed between diverse parties internal and external to the organization. There are several key elements of concurrent engineering. Fast product innovators strive to eliminate the *throw it over the wall* phenomenon, where designers work in isolation from manufacturing, leading to designs which are difficult to manufacture (Garwood and Bane 1990).

The concept of *design without delay* seeks to shorten lead times by taking out all unnecessary delays and developing product specifications which are right for both the customer and the producer (Schonberger 1986). Tools, such as quality function deployment, help in achieving design without delay, through translating the "voice of the customer" into detailed technical requirements, prioritized with competitive data.

Competitive analysis involves purchasing and trying competitors' products and surveying competitors' customers (Schonberger 1990). It may also include activity in trade associations and specialty groups, hiring knowledgeable people from outside firms and benchmarking competitors' rates of improvement.

Concurrent engineering relies on the use of *overlapping product development stages*, rather than the sequential stages of development approach traditionally used (Takeuchi and Nonaka 1986). The traditional approach is analogous to a relay race, where each stage is specialized and isolated, passing the baton to the next stage upon completion. In contrast, the overlapping stages approach is analogous to a rugby game, where the team tries to go the distance as a unit, passing the ball back and forth.

Design for manufacturability. The ease of manufacture of a product design can be enhanced through a number of practices. *Reducing the number of parts* makes manufacturing simpler and products more reliable (Schonberger 1986). *Modular designs* minimize the disruptive effects of product line-flexibility (Hartley 1992). Each module is designed to be a "vanilla" design, which can be mixed to satisfy a variety of customers through the quick and easy addition of snap-on, bolt-on and plug-in modifications.

Design for manufacturability includes the *avoidance of overspecification*, focusing on loose tolerances tightly enforced, rather than tight tolerances loosely enforced (Hartley 1992). CAD systems allows designs to be tapped by designers located at plants in different cities, permitting the use of company-standard parts, which are proven parts, rather than constantly inventing new parts, helping to reduce time to market.

QUALITY MANAGEMENT

Quality foundation for fast product development

Ferdows and DeMeyer (1990) have suggested that quality performance forms the foundation for the development of lasting manufacturing capabilities. Other strategies, such as speed, dependability and cost efficiency may be used to achieve a competitive advantage at a given point in time, however, quality improvement is the base which supports these initiatives. Many manufacturers have rushed to market with a new product, only to find that quality considerations had not been fully developed and that they were unprepared for high volume production. Thus, it is suggested that the effective implementation of fast product development can only be achieved in the context of quality management (Hayes, Wheelwright, and Clark 1988; Wheelwright and Clark 1992; Clark and Fujimoto 1991; Takeuchi and Nonaka 1986).

Applying the concept of organizational culture helps articulate the commonalities between the many approaches to quality management by focusing at the level of values, rather than at the level of specific practices, tools, or behaviors. Thus, although there are numerous approaches to quality management, this chapter proposes that there is a common value system which forms the foundation of the many diverse sets of practices associated with quality management. The culture of an organization is defined as:

> A pattern of shared basic assumptions that the group learned as it solved its problems . . . , that has worked well enough to be considered valid and, therefore, to be taught to new members as the correct way to perceive, think and feel in relation to those problems. (Schein 1992, p. 12)

It is the contention of this chapter that the implementation of quality management practices directs an organization's culture towards a common set of values and underlying assumptions, a position similar to Juran (1986), who suggests that management should work within the present culture to achieve quality improvement.

Quality management values

According to Rokeach (1973, p. 5), a value is defined as "an enduring belief that a specific mode of conduct or end-state of existence is . . . preferable to an opposite or converse mode of conduct or end-state of existence." Thus, quality management values are those beliefs that hold that certain quality end-states are preferred to the opposite; i.e., processes in control are preferred to out-of-control processes. While actual behavior may not be consistent with the values that are stated and genuinely held, this does not negate the fact that values are used to set goals and objectives and to guide behaviors that certain quality end-states are preferred to the opposite; i.e., processes in control are preferred to out-of control processes.

Although the Malcolm Baldrige National Quality Award criteria are based on a set of seven widely publicized "core values," many of these are not truly values, according to Rokeach's perspective. For example, "Leadership" does not imply an opposite mode of conduct or end-state of existence. Like many of the other MBNQA "values" it is actually a set of practices, rather than a value.

A comparative analysis of the literature, including the writings of the quality "gurus" (Crosby 1979; Deming 1982, 1986; Juran 1964, 1986), the Malcolm Baldridge Award Criteria (1997) and academic literature related to quality management (for example, Anderson, Rungtusanatham and Schroeder 1994; Dean and Bowen 1994; Dean and Snell 1991; Flynn, Sakakibara and Schroeder 1995; Saraph, Benson and Schroeder 1989), led to the extraction of nine values which underlie the various approaches to quality management (Amundson, Flynn, Rungtusanatham, and Schroeder 1997). They are stated below, in the form of what a quality-oriented organization "should" do or be like.

The first value, *Long-Term Orientation*, states that organizations should plan for the long-run, as opposed to focusing on short-term results. Anticipating and planning to meet the evolving expectations of customers can help an organization adapt to and survive in a changing external environment. Thus, the maximization of short-term performance may not necessarily result in maximization of long-term performance.

Continuous Improvement and Learning refers to perpetual advancement and refinement of all products and processes. This value implies that improvement of a product or process is never complete; there is always opportunity for further incremental improvement. Through continuous improvement, an organization is able to establish a moving performance target, which is difficult for competitors to attack.

The third quality management value is *Cooperation*. This value suggests that cooperative relationships will lead to better performance than adversarial relationships, and that the need for cooperative relationships extends to both employees and external partners, such as suppliers and customers.

Quality management approaches are built on the belief that people are inherently good (*Human Goodness*) and want to help the organization achieve its long-term goals and objectives. The fundamental goodness of people can be nurtured through training. This value refers to people who are employees of the organization, as well as those who are employees of customer and supplier organizations.

Customer Focus urges organizations to continually strive towards satisfying or exceeding customers' expectations. Thus, it implies that organizations

---

should be proactive in anticipating customer needs, and that customers are the best judge of their needs and wants.

Fact-Based Management refers to the use of objective data and the scientific method as the basis for decision making, rather than intuition, rules-of-thumb, tradition, opinion, or dogma. It implies that employees will make better decisions if they are trained in data gathering and analysis tools, such statistical process control, design of experiments, and cause-and-effect diagrams.

Process Emphasis refers to the extent to which organizations measure, manage, and hold processes accountable. Organizations are challenged to adopt the perspective of the process as the primary source of error and variation, rather than the people performing the process; as a result, the process is the primary opportunity for improvement.

Prevention prescribes that an organization should prevent errors and defects upstream in the process through designing quality in, rather than repairing or reworking defective products or services. Crosby (1979) indicates that it is always less expensive to produce only good product rather than some percentage defective, a position in conflict with the traditional "Cost of Quality" models which juxtapose quality prevention and inspection costs to find the optimal minimum cost of quality.

The last value identified is an *Organization-Wide Approach* to the implementation of quality management. Quality management should be the responsibility of everyone in the organization, and the quality department should take on coaching efforts, teaching people how to implement quality management in their own area of responsibility. This is in contrast with the traditional, technical-specialty approach to quality management, where the implementation of quality management efforts was considered the sole responsibility of the quality department.

CASE STUDIES

In order to better articulate the relationship between quality management and fast product development, a set of case studies was developed. Eight new product development projects, associated with large, well-known firms in the US electronics industry were visited. During each visit, a set of interviews and focus groups was conducted with members of the development team, as well as various levels of management and product development support functions, including quality and procurement. Each site was toured and a number of documents made available by the organizations were examined.

The case studies are briefly summarized below. The names of the organizations are disguised, and the cases are identified by product name only. They are divided into the projects which were identified by their organizations as much faster than the organization's "typical" projects, and those which could be considered more typical in their development speed. The core quality values which were most salient to each project are indicated in italics. Table 10.1 provides a brief summary of this information.

Table 10.1 Case summary

Project	Development speed	Quality level	Key values
Mainframe Computer	Fast	High	Customer focus Process emphasis Cooperation Organization-wide approach Human goodness Fact-based management Long-term orientation Prevention
Navigational Device	Fast	High	Cooperation Fact-based management Process emphasis Prevention Continuous improvement and Learning Organization-wide approach
Medical Device	Fast	High	Long-term orientation Customer focus Cooperation
Electronic Sensor	Fast	High	Long-term orientation Customer focus Cooperation Process emphasis Organization-wide approach Continuous improvement and learning Human goodness
Electronic Guide	Typical	High	Cooperation Fact-based management Prevention Long-term orientation Process emphasis
Software Product	Typical	High	Process emphasis Long-term orientation Human goodness Organization-wide approach Customer focus
Implantable Device Component	Typical	High	Process emphasis Cooperation (problems) Organization-wide approach Continuous improvement and learning (problems) Human goodness (problems)
Network Data Processor	Typical	High	Process emphasis Cooperation (problems)

"Fast" product development projects

Mainframe computer

This product was a small mainframe computer, designed to fill a niche between PC's/minicomputers and large mainframe computers. It also filled a technological niche by building upon existing architecture, and was seen as a bridge to the next generation of computer technology, through adding CMOS technology and SCSI peripherals to its existing product features (*long-term orientation*). What enabled this computer to be seen as a small mainframe was that it reduced the number of chips needed by 90 percent (from 197 to 18), while maintaining the same capacity as mainframe computers. In general, the market is very competitive at the top end, and it is a global market, with one-third of its sales in Europe. The product was the top priority of this division.

The organization had a formal customer advisory board (*customer focus*). This board was consulted regularly during the project initiation and development process. The development process was a phased process (*process emphasis*). The review at the end of Phase I was considered a major threshold, because it served as the firm's commitment to fund the project. Thus, the review was part of its business process. The transitions between stages were evolutionary, with the next stage starting long before signoffs. The formal exit from a stage was seen as the firm's commitment to complete the next stage. Review books were put on-line during the project, and all reviews are now on-line. When the project was completed, there was an in-depth review of the process, with suggestions for improvement in subsequent projects.

The project team was a cross-functional dedicated team. Many of the team members had worked together before. Twelve teams, in various functions, made up the project. Typically, there were four members per subteam, with leadership rotating among the members. The program manager had 15 project managers who reported to him.

Weekly progress reviews were held by the entire team. They became, by intent, sessions where only problems and delays were discussed, rather than going over subteam progress reports each week. Their focus was on how the entire team could provide resources and expertise to overcome any difficulties which had been encountered. It was a "no-blame" atmosphere (*process emphasis*). In addition to the weekly reviews, mileposts and progress were noted in the Microsoft Project notebook. Notes could be posted for all parties to read and respond to, between meetings, or prepare a response for the next weekly meeting.

In addition to being the top priority project in the division, the project enjoyed immense support from the organization. Rewards were based on meeting the schedule, performance standards and cost. Additional resources were made available, when required, to help the project meet its schedule. The facility's matrix structure supported the project's team approach.

The firm had very strong relationships with the project's suppliers (*cooperation*). These relationships were formalized early in the project's life, and they were seen as key strategic tools in the success of the project. For example, a major supplier was involved early, sharing its CMOS technology.

The quality system of the organization was extensive (*organization-wide approach*). At the corporate level, each division competed for an internally sponsored quality award, which is modeled after the Malcolm Baldrige National Quality Award. In addition, the division was ISO 9000 certified. This emphasis on a comprehensive quality system was seen in the project, as well. From its initiation, it was driven by the theme, "The customer comes first," with all actions directed towards satisfying customer needs (*customer focus*). In satisfying these needs, a zero-defect standard was enforced. The project's orientation was problem solving, from the project's mission of serving customer needs to addressing problems encountered during the project. Each part of the project team fully recognized that success was only defined at the project level. In addition, the project was managed with a "no blame" approach to problems (*human goodness*).

Decisions made throughout the project were fact-based, using data generated in the extensive record system discussed above (*fact-based management*). This information system also supported use of quality management tools throughout the project.

This project provided several characteristics which may prove to be significant factors which contributed to its success.

1   The project was the sole responsibility of the team members, rather than splitting their time and efforts between multiple projects.
2   The team members had a history of working together on an earlier project. This allowed members to focus on the technical aspects of their assignments.
3   The team was managed with the superordinate themes of customer focus and an "all-of-one" orientation, which resulted in the energies of the team being directed at solving problems, rather than assigning blame.
4   Centering the reward system on performance in satisfying the project's objective helped provide a strong focus for the project.
5   There were clear statements of the project's objective, as well as how each group contributed to the team's success (*prevention*).
6   The project was a merger of the firm's capabilities with those of its suppliers, bringing multiple capabilities, expertise and technological advances to the project.
7   The project benefited from the organization's willingness to provide the resources it needed to meet its objectives.
8   The project had a strong champion, who played the dual role of cheerleader and resource acquirer. He was able to ensure the project had the necessary resources and that people with appropriate skills and knowledge could address satisfying the project's objectives.

Navigational device

This organization undertook a special effort to obtain a new development program being awarded by the US Department of Defense (DoD), where a new generation of a product was being funded. The navigational device is used on an offensive aircraft, and helps the pilot to "see" under special conditions. This was a new generation of a product, incorporating new technologies and far superior capabilities to the existing product. The organization had been one of the primary providers of the old generation of the product. Technologically, the new product bore almost no resemblance to the older product, having gone from almost 12,000 parts to about 8,000 parts.

This development project was awarded as a result of the traditional RFP process. The prime contractor and the DoD were involved in administering the proposal competition and providing feedback to the various competitors. The organization had spent a great deal of time during the two years prior to contract award developing parts of the new generation of the navigational device. They had worked extensively with the DoD to try to influence the DoD's specifications (*cooperation*). They showed the DoD new features that they had developed, trying to persuade the DoD to incorporate the organization's developments into the specifications. They also worked extensively with the prime contractor. The new technology was based on proprietary designs, as opposed to the older technology, which had greater ability to interface with other vendors' products. Competition for this particular project was fierce, with over a dozen responses to the RFP process.

After receiving word that it had been awarded the contract, but before the actual award date, the organization collocated over 100 people and started them on the project. The organization was willing to provide advance funding for development time and also for supplier's prototypes, which enabled significant reductions in development time. The project team was organized with a core team and over 18 subteams, and the number of full time people on the project at its peak was over 100. The project team functioned very well, but was not without difficulties. One subteam, in particular, encountered relationship difficulties, which resulted in a small delay for the project. According to one subteam leader, this was the first project in which people had really worked together as a team, rather than working on individual, independent assignments in a group setting.

The project team leadership split the administrative and technical aspects of the project between the program manager and the systems engineer. The systems engineer was viewed as having had a particularly critical effect on project time and quality, because his vast technical expertise reduced the need to redesign component parts.

The organization made extensive use of simulation and rapid prototyping (*fact-based management*). Prototype testing equipment was used, so that at least partial information was available at the earliest time possible. Design and test engineers worked three shifts during time periods when interactive cycles between design and testing were on the critical path. Designers would work on the prototype units during first and second shifts, and the test engineer would run tests overnight. The organization used a flexible system for project planning and control, where the project team selected those tasks to be tracked from among several thousand possible tasks (*process emphasis*). Only the tasks selected early in the project were tracked and managed, and other tasks were either not done or received informal attention.

Manufacturability was given special attention in this project from the beginning. The organization felt that it had been weak in the area of design-to-manufacturing transitions in the past, and resolved to improve that aspect of this project (*prevention*). An engineer was assigned responsibilities for manufacturability six months before contract award, and he and his staff were credited with superior manufacturability performance on this project. The manufacturability engineer and his staff selected standardized parts and encouraged design engineers to reuse parts whenever possible. They also took on simple mechanical design tasks, such as connectors and other relatively standardized parts, which were parts that were important for manufacturability goals and tended to be aspects of the design less interesting to design engineers.

Design software that promised the generation of assembly drawings was used. Unfortunately, the drawings were not appropriate for military specifications, and the use of this particular design software generated many problems for the project team. The design software was new, but the team believed that using the software generated a better result than if they had not used the software (*continuous improvement and learning*). The software did not, however, work as promised, and a great deal of time was spent working with the software to make it produce what was required. An additional software tool used on this project was a public database used by engineers to post drawings and design information. All engineers would update the data base at least weekly, and the manufacturability, purchasing, and other concerned parties would review all postings every week. This enabled correct, current information to be shared widely, expediting problem identification and problem solving (*process emphasis*).

The organization had a very strong quality system in place, and had a reputation for excellence in the area of quality management (*organization-wide approach*). It had implemented a design analysis program, which aided in examining the design process and estimating the expected number of problems in a design. The organization's quality system was quite mature, and it had been used as the base for additional efforts aimed at development time reduction and profitability.

Software development on this project was extraordinarily successful. Software developers were 4 to 5 times more productive than was typical for this company. Upon initially being involved in the project, the software lead engineer determined that it would be impossible to complete the software development life cycle within the one-year time frame allotted for this project. Therefore, he eliminated all tasks to be done except for those that were absolutely necessary, eliminated all paper generation and insisted that all reviews be on-line, and created standardized processes by which all designers were to work (*process emphasis*). Also, many formal approvals for software changes were eliminated, and software engineers incorporated changes based on their interactions with others on the development team. The software was integrated with the hardware much earlier than usual, and the simulator was also helpful in saving time.

Engineering quality testing contributed to reductions in development time and improvements in quality by pursuing a strategy of buying more test equipment from outside, rather than building it. The purchased equipment was quicker to obtain and more reliable.

Total development time for this project was 11 months, for what would normally have been a 3 to 5 year effort. The insights learned from this project that contributed to such substantial development time reductions and quality performance include:

1   Marketing efforts were important in defining realistic and manufacturable specifications.
2   The role of off-line development efforts.
3   The role of advance funding, given appropriate justification.
4   Around-the-clock design and testing cycles, purchased test equipment, standardized software development procedures, manufacturability efforts, and management support all contributed to the development of a product that was both very high in quality and very fast to develop.

Medical device

This organization produces a medical device designed to save lives. This project was aimed at producing a line of this medical device at a lower cost than previously, in order to compete in an increasingly price sensitive global market (*long-term orientation*). The emphasis was on a modification of an existing product design that could then be economically produced by a new, highly automated manufacturing process. The existing product was already a market leader, due to its advanced product technology. By improving the manufacturing process, it was believed that the company could gain considerable cost advantages over its competitors. Production was planned for a remote site, away from the design team and corporate headquarters. This separation caused considerable difficulty, since the organization had never done this before.

The product development process consisted of five phases: business analysis, commitment, development, clinical trials and product introduction. Because of the medical nature of the product, the organization required strict adherence to the phase development process and management signoffs at the end of each phase (*process emphasis*). Considerable overlap between phases was used as a way of reducing the total development time. Management's objective was that the normal planned development time for this type of product be cut in half.

Part way through the development process, it was decided that a more competitive product could be developed by adding new features, in addition to lowering cost. The product development team was convinced that this was a "smart" move and convinced upper management. As a result of the changes, the product went back through the business analysis and commitment phase a second time and the schedule was extended slightly to accommodate the new product features.

The product development process used a team approach. There was a core team, consisting of twelve people, who were assigned full-time to the project. These people represented all of the critical design skills. In addition, engineers were assigned part-time, as needed, for specific design tasks. Altogether, two hundred people were involved in the project at some time during its development.

The team consisted of a mix of experienced and new people. It was very helpful that certain key individuals who had worked together before and were familiar with this particular product were assigned to the core team. Their familiarly helped to speed up the development process and improved the teamwork and coordination.

In addition to the core team, there was also a team located at the remote production site. This team consisted of manufacturing engineers and technicians who helped design and build the new production line. It was critical that the remote team and the core team work closely together. However, this was not always the case, due to the long distances involved and the lack of familiarly between teams.

The project leader was a very strong manager, who was able to work well with everyone on the team and with upper management, when additional resources or support were needed. The leader was very dedicated to bringing the project in on schedule. When problems arose, it was the leader's responsibility to help the team find a solution within the existing time schedule.

The customers for this product were doctors and, ultimately, patients. A panel of doctors was used to gain input into product design (*customer focus*). Physician input and evaluation was also obtained during the clinical trials for the product.

There were several critical suppliers, who were involved with the design team, in a partnership (*cooperation*). They developed several designs for components in parallel, in order to help protect the project schedule. While this involved some additional cost, it saved time when the final design was selected.

Risk was managed in this project in several ways. First, no risk was taken on the quality of the product in terms of its performance, reliability, durability, etc. It was part of the company culture to never take risks when lives were at stake. Downstream development was also started before upstream development was completed. While this practice elevated the risk that some redesign might be needed, downstream engineers found they could suggest upstream design changes before the design was frozen. In order to meet such an aggressive development schedule in half the normal time, things were done differently. This required considerable leadership from the project manager to convince people that the new way was a better way.

Quality was ingrained into the organization's culture. It had a customer-focused quality program and had historically valued quality as a corporate value. The importance of quality became a corporate value early in the company's history, when a product recall resulted in considerable loss of market share and severe financial problems. This failure and the concern for human life have made quality critical.

As a result of this fast product development project several lessons were learned:

1   The product description can be changed during development without sacrificing the schedule. This is contrary to conventional wisdom, which holds that product specifications should be "frozen" during the development process. All proposed product changes were subject to review, and those that could be incorporated without causing project completion delays were included. Those that would cause delays were held off for future product generations (*long-term orientation*). Incorporating these changes resulted in a superior product at low cost, providing the company with a one-two punch in the market place.

2   Downstream functions can start earlier. It is not always necessary, or desirable, to complete upstream development first.

3   It was necessary to challenge the organization's norms to speed up product development. This involved managing risk in a different way than before.

4   A corporate quality culture helps save time, by not having to do things over.

5   Quality is a multi-dimensional construct. While product performance and reliability may not be sacrificed for speed, some product features may be delayed until future product generations.

6   A capable project manager is the key to reducing time. Good human relations skills, technical knowledge, and project management experience are essential.

7   Fast projects can create stress on the project team, with team members asked to work overtime and put in extra effort to protect the project schedule. As a result, some team members experienced job stress from this project.

Electronic sensor

This product was a new venture for the organization, which was well-established in the electronics business. It is an electronic sensor, designed to be a component in a household appliance. It has the potential to revolutionize the market for the household appliance. Concurrent with the development of the sensor, it was known that a major competitor for the household appliance was developing a sensor with similar capabilities; thus, timely development of the sensor was critical.

The electronics firm had a long history in the controls industry and was interested in pursuing new directions, particularly with sensors (*long-term orientation*). Although it knew that it had both the technology and knowledge to develop a variety of sensors, it had little experience or interest in developing the end products in which they ultimately would be used. It solved this problem by contacting several manufacturers of household appliances and other applications, presenting its abilities and potential for developing sensors, and soliciting ideas. The customer ultimately chosen had wanted to create a high-end product, while meeting pending energy efficiency requirements; the sensor provided the customer with the ability to meet both goals (*customer focus*). Thus, this sensor represented a "win–win" opportunity for both organizations. The electronics firm was able to demonstrate its ability to work with cutting-edge technology and break into a new product line, while the household appliance company was able to achieve a competitive advantage in the high end of its market, as well as be proactive about impending government requirements.

In fully developing the sensor, the electronics firm worked together with the household appliance manufacturer on a dedicated team, which worked only on this project (*cooperation*). It began meeting with only a handshake between the parties involved, although the final legal agreement eventually took eight months to be developed to the satisfaction of both parties. The product team contained three distinct groups: members from corporate research and development, members from the division core team and members from the household appliance manufacturer. The team was so tightly integrated that, when a joint presentation was made to the household appliance manufacturer's vice presidents, they couldn't tell which members of the team were from which organization. The organizations described this relationship as a "co-destiny" relationship, which they defined as, "Two companies acting as one, using their combined knowledge to create responsive solutions that meet our customers' needs."

The product development process contained four phases, with a template of suggested activities for each of the phases (*process emphasis*). Suggested activities were viewed strictly as guidelines, rather than requirements. There was considerable overlap between the phases; team members described the phases has having a broad gray zone between them. Because of the formal review at the end of the stage, the team members felt that it was easier to discern the end of each stage. However, the team was often well into the following stage when the formal end of the previous stage occurred.

This organization was strongly committed to the implementation of quality management. It had received a site visit score of over 700 on the Malcolm Baldrige National Quality Award (*organization-wide approach*). The quality thrust was focused on the results of a customer survey which asked customers about quality, product performance and responsiveness. The organization scored well, relative to competitors, on all three dimensions; however, they selected responsiveness as the focus of their initiative because of its somewhat lower score relative to what customers wanted.

The environment in which the development team operated exemplified *continuous improvement and learning*. Team members described it as a blame-free environment, where they were not afraid of making mistakes. Although they worked through some difficult challenges, they described the bonding and learning which occurred, as a result. They felt that similar learning occurred from working cross-functionally. The team leader was described as having a "can-do" attitude, prone to statements like "Let's see what we can do to make that work" (*human goodness*).

There were several key themes which emerged from this project.

1   There was an extremely strong partnership with the customer, to the point where the home organization of the team members was sometimes difficult to determine. This led to a number of benefits in terms of development speed, including the availability of two sets of resources for solving problems and excellent knowledge of the details of the customer's needs.

2   The blame-free environment encouraged the sort of experimentation which was key to this product, which represented a totally new and untested concept.

3   The end-date for the project was non-negotiable. The team was willing to do whatever needed to be done, in order to meet the end-date, including adding resources where needed and working a tremendous amount of overtime, as needed.

4   The team was dedicated to working solely on this project alone. This permitted them to focus their complete attention on the project and eliminated time conflicts with other responsibilities.

The uniqueness of this project and the organization of the team led to the members having a perception of being "special."

Products with "typical" development time

Electronic guide

A defense division of an electronics company undertook a new development program for the US Department of Defense (DoD), called "electronic guide," which is part of an offensive aircraft's navigational system. This product included stringent specifications, due to the nature of the stressful military environment in which it would be used: no moving parts, specified size, shape, and weight, and very high reliability and durability. The development program was subject to a strict DoD-imposed project management system involving multiple steps and milestones, and included coordination between the US military, a prime contractor, and suppliers.

The division made a strong effort to win the project. Not only were significant division resources dedicated to creation of the proposal, but substantial coordination with the prime contractor and the military was required (*cooperation*). The organization participated in a process in which eight companies were initially selected to compete for the project. The selection process included several phases; at the close of each phase, half of the organizations were eliminated from the competition. Both of the final two competitors worked extensively with the prime contractor and the DoD for about three months, finalizing performance and design specifications and detailing what the product would look like, including unit production cost, a proposed bill of materials, and schedule. The result was a relatively small 40 page proposal, which team members indicated was far superior to previous very large proposals, because it contained only meaningful information. Specifications, costs, and schedules in the proposal were realistic, which reduced the need for discussion of contingent conditions in the proposal (*fact-based management*). For example, the unit production cost and bill of materials in the proposal were later shown to be accurate within 2 percent.

The project used a collocated, tightly integrated team. It worked behind closed doors at their company site, and used a dedicated conference room at the prime contractor's site. The team included representatives from manufacturing, quality testing, and design, with other functional areas contributing on an as-needed basis.

Team members reported that typical relationships between functional areas were changed in the team environment. In particular, the engineering quality testing function no longer engaged in the role of "policeman," where their position was "It can't be done until I sign off on it." Rather, engineering quality worked cooperatively with the designers to create appropriate tests and to help create designs that would meet testing requirements (*prevention*). The proposal development process was much faster than was typically the case, resulting in far fewer design changes later in the process.

After submitting the proposal, several months elapsed before the organization learned that it had won the contract. During that time, a number of the team members left the team, but some remained with the project, providing valued continuity. This proposal had been considered a "must-win" proposal for the organization, and the best resources were provided. Also, the organization's performance had not been exemplary with this particular prime contractor, in the past, and efforts were made to improve relationships with the prime contractor, which could be critical to future business (*long-term orientation*). To address the problem with reputation, the organization's management team visited the prime contractor's management team and committed themselves to improve their performance. In addition, the organization worked with its critical suppliers prior to submitting the proposal, obtaining their agreement on crucial issues.

Initially, the project manager had six project teams reporting to him, and felt that this impeded project progress. Later, a dedicated leader was selected for the team. For many members, this project provided the first experience with a true cross-functional project team, and the initial tendency of team members was to interact using their "old" roles. For example, the design engineers tended to dominate the decisions, with the manufacturing representatives less assertive about providing manufacturability input into the design process. Because the traditional role of manufacturing had been to take the design provided and work to build it, encouragement was required to change old patterns of communication, power, and influence.

The project was a high priority (*long-term orientation*). The electronic guide was part of one of the few aircraft for which significant production remained, and the technology used in the product was part of the organization's core competency. Progress was reviewed twice weekly by the general manager and a vice president; the reporting relationships skipped a layer so that reporting was direct to the top management team.

In working on proposal preparation and development, the military made a strong effort to eliminate rules and regulations that added time and cost and were non-value-added (*process emphasis*). According to team members, every MIL Spec was violated, but not FARS and DARS (more specific legal and accounting requirements that the military uses for projects).

This division was not one with a particularly strong quality system. A Baldrige self-assessment performed one year prior to the development effort had scored the division at about 200 out of a possible 1000 points. Quality systems in the division were traditional in some respects, since the division developed and manufactured products for the military, and the quality systems were oriented towards meeting those requirements. In this particular situation, the division seemed to be able to achieve very significant product development time reductions independent of the level of excellence of the quality system.

During the project, the team used very high level project planning systems, involving little detail. The critical dates for the team were customer driven reviews, and peer reviews were used periodically to keep the project on schedule and to assure that the team members were on the right track (*process emphasis*). Predefined phases overlapped substantially, even in those situations when the military project planning system specified that a new phase could not be started until the prior phase was completed.

Simulation was used extensively during the project for testing (*fact-based management*). New simulation software was used, and team members learned the new simulation software along with performing their testing tasks. Simulation software vendor representatives were at the organization's site, as needed, which greatly reduced product development time. The team members also agreed that there was further potential for significant development time reduction through better use of simulation. Team members were unable to simulate all aspects of the hardware, but they believed that they could have simulated the existing hardware more accurately and thereby generated more accurate test results, saving time during the hardware-software integration phase.

Development time for a project of this type would have been estimated to be about 48 months using normal business practices if the project had been undertaken several years ago. However, the time has now been compressed into 18 months, and the industry is moving towards a 12-month development time on projects of this type.

This development project provided several insights into rapid new product development and quality.

1   Quality was never compromised during the project, regardless of development time. High quality was expected, and the project was not considered completed until the high quality standards embodied in the specifications were met.
2   The nature of the relationship between the organization, the prime contractor, the military, and suppliers highlights the importance of cross-organizational cooperation in speeding product development time and also improving quality.
3   The process of negotiating specifications on the front end of the product created a clear definition of the project for the development team. As a result, fewer changes to the contract were made after development had begun.
4   The utilization of tools, in this case simulation, for testing, has improved quality while reducing development time.
5   The organization's quality system seemed to be relatively independent of product development time. Product quality was very high and development time was accelerated, but the quality system within the division was not outstanding relative to peers and competitors. This result suggests that it is possible to reduce product development time substantially without having a premier quality system in place.

Software product

This product was a new software product, aimed a assisting electronic circuit designers in developing new chips. These design kits were provided to customers by all chip suppliers in the industry, in the hope that increased sales of their chips would occur. All of the technology to construct this product was already available in the company, but there were some design challenges to be met. The organization was already late entering the market with its design kit, so time was of the essence.

The development process placed a strong emphasis on schedule. The organization used a "bulls-eye" system for scheduling. This system required that the project team identify the completion date (the bulls-eye) and then report each week to upper management whether they were ahead of schedule or behind schedule relative to it (*process emphasis*). The bulls-eye was constructed using bottom-up planning, so that a great deal of information and commitment were obtained from the engineers and technicians during the planning process.

The development process was well integrated with the division's strategic planning. This resulted in priority setting for allocating resources among the various projects (*long-term emphasis*). As a result, projects which needed resources and were high priority received the resources needed to achieve their schedule.

The company was very strong in using teams for business purposes and provided a great deal of team training (*human goodness*). This project had a core team of ten collocated people. During the peak, as many as 100 people were assigned to the project.

Resources were generally available to support the project. The schedule was always considered the top priority and managed to the bulls-eye objective. Quality was defined by the product development document established in the beginning of the project and was never sacrificed for schedule.

The division developing this product had a very good quality system, probably at a world class level. This was reflected in the team training, which was highly diffused in the division, a strong level of strategic planning, and the disciplined planning and control practices which were used (*organization-wide approach*).

During the project, the development team maintained close contact with a few key customers (*customer focus*). They felt that it was essential to stabilize the customer specification and not change it during the project. Virtually no outside suppliers were involved in this product development.

There were several keys to success in this project.

1 There was a clear definition of owners of the process (the development team) from the very beginning of the project (*human goodness*). There was a marketing strategy that remained constant and an early definition of project priority. There was a quality system in place, which supported disciplined product development.

2 The product development methodology had some unique attributes. Bottom-up schedule and resource needs were used, resulting in greater commitment and input by the team members. The "bulls-eye" charts, along with weekly program reviews, were effectively used to control the ability to achieve the schedule.

3 Teams were rewarded for their results. The use of group reward systems was very important in establishing effective teamwork on all development projects.

5 This project is a good example of strict project control. There was no question in anyone's mind that the project would be finished on time and meet the quality standards established by the project development document.

6 Cost was viewed as a possible variable, to protect quality and speed objectives. Time reduction was not critical in its own right, but was viewed as meeting the "bulls-eye," once the target was set.

7 This project was typical, in terms of its product development time, but could have been accelerated, had the bulls-eye been set more

aggressively and the priority for resources raised. In other words, the system for fast product development is in place in this organization, if the company needs it for a particular project.

Implantable device component

This product is a component of an implantable medical device, which sells for around $5,000 apiece. Although the component has existed previously in various forms, the current version was made of a new material which offered a number of significant advantages to both the surgeon and the patient. The market is considered highly competitive and time-sensitive; in fact, it was known that both primary competitors were working on similar products.

The development process followed the standard product development protocol used in the organization, which proceeded in a serial fashion (*process emphasis*). One unique feature of this particular component was that it was developed as a "split build" with an organization in France; it was designed so that initial operations would be performed in the US, while final operations and packaging would be performed in France. In addition to offering some efficiencies, this approach helped to gain entrance to the European market.

The development process was fairly lengthy, with several reasons being cited. First, federal Food and Drug Administration (FDA) regulations were described as being "a mystery." The organization had a difficult time determining, in advance, how the FDA would react to certain procedures and even which would ultimately be required (*cooperation* – problem). An error in anticipating FDA requirements could add six months to a year to the schedule. Second, because this was an implantable device, four to five months of animal studies were required. At the time that this product was being developed, there was some difficulty in finding healthy animals of the right age. Finally, a six month dose of Gamma rays was required for products sold in the US, which further delayed introduction.

In terms of quality, this organization was unbending in its stance that quality would not be compromised for anything, including the intended product release date. This was borne out by the evidence; 250,000 of the devices had been implanted with no failures. The organization is ISO 9001 certified and scores in the 500–600 range on an internal assessment similar to the Baldrige assessment (*organization-wide approach*).

For this organization, its relationship with its supplier was critical (*cooperation* – problem). The new component was made of a new and highly beneficial material, which was its distinguishing feature. The supplier had a virtual monopoly in the new material, controlling 85 percent of the worldwide implantable medical device market. Because the buying organization was a relatively small player in the worldwide market for this device, it found that the supplier was not very responsive to its needs, in terms of pricing and scheduling. The supplier also sold to this organization's competitors, frequently on more favorable terms. Clearly, the supplier relationship was far from a partnership.

There were also some difficulties within the product development team. There appeared to be some confusion about responsibilities of team members, particularly early in the project (*human goodness* – problem), as well as debate about whether this project should proceed or not. In addition, most of the members were assigned to multiple projects simultaneously, causing confusion about relative priorities.

The organization felt that there were a number of lessons learned from this project. They believed that it could have been expedited by:

1 Making a faster decision to move forward with this project.
2 Working more synergistically with the FDA.
3 Revising the product development protocol to allow more overlap between stages, as well as more creativity.
4 Learning more from other projects, through systematic study of what went well and what didn't (*continuous improvement and learning* – problems).
5 Employing a dedicated and collocated team, rather than assigning people to several projects, simultaneously.

Network data processor

The purpose of the project was to develop the next generation of an existing network data processor. It was designed to be quieter, easier to use and more reliable than the current version. The project was part of a larger strategy to promote the use of its new mainframe computers.

The market for this type of network data processor was changing, and while this product was designed to set new standards, there was a clear market leader, also developing its own new product, which the organization felt it could only marginally surpass. The market was characterized by segmentation, according to speed of the processor and customer size. The project was initiated and early stages completed, at the end of a major round of layoffs within the division and this facility. Downsizing had been ongoing for the division and facility for several years, with waves of layoffs occurring before and after the visit of the research team.

Project reviews were precipitated by the accomplishment of milestones and hurdles encountered. The project employed many metrics, which were posted in open areas and hallways, making them both public and easy to review (*process emphasis*). Project developments passed through frequent inspection.

The project team had two notable features: project leadership and team membership. During the project's first few months, the project manager also managed two other projects. During this time, the project fell far behind schedule. Roughly nine months into the project, a new leader, with sole assignment to the project, was appointed. Under his leadership, the project progressed very rapidly, and prototype testing was only a few weeks late. Team membership was not particularly large, with 19 in the core team. Team members were also assigned part-time. Assignment to the project was not predetermined; rather, it was done from the pool potentially available, when a particular type of function was needed.

While not managed as a set of independent steps, the transitions were relatively discrete. Once one subteam was ready to hand their part off, it was out of the picture. This was observed during the interviews, where the conversation was not a group conversation, but rather a dyadic conversation between the researcher and the person representing each specific stage. There was little interaction with other members of the project team (*cooperation* – problem).

The project had both strong and weak relationships with buyers and suppliers. For example, some customers were willing to be test sites, letting prototypes of the product replace their current machines. However, there was not a general sentiment reflecting a partnership with other customers. The relationships were cordial, but not intimate (*co-operation* – problems).

Suppliers were initially selected based on their track records. Later, this was changed because of corporate policy, and the relationship with suppliers soured (*cooperation* – problems). This change in corporate policy had the additional effect of segregating the purchasing personnel from the rest of the project team. Suppliers requiring long lead times were identified and contacted early.

The quality management effort followed the corporation's procedures and guidelines. This was noted in the extensive use of metrics, reviews, and their public posting. However, the quality orientation was hindered by the lack of data integration. There was an incompatibility between the production and design systems, which limited the speed and effectiveness of communication.

The project was given consistent priority, but not necessarily the highest priority. In the early stages especially, priority was placed on other projects which needed to be completed.

There were a number of insights from this project.

1 An obvious pair of observations are the need for a full-time project leader and a procedure for assigning people to a project, prior to the time they are needed. Both should have a strong impact on speed and quality.

2 This project indicated the need for a comprehensive infrastructure to support organizational quality management initiatives. There were both corporate and divisional characteristics, including highly centralized purchasing rules and reporting relationships, incompatible data systems and a downsizing environment. These had the unintended consequence of slowing the project down.

3 An external factor worthy of recognition is the constraints a clear market leader may impose. Even though the market wanted increased quality features, noise reduction and a more ergonomic design, the

market leader appeared to create the specifications which those improvements could not exceed.

4   Finally, the nature of the transitions between stages in the project's life is worth noting. This project clearly represented more of an "over the transom" approach, as opposed to a merged or integrated transition.

Conclusions and Generalizations

A number of the practices which distinguished between the fastest and the more typical projects embodied many of the core quality values. Thus, it can be concluded that there is a common foundation for quality management and fast product development. For example, the fastest projects were built on a foundation of *cooperation*, both within the project team and organization, as well as with suppliers and customers. These teams were integrated, with strong cross-functional membership, and provided many examples of close relationships with customers and/or suppliers. In contrast, while the typical speed projects may have had a small number of strong relationships with customers or suppliers, most of their relationships could not be characterized as strong, and in some cases, were adversarial. In addition, the fastest projects were able to overcome the impositions of their external regulating agencies (military organizations or the FDA) through cooperating with them, while the typical speed projects seemed baffled by the external requirements or felt that they provided an excuse for their lack of speed. Finally, several of the typical speed projects opted to divide their product development efforts between two geographically separated locations, leading to logistical problems.

The foundation provided by a belief in *human goodness* is illustrated by the blame-free culture in several of the fastest projects. When problems arose, there was the belief that the team could solve them, although the solution may have not been immediately apparent. Human goodness is also illustrated by the use of team training in some of the fastest projects; this exemplifies the belief that, although team members may not immediately have the necessary skills, they can be developed.

Customer focus was illustrated by the fastest projects drawing on the customers as a source of design ideas, through the use of advisory boards and environmental scanning by the sales force. In contrast, the typical speed projects had a "catch-up" mentality, using competitors' actions as the primary determinant of the features of their new or next-generation product, with a goal of imitation, rather than innovation.

There was a strong emphasis on *fact-based management* evident in the fastest projects, with a substantial amount of testing, simulation runs and rapid prototyping used as the basis for where to proceed next. These projects were also characterized by frequent (often weekly) progress reports to management or the full team. Through the provision of information about the project to management and team members, better decisions could be made by all parties concerned.

The fastest projects put considerable effort into streamlining their procedures, illustrating their *process emphasis*. In this same light, while they followed corporate product development protocol, they were more willing to relax it somewhat, allowing the overlap of stages. In contrast, the typical speed projects tended to follow their corporate product development protocol in a more serial fashion.

Prevention was shown through the initial specifications for the projects. The fastest projects were very clearly defined initially, with the entire team sharing the vision for the project. In contrast, the more typical projects tended to be ill-defined initially, costing valuable time to hammer out their details.

Long-term orientation is reflected in the perspective taken towards planning for product families and technology bases, which serve as the underlying foundation for rapid, high quality product development. When hardware and software technologies are planned across generations of products, the organizations were able to carve out multiple fast product development efforts, allocating risks and problems across projects and to products only after such issues had been solved off-line; that is, off the critical path of the development project. It was the careful planning and problem solving off-line that enabled project managers to very quickly develop high quality products. In addition, the fastest projects had higher levels of resources available to them, while the typical projects had to compete for their resources and perceived that they were more limited. This may have been because the fastest projects were all considered to be the top priority of their organization's development efforts. The more typical projects, while not low priority, were not their organization's top priority, either.

Continuous improvement and learning was evident in the emphasis of the fastest projects on thinking about the development process as a source for improvement. These projects often discussed when it was appropriate to deviate from the corporate product development protocol and had periodic meetings to discuss the lessons learned, which could be transferred to future projects. However, the fastest projects also experienced delays and difficulties due to the fact that they were working with leading edge technologies and processes. They managed these risks, however, confident that they needed to be continuously learning and improving so that they would be ahead of their competitors on the next development project. They strongly believed that they needed to be ahead of their competitors, in terms of learning and their knowledge base.

Thus, it can be tentatively concluded that the values which underlie the practices and procedures associated with quality management also provide a foundation for fast product development. The differences between the projects were clearly *not* at the level of practices; most of the projects were associated with organizations which had coherent and well thought-out quality initiatives. These initiatives, however, may not have been fully embraced by all units of these organizations, because the values which they are built upon were not reflected equally. Rather, it was at the level of the values which are genuinely embraced by the members of an organization and are ingrained in them as a way of thinking, that the true differences emerge. Those teams which strongly embodied the value system which underlies quality management were also the teams which were able to complete product development projects with the greatest speed. The fastest teams tended to reflect more of the core quality values, as well as a more thorough embodiment of them. In contrast, the typical speed teams reflected fewer core quality values or had problems as a result of not embracing a particular value. Thus, there is a strong overlap between quality management and fast product development, at the level of values which are genuinely held.

References

Amundson, S. W., Flynn, B. B., Rungtusanatham, M. and Schroeder, R. G. "The Relationship Between Duality Management Values and National and Organizational Culture." Working Paper, 1997.

Anderson, J. C., Rungtusanatham, M. and Schroeder, R. G. (1994). "A Theory of Quality Management Underlying the Deming Management Method." *Academy of Management Review*, 1991, vol. 37, no. 9, 1107–24.

Clark, K. B. and Fujimoto, T. *Product Development Performance*. Boston: Harvard Business School Press, 1991.

Clark, K. B. and Wheelwright, S. C. *Managing New Product and Process Development*. New York: The Free Press, 1993.

Crosby, P. *Quality is Free*. New York: Mentor Publishing, 1979.

Dean, J. W., Jr. and Bowen, D. E. "Management Theory and Total Quality: Improving Research and Practice Through Theory Development." *Academy of Management Review*, vol. 19 (July, 1994), no. 3, 392–418.

Dean, J. W., Jr. and Snell, S. A., "Integrated Manufacturing and Job Design: Moderating Effects of Organizational Inertia." *Academy of Management Journal*, 1991, vol. 34, no. 4, 776–804.

Deming, W. E., *Quality, Productivity and Competitive Position*. Cambridge, MA: Massachusetts Institute of Technology, Center for Advanced Engineering Study, 1982.

Deming, W. E. *Out of the Crisis*. Cambridge, MA: Massachusetts Institute of Technology, Center for Advanced Engineering Study, 1986.

Ferdows, K. and DeMeyer, A., "Lasting Improvements in Manufacturing Performance: In Search of the a New Theory." *Journal of Operations Management*, 1990, vol. 9, 168–84.

Flynn, B. B., Schroeder, R. G. and Sakakibara, "The Impact of Quality Management Practices on Performance and Competitive Advantage." *Decision Sciences*, 1995, vol. 26, no. 5, 659–92.

Garwood, D. and Bane, M. *Shifting Paradigms: Reshaping the Future of Industry*. Marietta, GA: Dogwood Publishing Company, 1990.

Hartley, J. R., *Concurrent Engineering*. Cambridge, MA: Productivity Press, 1992.

Hayes, R. H., Wheelwright, S. C. and Clark, K. B. *Dynamic Manufacturing: Creating the Learning Organization*. New York: The Free Press, 1988.

Juran, J. M., "The Quality Trilogy: A Universal Approach to Managing for Quality." *Quality Progress*, 1986, vol. 19, no. 8, 19–24.

Juran, J. M. *Managerial Breakthrough*. New York: McGraw-Hill, 1964.

Malcolm Baldrige National Quality Award 1997 Award Criteria. United States Department of Commerce, Gaithersburg, MD, 1997.

Maskill, B. F. *Performance Measurement for World Class Manufacturing: A Model for American Companies.* Cambridge, MA: Productivity Press, 1991.

Rokeach, M. *The Nature of Human Values.* New York: The Free Press, 1973.

Saraph, J. V., Benson, P. G. and Schroeder, R. G. "An Instrument for Measuring the Critical Factors of Quality Management." *Decision Sciences,* 1989, vol. 20, no. 4, 810–29.

Schein, E. H. *Organizational Culture and Leadership.* San Francisco: Jossey-Bass, 1992.

Schonberger, R. J. *World Class Manufacturing: The Lessons of Simplicity Applied.* New York: The Free Press, 1986.

Schonberger, R. J. *Building a Chain of Customers: Linking Business Functions to Create a World Class Company.* New York: The Free Press, 1990.

Snell, S. A. and Dean, J. W., Jr. "Integrated Manufacturing and Human Resource Management: a Human Capital Perspective." *Academy of Management Journal,* 1992, vol. 35, no. 3, 467–504.

Stalk, G. "The Strategic Value of Time. In J. D., Blackburn, *Time-Based Competition: the Next Battle Ground in American Manufacturing.* Homewood, IL: Business One Irwin, 1991.

Stalk, G. and Hout, T. M. *Competing Against Time: How Time-based Competition is Reshaping Global Markets.* New York: The Free Press, 1990.

Takeuchi, H. and Nonaka, I. "The New New Product Game." *Harvard Business Review,* 1986, January–February, 137–46.

Wheelwright, S. C. and Clark, K. B. *Revolutionizing Product Development: Quantum Leaps in Speed, Efficiency and Quality.* New York: The Free Press, 1992.

11 | Building the Lean Enterprise

Thomas G. Greenwood and Kenneth E. Kirby

Abstract

The accelerating movement toward implementing lean production processes in US industry coincided, in large part, with the release of the book *The Machine that Changed the World* by Womack, Jones, and Roos (16). Even though the book was short on specific strategies about how to make the transition from traditional to lean manufacturing, it served as an early guidebook for many companies looking for ways to make the most of their resources – and stay competitive.

Research over the past few years has provided more insight into how companies can effectively make this transition. Typically, companies that have successfully made this transition adhered to the following principles:

1 Focused on what their customer valued
2 Identified and organized their delivery system (value stream) by product
3 Redesigned their product delivery system to remove waste
4 Simplified and aligned the flow of material, information, and processes
5 Made the value flow more quickly and continuously as pulled by their customer
6 Executed operations with teams and relentlessly pursued perfection
7 Used shared measures to gauge performance

What will you gain from reading this chapter?

The chapter will show you how executives and managers can help redesign their company's product delivery system and move effectively from a traditional mass production model to a lean enterprise model. In the process, you will begin to understand why the traditional model is failing in today's business environment and how the lean enterprise model can help you make the most of your company's resources.

How the chapter is organized

This chapter is aimed at executives and managers in manufacturing companies. It is designed to be a practical explanation of and resource for implementing lean enterprise strategies in today's US manufacturing environment.

The first part of the chapter discusses some of the problems found in the traditional product delivery process and why this process is ineffective in meeting the demands of today's competitive business. Once you understand the problem, it is easier to understand the solution – the lean enterprise model.

The second part of the chapter provides you with a strategy for implementing changes that will help your company move from a traditional to a lean enterprise process. The recommended strategy you will find here is designed for an organization that is at ground zero in terms of moving from the traditional to the lean mode. If you are not at ground zero, but have initiated an implementation methodology, you should be able to assess where you are and utilize some subset of the recommendations to help in moving forward.

PART 1 THE PROBLEM WITH TRADITIONAL MANUFACTURING

Does your company suffer from any of these symptoms?

- Products are delivered late.
- Warehouse contains inventory that is the wrong finished product.
- An almost constant state of emergency where the "best" people tend to spend the majority of their time putting out fires or expediting orders.
- Mounds of paperwork that controls the flow of material, information, and products.

These symptoms represent just a few of the typical problems found in companies using the traditional product delivery system. All kinds of excuses prevail when it comes to explaining why these problems exist. No doubt, you have heard them all before: Forecasts were wrong. Suppliers inept. Equipment was continually breaking down. Critical people were away on vacation or out sick. The order was passed incorrectly or, worst of all, the customer simply changed their mind. Imagine that!

A Close Up of the Traditional Forecast Process

These symptoms are real – but they are not the problem. The problem is the design of the product delivery system being used. The system is simply not tolerant or robust enough to handle the changes in plans that can occur on any given day. In fact, some actions are dramatically self-destructive. Take, for example, the demand forecasts that are generated months in advance. Very little attention is paid to the forecast process itself and the underlying assumptions used to forecast needs.

- Meetings are held monthly rather than weekly to forecast needs.
- Individual salaries or performance bonuses are not directly tied to how accurately forecasts are generated.
- A distorted picture of true demand is generated, in some cases, when a company bases its forecast on upstream movement data (internal) rather than true customer or consumer demand (external).
- Stocking plans and distribution promotions swing the numbers wildly. Similarly, overbooking to accommodate other short-term needs (e.g., anticipation of seasonal shortages and monthly/quarterly closeouts for performance reporting, annual inventory and shut down periods, phase outs, and new production introductions) further cloud the true picture.

All of this happens because no mechanism exists to capture actual demand data from a reliable point-of-sale system. But, unfortunately, the self-destructive process is not complete.

- A number is picked for a production plan with no margin for error.
- Discrete orders are given to perhaps 100 suppliers based on the one "point" estimate. This is done even though we all know that the only sure thing about a forecast is that "it will be wrong."
- Suppliers are then given a target date to ensure materials arrive just in time to start production as scheduled. However, these schedules are never executed as planned, which results in a tremendous imbalance in materials.

Attitudes and mentality that result from traditional systems

Companies using the traditional product delivery system often find the absorption mentality alive and well. The system itself produces organizational philosophies and a structure that only reinforce the system – and the problems. For example, in a make-to-stock organization with product seasonality some of the following could occur:

- Throughput is at the top of the priority list. Large batch sizes are still considered necessary to minimize cost and maximize efficiency.
- After-market and replacement components are only run during low demand periods because of the impact on the bottom line.
- High labor content units are produced during low demand periods – knowing they are not needed – to absorb overhead and burden.
- Work-in-process inventories are minimized at the expense of finished goods inventory, which is someone else's problem.

This mentality means that inventory and schedules are allocated to customers on a first come, first serve basis – as if all customers have the same product delivery expectations. In this scenario, service groups are usually organized by customer rather than process, which creates an internal competition for products that often leads to overbooking and cancellation of orders.

PART 2   DEFINING LEAN ENTERPRISE

Lean Enterprise is a relatively new system of commercial competition for companies worldwide – even though Japanese companies, like Toyota (Monden 1993) have been perfecting the use of its underlying principles for several years.

The Lean Enterprise process can be defined and understood from several perspectives. From the marketing perspective, it is characterized by individualized, highly variable combination of goods, information, and services priced according to the value perceived by customers. In essence, prices and quantities sold are determined more by the markets' perception of value and less by the suppliers' perception of value.

From the production perspective, it is a company's ability to produce a wide and rapidly changing variety of goods and services as ordered by the customer in small order quantities.

From the system design perspective, it is the methods and techniques a company uses to integrate supplier processes, production processes, customer relations, and the product's use and eventual disposal.

From an organizational perspective, it is a company's or group of companies' ability to achieve and integrate new productive capabilities that are based on necessary business processes and the expertise of people and physical facilities, regardless of their location.

From management's perspective, it is a shift from the command and control philosophy inherent in the traditional industrial corporation to one of leadership, motivation, support, and trust.

From the employees' perspective, it is the emergence of a knowledgeable, skilled, entrepreneurial, and empowered total workforce, which is the ultimate differentiation between successful and unsuccessful companies.

FIVE MAJOR COMPONENTS OF THE LEAN ENTERPRISE

In a somewhat narrower sense, the Lean Enterprise consists of the six major components identified in figure 11.1.

1   Understanding Customer Values
2   Lean Production
3   Rate-Based Demand and Production Planning
4   Rate-Based Order Management
5   Supplier Process Integration
6   Distribution Channel Integration

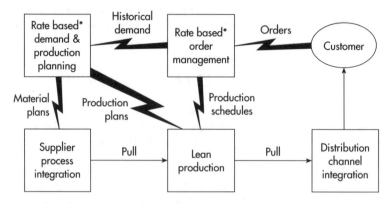

* Rate-based planning provides a technique to balance production with demand variation.

© 1977, Lean Enterprise Systems Design Institute, The University of Tennessee

Figure 11.1   The lean enterprise

PART 3   MARKET SCOPE AND CUSTOMER VALUES

To be successful, the customer's desires and values must drive the design (or redesign) of the enterprise. Once you understand your customers' needs, you can initiate major design changes on the factory floor (i.e., lean production). But, changing the capabilities and flexibility on the factory floor result in a domino effect of changes throughout the organization. The next step is to change the internal processes that support the floor such as production planning, scheduling, and order management.

Once the factory floor has increased capabilities, and changes to the support processes are in place, then the way material is supplied and products are distributed must be changed. It is important to engage suppliers early in the change process. If you do not, suppliers can act as an initial major constraint as you implement your early changes.

The scope of your market as well as the needs and values of important customers should drive how you redesign your product delivery system. The first step in gathering this information is to identify the major product lines within each market segment that your business unit (BU) provides. Examples of the type of information you should use to identify product lines within each market segment include:

- sales dollars;
- units of product sold;
- gross and net margins;
- share of market by segment.

Second, identify key customers – for example, the top 20 percent – for each product line and market segment. You can use these customers later to help you validate the value structure for the product line and market segment. Obviously, you will want to project expected growth or decline for various products as well.

Third, identify and objectively examine the strengths and weaknesses of the current product delivery process, relative to customer needs. This analysis will help you decide how to best redesign the delivery system.

Fourth, review your marketing strategies and make sure these strategies complement the strategies used to manufacture the product. The following questions should help you examine and compare these strategies:

- Does the business unit have a strategy to differentiate product brand(s)? If so, is it successful?
- Are brand differentiation objectives being achieved that fit the current product delivery process? If not, what changes are needed to improve the process?
- Is the full line being offered or some niche segment? How will this affect the design of the product delivery process?
- How does the business unit stack up against the competition?
- Does the competition have an advantage that will heavily influence the design of the product delivery process?

Fifth, carefully examine the business unit's product strategy. Determine if the business unit has a product strategy that is primarily based on the unit's ability to introduce new products and retire products that are obsolete. If not, develop a procedure that will give you a way to consume existing inventory before new products are introduced and distributed. And, more importantly, make sure the process is invisible to the customer.

PRINCIPLES OF A SUCCESSFUL DEVELOPMENT

Use all the information available to you about the scope of your market when you establish an initial product family (or line). The success of the implementation strategy you develop depends upon consistency of purpose. You must select a product line and develop an implementation plan that considers all activities of the enterprise – from suppliers to distributors. This approach enables the business unit to replicate achievements with other product lines.

Carefully coordinate implementation activities

Several implementation teams will be active at any given time. It is important to develop a roadmap to coordinate and integrate their actions. Make sure implementation events are linked to ensure a logical progression of improvement over time. This approach is particularly important in plants that manufacture multiple products.

Collect and use point-of-sale data to forecast accurately

From the very beginning, you must carefully consider how you can collect and use point-of-sale data – rather than relying solely on a forecast – to help you design the new system. If point-of-sale data is difficult to obtain, then it is imperative that you find a way to capture production plans as far in advance as possible. The importance of this data will become more apparent when changes to the production planning and scheduling processes are discussed.

Capture variations in customer demand

Data must be captured for each product concerning demand variation levels. Understanding variations in short-term levels of demand will help you decide how to handle the variation. For example, you would use this information to decide if the BU needed to be more flexible, carry more inventory, or offer long lead times.

Identify Time-Based Demand Profiles

Data must be captured to identify Time-Based Demand Profiles. All customers are not the same and it is important for you to understand how each customer is different. How? The best way is to monitor and observe the patterns that develop based on customer orders. Over time, you will begin to see some relative distribution of lead times develop (e.g., time between receiving and delivering the order) for a given product family. These patterns and distribution of lead times translate into different customer needs. This type of information is important because it helps you focus on what your customer wants – and how quickly you can deliver it. In short, your process becomes driven by what your customer actually wants – and not by what the Customer Service department can offer your customer.

Construct model planning bill-of-material (BOM)

After selecting the initial product family, you can construct model-level Planning Bill-of-Material's (that is, BOM's for each product). These BOM's

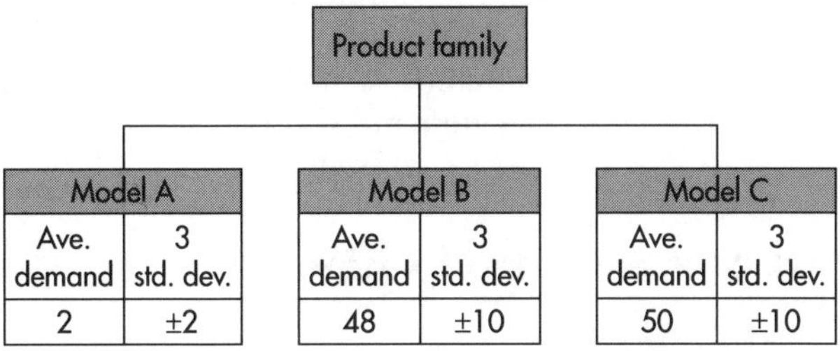

- The model-level planning BOM shows the model demand level and variation per model.
- It helps to identify which models are repetitive and should be produced more frequently.
- The average demand and variation must be tracked over time for stability.

© 1977, Lean Enterprise Systems Design Institute, The University of Tennessee

Figure 11.2 Model-level planning BOM

capture and help you identify the mix of products (i.e., model mix) and model variation levels your customers want. Eventually, you will use the information to improve the accuracy of your forecasts and help you decide which models you want to produce more often.

Figure 11.2 shows an example of a product family with three models. Models B and C represent products that might be produced more often (e.g., daily or twice a week). Model A is one that might be produced less often (e.g., weekly) or in a make-to-order situation that requires longer lead times.

The plus and minus values following the average demand values show the level of variation for each model. For example, assume the demand values are captured for each model on a weekly basis. Each model's level of variation is generated by estimating the standard deviation for each set of weekly demand, as follows:

Assuming a normal distribution for the sets of weekly demand, all data values will be captured within plus and minus three standard deviations of the mean. Here is how it would work:

1 The average weekly demand for all three models has been 100.

$$\overline{X_A} = 2$$
$$\overline{X_B} = 48$$
$$\overline{X_C} = 50$$

2 The average demand for model B is 48. Given the average demand and variation in demand, the maximum weekly demand will be no more than 58, the minimum weekly demand will be no less than 38.

3   The standard deviation of demand for model B is 3.33, since 3* Std. Dev. = 10.
4   The minimum weekly demand for model C will be no less than 40 and the maximum weekly demand will be no greater than 60.

What causes demand variation?

It is important to keep in mind that the *source* of variation in demand differs from one type of industry to the next. The following examples identify how three different sources can impact a BU.

Example 1: manufacturer of room air conditioners

A manufacturer of room air conditioners may receive orders from hundreds of independent customers every week. The manufacturer must decide what level of inventory must be maintained to respond effectively to all customers. The demand for any particular model varies each week, depending on the actual orders placed by all of the independent customers. If the manufacturer does not have the component parts available to handle the weekly variation, customers may very well go elsewhere to satisfy their needs. To determine the appropriate inventory level, the manufacturer captures the variation in the daily or weekly demand by model (i.e., orders and/or units) and tries to maintain the minimum level of inventory needed to meet the demands of its large customer base. For long lead time items, this manufacturer must also use forecasts to project future demand. In this case, forecast error must then be used to establish an inventory position for those parts or subassemblies.

Example 2: manufacturer with OEM customers

On the other hand, a second manufacturer might have a very small number of customers that are original equipment manufacturers (OEM). These customers typically provide the manufacturer with a projection of needs (i.e., potential demand) for several months into the future. The manufacturer interprets the projections to be orders that the customer will place within some reasonable period of time. In this case, the manufacturer captures the variation between the projected need and the actual demand (i.e., orders placed). Material and capacity are positioned according to the projected need. If the actual demand is greater than projected during a given time, material and capacity must be made available. Again, particularly for materials with long lead times, the difference between projected and actual demand (forecast error) is captured and used to establish safety inventory to ensure that material is available as needed.

Example 3: how demand signal processing can create variation

Several factors might affect demand variation in example 2. For example, it has been shown that "demand signal processing" creates variation as one moves along the value stream further away from actual customer demand. Demand signal processing refers to that case where each entity in the value stream generates a forecast based on their respective customer orders rather than on the end customer in the value stream. The demand observed from the customer is transmitted to each supplier in an exaggerated form as you move back along the value stream. Extended lead times amplify this variation.

CUSTOMER VALUE AS THE NORTH STAR

A company or business unit (BU) must translate lean principles into a total business strategy. Although the words may vary, the strategy focuses on customers, processes, and people. As illustrated in figure 11.1, a successful start involves finding some way to capture what customers value. This cannot be solely an internal activity. The BU's management team might project what customers value and use this information to provide initial guidance. However, management's perception of product cost and achieving a "reasonable" margin heavily influences this projection.

Eventually, the quest to understand customer value must involve real customers in real conversations. Engaging the customer is the only way to identify past assumptions and either validate or destroy them. The customer's perception originates from experiences associated with "having the product" or "receiving the service" – a perspective that is very different from the BU's management team.

Understanding what customers value is ongoing work. Today's customer is more sophisticated and demanding than ever before. The ability to discover, understand, and confirm customer perceptions and ultimately exceed their expectations must not be left to chance. Furthermore, the only thing that is certain about customer value is that values change. Tomorrow's customer will be more demanding than today's customer as your own capabilities and those of your competition grow.

How to capture customer value

Typically, customer values are captured by market segment. Goldratt (1994) defines market segment as "two sections of the market are called segmented from each other if and only if changes in prices in one section do not cause any changes in the other section."

A single, fair price and value structure may not exist for a given product or service if different market segments have different needs. You see this

principle when you make a reservation for an airplane flight. Each flight
has several different prices, depending on several factors. Price depends
on where and when the ticket is bought and if the ticket was bought as a
group or as an individual ticket. Other factors like how long you intend to
stay at the intended destination also influence the price. None of these
factors have anything to do with the space you occupy on the airplane.
The airlines made the effort to segment the market or they would not
have survived.

Southwest Airlines is a specific example of how a company can target
a market segment, identify product or service attributes that are valued
by that segment, and design a delivery process to provide the desired
attributes. Southwest's core competencies can be summarized as:

- Make very low ticket prices available by offering limited passenger
  service and high utilization of aircraft.
- Provide frequent, reliable departures by having lean, highly productive ground and gate crews.
- Make short-haul, point-to-point routes available between mid-size
  cities and secondary airports.

Other, tightly linked activities that generally support these core competencies are identified as:

- Do not provide meals, seat assignments, or connections with other
  airlines.
- Turnaround in 15 minutes.
- Use a standardized fleet of aircraft.
- Make limited use of travel agents.

This example clearly shows that you must either (1) find your market
niche and offer services that differentiates you from the competition or
(2) offer services in a way that makes it clear to the customer that they
should always come to you first because of your world class reputation.

SUMMARY

You must put in place a process that will provide you with continuous
feedback about your customers and what they value and need. Without
this information, you may very well design a product delivery process with
capabilities that your customers do not value. Even worse, you may end up
with a design that does not have the capabilities you need to compete in
the future. The key point is that you must design your product delivery
process to meet the needs of each customer segment with respect to lead
times, delivery expectations, performance, quality, and other performance
metrics.

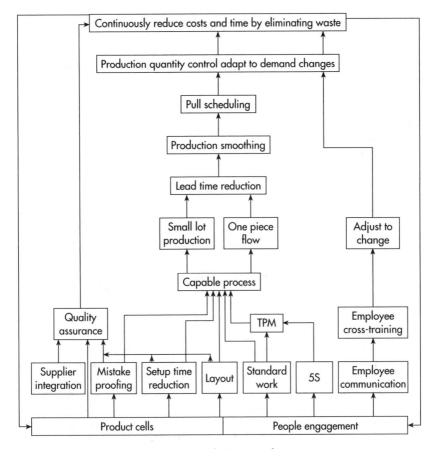

© 1977, Lean Enterprise Systems Design Institute, The University of Tennessee

Figure 11.3 Integrating the elements

PART 4   LEAN PRODUCTION

Typically, redesign activities start on the factory floor – and focus on how work is routed and streamlined, and how work centers are grouped into a lean production cell. These activities usually result in moving away from departmental or functional factory layouts and batch processing to more focused, product-oriented cells, and one-piece processing. Customer demand drives the volume of products produced in a cell – with the ultimate result being that the sequence of products (i.e., models) is intentionally mixed to provide a smoother demand on internal and supplier processes.

Several slightly different approaches can be used to convert from a batch manufacturing mode to lean production cells. Figure 11.3 lists some of the principles that apply during the transition.

Baseline the current process

The first step is to baseline the current process. During this step, your goal is to capture data about the current process and establish measures to help you evaluate any performance improvements made. Baselining steps include:

1 Conduct five "S" and safety checks.
2 Flowchart the process and identify activities that do not add value.
3 Identify required tasks, the sequence of the tasks, and record time observations of operator and machine activities.
4 Establish takt time for the cell being studied.
5 Identify and record performance measures.

Conduct five "S" and safety checks

It is very natural to start your improvement efforts by implementing the five "S": Sort, Storage, Shining, Standardizing, and Sustaining. It is also an excellent way to instill discipline in an organization.

1 *Sort* means you identify every item stored in and around a given work center and remove items that are not totally needed. One way to do this is to place "red tags" on all items that need to be removed.
2 *Storage* means every item (e.g., tools, gages, fixtures) needed in the work center is assigned a specific location for storage. Items used more often are ergonomically positioned nearest to the operator.
3 *Shining* means you establish ongoing procedures for cleaning the work center. Time for cleaning the work area is allocated to operators as part of their normal duties.
4 *Standardizing* means the operators maintain the workplace at a level that uncovers and makes problems obvious. The intent is to sustain sorting, storage, and shining activities every day. Develop standard practices to properly train operators and help supervisors ensure the standards are followed. The success of implementing standard practices effectively depends on involving associates (i.e., employees) early. Associates are much more likely to adhere to standard practices if they have a major role in developing the standards.
5 *Sustaining* refers to the training and development that leads to achieving a disciplined culture. It includes developing schedules and check lists that can be used daily.

Total productive maintenance program

It is very natural to combine five "S" with the beginnings of a Total Productive Maintenance program. In this program, work centers are taken out of service and components are evaluated to determine if they are working as designed. The intent is to bring the equipment to "original equipment" status and, then, identify the specific predictive and preventive maintenance practices needed to maintain the same condition over time.

As part of this initial analysis, establish downtime percentages (e.g., mean time to failure, mean time to repair) and process capability. You may find you need to buffer equipment or pieces of equipment that have availability (capacity) or quality problems with additional inventory to ensure the performance of the entire cell is not negatively impacted. Identify these deficiencies early and make sure you have the proper resources available to solve any problems. Make sure any buffer stock added is very visible, so you can remove it as soon as possible.

Emphasize safety

A significant characteristic of the five "S" process is that the safety of all equipment in a cell – along with any material-handling equipment – is addressed at the same time. In fact, some organizations refer to this as the six "S" process just to make sure that safety is given adequate consideration. Perform Failure Mode Effects Analysis (FMEA) on all equipment to identify the possible safety issues and consequences that could occur. Install mistake proofing devises such as guards and automatic cutoff controls as needed (e.g., tool breaks, part defects, etc.)

Flowchart the process and identify activities that do not add value

At this point, you will create a process flow chart to describe each step in the routing of a product line and to help identify activities that do not add value. Common flowchart symbols used when creating this flowchart are shown in figure 11.4.

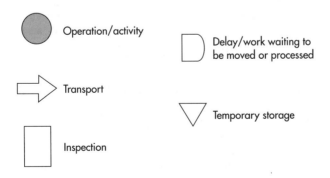

Operation/activity

Delay/work waiting to be moved or processed

Transport

Temporary storage

Inspection

© 1977, Lean Enterprise Systems Design Institute, The University of Tennessee

Figure 11.4 Process flowcharting symbols

Each symbol – with the exception of the Operation/Activity symbol – represents non-value added activities.

- Non-value added steps do not enhance the product or service (e.g., transport, inspect, etc.) and have no strategic or support function (e.g., training). Use these symbols to highlight activities for potential elimination.
- Use the Operation/Activity symbol to represent a value-added step. A value-added step is one that transforms or shapes a product or service toward that which satisfies your customer's real and perceived wants and needs.

Typically, a product line in the batch production mode has less than 5 percent of the total throughput time associated with value-added steps. Delays (e.g., wait in queue time), inspections, and rework represent the vast majority of the remaining time.

When you move to the lean production mode, a commonly accepted objective is that at least 80 percent of the total throughput time is associated with value-added activities.

Identify required tasks; identify the sequence of tasks; record time observations of operator and machine activities

The video camera is an excellent tool for capturing information about a current product line. Each work center is taped to capture the before and after process. When properly introduced, associates prefer to video tape their own process instead of using stop watches to capture cycle times. The reason is that video tapes can be revisited as needed to establish average labor content of each task that needs to be performed, as well as machine times. Using this technique to capture data is an excellent way to study tasks and machine times in a cell more closely – and ultimately discover ways to improve performance.

Establish takt time for the cell under study

After you establish the models (i.e., products) you want in the cell, you can calculate the takt time. Takt time is the "voice of the customer" in that it is the average time it takes to produce a unit. Some call this the "required drum beat." The formula for calculating takt time is as follows:

$$\text{Takt time} = \frac{\text{(Hours/Shift)} * \text{(Number of Shifts)}}{\text{Daily Demand at Design Capacity for all Products (Models)}}$$

Hours per shift are not reduced by any time other than scheduled times for lunch, breaks, clean up, and training. Scheduled downtime or quality problems are not allowed to reduce the available planned time. Why? The reason is simple. These problems should be highly visible. For example, overtime may be needed if serious problems exist in the cell. Overtime is rarely planned. When it occurs, management can readily recognize there is an issue that must be addressed.

Identify and record performance measures

Performance measures are the last item to address when you baseline current processes. Performance measures at the cell level must be aligned and be compatible with performance measures at the plant and the BU levels. An example of how such measures could be developed and used was a part of the final report of the Lean Aircraft Initiative. The measures reported there are not intended to focus exclusively on the aerospace industry, but are equally applicable to any type of industry. The enterprise level measures are shown in figure 11.5.

The use of these measures are intended to influence behavior toward the acceptance and use of twelve overarching practices, summarized as follows:

1   Identify and optimize enterprise flow.
2   Assure seamless information flow.
3   Optimize capability and utilization of people.
4   Make decisions at the lowest possible level.
5   Implement integrated product and process development.
6   Develop relationships based on mutual trust and commitment.
7   Continuously focus on the customer.
8   Promote lean leadership at all levels.

- Flow time
  Order to delivery time in months
  Product development cycle time/(industry comparative)/percentage reduction
- Stakeholder satisfaction
  On time deliveries
  Continuous cost/price improvement
- Resource utilization
  Output per employee
  Inventory turns
- Quality yield
  Scrap and rework rate

© 1977, Lean Enterprise Systems Design Institute, The University of Tennessee

Figure 11.5   Lean enterprise measures

9 Maintain challenge of existing processes.
10 Nurture a learning environment.
11 Ensure process capability and maturation.
12 Maximize stability in a changing environment.

The idea is to then establish lower level metrics that can be aligned with the overarching practices and the enterprise level measures. For example, for the first practice, "identify and optimize flow," some supporting metrics would be:

- Flow efficiency (as measured by actual work time divided by total flow time).
- Throughput rate in units per time period.
- Time from purchase order to point of use delivery time.
- Total product delivery cycle time (from concept to launch).

To assure seamless information flow, you could evaluate the commonality of databases, information retrieval time, and information sharing between customers and suppliers. Some of the measures may have to be qualitative in nature.

CREATE THE LEAN PRODUCTION CELL

The following list summarizes the typical work activity that occurs when you move to the next phase and create a manufacturing cell:

1 Establish the one-piece flow activities.
2 Plan for materials at the point-of-use (POU).
3 Detail the workstation design.
4 Establish standard work.
5 Establish visual controls.
6 Establish a pull scheduling system.
7 Generate and publicize before and after performance measures.

Establish the one-piece flow activities

A work center is an essential part of a lean production cell. Several work centers are grouped together to form a lean production cell. For example, a manufacturer of eye glasses might create a lean production cell by grouping the following work centers into one lean production cell: processing order center, lens identification center, lens grinding center, lens frames center, and polishing center. Each work center is needed to produce the final product: a pair of glasses.

There are a few significant factors that influence whether or not a work center can be placed into the one-piece flow.

Cycle time must be less than or equal to the takt time

To meet customer requirements, a work center's cycle time must be less than or equal to the takt time. This constraint is more prevalent in a machining cell than an assembly cell. For example, in an assembly cell with no significant machine time, tasks are assigned to an operator so that the total labor assigned is less than the takt time. Depending on the cell's design, it is usually possible to add operators if additional capacity is needed.

The same is not true in a machining cell. In this cell, the operator typically needs some manual loading time, followed by machine time. The sum of the manual time plus machine time generates the cycle time for that work center. If changes to the setup or tools are required, time for these activities must be added to the base cycle time, taking into consideration time and frequency of occurrence.

Percent capacity dedicated to product families not being considered for the cell

Generally, at least for a machining cell, one work center in the cell represents a bottleneck. If the bottlenecked work center's cycle time is greater than the takt time and cannot be alleviated, you may want to uncouple that work center from the cell and pull the parts from that work center's activities into the main flow. Other options, of course, are available.

- You can place equipment (redundancy) in the cell to achieve the desired capacity level.
- One machine center could run additional hours and accumulate inventory to balance the workload.

You may not want to include a work center in a cell if the work center consumes a small amount of capacity compared to the percent of capacity other product families use. In this situation, you must decide if there is an economic justification for providing redundant capacity.

Time to set up equipment (i.e., setup time)

The setup issue was discussed above. Basically, if the amortized setup time (i.e., setup time divided by the lot size) creates a cycle time that is greater than the takt time, the work center cannot be placed in the cell without some type of redundancy (e.g., redundant fixtures, tooling) or inventory buffering. Therefore, another key initiative is to apply techniques to reduce the time it takes to set up equipment.

Requirements for physically moving the work center

Last, some pieces of equipment stand as "living monuments" and are very difficult to move into the one-piece flow. Examples of such equipment include annealing ovens, heat-treat furnaces, paint lines, and various washing units typically shared by a major portion of all product lines. Some companies use these work centers as "seeds" and bring in mobile assembly equipment to achieve the benefits of a cell.

Plan for materials at the Point-Of-Use (POU)

To determine which materials you want at the POU, you must decide if you will schedule and produce products using segmented batch or mixed model techniques. Scheduling mixed model is much more prevalent on assembly lines where changeover times are generally less of an issue. If you want to run true mixed model, all parts for all models must be positioned on the line at the POU. Another option is to have feeder lines adjacent to the main line or cell to supply parts in the same part or model sequence as the main flow line in a synchronous fashion.

If you schedule segmented batch processing (e.g., so many A's, so many B's, so many C's and so forth), you can store common parts on the line at the POU. Then, pull unique parts needed for a given model from a "supermarket" located near to the line. Supermarkets allow you to position parts near the POU and see what parts are available.

The ultimate objective of storing materials at the POU is to have all certified suppliers use a pull system to replenish flow lines at the POU location as materials are consumed. The raw materials inventory will essentially vanish. Even though business units are not here today, this practice should be part of their vision.

Detail the workstation design

Detailing the design of the workstation includes identifying the physical location of all equipment, raw materials, and operators. For equipment, you need to identify tooling, fixtures, jigs, gages, instrumentation, test equipment, and so forth. For workstation design, you need to identify container design and, ultimately, the physical size and shape of the cell itself. For the layout of the cell, you need to identify at least the following:

- Location of machine centers.
- Location and number of units of standard work-in-process (WIP).
- Location of safety checks and quality checks.
- The footprint (work path) of each operator.
- Location of materials stored at POU.
- Location of material stored at a supermarket, as appropriate.

Establish time for standard work

Standard work is defined as a set of tasks grouped together so the sum of the individual task times is equal to or less than the takt time.

Knowing standard work time is important in a lean production cell. Standard work is used to balance the workload and achieve a daily output rate that is equal to customer demand. It also defines the amount of work each operator performs to achieve a balanced flow and linear output rate.

Once you determine standard work time, you can create and post method sheets and other standard practice documentation within the cell.

Establish visual controls

The factory should have as many visual clues as possible. Basically, six areas should be considered when you develop a visual factory (5).

- Team's territory.
- Visual documentation.
- Visual production control.
- Visual quality control.
- Display of indicators.
- Visible progress.

Team's territory

The team's territory identifies activities, resources, and products associated with the cell. Use markings on the floor to identify locations for incoming and outgoing materials. Assign and identify a location for all tools as discussed in the previous section. Likewise, identify all materials stored in racks near the cell. Use color coding schemes as much as possible. For example, a given color could designate common parts and an array of colors could identify unique parts for different models processed in the cell. Also, use a specific color scheme for material kanbans to indicate at a glance the source of supply. For example, you might use red for fabricated parts and yellow for supplier parts.

Designate a communication and rest area and use it to post pertinent daily communication notices. Also, designate an area where cleaning equipment can be stored.

Visual documentation

Visual documentation includes all manufacturing instructions and technical procedures. It also includes standard practices, method sheets, standard work and all instructions and acceptance criteria for testing performed.

Visual production control

Visual production control includes a computer terminal, if available, the production schedule, status against the production schedule, the maintenance schedule with check-off to indicate that prescribed work was completed. It also identifies inventories and work-in-progress.

Visual quality control

Visual quality control includes andon lights for each work center or cell. For example, a red light would indicate a quality problem exists and the line is stopped. A yellow light would indicate that quality is questionable, additional resources are requested, and the line will be shut down unless the problem is solved. A blue light would indicate the need for materials to be replenished. Post an SPC chart (or make one available via the computer) to monitor adherence to critical quality characteristics. You might use a Pareto chart to record and highlight quality problems.

Display of indicators

At the cell level you need to select performance indicators that are meaningful to the team. Examples are as follows:

- Performance against the daily production schedule.
- Linearity of the schedule over the month (same load per day, per week, etc.).
- A skills-matrix to display which operators can currently perform each job within the cell or operating area.
- A schedule of training that will increase the level of employee capabilities.
- Number of suggestions offered and accepted.
- Attendance records.

Essentially, how can you expect employees to be interested in what they doing if they are not informed of the results? I can't imagine a football team getting excited about discussing a game if they do not even know the score (5).

Visible progress

Designate an area where you can display the team's objectives and actual results. Present this information graphically, as much as possible, and include the following elements:

- Directly beneath or next to the objectives, include the specific improvement activities identified by the team to achieve the objectives
- Indicate timelines for each improvement activity
- Identify the team member taking lead responsibility

ESTABLISH A PULL SCHEDULING SYSTEM

Application of POU material storage, designing U-shaped cells that bring teams of associates closer together, establishing standard work, and developing visual controls are very powerful tools for improving product process and quality. The intent is (1) to develop very short feedback loops and (2) to have associates who are cross-trained on operating manufacturing processes and who understand the product's quality requirements at every stage of completion. Accountability for continuous improvement will be firmly established by moving raw materials into one end of a cell and moving finished product out of the cell.

A pull scheduling system is a visual signal to replenish materials. It is a simple system to use and is easily incorporated when you implement other visual controls. A kanban pull system is one of the more common pull systems and has the benefit of transferring ownership of replenishing materials back to the shop floor.

Kanban pull system

A kanban pull system consists of literally hundreds of individual material plans – not just one. With kanban, each part has its own replenishment process. You can achieve improvement with one part or one supplier at a time.

Using kanban cards

Although it is not always needed, many sites use kanban cards as the signal for replenishment. Two types of kanban card signals are available.

- The first is an *in-process kanban*. This type is used as a visual signal to pace the movement of products in a cell.
- The second type is a *material kanban* and represents a visual signal to replenish materials consumed in the cell.

Types of material kanbans

Three types of material kanbans exist: the *supplier kanban*, the *production kanban*, and the *withdrawal kanban*.

- The supplier kanban signals withdrawal from suppliers.
- The production kanban signals that materials for a given work center need to be replenished because portions of its exit-buffer inventory were consumed by a downstream work center.
- The withdrawal kanban signals replenishment from an upstream work center or raw materials inventory (Monden 1993).

Rules for using kanban

We recommend the following rules when using kanban.

- Nothing is made or transported without a kanban.
- Every part in the kanban must be of acceptable quality.

- The number of kanbans should decrease over time.
- Have only one partial kanban at a time, that is, do not pick parts from more than one kanban container at a time.

ACCOMMODATE FUTURE CHANGES

Using lean principles to redesign processes allows an organization to improve several dimensions of performance at the same time. Forming manufacturing cells and applying lean principles tends to promote improved quality by reducing the feedback time from inspection to detection of non-conforming product, reduce lead time by reducing transportation time and lot sizes, improve cost by reducing non-value added activities and so forth.

In closing, it is important to note that the work is not finished just because you complete the prescribed steps for creating a lean production cell. Cells will continue to be redesigned over time. To accommodate future changes, make sure your initial design includes the following elements:

- Utilities should be made very flexible. Drop down connections (i.e., utility sources located on the ceiling) for electricity, air, water and so forth will help encourage continual changes in cell design and enhance flexibility.
- Ongoing training for associates. Develop Kaizen action lists to identify and resolve issues that will undoubtedly remain. Many business units err in removing technical resources from a cell too early, rushing to begin the next cell.
- Continue to support team members as they begin to "jell" and take on additional responsibilities. The team must be facilitated to formulate improvement plans to ensure continuous improvement expectations are firmly planted.
- There must be planned status updates, where reports are made to management periodically.
- And, above all, make sure you celebrate along the way as progress is made.
- Establish an Area Team to support the implementation of lean production cells. The Area Team provides ongoing technical (cross-functional) support and is physically located near the point of production.

PART 5   RATE-BASED PRODUCTION PLANNING AND SCHEDULING

Typically, *production planning and scheduling* is the second component of the product delivery process that is redesigned. The intent is to leverage the capabilities of lean production in both directions of the value chain:

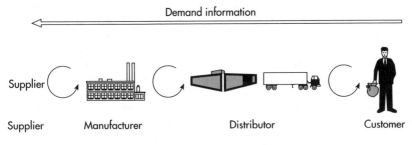

Figure 11.6 Aligning the value stream

forward to the customer and order management process and backward to the material supply channel. Figure 11.6 illustrates how the entire value stream must be aligned to take advantage of the benefits of implementing lean practices.

The concept is ambitious and cannot be achieved overnight. Leveraging capabilities in both directions requires short cycle times, small batch sizes (which implies small setup times, particularly for bottleneck operations), and flexible production. One element of this process is matching production with recent sales – in other words, make today what you sold yesterday. This is why point-of-sale data was identified earlier as being so important.

Set realistic expectations and goals

Making today what you sold yesterday is the goal. However, it is not a realistic expectation to believe that companies can achieve this from the start. A more realistic beginning is for companies to start scheduling this week what was sold last week. Adjustments may be needed for seasonality and changing safety stock levels. The next move would be to schedule over a period of two times per week and, ultimately, to schedule high volume items every day.

The number of adjustments made to the schedule decline as the scheduling period is reduced from one month to perhaps every day. Fewer adjustments are needed because there is less time between planning and execution – which means there is less opportunity for change. A shorter scheduling period means that you can place more emphasis on fulfilling customer needs – and less on the forecasting process itself (Maskell 1994).

Requirements for implementing rate-based planning

To implement rate-based planning, you need to understand what is constraining your company's flexibility to meet both short term and medium term customer demand variation. One way to start this effort is to consider a single product family. Plot the periodic demand for each model (monthly, weekly, and/or daily, depending upon how often you produce each model today) over time. Identify the internal constraints that reduce the frequency of producing the appropriate models. For example, setup times could be a constraint. If you produced your models more frequently, the increased times required for setups could create a lack of capacity. That would identify setup times as a target area. If you cut your setup times in half, for example, then you could double the number of setups you were able to perform. This would, in turn, double the number of times a given model is produced for a given time period. Another constraint could be downtime. The given level of current downtime may keep you from lowering batch sizes and running models more frequently. You could invoke Total Productive Maintenance to address that constraint. As you see, the path to increased flexibility evolves over time.

Obviously, you must consider external constraints. You cannot forget about customer ordering patterns. Customers may be ordering in truckload quantities in order to lower their cost of transportation. You must help them to understand that there are alternatives to full truckload shipments that other organizations are taking advantage of already. You must consider suppliers. It reduces the benefits of running every model every week if suppliers can only deliver once a month, or every other week.

In order to ensure that adequate progress is made in increasing flexibility, weekly rate-based planning meetings need to occur. Activities during these meetings would include reports on progress in increasing flexibility, progress in reducing forecast error, identifying model mix changes, and changes in levels of variability.

The following elements support rate-based planning:

- Developing model-level and component-level BOMs.
- Scheduling based on a mixed model sequencing method.
- Product Response Profile.

Moving to quantities of one

Building on the definition provided earlier, rate-based planning means you must stop thinking about your schedules as a way to produce large batches of product at maximum capacity. Instead, you must begin thinking about how to provide reserve capacity somewhere near 10 percent to 15 percent. Several studies have demonstrated the impact on throughput time and levels of work-in-process inventory when utilization levels move beyond 90 percent.

To establish and maintain the appropriate level of reserve capacity, you must start thinking in terms of producing models in quantities of one, that is, running every model every day. This means you cannot order raw materials from suppliers on a monthly basis and schedule the materials to arrive just before you need to run the corresponding batch of product. You must develop the available capacity in each scheduling cycle to adjust output to actual demand in terms of both quantity and mix. You will not get there overnight, but that is the mindset that must be diligently pursued if you are to make this transition successfully.

Developing a repetitive scheduling policy

To develop a repetitive scheduling policy, you must determine how often you need to repeat the model mix to satisfy customer demand flexibility requirements. In other words, determine if you need to schedule every model every week or every day.

Use the Planning BOM (which provides average demand and variation amounts for each model) and the Pareto principle to determine the type of response capability you need to develop. You may find that you can satisfy customer demand better with a two-tier response capability where you run high demand models every day and low demand models every week.

You can run very low demand models that require longer lead times as you receive the orders. To do this, suppliers must be able to make weekly deliveries in the mix and quantities determined by the component-level Planning BOM. During each scheduling period, you want the capacity and materials to make every model at the planned quantity, given the anticipated levels of variability.

Model-level bill-of-material (BOM)

As described earlier, the model-level BOM includes information about (1) the mix of models within a given product family and (2) the variation associated with each model.

As you work with models, you will find some are defined (meaning your customers do not want adjustments made to the product) and others are more customized. You can use the model-level BOM to help you plan requirements for both types of models.

Defined models

If the model you want to create is part of a finite number of defined products within a product family, you can easily establish the quantity of component parts necessary to build each product you want to produce in the appropriate quantity. Once the model quantities have been established supplier requirements are generated by exploding the model-level BOM in the Materials Requirements Planning (MRP) system.

1 Due to product line complexity of build-to-order and configure-to-order products we must use a first-level planning BOM based upon product family subgroups instead of individual models.

2 Begin with the first-level planning BOM used by marketing for forecasting:

Example: First-level planning BOM

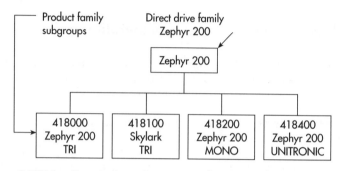

© 1977, Lean Enterprise Systems Design Institute, The University of Tennessee

Figure 11.7   First-level planning BOMs

Customized models

Other steps must be taken to accommodate build-to-order or configure-to-order product lines (where product customization does not allow for a finite number of distinct models). To accommodate these models, extend the model-level Planning BOM down to the component level to provide your suppliers with the component requirements. Figures 11.7 and 11.8 illustrate a component-level BOM.

Figure 11.7 identifies a product family (Zephyr 200) and four product family subgroups for a truck refrigeration unit where significant customization exists such that individual models are not clearly defined.

As shown in figure 11.7, the first level Planning BOM is configured around a product family instead of distinct models, in this case refrigeration units. The second level shows product family subgroups along with the mix distribution. The variation for each would be a required piece of information.

Figure 11.8 shows the component-level BOM for the same refrigeration unit.

Identifying all common and optional components formed the component-level BOM shown in figure 11.8. When you develop the variation for each component, keep in mind the mix variation needed for each subgroup within the product family.

Convert the first-level planning BOM to a component level Planning BOM by rationalizing the common components and optional components. This is determined by using the current historical percentage of consumption of optional components within each product family subgroup.

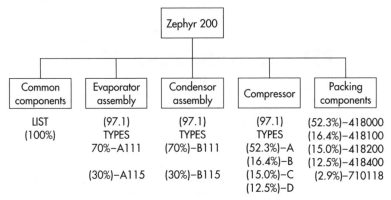

Zephyr 200

Common components	Evaporator assembly	Condensor assembly	Compressor	Packing components
LIST	(97.1)	(97.1)	(97.1)	(52.3%)–418000
(100%)	TYPES	TYPES	TYPES	(16.4%)–418100
	70%–A111	(70%)–B111	(52.3%)–A	(15.0%)–418200
			(16.4%)–B	(12.5%)–418400
	(30%)–A115	(30%)–B115	(15.0%)–C	(2.9%)–710118
			(12.5%)–D	

© 1977, Lean Enterprise Systems Design Institute, The University of Tennessee

Figure 11.8   Component level planning BOMs

Balance demand and flexibility

With rate-based production planning, you are trying to balance demand changes with plant and supplier flexibility. The only way to make sure you keep these elements properly balanced is to conduct Rate-Based Planning Meetings every week with Production Scheduling and Materials, Customer Service, and the Director of Sales. The main purpose of each weekly meeting is to coordinate activities and make sure no significant changes have occurred in the model mix and variation reflected in the first-level Planning BOM. You can generate updates as needed by comparing the actual order backlog to the Planning BOM.

Coordination meetings are essential to the success of rate-based planning. A best practice is to physically co-locate the Customer Service Manager and the Plant Scheduler in the same area. This closeness will facilitate easy communication between these two departments.

The model-level and the component-level Planning BOM will provide the information you need to develop minimum, plan, and maximum "to-build" schedules for models and components on a weekly and, ultimately, daily basis.

PRODUCTION SCHEDULING

Production scheduling follows rate-based production planning. When you develop a production schedule, your objective is to combine flexible

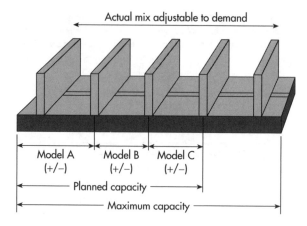

Actual mix adjustable to demand

| Model A (+/−) | Model B (+/−) | Model C (+/−) |

Planned capacity

Maximum capacity

The objective is to have flexible maximum capacity with flexible individual capacities according to the model-mix (i.e., want to be able to flex A, B or C)

© 1977, Lean Enterprise Systems Design Institute, The University of Tennessee

Figure 11.9 Production scheduling: provide maximum model-mix flexibility

maximum capacity with flexible individual capacities – based on the model mix. Figure 11.9 uses a large file drawer to help you visualize the capacity of a given product family.

Note that the level of planned capacity does not equal the level of absolute maximum capacity. More than likely, planned capacity will be less than or equal to 85 percent to 90 percent of the maximum capacity. The planned capacity for each model can vary for a given time. Use the Planning BOM to establish the planned level and the minimum and maximum levels.

Based on the true order pattern, actual mixed percentages are determined within the upper and lower bounds previously set. Orders are intentionally mixed to accommodate customer flexibility for changes, balanced workloads, and pull requirements for materials. Since computer programs are needed to actually calculate mixed model sequences in complex situations, the specific method for developing the sequence is beyond the scope of this chapter.

Minimum requirements for scheduling mixed models

Several factors must be considered in building a schedule that is situational specific (e.g., work center and material constraints, transportation costs, and customer priorities).

The ability to schedule mixed models is driven by effectively implementing lean production practices. The following list identifies minimum requirements needed to support mixed model scheduling:

- Setup time reduced
- Equipment availability increased by implementing Total Productive Maintenance
- Materials stored at the POU
- Suppliers deliver materials more frequently
- Quality throughput

Moving to mixed model schedules

Generally, mixed model schedules occur slowly over time. Many companies or BU's continue to schedule what is called a "segmented batch". This means that some batch production occurs for various models. Companies using this approach focus on shortening the time it takes to set up and slowly reduce the size of the batch segments as changes are implemented.

Another mode of scheduling that is not mixed model may also occur. High volume units are run as mixed models for a major part of the week and low volume units are run as segmented batches for the remainder of the week. Obviously, there are many possible scenarios. However, the primary objective should be to run as close to a mixed model schedule as possible.

Benefits of running mixed models

Why is it important to run mixed model? The benefits are many – from balancing the workload to providing more flexibility within the BU.

Balance workload within cell

Models that require high labor content would call for more people in the cell. Conversely, if you run a model that required less labor content, you would have fewer people in the cell. This means when you run segmented batches, you would need to change the number of people in the crew as different models are run.

Respond to variations in customer demand

Mixed model provides more flexibility for the customer. Customers can change their minds about quantity or mix and the mixed model will be able to respond. Running mixed model on an assembly line makes the daily and weekly work load for work centers or cells upstream more level – as well as the demand for parts and subassemblies from suppliers.

Reduce exposure to batch-related defects

Repeated changes to models foster productivity improvements and help to ensure quality by reducing the exposure to batch-related defects.

Create a robust delivery process

The intent of shortening the scheduling cycle is to define a controlled level of flexibility in the delivery process (that is, focus primarily on bottleneck work centers or suppliers). The delivery process you create must be robust enough to anticipate variations in short-term and medium-term demand. You will achieve this flexibility by establishing minimum and maximum bounds for future demand forecasts. The idea is that both the production facility and the materials supply channels will have sufficient capacity to accommodate demand swings that do not exceed established demand bounds. As future demands move closer to the production window, updated demand bounds are periodically communicated to the materials suppliers.

Demand bounding limits are enforced by your Sales or Customer Service departments when the order is received and the promise of delivery is made to ensure the rate-based production plan remains feasible. In essence, you must understand your short and medium term flexibility and your short and medium term demand variability – then, plan and schedule within those limits.

When flexibility exceeds the percentage of variation on the demand side, your product delivery process is "capable." When this is not the case, you must develop inventory strategies when the bounds are exceeded.

MEETING VARIATIONS IN DEMAND

As stated, the objective of rate-based planning techniques is to balance variations in demand with production and supply responsiveness. This can be seen graphically in Figure 11.10.

As you might anticipate, the error in the demand forecast is expected to increase as you forecast further into the future – as well as the BU's ability to respond to these changes.

Product response profile

The Product Response Profile can help you determine how quickly the BU can respond and react to unforeseen medium-term changes in market trends. Information in this profile is expressed in weeks and percent of flexibility.

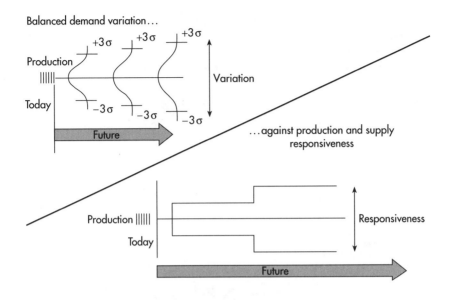

Balanced demand variation...

Figure 11.10 Objective of rate-based planning techniques

Prerequisite for generating a product response profile

Before you can generate a Product Response Profile, you must know the limitations of your factory and your suppliers. You determine these by creating the Factory Response Profile and the Suppliers Response Profile. The respective profile is used to help you define any constraining conditions in the factory and from your suppliers. Once you know these limitations, you can form the Product Response Profile.

Factory response profile

As noted, the BU develops the Factory Response Profile first. To do this, schedule a meeting to include representatives from production scheduling, sales, customer service, materials, and purchasing. The Factory Response Profile is a negotiated commitment among all parties represented. It is an explicit statement of what can and cannot be expected in terms of flexibility. It is a good idea to formally place these agreements in writing to avoid a case of "corporate amnesia". With these agreements in writing, this document can then become a written commitment to suppliers and to customer service. As the flexibility of the BU improves, you should review and update the document periodically.

- Schedule a meeting with the production manager to ducoment flexible production capacity
  - Document current flexible capacity
  - Document future capacities and the time to respond at those levels

Flexible production capacity

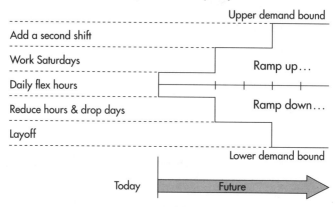

© 1977, Lean Enterprise Systems Design Institute, The University of Tennessee

Figure 11.11 The factory response profile

Figure 11.11 shows an example of a Factory Response Profile.

Assume the narrow boundary at the left of the profile is week 1 and the flexibility to react when only one week away is plus and minus 10 percent. The next larger demand bound can be assumed to be week 2 and might have a flexibility level of plus and minus 20 percent. The wider bound at the right might be week 3 and have a flexibility of plus and minus 30 percent. The Product Response Profile is divided into sections based on the width of the flexibility bounds. The upper and lower bounds do not have to be symmetric. The upper bound is the commitment to increase to meet customer needs. The lower bound is the downside commitment. The first forecast in each flexibility section is critical because it sets new limits (plus or minus some percentage of the forecast value). The profile becomes more constrictive as the production window gets closer. Previous bounds cannot be violated.

Supplier response profile

Establishing Supplier Response Profiles requires that you meet with the Materials department to identify components and suppliers that cannot respond to weekly schedules within lower and upper bounds. It should be noted that the Supplier Response Profile is based at the component level – unlike the factory profile, which is based on the final product. Obviously, the Factory Response Profile can be a starting point to inform the supplier of your expectations.

When you identify a constraint that will effect the factory, you also want to identify the product models that will be effected. Eventually, you must develop a plan to offset this restriction. Your plans might be to (1) obtain a new supplier, (2) establish an inventory plan to support the bounds at the supplier, or (3) work directly with the supplier to increase their capabilities.

Develop a unique response profile for a subset of your suppliers. This subset could be defined by criteria such as dollar value supplied, critical parts supplied, most delinquent on deliveries, etc. The response profile should include lead-time and the supplier's ability to adapt up or down for subsequent periods in the future. The objective is to drive suppliers to achieve response profiles that allow you to meet the demands of your customers.

PART 6   RATE-BASED ORDER MANAGEMENT

Even though rate-based planning enhances flexibility, it is controlled by upper and lower demand limits. To ensure success, Sales and Marketing departments must be informed of these limits to ensure they do not violate the maximum flexibility limits. You can accomplish this by controlling the order promising function.

If you control the order promise function, you will be in a better position to ensure the number of orders placed in the system during any given period is compatible with BU's ability to fulfill the orders – and, therefore, meet your customer requirements.

Rate-based order management does not preclude a company from accepting and responding to exceptional customer needs. You should always be ready to expedite activities in response to special circumstances. However, this should become the exception rather than the rule. The goal is to develop normal capacity bounds that are robust enough to absorb routine sources of variation. Remember that reserve capacity is considered part of the design of the finite capacity model, since unanticipated sources of variation can occur weekly and daily.

Eliminate transactions that do not add value

One of the benefits of rate-based order management is that it eliminates transactions that do not add value, but that seem to occur every day in the traditional product delivery process. These non-value added transactions would include urgent telephone calls, fax messages, e-mails, and customer promises that drain both energy and patience. With rate-based order management, reduced transaction costs occur because the Customer Service Representative has "real time" information. They know what agreements were made concerning what can and cannot be done. Knowing the maximum capacities guaranteed by upstream manufacturing and supplier channels allow order promises to be made quickly and with confidence.

Develop multiple order plans

Understanding and responding to customer expectations is a key principle of lean enterprise that significantly impacts on order delivery and flexibility. These expectations include customer time-based demands. As noted earlier, before you try to redesign the product delivery process, you should first develop a Time-Based Demand Profile for each product family in each market segment you are targeting. Figure 11.12 shows how such a profile plots the percentage of demand (i.e., orders) in time segments that are defined with respect to current response lead times.

If you understand customer demand expectations, you can develop multiple order plans and put in place appropriate delivery mechanisms that will ensure the new process yields true market benefits.

For example, one time-based response strategy might be to use limited finished goods inventories to provide immediate response to those customers that want immediate delivery – and, who may be willing to pay a premium. As mentioned earlier, being able to identify these customers is one of the primary reasons for using market segment to group your product lines. You could use a kanban system to replenish these inventories

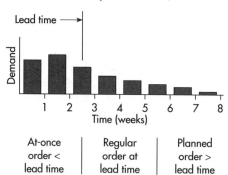

© 1977, Lean Enterprise Systems Design Institute, The University of Tennessee

Figure 11.12   Customer demand profiles by product family

at normal lead times – and, perhaps, receive a higher return to absorb the cost of offering the immediate service. The strategy becomes more viable as normal lead times are reduced, because the level of inventory needed to execute such a strategy becomes more reasonable.

Other order plans might include forward scheduling (at lead time) of the majority of demand requirements that are built-to-order and backwards scheduling for orders that are promised during periods beyond the current lead time. This possibility is attractive because you can offer a spectrum of order plans, each tailored to a segment of the market profile with respect to time. The eventual goal, of course, is to reduce lead times to the point that all demand is satisfied by building all units to order.

Link order promising and production scheduling

The final aspect of Rate-Based Order Management is to link order promising and production scheduling. A precept of the lean enterprise already discussed is the mixed-model smoothing of the production schedule. Producing to a mixed model sequence allows flexible balancing of the flow process and ensures a level demand "pull" across feeder cells, upstream processes, and through supply channels. It is a true challenge to achieve mixed-model flow production in a build-to-order environment and to do it in a way that is both transparent to the customer and compatible with distribution requirements.

PART 7 RATE-BASED MATERIALS MANAGEMENT AND SUPPLIER PROCESS INTEGRATION

A traditional product delivery system does not become a lean enterprise without establishing a new, more responsive supply and distribution channel. When dealing with suppliers, rate-based management calls for long-term relationships, more emphasis on joint development efforts (particularly as these relate to cooperation and technical support in product design), dedicated capacity or response capabilities and, most important, information sharing.

Several tools are used to ensure the right amount of quality materials will be delivered at the right place at the right time. Kanban's pull execution technique (visual signal) is coupled with electronic data interchange (EDI) and fax communication capabilities to broadcast to suppliers rate-based planning information and material releases. One key difference in the new process is that suppliers receive broadcasts indicating a range of expected product per period that include the minimum, plan, and maximum quantities.

DISTRIBUTION CHANNEL INTEGRATION

It is not enough to know what customer's value and to create that value. You must also deliver the product to the customer in a timely manner. You must ensure availability to establish effective channels of distribution. Some concepts of lean production (which may or may not be appropriate for different industries) include:

- Kanban replenishment of demand from the point of sale.
- Weekly direct shipments.
- Establishing milk runs (fixed transportation routings).

Fixed transportation routings are more attractive if the volumes of inbound and outbound shipments are larger. Some transportation companies recognize the potential application of this concept and now create routings for business units as part of their service.

INTEGRATED NETWORK

If you step back and view the entire product delivery process, you will see that the five process segments shown in figure 11.1 actually represent an integrated network of both planning and execution activities.

Each activity forms a critical link in the total process. The companies involved in the network, the suppliers, the manufacturer, the distribution channels, and ultimately the customer form an enterprise that must act together in becoming more competitive. The weakest link will constrain the entire value stream.

The role of the Manager in this blueprint is not to manage the process systemic. The process should be designed such that the systemic is delivered without the routine need for management intervention. Management's role consists of coordinating across functions to reduce sources of variation to the process and to handle the exceptions that arise.

IMPROVING NEW PROCESSES

The pursuit of world class performance is not a program or a project. It is an evolution. Management must focus on the following requirements to sustain momentum and to continually improve.

1   How to keep the organization aligned.
2   How to establish appropriate performance measures to gauge continued progress.
3   How to establish and equip cross-functional teams with the skills to manage change.

The toughest challenge in a fast-paced world is to sustain the alignment of managers, at all levels, behind the change process. After months have passed and gains are made, new books will be released touting the latest fad. The general feeling will be an urge to move on to the next frontier. To Alleviate this problem and keep your team on course, develop a progressive roadmap that clearly delineates the next and subsequent rewards. It is important to keep the team focused. A multitude of different initiatives tends to dilute the ability to concentrate on continuing to build what is now underway. Routine executive team presentations help in this regard. A continuous program of education for managers is needed to keep the necessary focus.

Another area of particular interest is the development of performance measures that are conductive, rather than inhibiting, to the cross-functional nature of process management. A silent phrase that many organizations act out is "now that I know what you are measuring, I know how I am going to behave." There remains a pressing need to kill some existing measures such as departmental efficiency ratings and utilization and replace these with different measures such as on-time delivery, lead time, and share of the market.

To survive in today's global economy, companies are rethinking the ways in which goods and services are manufactured and delivered. They recognize that they must think more broadly than they did in the past – and that the boundaries of the playing field must be broadened accordingly. Where appropriate, companies are changing the very nature and order of the activities that comprise their business processes. Lean enterprise concepts provide a blueprint for guiding these changes.

References

Dyer, "How Chrysler Created An American Keiretsu," *Harvard Business Review*, July–August, 1996.

Fisher, Hammond, Obermeyer, and Ramon, "Making Supply Meet Demand in an Uncertain World," *Harvard Business Review*, May–June, 1994.

Goldratt, E., *It's Not Luck*, The North Rover Press, Great Barrington, MA, 1994.

Greenwood, T. G., "Blueprint For Change: Lean Production Systems," *American Production and Inventory Control Society*, October, 1994.

Grief, Michael, *The Visual Factory: Building Participation Through Shared Information*, Productivity Press, c.1994.

Harper, "Integrated Supply Creates New Relationships," *Industrial Distribution*, May, 1996.

Kim and Takeda, "The JIT Philosophy Is the Culture In Japan," *Production and Inventory Management Journal*, First Quarter, 1996.

Kirby and Hild, "Planning for the successful Building of a Lean Enterprise," *Quality Observer*, August, 1996.

Kumar, "The Power of Trust in Manufacturer-Retailer Relationships," *Harvard Business Review*, November–December, 1996.

Maskell, *Software and the Agile Manufacturer*, Productivity Press, Portland, OR, 1994.

Monden, *Toyota Production System: An Integrated Approach to Just-In-Time*, Industrial Engineering and Management Press, Second Edition, 1993.

Pragman, "JIT II: A Purchasing Concept For Reducing Lead Times in Time-Based Competition," *Business Horizons,* July–August, 1996.

Swartz, *The Hunters and the Hunted; A Non-Linear Solution for Reengineering the Workplace,* Productivity Press, *c.*1994.

Upton, "What Really Makes Factories Flexible?" *Harvard Business Review,* July–August, 1995.

Wilson, "Henry Ford: A Just-in-Time Pioneer," *Production and Inventory Management,* Second Quarter, 1996.

Womack, Jones, and Roos, *The Machine That Changed the World,* Harpers Publishers, New York, *c.*1991.

Womack and Jones, "Beyond Toyota: How to Root Out Waste and Pursue Perfection," *Harvard Business Review,* September–October, 1996.

Womack and Jones, *Lean Thinking,* Simon and Schuster, New York, *c.*1996.

Venkatesan, "Strategic Sourcing: To Make or Not to Make," *Harvard Business Review,* November–December, 1992.

PART
IV

Continuous Improvement and Assessment

12 | Using the Baldrige Framework for Self-Assessment and Continuous Improvement

John P. Evans

Abstract

Many organizations in the United States have used the criteria for the Malcolm Baldrige National Quality Award as a starting point in the creation of internal assessment processes. While much assessment activity continues, legitimate attention is addressed to the matter of insuring that the value gained from assessment is worth the resources committed to doing it. Drawing on the practices and experiences of a number of organizations, this chapter has synthesized a series of ideas about assessment.

INTRODUCTION AND BACKGROUND

For today's reader the competitive situation that existed for US industry in the mid-1980s seems a bit distant. Not only US companies, but whole US industries had lost market share to competitors, particularly very successful Japanese manufacturing organizations. A timely *Business Week* article in 1987 documented comparisons between US and Japanese manufacturers in a number of different industries.[1] Fortunately, by 1987 a number of individual companies had begun to address these competitive issues aggressively through systematic efforts to improve quality, eliminate defects and waste, and (thereby) reduce cost. In addition the Congress of the United States approved the "Malcolm Baldrige National Quality Improvement Act of 1987" and the President signed Public Law 100–107 into law on August 20, 1987. While the future consequences of this act could not all be anticipated at the time, it seems fair to say that the Malcolm Baldrige National Quality Award created by this act has had a very substantial impact on the way in which leaders of organizations in the United States think about quality improvement.

At the time of its passage a national quality award was expected to be beneficial by:

1 Helping to stimulate American companies to improve quality and productivity for the pride of recognition while obtaining a competitive edge through increased profits.
2 Recognizing the achievements of those companies which improve the quality of their goods and services and providing an example to others.

3   Establishing guidelines and criteria that can be used by business,
    industrial, governmental, and other organizations in evaluating their
    own quality improvement efforts.
4   Providing specific guidance for other American organizations that
    wish to learn how to manage for high quality by making available
    detailed information on how winning organizations were able to
    change their cultures and achieve eminence.[2]

These objectives of bringing attention to quality as a competitive issue,
recognizing achievement, and providing for information transfer may be
the better known purposes of the Baldrige Award. Perhaps less well known
is the fact that the Act that created the Award also sought a vehicle that
would be useful for what we now call self-assessment (of quality systems).
The point is that the sponsors of the Act foresaw that applications for the
Award might turn out to be the tip of the iceberg, with self-assessment
occurring in many organizations without regard to external recognition.
In fact, by 1996 some 41[3] state awards had been created in the United
States and the Baldrige evaluation framework has been widely adapted and
emulated in the national awards of other countries. In addition numerous
companies have created mechanisms both for self-assessment and for
internal, corporate quality awards. The Baldrige framework and process
will be the point of departure for this chapter.

Let's establish a working definition of "self-assessment" to be used
throughout this chapter. By self-assessment (or simply assessment, within
this chapter) we mean

> Regularly evaluating the key systems, processes, and results of an organiza-
> tion by following an established framework and methodology in order to
> create a basis for the strategic and continual improvement of the organiza-
> tion's performance.

Several comments will help to clarify the scope and intent of this definition.

1   "Regularly" implies that we do not expect self-assessment to be a one-
    time or even only an occasional activity, but rather a process that is
    integrated into the way in which an organization runs and improves
    its performance. "Regularly" expresses the notion of successive cycles
    of assessment and follow-on actions to achieve improvements.
2   While assessment does not imply a literally exhaustive review of each
    system, etc., "key" is meant to indicate comprehensive review of an
    organization and not a more narrow, and possibly more detailed,
    audit of some portion of the activity.
3   Assessment is intended to encompass both breakthrough and incre-
    mental improvement actions.
4   Finally, we will typically have a business unit as the reference point,
    even though assessment could be applied to corporate offices, a
    corporate functional unit, or the plant level.

The general context and role that we envision for assessment could be thought of as the "Check" step in "Plan-Do-Check-Act" at the business unit level. Thus, the primary motivation for assessment considered here is to obtain a diagnosis to guide improvement. We will not address activities that are undertaken primarily for purposes of seeking some quality award, even though a number of organizations conduct self-assessments prior to applying for an external award. In a 1996 survey conducted by the Total Quality Management Center of The Conference Board 69 of 107 respondents (65 percent) reported that they are either doing or planning to do self-assessment.[4] In addition, the primary reason for these activity was reported as gathering information to guide efforts to improve key processes.

OVERVIEW OF THE MALCOLM BALDRIGE NATIONAL QUALITY AWARD

As noted above, the Baldrige process serves as a point of reference for this chapter. However, based on the author's observation of the practices of a number of organizations, it is now clear that value-adding assessment can be conducted effectively by a wide range of practices that vary considerably from the "standard Baldrige" model. The range of choices available to organizations conducting assessment will be addressed as we proceed through this chapter.

Since the first Award cycle in 1988, the criteria for the Baldrige Award have been revised through a systematic, annual cycle of improvement. From the first year the criteria have been organized into seven categories (see figure 12.1) with each category containing two or more items and several "areas to address" that support a detailed evaluation. In revising the criteria for the 1995 Award cycle, the criteria at both the category and item level were refined in order to establish more clearly the fact that "quality" is not something that is done "on the side", but should instead be considered integral to leading a business to excellent performance for its various stakeholders-employees, customers, shareholders, and society. Figure 12.1 presents an overall view of the Baldrige criteria at the category level. Appendix 1 lists the individual items that comprise the 1997 Baldrige criteria. These elements will provide the basis for discussion of a "manager's model" built from Baldrige items.

The items that comprise the Baldrige criteria fall into two groups.

(1) "Approach and deployment" items ask how an organization accomplishes a particular activity (e.g., determining customer requirements and expectations) and how widely that approach is practiced throughout the organization. Higher scores are assigned for systematic processes that are designed to prevent errors and waste and that are widely deployed throughout an organization.

(2) "Results" items ask for performance data for the metrics that the organization uses to track performance. The particular measures are not prescribed but rather should be chosen by the business unit to form a

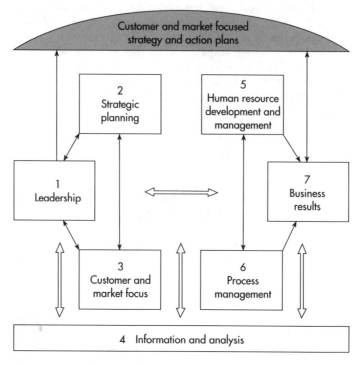

Figure 12.1   Baldrige award criteria framework (a systems perspective)

comprehensive set of measures that will be useful to management in evaluating performance. Higher scores are assigned to results that are at good performance levels, reflect improving trends, and compare favorably with external standards such as "industry best" or Baldrige Award winners.

DESIGNING AN ASSESSMENT PROCESS

Building on the definition proposed, the view taken here is that assessment is systematic, structured, and regular (rather than ad hoc, informal, and one-time). In addition the primary purpose for conducting an assessment is presumed to be to develop information that can be used to guide selection of improvement actions. If assessment is to play that sort of role, it could be viewed schematically as portrayed in figure 12.2. The output of an assessment is a collection of identified strengths and areas for improvement for the business unit. The typical experience is that the list of improvement opportunities is far longer than can realistically or usefully be attacked simultaneously. It is thus necessary to consider those opportunities in the context of the specific business unit. The value to the business of accomplishing any of the possible improvements and the time and resources

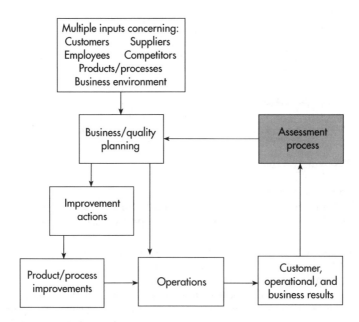

Figure 12.2 The planning-assessment link

required to do that must all be considered. Evaluation, prioritization, and conscious selection of which improvement opportunities will be attacked must all occur in some way. The outputs of an assessment are thus shown schematically in figure 12.2 as inputs to the planning process of the business unit. And the planning process is depicted as setting both an annual operating plan and a plan for improvement actions that have been selected from the "menu" created by the assessment.

In discussing assessment with various organizations that are either already involved or are contemplating it, the author has found it beneficial to use a process model as a vehicle for describing a series of key roles and decisions for the business unit. One of the choices available is following the Baldrige Award process. This would entail developing a document like an Award application (possibly running to 50 pages or more) which is then evaluated by one or more people performing the role of Examiners, who prepare a list of strengths and areas for improvement which is then transmitted to the leadership of the business unit in some way. While some organizations follow this approach, others, particularly at early stages of either their quality effort or their experience with assessment, seek some way to gain most of the benefit from assessment without having to copy the Baldrige process in its full detail.

Figure 12.3 presents a schematic model of an assessment process as a basis for describing the choices that should be considered in designing an assessment process and also for suggesting what appear to be good practices. The building blocks of an assessment process are the following:

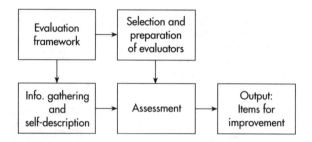

Figure 12.3 An assessment process

- *Framework for evaluation*
  The framework sets the overall agenda for the assessment by indicating what issues will be reviewed. The point is to make this choice in advance so that the agenda and scope for the assessment are defined rather than ad hoc. The result could be the full Baldrige criteria but other choices will be described below.
- *Information gathering and self-description*
  The necessary information may already exist in peoples' minds, in documents, and in data bases, but will not necessarily fit any particular assessment framework. The organization that plans to conduct an assessment will want to make choices here that are consistent with the purposes for which the assessment is being conducted and that balance the resources required with that purpose. The tasks of compiling and organizing information according to the assessment framework, plus any writing, compressing, and editing can be consequential. The typical experience of an applicant for the Baldrige Award is that a great deal of work goes into writing the 50-page application, even though this experience usually has considerable value in itself.
- *Evaluators (Examiners)*
  The evaluators apply the framework for evaluation to information about the organization. They prepare a summary of strengths and areas for improvement. They may also be asked to prepare a feedback report, possibly to be delivered in writing. "Evaluators" is used here deliberately to distinguish these people from individuals who have preparation equivalent to Examiners for the Baldrige Award. Whoever these people are, they must be oriented to the framework and they must already have or have access to the necessary information about the organization. They might be "examiner-equivalents" but other choices are possible.
- *Assessment*
  This step in the assessment process creates the list of specific strengths and areas for improvement that pertain to the business unit being assessed. As will be discussed in more detail below, this work can be accomplished in a variety of ways. Some choices will be more

applicable to an organization's situation and purpose than others. Some organizations assign a score or "quality maturity level" to each item in the framework. When completed the result is an overall profile of current status and it provides a basis for comparison with other assessments.

■ *Assessment Output*
This is the specific list of strengths and areas for improvement for the business unit. If the assessment is viewed as analogous to an annual physical exam, the assessment output is the doctor's diagnosis of the characteristics that are within normal ranges and those that are not and may therefore warrant attention (improvement).

From the material above it can easily be seen that the evaluators play a key role in the assessment process. Another key role, which here will be called the Process Owner, is implicit in the material above. The decision about who will do the evaluation is a central one which then drives many key features of how an assessment will actually be accomplished. As a result, this decision, while probably made by the Process Owner, also influences the work of the Process Owner.

Let's consider several options for choosing evaluators and the implications of those options. The range of choices can be illustrated by the list below.

■ senior managers (and possibly others) from within the business unit;
■ managers from outside the business unit but within the corporation; and
■ individuals from outside the business unit, or even outside the corporation, who might be "examiner-equivalents" (meaning that they have preparation comparable to that of Examiners for the Baldrige Award).

Obviously, the people within the business unit being reviewed should be knowledgeable about the systems, processes, and measurement system of that unit. They are less likely to be familiar, at least initially, with using a specific evaluation framework and approach to assessment such as the Baldrige framework or an adaptation of it for use by the business unit. One of the tasks for the Process Owner will be to provide those individuals with a thorough orientation to the framework to be used and to how the information is to be gathered and the assessment performed.

In contrast, external evaluators could be chosen for their familiarity with the particular evaluation framework that is to be used, for their understanding of what the Process Owner expects from evaluators as the product of their work, and for their knowledge of good practices in other organizations. These external evaluators would not likely be knowledgeable of the business unit's systems and processes. Thus, the Process Owner will necessarily be responsible for overseeing the compiling and organizing of information into a package that the evaluators can evaluate. In addition, it will be important to consider in advance how people within the business unit will receive the outputs from the work of these evaluators. External evaluators can be expected to provide a report in a great deal of detail, but how senior managers respond to it may depend on whether steps are taken to increase the likelihood that they understand, accept, and take ownership of the results.

To summarize briefly, the Process Owner who is designing an assessment process for a single business unit or for a group of them has important choices to make for each of the primary elements of an assessment process. These will be addressed more extensively below. However, the decision about who does the evaluation is central and it drives a great deal of what the Process Owner does to facilitate and support the assessment process. Therefore, this decision should be made early and should support the purposes for which the assessment is being conducted.

The most obvious purpose for conducting a self-assessment is to compile information that will then lead to focused improvement actions. These actions should be focused on improving key processes so that business performance will improve over time. However, experience in organizations that have done assessments suggests that additional issues should be considered. In our definition of assessment we described it as a regular, i.e. repeated, process. At the time of the first assessment, however, no guarantee exists that a second one will occur. This makes building knowledge and understanding of the assessment process a secondary objective of the assessment. In other words, if an assessment can help the managers of a business unit to improve their understanding of a "model for success" in their business, assessment is more likely to be seen as an activity that can advance the achievement of that success.

In each of the elements of the model of an assessment process, the choices available to the Process Owner will be described below as ranging along a spectrum from informal and loosely structured to more formal and tightly structured. In all cases the more formal versions bring certain advantages, but typically at the cost of greater resource use to accomplish the assessment. Figure 12.4 below shows relationships that the Process Owner should consider in making these key decisions.

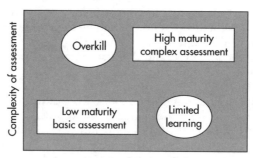

Figure 12.4 Matching maturity and approach to assessment

In the upper left-hand corner of figure 12.4 a complex assessment is associated with a quality effort in its relatively early stages. While this combination should produce a great deal of useful information, this organization may benefit more from a more basic analysis that identifies and concentrates on a relatively small number of important improvement issues. This combination also may run the risk of discouraging managers from conducting additional assessments. On the other hand, if a relatively simple assessment model is used for an organization that has a mature quality effort (lower right-hand corner of figure 12.4), the result may be limited insight into where to concentrate improvement efforts. An advanced quality effort may have many of the building blocks in place, but may be able to use an assessment to evaluate the extent to which those elements are functioning effectively as a linked system. This is likely to require a relatively sophisticated approach to assessment. Experience suggests matching the approach to assessment and the maturity of the organization's quality effort so as to be on the southwest–northeast diagonal in figure 12.4. Later in this chapter we suggest some prototype assessment processes for different situations.

A STEP-BY-STEP APPROACH TO DESIGNING AN ASSESSMENT

Step 1: establish the purpose

A first assessment might be used to review the primary building blocks of the business unit's quality effort. The output desired may be a list of the main strengths and areas for improvement for the key processes. A unit that has reached an advanced level of maturity with quality improvement may want to concentrate on linkages among the various elements of its quality system and it may want a validity check by people external to the unit. This will calibrate assessments that have previously been done internally against the experience of the external evaluators. Table 12.1 below gives a flavor of the range of choices for three hypothetical levels of maturity for a quality effort.

Table 12.1   Three hypothetical levels of maturity for a quality effort: choices

Early	Maturing	Advanced
1 Evaluate key processes. 2 Build understanding of and support for assessment.	1 Conduct a thorough diagnosis. 2 Demonstrate value for improving the business.	1 Obtain a thorough evaluation with validity check. 2 Capture learning from outside perspectives.

Process owner's role: Engage appropriate senior members of the business unit in this decision by considering the issues suggested in figure 12.4.

Step 2: identify the evaluators

The pivotal role that the decision about evaluators plays was described earlier. An important point to remember is that this choice should be consistent with the organization's effort and also with the purposes of the assessment. As table 12.2 below suggests, assessments can be used not only for diagnosis but also to improve managers' understanding both of an assessment process and also of the level of performance that the organizations' key processes have reached.

The advantage of internal evaluators is presumably knowledge of the systems and processes that already exist, so the group of evaluators needs to be large enough to provide that coverage. This can easily require eight to a dozen people and some organizations use internal evaluation teams of 15 to 18 people. The "diagonal slice" referred to in the table below is a way to cover multiple functions and levels of an organization while still keeping the group at a manageable size. This option will reappear in material to follow. As the emphasis shifts in the direction of external evaluators, the size of the group involved can usually be decreased. A group of at least three is advisable and for effective coverage of the business and the assessment agenda it may expand to five to seven people.

Process owner's role: At the time of the decision, bring key senior managers into the discussion so that they understand the choice and the reason for it. As the work of the assessment progresses, orient internal evaluators to their responsibilities or coordinate the preparation of information and the work of any external evaluators.

Table 12.2   Three hypothetical levels of maturity for a quality effort: assessments/lack of performance

Early	*Maturing*	*Advanced*
All evaluators are internal to the business unit. A first assessment might use only managers.	Early assessment might use only internal evaluators. Consider using a "diagonal slice".	Select some evaluators, if not all, external to the business unit.

Step 3: choose the evaluation framework

Guided by the maturity of the quality effort and the purposes of the assessment, determine the breadth and level of detail for the assessment "agenda". The Baldrige framework, consisting of seven categories and

Table 12.3 Three hypothetical levels of maturity for a quality effort: prototypical choices

Early	Maturing	Advanced
Select Baldrige items of primary interest. Tailor the language of the items for easy understanding within the business unit.	Select the full Baldrige scope (expand as relevant). Tailor the language for easy understanding within the business unit.	Select the full Baldrige scope and use the standard version, particularly if evaluating progress relative to known scores.

20 items, serves as a point of departure point for these decisions. Because it already exists, has been refined annually since 1989, and has been validated through extensive use, it may appear to be an easy choice. A number of organizations that are now experienced with self-assessment have modified this framework in a number of ways. The scope of the coverage could be reduced to emphasize a small number of key issues in an early assessment or expanded to include or emphasize issues of particular importance to the business unit being reviewed. For example, some organizations have built ideas from ISO 9000 into their self-assessment agendas. On the other hand, the language of the Baldrige framework can be adapted to the internal vocabulary of the business being reviewed. This latter step can be particularly useful for internal evaluators who will have significant responsibilities in the information gathering portions of the self-assessment (more on this below).

Whether or not results of the assessment are to be compared with those for other business units may become a factor in this decision. If comparability is to be sought across several units, a consistent framework should obviously be chosen for all of those units. To the extent that comparisons with external reference points are sought, it will be desirable to adhere closely to the Baldrige framework, simply due to its wide deployment.

Table 12.3 is intended to suggest only prototypical choices, not prescriptive ones. However, these choices fit generally with the three sets of purposes outlined earlier. With regard to assessments for an "early" company, this author's bias is still to use all seven Baldrige categories, even if in simplified language, because of the comprehensiveness of the Baldrige model. Alternatively, the Baldrige framework may be replaced by one developed within a large corporation for consistent use in all business units over time, so that any scores that are developed can be compared meaningfully.

Process owner's role: Facilitate a discussion among senior managers concerning this decision. This may take the form of proposing and explaining a particular choice. The Process Owner has an important role here in adapting the methodology to the needs of the business unit. And, once the decision is made, he or she would be the developer of the modified language. An option might exist to "import" an evaluation framework from some other environment (e.g., another company), in which case the Process Owner has the task of studying and then explaining that framework. Other responsibilities related to this choice will appear in the discussion below.

Step 4: determine how the assessment is to be conducted and how information will be gathered

This step actually represents two sets of decisions, but because they are related, they are represented as one step.

For what we have called an advanced assessment using outside evaluators, the actual evaluation would typically be conducted by each of several evaluators first working independently and using a written summary (such as a pro forma Baldrige application) as the basis. For this case, the decision to use outside evaluators drives a number of other decisions and much of the preparation for an assessment will take the form of preparing the written summary of systems, processes, and results in accordance with the evaluation framework that has been adopted.

If the decision has been made to use evaluators who are internal to the business unit, some interesting variations are possible for conducting the assessment and gathering the input information. The least formal approach, which is well-suited to a first assessment, might involve a facilitated meeting in which the evaluators are first provided an orientation to the meaning and scope of each item in the assessment framework. The participants are then asked to identify strengths and areas for improvement for each item to be discussed. The emphasis here could be on identifying whether a systematic approach exists for key processes and the degree to which that approach has been fully deployed throughout the business unit. Adopting this level of informality for a first assessment places a special burden on the facilitator of the meeting to provide a clear orientation to each item and then to be thorough in leading the discussion of strengths and weaknesses. This approach also imposes substantial burdens on the participants to be objective about the maturity and deployment of the approaches that are in place. Relying on the memory of participants for discussion of results items (e.g., the levels and trends of customer satisfaction data, performance of key processes, and the like) runs the risk of incorrect or incomplete recall.

A facilitated meeting can be raised to a higher level of formality by identifying evaluators in advance and making clear assignments of information to be gathered in advance of the assessment meeting. An interesting use of the diagonal slice approach to evaluation is to divide a team of 15 to 18 individuals into three sub-teams and then to divide the work of information gathering among the sub-teams as outlined in the matrix shown in table 12.4.

Table 12.4   Information-gathering matrix for lead and back-up teams

	Team A	*Team B*	*Team C*
Lead	Categories 1, 3, 4	Categories 5, 6	Categories 2, 7
Back-up	Categories 5, 6	Categories 2, 7	Categories 1, 3, 4

Lead responsibility means that the team is to prepare the primary analysis of those items, identify the strengths, areas for improvement, and assign an evaluation or score (if that is part of the process). Information for this analysis would be gathered in advance, but the actual assessment could be done either as pre-meeting work or in a preliminary portion of the assessment meeting and then presented by the lead team. The team with back-up responsibility is expected to acquire the same knowledge and then simply to complement the lead team's presentation by identifying additional comments for the assessment and possibly providing another perspective on the score. For each item there is a third team that has no advance assignment. This team can play a constructive, but devil's advocate role, concerning whether an approach is truly systematic or well-deployed, or whether the results data presented are complete. Forming each sub-team as a diagonal slice of the organization helps to achieve good coverage of the activities of the business unit.

"To score or not to score" is an important question for the assessment process. If the emphasis is really on capturing information to guide improvement, the areas for improvement constitute the crucial product of the assessment meeting. For a first assessment it might be desirable to omit scoring in order to concentrate on the diagnostic role of the activity. Eventually, and even for a first assessment, a desire for some overall measure of maturity or progress is likely to be desired. The Baldrige process enables this summary by allocating 1,000 points among the 20 items and also calibrating a scoring scale for 0 to 100 percent for each item. At the end of the assessment, these item percentages can be multiplied by the item point allocations and summed to achieve an overall weighted score (out of the maximum possible score of 1,000).

The training for Baldrige Examiners allocates a considerable amount of effort to the task of calibrating Examiners to the scoring scale. General purpose Baldrige scoring guidelines have been developed with separate segments for approach-deployment and results items. If external evaluators are used, they can be chosen from a group that has already received this calibration. If internal evaluators have not had this preparation in advance, it will be useful to provide it in order to reduce variation among evaluators in assigning scores. In various corporate assessment processes, a couple of devices have been used effectively to help evaluators through this aspect of the work. The devices are variously called "scoring thermometers" or "Quality Maturity Ladders." In versions of these tools that are

Table 12.5 Three hypothetical levels of maturity for a quality effort: typical choices for different levels of maturity

Early	*Maturing*	*Advanced*
Assessment conducted in a facilitated meeting with a small set of managers serving as evaluators.	Assessment conducted in a facilitated meeting using a diagonal slice team as evaluators.	Assessment conducted by external evaluators using a written summary of processes and results.
Evaluators are oriented to the evaluation framework, but rely on memory of processes and results data.	Evaluators are oriented to the evaluation framework and given advance assignments for data gathering.	Process descriptions and results data are organized into a formal written summary for the evaluators.

in common use, the thermometers happen to involve 100-point scales (with 10-point steps) and the ladders happen to involve 4-point scales. However these details are handled, the basic point is to create *for each item* an association between the progress that has been accomplished and a score or maturity level. These tools can be extremely valuable in reducing debates about what score to assign to an item because they help to keep the evaluators focused on the comments (strengths and areas for improvement) that describe the organization's situation for each item.

The desire to have an overall score at the end of an assessment is easy to understand. This supports comparison over time and it also supports comparison to levels of performance that might have been created in internal corporate quality awards or identified with various external awards which associate various levels of recognition with a particular score. However, the decision to assign scores brings with it the task of calibrating the evaluators and the work of doing that must typically be supported by the Process Owner. Table 12.5 outlines choices that might be typical for different levels of quality maturity.

Process owner's role: Select the methodology in discussion with appropriate senior managers so that the purposes of the assessment can be considered along with the level of resource commitment required to execute it. When internal evaluators are to be used, provide the necessary orientation, plan the assessment meeting, and then facilitate it. If scoring is to be done, prepare any materials that will be used to provide calibrations. When external evaluators are to be used, select those evaluators and establish expectations with them. Also, manage the preparation of the written summary that is to serve as the basis for their work.

A number of organizations have found Assessment Workbooks to be an effective way to prepare for and then execute this work. Once the assessment framework has been determined, the Assessment Workbook might typically have the following organization for each topic (item) to be evaluated.

- A concise statement of the topic or item (e.g., Leadership System or Customer Satisfaction Results).
- A statement which expands and illustrates the issues to be considered.
- Space for the evaluator to make notes and to identify specific strengths and areas for improvement within the scope of this item.
- Descriptive statements that reflect successive levels of maturity or performance along with the score or maturity level associated with that level.
- Space to record the score or maturity level assigned by the evaluator.

Assessment Workbooks are useful vehicles for orienting internal evaluators and they also help to create some consistency in the approach taken by these evaluators as the assessment progresses.

Step 5: conduct the assessment and obtain/prepare the assessment output

This is largely a matter of executing the plans that have been made in the preceding steps. Whatever those choices were, one result of the assessment work should be a list of strengths and areas for improvement for each item that is covered in the evaluation framework. If scoring was included in the planned outputs, some consideration should be given to how variation among evaluators will be handled. The Baldrige process, of course, encompasses a "consensus" stage that is used to explore and reduce variation in scoring. The details of that need not concern us here, but the point is to reduce the variation among scores assigned by improving the shared understanding of both the facts and also how those facts relate to the item of evaluation and the scoring scale. With internal evaluators working in an assessment meeting, a consensus discussion can occur as each item is processed. With external evaluators the choices include omitting the consensus process, conducting consensus by conference call (as the Baldrige process does), or having a consensus meeting of the evaluators (as some state awards do).

For an informal assessment meeting, the outputs may be as informal as information captured on flip chart sheets for each item. In this case, a follow-up transcription of this material will be important. If internal evaluators have been asked to prepare summaries of strengths and areas for improvement in advance of the assessment meeting, these working papers provide the basis for a summary of the assessment activity. When external evaluators are used, each evaluator would typically prepare a written set of comments (strengths, areas for improvement, and scores). A synthesizing process might be used to reduce these separate summaries to a single assessment report.

In addition to this, relatively obvious work of creating an assessment report, as the level of maturity of the business unit's quality effort advances, the level of sophistication sought from the assessment is likely to escalate as well. The comments on individual items then become the raw material for a synthesis of important themes and an opportunity to test whether the various elements of the organization's activities are functioning as an effective system. Here various linkage questions can be asked. Examples include:

> Is the unit using customer satisfaction data to check whether a clear understanding of customer requirements exists? Is the unit using those same data to provide inputs to the design and creation of products and services?
>
> Is the unit using other kinds of feedback from customers (e.g., complaint data, warranty activity, requests for help, etc.) as a source of insight into processes that should be improved?
>
> Does the unit's information system provide measurements of the key processes that determine perceptions of customer value?
>
> Does the unit match evaluations of the important capabilities of the work force against projections of those capabilities needed for the future as a starting point for formulation of action plans?
>
> Does the unit use its employee survey to obtain feedback on the completeness of training and on the level of support from supervisors and managers?

As the processes that are the subject of individual items in the evaluation framework become well-documented, systemically followed, and well deployed, these more sophisticated questions become important. External evaluators can be asked to address this in a summary of the evaluations of individual items. When internal evaluators are used, this synthesis can be conducted at the conclusion of the assessment meeting. Alternatively, this can be a follow-on activity conducted or coordinated by the Process Owner.

Once the assessment has been completed, it is important to take steps that will cause the organization to view the assessment not as some add-on activity that is independent of achieving the desired performance from the business, but an integral part of that activity. This can be difficult but it can be helped by a variety of activities suggested in the list below.

- Involve senior managers in the assessment meeting, including the discussion that synthesizes important themes and opportunities from the detailed assessment of individual items.
- Formalize use of the assessment outputs at an early stage of the unit's planning process.
- Have the evaluators (whether internal or external) make an oral presentation of feedback to senior managers.
- Invite evaluators to provide prescriptive feedback once the detailed evaluations have been completed.
- Reorganize the assessment results along lines suggested by the following section of this chapter as a means to improve the insights into improvement opportunities.

Table 12.6 Three hypothetical levels of maturity for a quality effort: assessment discussion and feedback

Early	*Maturing*	*Advanced*
Capture the key strengths and areas for improvement from the assessment meeting as a follow-up action.	Designate one or more people to capture the assessment discussion and edit it into a summary report.	Have the external evaluators prepare a single feedback report, including key themes in an overall evaluation.

Process owner's role: Plan in advance what the products of the assessment work are to be and make the assignments that are necessary to obtain them. Discuss with senior managers how these assessment outputs will be used to identify specific actions to improve key processes.

Table 12.7 below recaps the preceding discussion. It should be noted that these guidelines should be viewed as suggestions, not as a prescription. The objective in each column is to provide ideas for each step in the process that are consistent with the maturity level and objectives represented by that column.

BUILDING A MANAGEMENT MODEL BASED ON THE BALDRIGE CRITERIA

Assessment is not, of course, an end in itself. Assessment should really facilitate and leverage managers' efforts to improve the performance of an organization. The Baldrige framework is organized to highlight seven functional themes that are clearly an important basis for business performance. This framework is organized around the principles and concepts of quality improvement that have been applied and tested in many organizations. This section creates a management model from the Baldrige framework in order to emphasize a number of important linkages. As these linkages become effective, an organization moves from the "basic building blocks" stage of quality in the direction of an integrated, learning and improving organization.

The material in this section could be used in either of two ways:

1 To plan where emphasis should be placed during an assessment; and
2 To organize the summary and synthesis of assessment results.

The model groups the items around six themes:

- Leadership: vision, values, systems.
- Value chain items (meeting current requirements).
- Support items and feedback (related to current requirements).
- Direction setting: input items.
- Direction setting: outputs.
- Leadership: closing the loop with feedback.

Table 12.7 Summary of the step-by-step approach to designing an assessment process

Process step	Early	Maturing	Advanced
Step 1: Establish the Purpose	1 Evaluate key processes. 2 Build understanding of and support for assessment.	1 Conduct a thorough diagnosis. 2 Demonstrate value for improving the business.	1 Obtain a thorough evaluation with validity check. 2 Capture learning from outside perspectives.
Step 2: Identify the Evaluators	All evaluators are internal to the business unit. A first assessment might use only managers.	Early assessment might use only internal evaluators. Consider using a "diagonal slice."	Select some evaluators, if not all, external to the business unit.
Step 3: Choose the evaluation framework	Select Baldrige items of primary interest. Tailor the language of the items for easy understanding within the business unit.	Select the full Baldrige scope (expand as relevant). Tailor the language for easy understanding within the business unit.	Select the full Baldrige scope and use the standard version, particularly if evaluating progress relative to known scores.
Step 4: Determine how the assessment is to be conducted and how information will be gathered	Assessment conducted in a facilitated meeting with a small set of managers serving as evaluators.	Assessment conducted in a facilitated meeting using a diagonal slice team as evaluators.	Assessment conducted by external evaluators using a written summary of processes and results.
	Evaluators are oriented to the evaluation framework, but rely on memory of processes and results data.	Evaluators are oriented to the evaluation framework and given advance assignments for data gathering.	Process descriptions and results data are organized into a formal written summary for the evaluators.
Step 5: Conduct the assessment and obtain/prepare the assessment output	Capture the key strengths and areas for improvement from the assessment meeting as a follow-up action.	Designate one or more people to capture the assessment discussion and edit it into a summary report.	Have the external evaluators prepare a single feedback report, including key themes in an overall evaluation.

Each of these groupings consists of several items from the Baldrige criteria. Each Baldrige item appears at least once. Some appear more than once because they logically contribute to more than one section. Each section of the model is described and discussed below.

Leadership: vision, values, systems

The logic of this section is to pull together the items that are of most direct significance to senior leadership and that are most directly influenced by that group. While decisions of senior leadership can clearly influence any portion of the organization and its operation, the premise here is to concentrate on those items where the influence of senior leadership is most immediate. The elements of this section of the model are described first in brief statements and then linkages are outlined for the most closely related items from the 1998 version of the criteria for the Baldrige Award.

Leadership system (1.1)

How senior leaders guide the company in setting directions and in developing and sustaining an effective leadership system.

Strategy development process (2.1)

How the company sets strategic directions to strengthen its business performance and competitive position.

Company strategy (2.2)

The company's strategy and action plans, how they are deployed and how performance is tracked.

Key performance requirements and measures; an outline of overall human resource plans.

How the company's performance projects in the future relative to competitors or key benchmarks.

Customer satisfaction results (7.1)

Results for key measures of customer satisfaction, dissatisfaction, and satisfaction relative to competitors.

Financial and market results (7.2)

Results for key measures of financial and market performance.

Human resource results (7.3)

Results for key measures of human resource issues, such as employee development, well-being, satisfaction, and work system performance.

Supplier and partner results (7.4)

Results for key measures of supplier and partner performance.

Company-specific results (7.5)

Results for key measures that significantly contribute to customer satisfaction, operational, financial, and marketplace performance.

A diagram that reflects the relationships for this section appears below as figure 12.5. This portion of the model emphasizes the direct influence of senior leadership on the selection of mission (e.g., businesses in which to compete), vision, values, organization, communication, and planning. It shows "execution" (without detail) as being driven by the company's strategy with performance results from this combination of activities. As decisions are deployed into expectations and accountabilities throughout the organization and reinforced by the communications and other actions of senior leaders, all facets of the organization are affected. This section of the model suggests the direct involvement of leadership in creating the environment, culture, and high-level approaches that will be used within the organization.

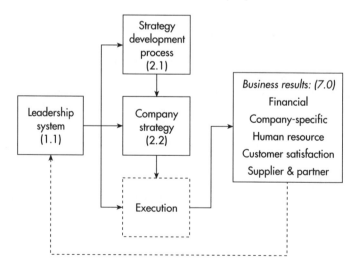

Figure 12.5 Leadership: values, directions, and systems

Value Chain Items

Customer and market knowledge (3.1) (emphasis on requirements of current customers)

How the company determines the requirements, expectations, and preferences of customers.

Management of product and service processes (6.1)

How products and services are designed, implemented, and improved.

How processes for production and delivery of products and services are designed, managed, and improved.

Management of supplier and partnering processes (6.3)

How supplier and partnering processes and relationships are managed and improved.

Customer accessibility and complaint management (3.2)

How access and information are provided so that customers can easily seek assistance, conduct business, obtain service, and make complaints.

Measuring performance relative to current requirements

Customer satisfaction results (7.1). Results for key measures of customer satisfaction, dissatisfaction, and satisfaction relative to competitors.

Human resource results (7.3). Results for key measures of human resource issues, such as employee development, well-being, satisfaction, and work system performance.

Supplier and partner results (7.4). Results for key measures of supplier and partner performance.

Company-specific results (7.5). Results for key measures that significantly contribute to customer satisfaction, operational, financial, and marketplace performance.

A diagram that presents the relationships among the items in this portion of the model appears below as figure 12.6. This section focuses on the flow from knowledge of customer requirements and expectations, through design of products and services, through delivery processes (including supplier activities), to post-sale activities (ranging from service to complaint resolution) to results that both summarize performance and provide information that can be used for the improvement of all of these processes.

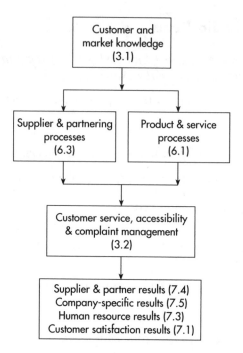

Figure 12.6 Value chain items

Items that support the value chain

Selection and use of information and data (4.1)

Selection, management, and use of information and data needed to support key business processes and action plans and to improve company performance.

Management of support service processes (6.2)

How key support services processes are designed, implemented, managed, and improved.

Work systems (5.1)

How work and job design, along with compensation and recognition systems enable and encourage employees to contribute effectively to achieving the company's performance and learning objectives.

Employee education, training, and development (5.2)

How education and training support key company plans and needs, including building knowledge, skills, and capabilities, contributing to improved employee performance and development.

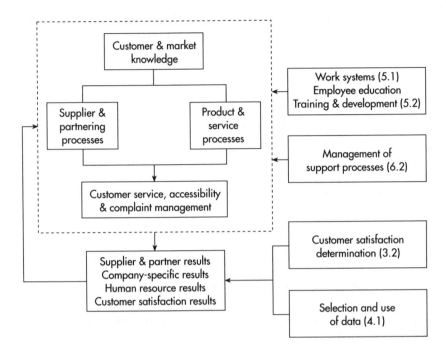

Figure 12.7   Support items and feedback loops

Customer satisfaction determination (3.2)

How customer satisfaction is determined.

A diagram that presents the linkages for this portion of the model appears as figure 12.7. While the topics included here under the heading of support items span a diverse range of issues, they address explicitly a number of processes or capabilities that must be in place in order not only to execute activities on the value chain, but also to be in position to improve those activities in a systematic way.

Direction setting: input items

In this section we shift the focus from how a company executes its current revenue producing business to how it prepares for the future. This section summarizes a broad range of inputs that a company might incorporate in its planning.

Customer and market knowledge (3.1)

How longer-term requirements, expectations, and preferences are determined for target and potential customers and markets.

How the company attempts to understand and anticipate needs and how it develops and evaluates business opportunities.

Selection and use of comparative information and data (4.2)

How comparative data that are used to improve performance and competitive position are selected, managed, and used.

Analysis and review of company performance (4.3)

How the company analyzes and reviews performance to assess progress relative to plans and to identify key areas for improvement.

Company responsibility and citizenship (1.2)

How the company addresses its responsibilities to the public and how the company practices good citizenship.

Employee well-being and satisfaction (5.3)

How the company maintains a work environment and work climate that support the well-being, satisfaction, and motivation of employees.

Customer Satisfaction Results (7.1)
Financial and Market Results (7.2)
Human Resource Results (7.3)
Supplier and Partner Results (7.4)
Company-Specific Results (7.5)

Descriptions of these items appeared earlier.

A diagram that reflects the linkages of this portion of the model appears below as figure 12.8. This section of the model summarizes a wide range of information that might logically be used as inputs for a company's planning process. Once an assessment process is in use on a regular basis, results from the most recent assessment as well as progress reports on improvement actions would also constitute information for consideration in the early stages of the planning process.

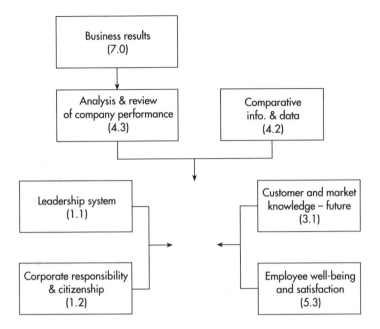

Figure 12.8 Direction setting – input items

Direction setting: outputs

This section of the model consists of two elements presented previously within the section on Leadership: Vision, Values, and Systems.

Strategy development (2.1)
Company strategy (2.2)

Descriptions of these items appeared earlier. The relationship of these items to the input items is described below in figure 12.9. Outputs of these planning activities might typically include an Annual Operating Plan that identifies key operating objectives for the coming year. However, the direction and momentum for improvement typically come from supplemental information that emerges from the planning process. Key business drivers state the high priority capabilities and performance levels that are intended to take the company to its next desired level of performance, not just in financial results, but also with regard to capabilities that have been identified as instrumental to meeting emerging customer requirements and market opportunities. Consequently, these planning outputs could be aimed at virtually any portion of an organization. These outputs should be capable of translation, or deployment, to at least one of the items identified earlier in this model. Some examples follow:

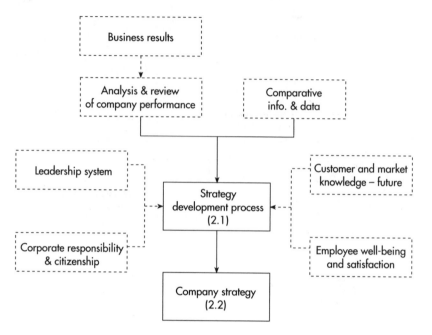

Figure 12.9   Direction setting – outputs

- Activities related to creation and delivery of products and services
  Category 6.0   Process Management
- Activities related to the capabilities of the organization's work force
  Category 5.0   Human Resource Focus
- Organizational structure, and communication
  Item 1.1   Leadership System
- Measurements used to track performance of key processes and
  activities Item 4.1   Selection and Use of Information and Data
- Customer support, development of customer relationships, or meas-
  urement of customer satisfaction
  Item 3.2   Customer Satisfaction and Relationship Enhancement

Leadership: closing the loop with feedback

This section uses the earlier material on leadership but this time with
emphasis (see figure 12.10) on the feedback from business results that
might be used to guide and drive improvement of the leadership system of
an organization.

Now let us relate this model to the earlier discussion of approaches to
assessment. For a company that is relatively early in the development of its
quality initiative, an assessment might concentrate on a number of basic
building blocks. Examples of these building blocks would include the level

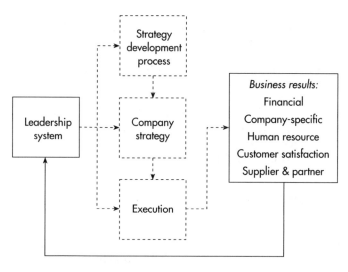

Figure 12.10   Leadership: closing the loop with feedback

of leadership for the overall effort, the methods for measuring customer satisfaction, approaches in place to reduce errors, defects, rework and other waste in production and service processes, and the like. A listing of several of these basic building blocks appears as figure 12.11.

- Leadership: mission, vision, values
- Customer satisfaction measurement: method
- HR practices for quality improvement
- Customer expectations: method
- Customer service training
- Quality improvement linked to planning
- External reference points: competitive
- Defect, cost, time reduction
- Design of products and services for quality

Figure 12.11   Examples of building blocks

A company that is more advanced in its quality effort might be more interested in some of the key linkages that are indicated in the model of this section. Examples might include the issues in the following list:

■   How effectively is knowledge of current customers and their requirements captured in the design processes for products, services, and delivery processes?
■   How effectively are the approaches to training and education preparing employees for the work systems that are to be used?

- How effectively is the organization capturing and using information about the external competitive environment for planning as well as for the improvement of key processes?

Of course, these examples are simply illustrative. However, they suggest how this management model can be incorporated into an organization's planning for its next assessment.

Finally, a company in which the quality effort has achieved a high level of maturity will be interested in evaluating whether its overall effort is becoming an integrated process for improvement not just of individual processes but of overall business performance.

CONCLUSION

Many organizations in the United States have used the criteria for the Malcolm Baldrige National Quality Award as a starting point in the creation of internal assessment processes. While much assessment activity continues, legitimate attention is addressed to the matter of insuring that the value gained from assessment is worth the resources committed to doing it. Drawing on the practices and experiences of a number of organizations, this chapter has synthesized a series of ideas about assessment. A brief summary of key points follows.

- The Process Owner of the assessment has a series of key decisions to make which, when made, determine in large measure how the Process Owner will work to support the process.
- Evaluators play a key role in each assessment; deciding who will perform this function is a central decision.
- The maturity of the organization's quality effort and the objectives of conducting an assessment should be considered in making the various decisions that have been reviewed in this chapter.
- An overall model that indicates how various processes within an organization interact can be useful in determining which activities to emphasize in planning an assessment and also later in summarizing what has been learned from the assessment.

APPENDIX – 1998 CRITERIA FOR THE MALCOLM BALDRIGE NATIONAL QUALITY AWARD

1.0 Leadership
   1.1 Leadership System
   1.2 Company Responsibility and Citizenship

2.0 Strategic Planning
    2.1 Strategy Development Process
    2.2 Company Strategy
3.0 Customer and Market Focus
    3.1 Customer and Market Knowledge
    3.2 Customer Satisfaction and Relationship Enhancement
4.0 Information and Analysis
    4.1 Selection and Use of Information and Data
    4.2 Selection and Use of Comparative Information and Data
    4.3 Analysis and Review of Company Performance
5.0 Human Resource Focus
    5.1 Work Systems
    5.2 Employee Education, Training, and Development
    5.3 Employee Well-Being and Satisfaction
6.0 Process Management
    6.1 Management of Product and Service Processes
    6.2 Management of Support Processes
    6.3 Management of Supplier and Partnering Processes
7.0 Business Results
    7.1 Customer Satisfaction Results
    7.2 Financial and Market Results
    7.3 Human Resource Results
    7.4 Supplier and Partner Results
    7.5 Company-Specific Results

Acknowledgments

Work for this chapter has been supported in part by grant number SBR-9422262 from the National Science Foundation as part of its Transformations to Quality Organizations research program. The author gratefully acknowledges this support.

The author gratefully acknowledges the participation and contribution of the following organizations as sources of information about assessment practices as well as discussions that were used to develop insights about good assessment practices: AlliedSignal Inc., American Express, Amp Incorporated, AT&T, Chevron, Corning, Inc., Henry Ford Health System, Honeywell, Inc., IBM Credit Corporation, Johnson & Johnson, McDonnell Douglass Corporation, The Procter & Gamble Company, Texas Instruments, Union Pacific Railroad, Unisys, and Xerox Corporation.

The author also expresses appreciation for the opportunity to serve as an Examiner, Senior Examiner, and Judge for the Malcolm Baldrige National Quality Award. The views expressed in this chapter are those of the author and do not, therefore, necessarily represent the views of the Quality Award Office of the National Institute of Standards and Technology of the U.S. Department of Commerce.

In accordance with the Policy on Conflicts of Interest and Commitment of The University of North Carolina at Chapel Hill, the author indicates that he holds what is defined under that Policy as a "significant financial interest" in one of the companies that has participated in this work. This situation has been reviewed by the University's Committee on Conflicts of Interest and Commitment and the work has been approved for continuation.

Notes

1   "The Push for Quality," *Business Week*, June 8, 1987.
2   Malcolm Baldrige National Quality Improvement Act of 1987.
3   "Malcolm Baldrige National Quality Award: 1998 Criteria for Performance Excellence", Quality Award Office, National Institute of Standards and Technology, U.S. Department of Commerce.
4   J.P. Evans, and A. Powell, "1996 Survey of Self-Assessment," Members' Report Number 9 of the Total Quality Management Center, The Conference Board, 1996.
5   A. M., Weimerskirch, "Baldrige for the Baffled: A Friendly Guide to the Malcolm Baldrige National Quality Award Criteria", Honeywell Inc., 1996.
6   M.C., Brown, Baldrige Award Winning Quality, Seventh Edition, ASQC Press, Milwaukee, 1997.

13 | Using ISO 9000 and the European Quality Award Approach to Improve Competitiveness

John J. Kirchenstein and Reg Blake

Abstract

The challenge to improve competitiveness, preserve social achievements and maintain economic growth is a major undertaking of the European Union. A leading remedial strategy is the encouragement of all industry sectors to adopt quality principles. The goal is to improve competitiveness and thereby reduce unemployment.

In the vanguard of the European Union's quality promotion programme is the encouragement of companies to demonstrate excellence in striving for continuous improvement by self-assessment against the criteria of the European Quality Award. Incorporating ISO 9000 early-on in the management of the company's quality system, with follow-on application of TQM improves this process. A review of Total Quality Management (TQM) as a workplace practice indicates that improvements accrue in financial performance and customer satisfaction upon its adoption.

The route to quality is dependent upon the commitment by top management. The self-assessment approach of the European Quality Award is an effective analytical means to identify the company's shortcomings which need management's remedial attention. The ISO 9000 matrix is useful in developing quality management systems which will serve economic, social or environmental purposes.

INTRODUCTION AND OVERVIEW

Concerns about competitiveness, quality of life, unemployment and related social, economic and environmental factors are of global interest. The unique challenge is to concurrently improve competitiveness, preserve social achievements and maintain economic growth. In the European Union (EU) there has been significant movement in seeking a solution. The European Council Meeting in Copenhagen during June of 1993[1] clearly foresaw that continued high unemployment and stagnant economic growth in the European Union could spell economic and social disaster in the not too distant future. The Council invited the

European Commission to formulate remedial strategies to improve growth, competitiveness and employment.[2] By December, 1993, the President of the Commission, Jacques Delors, presented a White Paper which reviewed the causes of the economic and social situation that endangered EU cohesion and put forth a strategy for competitiveness and employment. A Council resolution followed on November 21, 1994.[3] It pressed for the EU industrial policy to be recast as "market driven" and responsive to "global challenges with the aim of substantial improvement of the competitive position of European industry in global markets." Also, as a particularly urgent issue, was the encouragement of all industry sectors to adopt *quality* principles.

The linkage of competitiveness and quality spurred the formulation of a broad and innovative quality policy which addresses certification of quality systems, strengthening the European Quality Award, incorporating quality training in educational courses and the universities, and improving the European productivity apparatus.[4] To accomplish the latter, competitiveness of the European economy (internally and on the world market) would be increased through technological innovation, industrial design, improvement of the quality of products and services; and research and development of new control technologies and management methods.[5]

There are benchmarking possibilities to be gleaned from the European experience. This chapter draws heavily on the European Councils' initiatives and the European Quality Promotion Policy that are being pursued to strengthen overall competitiveness of European firms world-wide. The effectiveness of some of the innovative work place practices are examined in the light of recent research by accountants about the financial return on investments in such initiatives, especially in quality management areas such as TQM and ISO 9000. The benefits of the self-assessment structure of the European Quality Award are reviewed and the procedure introduced as a suggested first step on a path towards quality improvement.

Inasmuch as the continuing theme throughout this chapter is *quality*, and there are numerous definitions and interpretations of the meaning of the word, for common understanding the internationally agreed upon basic definition contained in ISO 8402[6] will be used:

> Quality: The totality of characteristics of an entity that bear on its ability to satisfy stated and implied needs. [per note 6 under the definition, quality is referred to as "fitness for use" or "fitness for purpose" or "customer satisfaction" or "conformance to the requirements."]

The European Council call for improved competitiveness required action on a broad front. The resultant introduction of quality as the binder of the various initiatives has attracted a few bottom line concerns for managers to address. Some of the attendant issues are examined in this chapter. Quality itself, for example has been applied beyond the parameters of the definition quoted above. It was always associated with products and services. Now quality is *lingua franca* for managers in all sectors – economic, social and environmental alike. The discussion about ISO 9000 as a universal foundation for quality initiatives addresses this development towards the end of the chapter.

European quality promotion policy plans include efforts to stress the importance of a European quality image and culture. For example, an annual European-wide quality week is held. It's a campaign to raise public awareness, promotion and demonstration of the advantages and importance of quality for the competitiveness of the European Union and non EU member economies. The spirit of "quality" has also been introduced in consumer thinking through these measures as exemplified by the advertisements of K. L. Ruppert, a Munich, Germany based sports apparel firm.[7] Ruppert takes advantage of a Eurobarometer survey result (No. 41 of 1994) which reports that "quality has now overtaken price" as the governing factor in the consumer purchasing decision process. Accordingly, Ruppert proclaims that *"Qualitaet ist in. Teuer ist out."* This anglicized German statement translates as follows: Quality is "in" and expensiveness is "out." The statement follows the EC quality promotion effort that quality provides customer satisfaction, and the price need not be expensive. The statement also infers that *quality* will make an item more competitive as the consumer will be attracted to it and be satisfied when using it. This thought is further supported by the European Commissioner for Industry, Martin Bangeman[8] who in confirming that quality is now well established as a pervading concern for consumers, further argues that European organizations and industry must now aim for excellence and not just conformity.

The 1996 European Quality Week was aggressively marketed. The *European Quality Platform* composed of the Switzerland-based European Organization for Quality (EOQ) and the European Foundation for Quality Management (EFQM), with financial support of the European Commission (EC) has estimated that actual participants in events related to the 1996 Week exceeded one quarter million. However, the estimated number of persons who heard about the Week via television, radio, daily newspapers and in general conversations ran into the millions. The campaign was pursued in each of the fifteen European Union member countries and in the following non EU member countries: Croatia, Czech Republic, Hungary, Iceland, Latvia, Macedonia, Malta, Norway, Poland, Romania, Russia, Slovakia, Slovenia, Switzerland, Turkey, and the Ukraine.[9]

The types of Quality Week activities included conferences, workshops, seminars and exhibitors. Also, both local and national media carried articles on standards, environmental management, performance measures, customer focus, and the various on-going educational programs. National quality organizations managed to acquire radio and TV coverage of the Weeks events. The main purpose of the Week, to make people aware of quality and engender an increased recognition of the importance of the implementation of Quality in European industries and services, proved to be quite successful.[10] In the words of Deputy Director General of DG III, Industry, of the European Commission Magnus Lemmel, "in its promotion of quality as an important element in improving the competitiveness

of European enterprises and organizations, the European Commission
aims to create the conditions in which a thousand initiatives can blossom."[11]

With the globalization of economies and markets, boundaries between
industrial sectors are blurring as firms engage in production or provide
services both home and abroad. The World Trade Organization Secretariat
reports that with globalization of the world economy, trade growth figures
continue to exceed world production growth by large margins (projected
in 1995 by a factor of almost three, and for 1996 close to double).[12] Such
projections further stimulated the European Council to urge EU industry
to improve competitiveness by paying attention to quality. This chapter
reviews such linkages between quality and competitiveness.

INVESTING IN TQM AND ISO 9000

Perhaps the largest investment in innovative quality management workplace
practice in the quality management field has been in Total Quality Management (TQM) techniques. Of almost equal interest has been ISO 9000
implementation, a matured quality management approach.

However, despite a number of studies, it is very difficult to relate specific
improvements in financial performance directly to adoption of TQM. One
reason is that TQM approaches and application vary from company to
company.

Nevertheless, the accounting firm of A. T. Kearney addressed such concerns in a survey of over 100 UK firms. They found no significant change
in performance because of TQM.[13] Likewise, the Arthur D. Little firm
looked at 500 US firms and corroborated the UK observations upon finding
"zero competitive gain" because of following TQM.[14] *However*, these surveys
included a very wide spectrum of companies, both large and small, and
those with both short- and long-term implementation of TQM practices.
On the other hand, in more focused studies (a preliminary review by Sherry
Jarrell and George Easton;[15] and a 1994 study by Thomas Heller[16]) of
firms noted especially for sustained or above average implementation of
TQM practices, *consistent increases in returns were found*. These firms outperformed the Standard & Poor's 500 list by an average of one to two percent
per year from 1989 to 1992, with some accruing excess of 15 percent
financial return over five years after the start of their TQM programs.
Broad snapshot statements about the benefits of TQM to a firm are not
possible. Apparently *persistent* pursuit of TQM practices (strong management involvement?) has produced financial benefits.

But what is TQM? It can mean many things to many people. Also,
alluding to follow TQM philosophy are numerous improvement schemes,
approaches and tools in use, so measurement or compliance of any of
them to an agreed set of principles or standard is not practical. When it
comes to finding a definition of TQM to reference, the ones by the International Standards Organization (ISO 8402), the British Standards Institution (BS 7850),[17] and the US Department of Defense (DOD 5000.510G),[18]

are probably the few which are published at international or national levels. On the other hand, almost every quality practitioner, quality management writer, or quality-oriented organization has its own definition. This further contributes to the diversity of the *TQM philosophy* and frustrates measurement. Because of its international significance, the definition of TQM as contained in the *ISO 8402 Quality Management and Quality Assurance Vocabulary* is quoted for reference: "A management approach of an organization, centered on quality, based on the participation of all of its members and aiming at long-term success through customer satisfaction and benefits to the members of the organization and to society."

Despite the perplexity about TQM and the diversity of circumscription, the attention to *quality* itself continues to be strong worldwide with TQM as the most popular workplace practice. In support of a 1992 American Quality Foundation and Ernst & Young International Quality Best Practices Survey,[19] over 500 US, Canadian, German and Japanese firms were contacted and over half reported that they conduct monthly evaluations of the consequences of quality upon their businesses. The firms were generally large and above average, well established and good performers. The paper did not disclose statistical data because of proprietary reasons. However, interpretations of the study hinted that *in order for low performing firms to reap the benefits of quality initiatives, they must first master the most elementary techniques before any advanced ones could be beneficially applied and become effective.* Based on the above, it would be unwise to support general contentions that TQM is ineffective. By the same token, adopting an ISO 9000 approach in developing a basic quality system might be a sound step towards TQM.

The ISO 9000 series of Quality Management and Quality Assurance Standards is a family of five written standards, but conformity can only be certifiable to three (ISO 9001, 9002 and 9003). The certifiable quality elements of the three are shown in table 13.1. The other two standards (ISO 9000 and 9004) contain guidance. ISO 9000 standards have been adopted by over 90 countries as National Standards and reflect industry agreed upon quality elements for quality management systems.[20] In Europe, the CEN/CENELEC adopted them as EN-ISO 29000. Following the ISO 9000 standards in setting up a bare bones quality system can be regarded as a first step towards overall quality management. In such instances enhancement with more sophisticated TQM methodologies would be the follow-on steps.

Conformity with ISO 9000 requires that all procedures and processes affecting quality be documented. Inherently this *documented procedures* requirement facilitates measurement. Thus, company quality management systems set up along the "bare bones" lines of one of the certifiable ISO 9000 standards can be audited and "certified" as being in conformance. The need for certification of quality systems is an action high among the European Union's quality policy initiatives supporting competitiveness improvement.[21] Although registration of ISO 9000 conforming quality management systems is voluntary, the European Council in a 1989 Resolution[22]

Table 13.1 The certifiable quality system elements of ISO 9000 (all are contained in ISO 9001; as indicated, some are not in ISO 9002 or ISO 9003)

4.1	Management Responsibility
4.2	Quality System
4.3	Contract Review
4.4	Design Control (not required in ISO 9002 or ISO 9003)
4.5	Document and Data Control
4.6	Purchasing (not required in ISO 9003)
4.7	Control of Customer Supplied Product
4.8	Product Identification and Traceability
4.9	Process Control (not required in ISO 9003)
4.10	Inspection and Testing
4.11	Control of Inspection, Measuring and Test Equipment
4.12	Inspection and Test Status
4.13	Control of Non-conforming Product
4.14	Corrective and Preventive Action
4.15	Handling, Storage, Packaging, Preservation and Delivery
4.16	Control of Quality Records
4.17	Internal Quality Audits
4.18	Training
4.19	Servicing (not required in ISO 9003)
4.20	Statistical Techniques

Source: ANSI/ASQC Q9001-1994.

concerning a global approach to conformity assessment, recommended that the ISO 9000 standards (EN 29000) be used as references for quality systems.

Certification by an accredited third party Registrar is the preferred method of showing ISO 9000 conformance (certification itself is discussed in a paragraph below). It is estimated that over 95,000 companies worldwide have been registered by accredited registrars as certified.[23] According to a Mobil Oil Survey and the ISO-Geneva estimate (percentages are rounded) the United Kingdom leads with about 52 percent of the registrations, followed by 26 percent for the other European countries, about 7 percent each for North America and Australia/New Zealand. The Far East, including Japan, accounts for about 4.5 percent and the rest of the world 3.5 percent.

The value of adopting ISO 9000 varies among firms mostly by reasons for the adoption. The major stimulants to adopt ISO 9000 have been pressures by customers and defensive reaction against competitors, rather than an underlying quest for better quality. Associated with a "me to" rush to adopt ISO 9000, is the deep and irresistible longing to be "certified". Certification of a firm's quality system is a very tangible way to convey to all comers that the firm's quality management system has been measured and according to the certifier conforms to an international standard. *The inference message is that certification assures that the firms products or services are of higher quality.* Accordingly, a number of firms have sought and adopted ISO 9000 solely for the purpose of acquiring certification. Subsequently, they have learned that while certification may inspire initial confidence, prestige and advantage in the marketplace, certification in itself will not guarantee high quality of goods or services or repeat business. There needs to be constant management commitment to quality and continuous improvement because quality is more than hanging a certificate on the wall. These factors are detected early on by accredited registrars and the superficial players lose certification after a surveillance visit or two by the registrars who detect loss of quality control by management. Such firms rarely seek or achieve re-certification.

In 1994, at the direction of the European Commission, the ISO 9000 certified quality management systems of a sample of firms in the European Union were examined by Bekaert-Stanwick to determine the added value of quality system certification. The study[24] found that there were *qualitative* advantages to firms which had certified systems. In order of importance, they were: *improvement of quality awareness, clarity in responsibilities, involvement of employees, confidence of customers, internal efficiency, image, and uniformity of performing tasks.* The study also indicated that achieving certification was an important first step towards overall quality management, especially at a time when competition has become truly global. The act of certification alone, it was recognized, in the study, does not provide all of the means necessary to sustain competitiveness.

Further research in the US on the market value of ISO 9000 certification by Anderson, Daly and Johnson[25] suggested that firms tend to seek ISO 9000 certification to ensure continuing access into both European Union and non EU Markets. The certification action is driven mostly by customer demands. To one's surprise, the study further revealed that certification provides higher market value for firms selling in the *non European Union* international market. Also, it was noted that medium- to large-sized firms which adopted the standard early on fared better in achieving higher market valuation benefits than similar firms that adopted later on. The suggestion that small to medium firms may not benefit as much as larger ones from early ISO 9000 adoption may be because such larger firms had retained their ISO values after establishing favorable and entrenched market positions.[26]

RESULTS OF ISO 9000 INVESTMENTS

Review of the Testimonial Data Base of the British Standards Institution,[27] a UK accredited Registrar, further supports the findings of the aforementioned studies as to the benefits of ISO 9000 adoption and subsequent provision of consistently high quality service to the customer. A few quotes from the files of the remarks by executives of registered companies in both the manufacturing and service sectors underscore this observation:

- Mr Ian Richards, Senior Manager and Quality Representative of Centra Automotive Ltd (UK) saw benefits of wider market opportunities and increased competitiveness "as a result of registration, but the marketing advantages and long-term orders are also noteworthy. Supplier quality surveys, allied to performance mentoring techniques, have enabled us to establish an improved vendor list. A welcome consequence of this is our ability to reward quality supply sources with further orders, while penalizing poor quality suppliers."

- Mr Randy Mitchell, Production Executive of Philips Consumer Electronics Company (USA), has noted fewer mistakes and increased customer satisfaction for its color TV sets. He states that "our BS5750/ ISO 9000 quality system has proven very effective in redefining our system to adopt what has become our primary business objective – Total Customer Satisfaction. The file failure rate for our Colour televisions improved by 49 percent in 1991 versus 1990 and was 33 percent lower again in 1991 to 1992. Warranty costs per unit in 1992 were 38 percent lower than 1990."

- Mr Dominic Proctor, Chief Executive of J. Walter Thompson Company, Ltd (UK Advertising Agency) reports better use of time and resources as well as increased customer satisfaction. He acknowledges the impression that "BS 5750/ISO 9000 is more appropriate to a manufacturing environment with constant repetitive processes and a factory line, but it is clear to us that there are very real benefits for an advertising agency too. It encourages proper disciplines in handling projects and should help to safeguard our client's money. In no way is it a barrier to creativity."

- Mr Edward Gillespie, Managing Director of the Steeplechase Company (Cheltenham) Ltd (UK racecourse) observes that "coping with over 60,000 visitors on a single race day, not to mention all the horses, jockeys, owners and trainers needs a great deal of organizational efficiency. We needed to implement a system which would improve our efficiency and make our business more effective. After all, in this business we have to get things right first time every time – there is no such thing as a second chance. We have an obligation to all our clients to provide the high level of service they require and it is up to us to ensure they feel safe and are looked after. Registration to BS 5750/ISO 9000 has drawn together all our members of staff and enables us to delivery a service that is right first time, every time."

BSI constantly conducts a "Customer Satisfaction Survey." The monthly reports for the period August 1995 to February 1996[28] contain many comments which reflect the BSI client's views of the benefits of BS 5750/ISO 9000 registration. A few of the reports from British firms which substantiate the following views are summarized below: "It improves productivity and almost always gives an immediate result in terms of productivity and efficiency, and that means cost reduction."

- "In the middle of a recession our order book is currently higher than at any time in our 27-year history, most of the work having come from blue chip companies who would not have touched us without BS 5750. We feel that registration provides tangible evidence that we at least try to get things first."

Martyn Goodard
Managing Director
International Uniforms Limited

■ "We have seen significant improvements results from systems installed for our BS 5750 registration. The status of all work in progress can be instantly ascertained. Constant analysis of non-conformance is enabling us to eliminate sources of error and identify potential improvements to our quality system. Complaints and product rejections are rigorously investigated and actions taken to eliminate their causes by improving processes or procedures. There has been a reduction in problems associated with non-conformance, freeing staff to concentrate on more productive work to the benefit of our customers."

Richard Brimley
Quality Manager
Tastemaker Limited

■ "A £15,000 saving was made in the first year in reduction in service rectification costs."

Tony Fox
Harratts of Wakefield

■ "NuAire is currently recovering the extra cost of quality twice over per annum because warranty costs have steadily fallen since the introduction of quality assurance. And it must be emphasized that this saving is being achieved by a company which, before the improvement, enjoyed a reputation for reliable products. In percentage terms, warranty costs have been cut from 0.45 to 0.15 percent turnover. Alongside the reduction in warranty costs, inspection staff have been reduced by 25 percent even though production has increased by some 25 percent in real terms. Striking figures which clearly illustrate the fundamental difference between quality assurance and quality control."

Brian Moss
Managing Director
NuAire Limited

THE QUEST FOR CUSTOMER SATISFACTION

Perhaps an established manufacturing firm or service provider adhering to time proven business practices could be a very successful and profit generating organization in the global marketplace. However, if the organization lacks a mechanism to alter processes to sustain continuous improvement and be responsive to customer needs, the organization will eventually decline in competitiveness.[29] To preclude these circumstances, the organization needs to introduce Total Quality Management with systems and controls for process management, document control and management direction. As a first step in establishing such total quality conditions, a bare bones structural framework of a ISO 9000 quality management system, should be installed. As conformance to quality guidance and consistency of processes is achieved, continuous improvement becomes possible given the availability of documented procedures for review by management. The formation of a dedicated quality management system further provides information on which to base actions that result in reducing customer complaint and improving satisfaction.[30] Conformity of the quality system to a ISO 9000 standard can be assessed by a third-party registrar and a certificate issued to record this fact.

While debates about TQM and ISO 9000 continue, the "latest magical elixir" to gain the attention of top management is *customer satisfaction*.[31] It has for some time been an objective in most TQM philosophies. Donald Shoultz, writing in the *American Banker* in 1989[32] found that of 700 top executives interviewed, over 60 percent ranked it as their top priority. Customer satisfaction also is emerging as the link between product quality and profitability and is a logical refinement of ISO 9000 emphasis on *conformance to requirements for customer satisfaction*. An examination of relationships between perceived quality, customer satisfaction, and returns on investment by Anderson, Fornell and Lehman[33] in 1993, concluded that firms *achieving high customer satisfaction likewise enjoy above average profitability*. A follow-on 1993 study[34] looked at 100 typical Swedish companies in 30 industry sectors. The results indicated that "an annual one point increase in customer satisfaction has a net present value of $7.48 million over five years" (or 11.5 percent per annum, given an average net income of the sample to be $65 million).

Satisfying the customer is becoming the preferred way of meeting competition. Providing the customer with a product or a service that satisfies a given need is well within the definition of quality. Management world-wide is striving to provide "customer satisfaction," and establishing the supporting quality system within the organization has become a basic management strategy. To best implement this goal, strict discipline with management in charge must exist to assure that controls are maintained. Thus, in an ISO 9000 conforming quality system, *documented procedures* are imperative but must be changed when required. Notwithstanding, the changes must be authorized and unauthorized changes prohibited. Only then can management remain fully involved and in control, and a documented paper trail kept intact.[35]

Figure 13.1 shows the relationship between a Quality Management System (QMS), ISO 9000, and TQM in meeting the continuous challenge to provide customer satisfaction. In this schematic, it is assumed that the organization has some sort of management system in place, which includes a few quality efforts that management believes gives it a QMS flavor. This first cut QMS is transformed into a bare bones QMS by the inclusion of

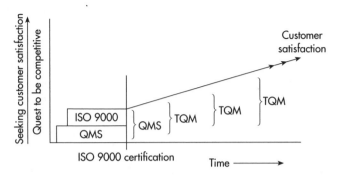

Figure 13.1 Meeting the continuous challenge to provide customer satisfaction – applying TQM

the ISO 9000 quality elements. After functioning smoothly for a period of time (usually between 3 and 9 months), the QMS is audited and if found to be in conformity with an ISO 9000 standard, can be so certified. Adding value by continuously improving to meet customers requirements, more sophisticated management tools and techniques are applied. The QMS begins to evolve as a TQM-oriented organization. As the quest to be competitive by providing customer satisfaction is elusive (customer wants and desires change), *continuous improvement of the product or services and refinement in TQM must be carried out to keep abreast with the customers desires.* Each "TQM" in the chart is a refinement of the previous one. No one ever fully captures TQM because the search to provide customer satisfaction never ends! As a foundation for TQM, a certified ISO 9000 quality management system is an important international message and means of proof that the ultimate objective of the company remains *quality* which will assure *customer satisfaction.*

CERTIFICATION, TESTING AND ACCREDITATION

When *certification* is mentioned, it is envisioned that the *certifier* guarantees or affirms that what has been stated is true *sans peur et sans reproche* (without fear to reproach). Likewise, the certifier is presumed to be an authority who possesses traits which exude confidence and ability to confer certification.

In the quality field, certification is generally associated with assessing a quality system where conformation is sought to ascertain that the system conforms to a standard or matches a model. In product certification, the aim is to assure the consumer that the ingredients or components in the product have met the required technical specifications or legislated demands.

As noted in the European Community study by Bekaert-Stanwick,[36] certification of quality systems as conforming to an ISO 9000 standard does not guarantee output of high quality goods and services. What is guaranteed is that the documented quality system would provide output which should consistently meet the customers stated requirements.

For the most part, registrars of quality systems in the EU are accredited by a national body. In the US there is no such national body, but the Registrar Accreditation Board (RAB), a private organization, performs this function.[37] In the EC study it was observed that the recent proliferation of non-accredited certifiers and other means to award certificates has resulted in public loss of confidence and trust in the certification process. Obviously, the veracity of the registration process is in question, which gives rise to the credibility of the certificates themselves. Consumers in particular are becoming wary about certification claims and seek reassurances.[38]

One of the absolutely essential quality initiatives of the European Commission is to strengthen the infrastructures for testing and certification as well as the accreditation network. As reported by Bakaert-Stanwick in the EC study, another is the need for a system to qualify quality professionals, managers and auditors. Similar concerns have been expressed by the American Society for Quality Control (ASQC) and the American National Standards Institute (ANSI), who are the co-sponsors of RAB.

Examining the EU accreditation network reveals that some of the infrastructure is already in place but needs to be strengthened. The UK provides a good model. At the top of the pyramid is the United Kingdom Accreditation Service (UKAS).[39] It was recently formed by the merger of the National Accreditation Council of Certification Bodies (NACCB) and the National Measurement Accreditation Service (NAMAS). Both had been authorized to use accreditation logos incorporating the Royal Crown. UKAS is set up as a private sector non-profit distributing company with no share capital. It is limited by guarantee and operates under the terms of a Memorandum of Understanding with the UK Department of Trade and Industry. DTI recognizes the unique national role of UKAS in the field of accreditation. UKAS is to provide a unified national accreditation service for *laboratories* performing tests and calibration, as well as *bodies* undertaking certification of products, personnel or systems. DTI also looks to UKAS to address environmental verifiers and inspection bodies. In other words, UKAS as the accreditation body in the UK, sets the rules and accreditation requirements that must be met by all comers seeking authority to provide certification services for companies and individuals within the domain of UK law. Such certification conferring organizations would be the British Standards Institution, Lloyd's Register, ABS Quality Evaluations, Inc. (a US company based in the UK), etc., who would operate as "Registrars," that is recording in a register or other permanent document those organizations that they have audited and confirmed as being in conformance with a standard (such as ISO 9000, QS 9000 and ISO 14000). To announce the registration, the Registrar issues a certificate of the fact. A similar procedure is followed in the examination of personnel seeking registration (certification) as auditors, or in the testing and calibration of equipment, or ascertaining conformity of products to specifications or meeting legislative requirements. The RAB operates similarly in the US, the Dutch Council for Accreditation (Raad voor de Acreditie, RVA) in the Netherlands and so forth.

Unlike UKAS, which has a link to the UK government through DTI, RAB being a private entity, has no stamp of approval from the US government (which would be the Department of Commerce's National Institute of Standards and Technology, NIST).

In 1994, six European national accreditation bodies signed a multinational agreement[40] agreeing to accept each others certificates in all matters. They were Mittatekniikan Keskus (Finland), Raad voor de Certificatie (RVC, Netherlands, now RVA), Norsk Akkreditering (Norway), SWEDAC (Sweden), Schweizerische Akreditierungstelle (Switzerland), and NACCB (UK) (now UKAS). All are members of EAC, the European Accreditation of Certification. The remaining EAC members are in the process of joining the multinational agreement[41] – Austria, Belgium (who has an MOU with Luxembourg and acts on its behalf), Denmark, France, Germany, Greece, Iceland, Ireland, Italy, and Spain and Portugal (who have a joint MOU).

The European Commission supports the EAC multinational agreement as a move to help growth of trade. When the multinational agreement is fully operational, it will be possible for European accreditation bodies (such as UKAS) to accredit certification bodies and Registrars outside the EU (such as RAB), subject to certain parameters.[42] An accredited Registrar in the EU may also act as a "Notified Body" (acting under authority of the European Commission), if required in determining conformity with harmonized EC Product Directives. These products in conformity with a Directive or Directives can carry the "CE" marking. Some conformity assessment requirements require the involvement of a Notified Body while others do not. There are some that require an in-place quality system "such as EN 29000" (ISO 9000). The individual EC Product Directives spell out documentation, marking procedures and other requirements. Generally, products which are regulated, and pertain to health, safety and the environment, are subjects of the harmonized EC Product Directives.

The European Commission looks to the European Organization for Testing and Certification (EOTC) to take the lead and strengthen the European accreditation network.[43] Through the work of the EOTC, the Commission hopes to attain universal mutual recognition of conformity assessment to European and international standards and a strong infrastructure for testing and certification. The goal is to facilitate the elimination of costly multiple tests and certificates of conformity or other proof of product compliance to standards and essential specifications. In other words, one-stop certification per product with the fact acceptable anywhere in the European Union and eventually in the global marketplace. A subset of the goal is the strengthening of the accreditation network to assure that testing and certification activities of all sorts in the Member States are accredited by nationally sanctioned bodies (such as UKAS).[44] This would, in time, eliminate the proliferation of unregulated certification bodies, re-establish the veracity of the certification process, and give purchasers the confidence they seek.[45]

The European Quality Award – Preparation to Improve Competitiveness

The effectiveness of quality programs tend to vary because of many diverse elements and different approaches. In constructing quality award programs or certifications, standards are provided to enable measurement and examiners determine conformity to the criteria. While not very obvious, there is a relationship between quality awards and financial performance (ISO 9000 does not accrue an "award," but rather is an achievement of conformance). There is evidence that improving quality processes (as reflected in seeking awards) brings on improved financial performance of the firm.

The announcement of independent quality awards, such as the Malcolm Baldrige award in the US or the European Quality Award in the European Union generally creates a positive market reaction. Hendricks and Singhal,[46] in a 1994 working paper, reported that first time US winners of awards gained significant market attention but subsequent winnings by these companies were not so important. It was also suggested that while *direct* financial improvement may not be obvious, it does not mean that investment in improving a process in order to compete was not worthwhile. The converse may have been more true – without the improvements, the financial results may not have turned out to be favourable. The European Commission recognized the need to improve economic growth, employment and competition throughout the EU. The Council resolution of November 21, 1994[47] viewed action by the Community and the Member States to be particularly urgent in a number of spheres, including the encouragement of all industry sectors to adopt quality principles.

The European Quality Award is in the vanguard of the EU approach to deal successfully with competitiveness and the challenges of modern society. The Award, together with the European Quality Prizes were developed in 1991 by the European Foundation for Quality Management (EFQM) in cooperation with the European Organization for Quality (EOQ) and with full support of the European Commission. Each year several prizes are awarded in the private sector with the company judged to be the best of the prize winners and the most successful exponent of TQM in Europe receiving the European Quality Award.[48]

The prize winners must demonstrate "how their approach to TQM contributed significantly to satisfying the expectations of its customers, employees and others over a number of years." The European Quality Award winner retains the trophy for a full year and all prize winners are presented a framed holographic image of the Award. Beginning in 1996, there were contenders also from the public sector, but none were prize nor award winners. It is expected that in 1997, there will be separate recognition categories for small- and medium-sized enterprises (SMEs) (organizations with fewer than 250 people) and also one for operational units of large companies.[49]

There is also a European Quality Award for Masters and Doctoral theses. These awards are individual awards intended to encourage TQM research and education. The subjects must be relevant to TQM, focus on management rather than technical aspects and have a reasonably wide range of application. There is one Award for each of the Masters and Doctoral categories. The prizes for the winning entries are: Master Thesis, ECU 2,000; Doctoral Thesis, ECU 3,000[50] (an ECU is approximately US $1.27).

With European Quality Prizes awarded to companies who demonstrate excellence in the management of quality as their fundamental process for continuous improvement, the European Commission believes the Award application experience is also an excellent way to improve a company's competitiveness. The model for the award, it appears, is also an appropriate matrix for self-assessment.[51] The Commission has taken note that the Award application self-assessment process involves highlighting the company's strong points and accomplishments, including doing something about those areas needing improvement in the company's search for continuous improvement and excellence. Taken together with benchmarking (that is, comparing selected aspects of a company against the best ones in the industry or another industry), self-assessment becomes the key to strategic improvement planning and subsequently competitiveness. It can also serve as a complement to certification by third parties.

The application procedure is straightforward. Sections A and B of the application (general information about the company) and fee are submitted by the end of January to the EFQM Secretariat. Applications with fewer than 500 employees submit a fee of ECU 1,000, and all others ECU 3,000. A separate "Application Document", which is the detailed self-assessment in a tightly prescribed format (and not to exceed 75 pages in total length), is to follow no later than the first week in March.

The application document format is aligned with the nine Award assessment criteria. These criteria comprise *the European Model for TQM*. The nine Award criteria in the model are grouped as "Enablers" (those criteria concerned with how results are being achieved), and by "Results" (which are criteria that pertain to what the company has achieved or intends to achieve).

Enablers and Results groups are each valued at 500 points. The value of each of the nine component criterion is as follows: The five Enablers – Leadership (100), People Management (90), Policy and Strategy (80), Resources (90), and Processes (140); and the four Results – People Satisfaction (90), Customer Satisfaction (200), Impact on Society (60), and Business Results (150).[52]

Essentially, the European Model for TQM shows that *"Customer Satisfaction, People (employee) Satisfaction and Impact on Society are achieved through Leadership driving Policy and Strategy, People Management, the Management of Resources and Processes, leading to excellence in Business Results"* (as stated in the current Application Brochure). The European Model for TQM, shown in figure 13.2, can also be taken as another definition of TQM.

An assessment team evaluates all application materials and creates a pool of finalists which are to be site visited. The finalists are subjected to a

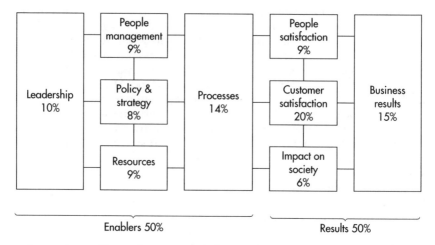

Source: Extracted from "The European Quality Award, 1997 Application Brochure", European Foundation for Quality Management, Brussels Representative Office, 1997, p. 9. Also displayed and referred to as the "British Quality Foundation Business Excellence Model". *BSI* News, July 1996, pp. 24–5.

Figure 13.2   The European model for TQM and self-assessment process

comprehensive assessment of their company's commitment to the criteria of the European Model for TQM. The on-site assessment team is composed of experienced managers, supplemented by a few practitioners and academics. After the assessment, it provides feedback highlighting the company's strengths and areas in need of improvement. It is indeed a prescription for movement ahead. This may explain why the demand for European Quality Award applications (actually a self assessment format) increased threefold from 1993 to 1994, which is a strong indication of quality awareness in Europe.[53]

After site visits with the most promising candidate company's, the Award winner and prize recipients are selected. The site visits are usually in late June. The Award and Prizes are presented at EFQM's Annual Forum, usually in September.

The past European Quality Award and European Quality Prize winners are all prestigious European firms.[54] In some instances they are also scions of multinational firms. The first award was in 1992. All past winners are shown in table 13.2 and those for 1996 in table 13.3. It is interesting to note that the 1996 Award winner and a 1996 Prize winner were from Turkey, a non-EU member state.

A commonality appears among the past winners, particularly during their preparation and posturing stages to improve competitiveness.[55] All had adopted or emphasized some TQM philosophy and most had participated in assessments or measurements, including ISO 9000 certification, to gain better appreciation of the quality process. This led to special focus

Table 13.2 1992–1995 winners of the European Quality Award and European Quality Prizes

1992	Rank Xerox Limited – Award winner
	BOC Limited, Special Gases – Prize winner
	Industrial del Ubierna SA, UBISA, Prize winner
	Milliken European Division – Prize Winner
	The 1992 Award was conferred by King Juan Carlos of Spain in Madrid.
1993	Milliken European Division – Prize Winner
	ICL Manufacturing Division (Now called D2D Limited) – Prize Winner
	The 1993 Award was conferred by Mr Vanni D'Archifari, European Commissioner for the Internal Market in Turin.
1994	D2D Limited-Award Winner
	Ericsson SA – Prize Winner
	IBM (SEMEA) – Prize Winner
	The 1994 Award was conferred by the President of the European Commission Jacques Delors in Amsterdam.
1995	Texas Instruments Europe – Award Winner
	TNT Express (UK Limited) – Prize Winner
	The 1995 Award was conferred by Juan M. Equiagaray, Acting President of the European Council of Ministers for Industry in Berlin.

Source: Fax from Vince Ellis, Manager – Assessment Systems, European Foundation for Quality Management, to John J. Kirchenstein, October 12, 1995.

Table 13.3 1996 European Quality Award and Quality Prize winners

1996	Brisa Bridgestone Sabanci Tyre Manufacturing and Trading, Inc. (Istanbul, Turkey) – Award Winner
	BT-British Telecommunications, plc – Prize Winner
	TNT Express (UK Limited) – Prize Winner
	Netas, Northern Electric Telekomuenikayson AS (Istanbul, Turkey) – Prize Winner
	The 1996 Award was conferred by Mr Karel Vinck, CEO of Union Minière and President of the European Foundation of Quality Management, and the Prizes were presented by Mr Bernard Fournier, CEO of Rank Xerox, Europe and Chairman of the European Quality Award Jury 1996, in Edinburgh.

Note: The 1997 Quality Award and Prizes Forum will be held in Stockholm, Sweden. It is expected that the Queen of Sweden will make the Award presentation in the Nobel Prize Winners Hall.
Source: Fax from Vince Ellis, Manager – Assessment Systems, European Foundation for Quality Management, to John J. Kirchenstein, March 28, 1997.

on identifying and defining critical business practices and establishing process ownerships within their organizations. It was directed towards correcting the weaknesses which could have adverse affect on competitiveness. The presence of management each step of the way was most evident.

The summation of the actions described above is *self assessment,* a practice which is vital for survival. Essentially, all of the winners engaged in this activity prior to and during the European Quality Award application phase. Self assessment information relevant to the business situation is brought out in the organizations Award application.[56] It shows (in the enablers section) how each element of the company approaches and takes action in every quality aspect, and (in the results part) what the company achieves with respect to each result. The findings are synthesized in the application.

The 1995 Award Winner, Texas Instruments Europe (TI Europe), offers a case study of in depth and rigorous application of self-assessment and follow-on continuous improvement.[57] The achievement of the Award culminated a year long period of self assessment of TI Europe's main and support organization against the criteria of the Award. This provided the input for strategic re-engineering plans, including fundamental changes in processes and structures. John Scarisbrick, President of TI Europe, in assessing the excellent financial returns of the company for 1994, attributed the success to the major one year restructuring and self assessment effort in preparation of the Application Document. However, he cautioned that it was still necessary when making change, to recognize *which* elements are appropriate to the particular activities. Total Quality (TQ) he said "is not a universal panacea, as it is not appropriate in all situations and on all occasions". Instead, he chose to follow 'TQ versus IQ" advice. Here everyone can get involved, he said, and adapt what is appropriate, not relying on just one thing. "Doing it better is a continuous improvement model and doing it differently is a process re-engineering model," Scarisbrick emphasized, "as common sense and business judgement still have to play a significant role, self assessment can serve this need."[58]

The 1996 Award Winner, Brisa Bridgestone Sabanci, the Turkish tire factory, provides an example of studied transformation from confrontation to cooperation, which recognized the need for change, building friendly and cooperative relations with the work force, injected the idea of continuous improvement into the production process, and encouraged total employee participation. Essentially, all of the aforementioned were accomplished through training and communication. Hazim Kantarci, past Brisa president, recalls the change in employee attitudal approach during the preparation of a radical collective bargaining agreement that ended a 109-day strike in 1990 (preceded by a 23-day strike in 1988).[59] Previously, managers, the union, or the workers addressed implementation of direction as "the company should do this or that." Now, Mr Kantarci observes, the attitude is "there is no company, we are the company. If anything has to be done, we all have to do it."[60] A new company slogan has appeared: "Let's change," which according to Ali Risa Orcunus, the quality assurance director has led to total customer focus, as exemplified in another statement: "The customer pays my salary, not my boss."[61] Mr Orcunus further observed that once everyone grasped the concept, both workforce and workplace "underwent a complete mental and physical facelift." The work areas were painted and enhanced with plants and other ornaments.

Continuous *planned* improvement, as suggested in quality circles spread rapidly. Previously, *rules* were used for enforcement and control, whereas under the newly adopted *kaizen* philosophy,[62] improvement happens by *consensus*. Product quality has become a matter of pride and cost reduction as part of the everyday agenda. The company's objective has become "carrying our quality to market."

According to Ahmet Piker, who became Brisa's president in 1996, continuous improvement changed the life of the company allowing it to gain massive competitive advantage through TQM. By 1993, Brisa had earned a gold prize from Renault as the top scoring supplier and the same year Brisa was the winner of the Turkish Quality Award. Using the EFQM business excellence model to put a strategic focus in its *kaizen* based manufacturing disciplines, with support from the managers and the employees in their shared destiny,[63] management was given impetus to submit the Award application without reservation.

Past European Quality Award and Prize winners continue to seek further improvements with resultant profit growth. The CEOs of these organizations are fully immersed in quality drives having accepted early on the leadership challenge. The rank and file visibly respond to positive inspiration and personal example. All stakeholders look towards continuous improvement because the results will be financially rewarding.[64]

The competition experience for the European Quality Award, fulfills most of the requirements and needs to improve competitiveness in the European Union.[65] Post award winners conferences are held throughout Europe at convenient locations and have become a part of the Award process. These conferences are well attended, usually presented jointly in conjunction with a national quality association. The Award and Prize winners make their presentations and an atmosphere of networking and education is easily attained.

ISO 9000, A UNIVERSAL FOUNDATION FOR QUALITY INITIATIVES

ISO 9000, briefly discussed previously, is an approach to quality which is most useful as an impetus to achieve excellence through TQM. It is interesting to note that the ISO 9000 Quality Management and Quality Assurance Standards have a British Standards Institution (BSI) heritage. The first quality system standard was published in 1979 as British Standard 5750-Quality Systems. From these beginnings, a series of standards evolved which were used as the basis for the ISO 9000 family of standards for quality management systems. They were first published by ISO in 1987 and subsequently reviewed and updated in 1994.

A similar path was followed for Environmental Management Systems (EMS) where BS 7750 became the basis for ISO 14001. Being a leader in the field of standards is natural to BSI and this is ably demonstrated by the publication of BS 8800: 1996 – Guide to Occupational Health and Safety

Management Systems. An integrated approach has been placed on the agenda which could well result in a single standard which incorporates quality, environmental and health and safety management.

ISO 9000

Although the ISO 9000 standards are voluntary standards, established by consensus, they have been adopted within the regulatory sector. In those instances their use becomes mandatory. They have been incorporated into European Directives as well as national legislation such as the United States Food and Drug Administration's Good Manufacturing Procedures (GMP's). Industry sector adoption has also occurred as with the US "Big 3" automotive manufacturers, Chrysler, Ford and General Motors who have, to a very large degree, harmonized their individual requirements and published them collectively as QS-9000.[66]

In terms of worldwide acceptance, the ISO 9000 family of standards is unquestionably the most successful as over 80 countries have adopted it as their national standards and this figure continues to increase. The great strengths of ISO 9000 are to be found in its generic and non-prescriptive approach and its ability to be used by all:[67]

- industry sectors including manufacturing, process and service,
- sizes of companies,
- types of business activities.

We do, however, need to place ISO 9000 in its proper context. It is very much the foundation and catalyst for quality management systems and presents executive management with a practical and effective tool for implementing a quality system approach within their organization. The prime objective for any organization should be the establishment of an excellent quality system that is well controlled, simple, effective and efficient. It should also accommodate the needs and expectations of both customers and the company itself and be capable of adding value, this can only be achieved by integrating ISO 9000 into the business in such a way that it compliments the strategic direction of the company while capturing best business practices. Although building a business solely around the ISO 9000 is not a sound strategy, integrating it into the business is. Adopting an ISO 9000 approach demands top management commitment and ownership by all, but if these two absolutely essential ingredients do not exist then the decision to proceed should be reconsidered. Used in the right way, for the right reasons and setting realistic goals and expectations will ensure that ISO 9000 brings significant benefit to its users.

A fundamental element of the quality scene today is the independent third party audit, registration and certification process. This has served industry well for nearly twenty years and has a major role to play providing and maintaining the highest standards of service, integrity and competence. This service must add value and is best achieved by a Registrar or Certification Body using highly qualified, competent and well trained auditors. These individuals need to adopt a pragmatic and flexible approach and develop partnerships with their clients which result in identifying opportunities for continuous improvement of the quality system, confirming top management commitment and motivating users to have ownership of the system.

QS-9000 quality system requirements (automotive)

Although not a standard, QS-9000 is a good example as to how ISO 9000 can be applied to a specific industry. It not only integrates in full ISO 9001, but sets a goal of continuous improvement with an emphasis on defect prevention and the reduction of variation and waste in the supply chain. It also requires the establishment of a formal, documented, comprehensive business plan that should consider, in addition to other aspects, such things as cost objectives, quality objectives, health, safety and environmental issues. QS-9000 emphasizes the importance of considering the three key foundations of a modern business, namely: *quality, environmental responsibility and health and safety*.

QS-9000 consists of three sections:[68]

Section 1   ISO 9000 based requirements
Section 2   Sector-specific requirements
Section 3   Customer-specific requirements

Section 2, being industry specific, covers continuous improvement requirements and addresses three main areas: the first being comprehensive continuous improvement philosophy; the second, quality and productivity improvements; and the third, and outline of techniques for continuous improvement.

ISO 14000 – environmental management systems

Much like the ISO 9000 series, the ISO 14000 environmental management systems series[69] will provide a structured approach to managing environmental compliance. The benefits from worldwide adoption of these standards should be improved environmental responsibility leading to organizational management efficiencies, reduction of waste, pollution prevention, improved environmental performance, regulatory compliance and a direct impact on economic and social well-being. Adoption of ISO 14001 will also permit a universally consistent approach to environmental management systems and will be capable of being independently audited for compliance.

Like quality management systems, environmental management systems need to be viewed strategically. Adopting this approach will ensure a proactive position is taken to developing an environmental policy which should anticipate regulation rather than just reaction.

The European Union has clearly identified the potential advantages of having organizations implement environmental management systems and accepts that there is a role for voluntary regulation within the European regulatory system. A good example of this is the European Commission's Eco-Management and Audit Scheme (EMAS). This scheme encourages voluntary participation and is based on establishing a structured approach to environmental management through the application of environmental management systems which are based on recognized standards such as BS 7750.

BS 8800 – guide to occupational health and safety management systems

Users of the above standards and requirements documents have seen the advantages of adopting the structured approach, controls and disciplines to managing quality and environmental activities. The common sense principles and philosophy of management embedded in ISO 9000, QS-9000 and ISO 14000 lend themselves to an application in the field of occupational health and safety management. Many organizations view management of OH&S as complementary to their other management initiatives.

BS 8800[70] provides guidance to management to help them integrate occupational health and safety management within their overall management system as well as assisting them in achieving compliance with stated OH&S policies and objectives. The standard explains that it contains guidance and recommendations and that it should not be considered a specification nor used for certification purposes.

Studies by the Health and Safety Executive (UK) indicate that the overall cost to employers of personal injury work accidents, work related ill-health and avoidable non-injury accidents is estimated to be equivalent to around 5 to 10 percent of all UK companies' gross trading profits. One study showed that, in the organizations studied, uninsured costs from accidental loss were between 8 and 36 times greater than the cost of insurance premiums. There are, therefore, sound economic reasons for reducing work related accidents and ill-health, as well as ethical and regulatory reasons. Besides reducing costs, effective OH&S management promotes business efficiency.

BS 8800 applies best business practices to improve OH&S performance by:

- minimizing the risk to employees and others;
- improving business performance; and
- assisting organization to establish a responsible image within the marketplace.

Many of the principles embedded in ISO 9000 and ISO 14000 are to be found in BS 8800 and it is reasonable to assume this approach will be reflected in any future OH&S standard that ISO may produce. As in the development of ISO 9000 and ISO 14000, the British Standard (8800) will probably become a significant contribution to the future international standard.

The future

The future direction of standards in the fields of management systems seems to be one of convergence between the various standards of quality assurance, environmental management and health and safety. This appears to be a very logical step as the one constant in the equation is management. Furthermore, there is much similarity and sharing of common management systems principles and philosophies within the ISO 9000 and ISO 14000 families of standards and requirements documents such as QS-9000.

However, without true management commitment and leadership the pursuit of quality initiatives within an organization is flawed. Quality management is without a question a strategic issue which resides in the domain of executive management. It should be an essential element of any organization's strategic planning and should encourage a realistic, proactive, measurable and preventive approach to quality. If addressed in this way then the company will experience significant benefits in economic, social and environmental terms. Reasonable arguments can be made as to the positive impact ISO 9000 has had in providing a universal foundation on which to build quality initiatives. However, we must appreciate that ISO 9000 is not the "be all and end all." In the words of Sir Winston Churchill, as applied to ISO 9000. "This is not the end. It is not even the beginning of the end. But it is, perhaps, the end of the beginning."

Relating to the European Quality Promotion Policy to competitiveness in international markets and ISO 9000, Magnus Lemmel, Deputy Director General of DG III, Industry, European Commission, commented that:

> the Quality Promotion Policy demonstrates to member states and enterprises that quality needs to be considered as an element of the overall strategy of companies if they want to compete in international markets. This approach goes far beyond the certification of purely technical product quality. While certification of a company's quality system is an important way of proving it can meet specified requirements . . . , it must not be regarded as an end in itself. The use of ISO 9000 can be regarded as the first step towards a more global management of companies based on a continuous improvement strategy.[71]

SUMMARY AND CONCLUSIONS

Over the last ten years there has been a definite trend towards globalization of the international market place and global competition has become a reality for many companies. Today, world-class companies have to adjust quickly to a constantly changing and competitive environment. They also understand the need for having structured and responsive systems that promote timely product development linked to sound and well-researched marketing strategies. A fundamental and essential part of any business strategy is to understand and recognize the importance of quality of product or service provided. It may or may not be coincidental that ISO 9000 is of a similar age and has developed and matured in line with best business practices over this same period.

To be competitive in the global market-place, an organization requires a number of weapons in its arsenal so that it has an even chance of success whether it chooses to fight its battles. One such weapon is quality where the degree of excellence of the product or service meets, and whenever possible, exceeds the customer's needs and expectations. The road to excellence has many milestones, adopting an ISO 9000 approach to quality is an excellent start through Total Quality Management (TQM) or as is often referred to today as "business process improvement," "business excellence"; "organizational excellence," etc.

One particular regional market that has experienced significant change over the past two decades is the European Common Market, later the European Community and now known as the European Union. The European Commission has placed particular emphasis on quality and has enacted numerous European Product Directives to ensure that products being placed on the market meet the essential minimum requirements for safety and quality. The Commission's plan depends, to a large degree, on the application and use of international and national standards. This in turn is supported by the use of third-party registration and certification schemes that demonstrate compliance with recognized standards and adequacy of quality systems. ISO 9001; ISO 9002 and ISO 9003 are the quality systems standards called up in European Product Directives.

The encouragement of all industry sectors to adopt quality principles is a pillar in the European Union's quality policy. The underlying purpose is to improve European competitiveness in the world market place by presenting better products which will assure customer satisfaction; and through this approach increase demand and thereby reduce unemployment. Concurrently, the European Union initiated a coordinated European quality promotion plan to stress the European quality image.

In the vanguard of the European Union's approach to emphasize quality as the tool to deal successfully with competitiveness and the challenges of modern society, is the European Quality Award. Firms seeking this recognition are required to demonstrate excellence in the management of quality as a fundamental process for continuous improvement. The self-assessment approach embodied in the European Quality Award process (following the European Model for TQM) is an effective analytical means to identify the company's shortcomings which need remedial attention. In this context, the ISO 9000 matrix is useful in developing quality management systems which will serve economic, social or environmental purposes. The Award's detailed self assessment matrix is an excellent check list to use in evaluating a firm's quality management system. All applicants competing for the Award are obligated to closely adhere to this detailed self assessment matrix.

The quest for customer satisfaction must be the top priority issue for management. The combined efforts of TQM and ISO 9000 are essential in achieving this goal. Thus, ISO 9000 can be viewed as having market value. Specific improvements in financial performance can be attributed to the innovative application of ISO 9000 and TQM as workplace practices. The prime consideration is to use ISO 9000 at inception when building a quality management system.

Not only does ISO 9000 find a niche in the manufacturing and services sector, its tenets extend as well to environment management, occupational health and safety, and automotive fields. In all instances, top management support is essential and without it no quality management efforts can survive.

All indications are that following TQM practices, consistent increases in return will be found. The pre-condition in such instances had been an inplace functioning QMS based on ISO 9000. Customers are increasingly becoming concerned about assurances of certification claims as to product or service capabilities or attributes. The credibility of the certificate is at stake, which lays open the questions of the confidence and trust in the certification process. The strengthening of the infrastructures for testing and certification as well as the accreditation network are on the European Union's agenda to improve competitiveness. Multinational agreements are being formed to establish criteria and the acceptance of each others certificates on a common basis.

Likewise, multinational agreements are being relied upon to help the growth of trade. Conformity to product directives spelling out minimum essential requirements for health and safety assurance is being emphasized. The existence of in-place quality systems, such as EN 29000 (ISO 9000) is required for some regulated products, and conformity assessment requirements are specific as to how this will be ascertained. The veracity of the certification process is being reestablished to give the consumers the confidence they seek.

All efforts to instill or improve quality and achieve subsequent advantage in competitiveness are derived from the commitment by management to excel. As the Romans experienced, skill and discipline are vital to success. Vegetius,[72] a Roman military historian and author who flourished in the fourth century, emphasized that *"Victory in war does not depend entirely upon numbers or mere courage; only skill and discipline will insure it."*

The maxims of Vegetius are applicable to modern business. The need for leadership is ever present to provide guidance and direction, enforce compliance and adherence to plans to be executed. All is underscored by a discipline and competence to follow through. The manager or leader must inspire all to work as a team to accomplish the goals.

Notes

1   European Council in Copenhagen, June 21–22, 1993, quoted in *The European Councils – Conclusions of the Presidency, 1992–1994.* Directorate General for Information, Communication, Culture and Audiovisual. European Commission Brussels, 1995.

2   Bulletin of the European Communities, Supplement 6/93. "Growth, Competitiveness, Employment – The Challenges and Ways Forward into the 21st Century (White Paper)". Office for Official Publications. Commission of the European Communities. 1993.

3   OJ No C 343/1. Council Resolution of November 21, 1994 (94/C 343/01).

4   Doc Certif 95/1. Working Document on "A European Quality Promotion Policy", 17/2/95, Directorate General III, European Commission, Brussels.

5   Doc Certif 95/1.

6   International Standard ISO 8402: 1993 *Quality Management and Quality Assurance Vocabulary*, International Organization for Standardization, Geneva, Switzerland.

7   K L. Ruppert, Munich, Germany, sports apparel firm advertisement, Spring 1996.

8   Martin, Bangemann, "Aim for Excellence." *European Quality Award Special Report.* European Quality Publications Ltd., London, 1995, 7.

9   *European Quality Week, 1996 Report.* EOQ Secretariat. Bern, Switzerland. February 1997.

10 *European Quality Week, 1996 Report.*

11 Magnus, Lemmel, "Nurturing Competition." *European Quality Award Special Report, 1996.* European Quality Publications Ltd., London, 1996, 8–9.

12 "High Rates of World Trade Growth Continue to Outstrip Output Growth." *World Trade Organization* Press Release 29, November 2, 1995. The WTO Secretariat, in Press Release 71 of April 4, 1997, further projects value of world merchandise exports to increase in 1997 from $5,000 billion to $5,100 billion.

13 Independent survey reports by A. T. Kearney and Arthur D. Little, as reported in Sarah C. Mavrinac, Neil R. Jones, and Marshal W. Meyer "The Financial and Non-Financial Returns to Innovate Workplace Practices." Ernst & Young Center for Business Innovation working paper. Boston, 1995.

14 Independent survey reports.

15 Sherry L. Jarrell, and George S., Easton "An Exploratory Empirical Investigation of the Effects of TQM on Corporate Performance," in *The Practice of Quality Management*, edited by P. Lederer, Harvard University Press, Cambridge, MA (forthcoming).

16 Thomas, Heller, "The Superior Stock Market Performance of a TQM Portfolio." *The Center for Quality Management Journal*, 3:1, Winter 1994, 23–32.

17 British Standard BS 7850: Part 1, 1992, *Total Quality Management Guide To Management Principles*, BSI Standards, Milton Keynes, UK.

18 DOD Directive 5000.510G, Department of Defense, Washington, D.C.

19 "Evaluation of the Systems for Certification by Third Parties of the Quality Systems Set Up by Businesses in the Community," Bekaert-Stanwick, 1994. As reported in Doc. Certif. 95/1, working document on "A European Quality Promotion Policy," 17/2/95, Directorate General III, European Commission, Brussels.

20 There are five ISO 9000 series standards in the 1994 international revision: ISO 9000-1, ISO 9001, ISO 9002, ISO 9003, and ISO 9004-1. These international standards correspond to the American National Standards which are

designated ANSI/ASQC Q9000-1-1994, ANSI/ASQC Q9001-1994, ANSI/ASQC Q9002-1994, ANSI/ASQC Q9003-1994, and ANSI/ASQC Q9004-1-1994. The use of the generic identifier "ISO 9000" is very popular. In practice, national standards are still retaining their own designations of the ISO 9000 standards. For example, the British continue to refer to them collectively "BS 5750", and ISO 9001, ISO 9002, ISO 9003, and ISO 9004 as "Part 1, Part 2, Part 3, and Part 4" respectively.

21 Doc Certif. 93/2, Rev 2. "Elements of a Community Quality Policy," 12/01/94, Directorate General III, European Commission, Brussels.

22 OJ No C 10/1. Council Resolution of December 21, 1989 (90/C 10/01).

23 Doc Certif 95/1, and Mobil Europe Ltd, *The Mobil Survey of ISO 9000 Certificates Awarded Worldwide* (fourth cycle), August 31, 1995.

24 Bakaert-Stanwick. See note 19.

25 Shannon W., Anderson, J. Daniel, Daly, and Marilyn F., Johnson, "The Value Relevance of Non-Financial Performance Measures: Evidence on ISO 9000 Quality Certification." University of Michigan Working Paper, Ann Arbor, 1994.

26 American Quality Foundation and Ernst & Young. *The International Quality Study: Best Practices Report*: 1992.

27 Client testimonials extracted from the British Standards Institution Testimonial Data Base of July, 4 1995, London. File M4. Centra Automotive Components Ltd., of June 7, 1995; File M12. Philips Consumer Electronics Co., of June 13, 1995; File S5. J. Walter Thompson Co., Ltd. Undated; File S13. The Steeplechase Co. (Cheltenham) Ltd. of June 12, 1995.

28 Client's views, extracted from the British Standards Institution's "Customer Satisfaction Survey" for the period of August 1995 to February 1996, as reported as of April 18, 1996, London.

29 AQF and Ernst & Young. See note 26.

30 AQF and Ernst & Young.

31 Kenneth L., Bernhardt Naveen, Don Thu and Pamela A., Kennett, "The Relationship Among Customer Satisfaction, Employee Satisfaction, and Profitability: A Longitudinal Analysis." Georgia State University Working Paper, Atlanta, 1994.

32 Daniel, Shoultz, "Service Firms are Customer Driven: Study." *American Bankers*, February 1989, pp. 17–18.

33 Eugene W., Anderson, Claes, Fornell and Donald R., Lehman, "Customer Satisfaction, Market Share and Profitability: Findings from Sweden." *Journal of Marketing*, July 1994, p. 30.

34 Eugene W. Anderson and Mary W. Sullivan. "The Antecedents and Consequences of Customer Satisfaction for Firms." *Marketing Services*, 12:2 Spring, 1992, 125–43.

35 Bakaert-Stanwick. See note 19.

36 Bakaert-Stanwick.

37 "ISO 9000 Worldwide Recognition System Set for Launch" *On Q*, ASQC, May 1995, p. 8.

38 Letter from Benedicte Federspiel, Executive Director, Danish Consumer Council and Member of the Consumers Consultive Council of the European Commission, to John J. Kirchenstein dated October 17, 1995.

39 "DTI Appoints Chairman for New National Accreditation Service." *TickIT International*, 2Q95, p. 11 and "Business as Usual: UKAS Supersedes NACCB." *TickIt International*, 3Q95, p. 9, pp. 27–8.

40 "International Agreement." *TickIT International*, IQ95, p. 12.

41 "International Agreement."

42 "International Agreement."

43   Letter from Alan Barber, Assistant to the Secretary General for EOTC, to John J. Kirchenstein, dated, September 26, 1995.

44   "May 1995 Newsletter," *EOTC*, Brussels.

45   "International Agreement."

46   Kevin B. Hendricks, and Vinod R. Singhal, "Quality Awards and the Market Value of the Firm: An Empirical Investigation," Ernst & Young LLP Working Paper, Boston, 1994.

47   Council Resolution of 21 November.

48   "European Quality Award – Application Brochure." European Foundation for Quality Management. Brussels Representative Office, 1995/6 and 1997.

49   Faxes from Vince Ellis, Manager-Assessment Systems, European Foundation for Quality Management, to John J. Kirchenstein, October, 9 1995 and March 28, 1997.

50   "European Quality Award for Theses on Total Quality Management – Call for Applications." European Foundation for Quality Management, Brussels Representative Office. 1995/96.

51   "Across the Board Improvement." *European Quality Award Special Report*, European Quality Publications Ltd., London, 1995, 38–9; and "Improvements with Competitive Edge." *European Quality Award Special Report*, European Quality Publications, Ltd. London, 1996, 12–13.

52   "European Quality Award – Application Brochure."

53   Martin, Bengemann. See note 8.

54   Letter from Max Conrad, Secretary General for the European Organization for Quality, to John J. Kirchenstein dated July 20, 1995.

55   Geert de Raad, "The Leadership Challenge." *European Quality Award Special Report*. European Quality Publications Ltd., London, 1995, 1.

56   EQ Award-Application.

57   "Transnational Excellence." *European Quality Award Special Report*, European Quality Publications Ltd., London, 1995, 54–60.

58   "Transnational Excellence," p. 56.

59   "On the Road to Excellence," *European Quality Award Special Report, 1996*. European Quality Publications Ltd., London, 1996, 16–20.

60   "On the Road to Excellence."

61   "On the Road to Excellence."

62   *Kaizen.* The Japanese concept of continuous improvement where major changes are effected over time by small changes done continuously. Masaaki, Imai *Kaizen: The Key to Japan's Competitive Success*. Random House, New York, 1986.

63   "On the Road to Excellence."

64   Geert de Raad, p. 1. See note 55.

65   Geert de Raad.

66   QS-9000 Quality System Requirements – Copyright 1994; 1995; Chrysler Corporation, Ford Motor Company, General Motors Corporation.

67   Vision 2000: The Strategy for the ISO 9000 Series Standards in the '90s – Quality Progress, May 1991.

68   QS 9000.

69   The ISO 14000 Handbook – CEEM Information Services.

70   British Standard BS 8800: 1996, *Guide to Occupational Health and Safety Management Systems* – British Standards Institution, Milton Keynes, UK.

71   Magnus, Lemmel, "Nurturing Competition." *European Quality Award Special Report, 1996*. European Quality Publications Ltd., London 1996, 8.

72   Vegetius, *Military Institutions of the Romans*, translated from the Latin by Lieutenant John Clark, Stackpole Company, Harrisburg, PA, 1944.

14 | The Competitive Advantages of the TQM Firm

John W. Mogab and William E. Cole

Abstract

During the last quarter century, some Japanese firms have become world-class competitors based on innovations in organizational design and management systems often referred to as Total Quality Management (TQM). The Economies of Quality Index is used here to illustrate their competitive advantages *vis-à-vis* the mass production (MP) firm. In response to these advantage, many western firms have responded with cost-cutting strategies and adoption of some TQM features. While these responses and Japan's economic difficulties have given new life to MP firms, the TQM firms are and will continue to be formidable competitors.

INTRODUCTION

Half a century ago and more the British were acknowledged as the foremost shipbuilders, watch-making was associated with Switzerland, German cameras makers reigned supreme, and the US producers excelled in consumer electronics and automobiles, among other things. Within a few decades, however, Japanese manufacturing was "king of the hill" in each of those sectors and in steel-making as well. Their competitive advantage was acknowledged to stand upon a foundation of high quality goods marketed at competitive prices. Furthermore, their advantage has not been static because the quality of their products has continually increased while costs of production have fallen. Many analysts have studied this phenomenon and a preponderance of them have identified certain organizational designs and management systems, often referred to as Total Quality Management (TQM), as being responsible for producing this revolution. The initial impetus for those designs and systems, claimed by some to constitute a new manufacturing paradigm, is said to rest with American pioneering thinkers such as W. E. Deming and J. M. Juran.

The past quarter of a century has featured a competitive scramble on the part of firms worldwide as they have tried to overcome the Japanese advantages. Some western firms have tried to copy the methods of TQM; some have taken their mass production methods to extreme lengths in efforts to reduce costs, and others have engaged in some of both. The impact of the TQM methods has not been limited to the US and Europe.

Indeed, there is probably not one country on earth that has not been infiltrated by the jargon of TQM, if not by the substance.[1]

In recent years, the competitive edge of the Japanese firms has been dulled somewhat, partly by improvements achieved by some western firms and, partly, by the appreciation of the Yen. For example the persistence of an export trade balance for Japan and an import trade balance for the US has changed the dollar/yen ratio to such an extent that the dollar equivalent of a 2,500,000 yen Toyota would have risen from $10,000 in 1985 to $25,000 in 1996. For several years the western firms tended to raise their prices as the yen appreciated in value, but more recently they have held back, allowing a price gap to develop, thereby enhancing the relative net customer value of their products. Some have mistakenly taken these events as proof that the new paradigm is a "flash in the pan" and that true gold is still found in the standard mass production/scientific management systems. These observers give credit to the cost-cutting strategies and overlook the fact that the relative cost changes have also come from exchange rate trends.[2]

What can we deduce from these recent trends about the relative merits of the TQM methods compared to traditional mass production/scientific management (MP/SM) methods? To answer in the most blunt terms, the recent resurgence of MP/SM firms is in large part an artifact of the particular global monetary institutions that are in force. If it were that the countries of the world utilized a single currency, the likelihood is that many currently thriving MP/SM firms would be competing in a much more hostile market environment. If a firm's earnings depended not at all on movements in the exchange markets, TQM firms that excel at improving net customer value would have a long-term strategic competitive advantage over firms that focused on improving stockholders' value through cost-cutting alone.

Succinctly put, the essence of the new paradigm is a constant striving on the part of the firm to improve quality, flexibility, and cost of production so as to persistently offer the customer the best net customer value available in the market at prices that yield a profit. This does not mean that success will come to every firm adopting a TQM strategy. As in any competition, the cup goes to the one who does it best.

NET CUSTOMER VALUE IS THE NEW COMPETITIVE ARENA

According to Carothers and Adams (p. 34), net customer value is the total value realized by the customer from the purchase and use of the good or service less that which must be sacrificed (given up) to obtain and use it.[3] Net customer value is therefore enhanced from two basic sources: (1) an increment to customer value provided by an improvement in the product itself, and (2) a reduction in the amount that the customer must give up to obtain and use the product. In measuring the amount given up, price may be viewed as a first approximation, but often there are opportunity costs other than price that are borne by the customer which are not reflected in the price.[4] If, for the moment, we take price as an approximate measure of the amount given up by the customer to purchase and use the product, it can be seen that for a given level of value, the lower the price the greater will be the *net* customer value.[5]

A customer's choice among relatively similar products will be made on the basis of net customer value. In searching for a decision rule, we can flatly say that between two competing products requiring the same opportunity costs, a customer with full information will always choose the one offering greater customer value. Similarly, of two products that are perceived to offer the same value, the informed customer will choose the one featuring the smaller opportunity cost.[6] Perceived value differences among competing products, therefore, serve as a basis for establishing competitive advantages or disadvantages. We can say then that in the face of full and free information, the difference in price must fully reflect the difference in customer value[7] if the lower quality producer expects to stay in the market. The difference in value, therefore, becomes a wedge between the price of the product that leads in providing customer value and the price of the product that lags in value.

The TQM firm that follows a strategy of providing best net customer value to its logical conclusion will strive to differentiate the market to the greatest extent possible. To do this the firm must develop flexibility. Indeed, it can be said that a fully developed ideal type TQM firm would be able to produce a unique product for each customer while still enjoying economies of scale.

Beyond the product features and reliability aspects of quality, another dimension of value is the ability to provide the customer with the product when the customer wants it. This aspect, known as just-in-time delivery, is achievable at competitive costs only when very high levels of quality are found at each stage of production. Indeed, it is the hallmark of TQM to continually produce improvements in the production process that simultaneously provide reductions in cost, improvements in product quality, increased flexibility, and enhanced ability to deliver according to the customer's schedule.[8]

THE DYNAMIC ECONOMICS OF TQM

A crucial starting point for analyzing the dynamics of TQM, or the continuous improvement firm, is understanding that all aspects of net customer value may be improved simultaneously. More specifically, we see, over and over, examples where the same improvement activity enhances quality, reduces cost, and provides more of the flexibility necessary to provide for each customer's needs (including delivery time). This stands in stark contrast to firms that utilize cost-cutting as their principal competitive weapon. Where cost reduction is the single-minded goal, downsizing

activities not only fail to improve quality, they are not intended to do so.[9]
After all, the standard mass-production firm adheres to the outdated maxim
that "quality costs."[10]

The essential difference between the continuous improvement and cost-
cutting strategies can be illustrated with a tool we call the Economies of
Quality Index (Q*) which is given in equation 1.

(1) Q* = (Net Revenue Index/Total Cost Index) × 100

The numerator of equation 1, in turn, is defined as follows in equation 1a:

(1a) Net Revenue Index = (Net Revenue in Current Period/
                          Net Revenue in Base Period) × 100

And, the denominator is defined below in equation 1b.

(1b) Total Cost Index = (Total Cost in Current Period/
                         Total Cost in Base Period) × 100

At the outset, it should be noted that the measure Q* is completely
consistent with standard measures of productivity. As a "stand alone" *ex-
post* measure, it gives no more or no less information than those standard
measures. The additional benefits of Q* become obvious only when it is
decomposed in a way that allows us to trace the components of change
back to their origins.

When decomposed, net revenue is the total value of output minus
the value of returns. The value of total output is essentially a function
of product prices, line speed, the number of production lines, and the
throughput[11] quality. Product prices are dependent on the buyers' perceptions of the customer value provided by the products minus the non-price
opportunity costs, and the prices of substitute products available in the
market (this aspect is discussed below under the topic of the customer
value wedge). Line speed, in turn, is a function of the organization of the
work processes and extent of machine "down-time." Machine down-time,
in its turn, is influenced by, among other things, the machine maintenance practices, operation policies and methods, and the time required to
make the line changeovers needed to match the composition of output
with that of customer orders. The organization of work may be affected by
the product design, which in turn, is determined by the customer's needs,
the beginning point for all contemporary manufacturing. Quality of
throughput is a function of how closely manufacturing processes can
adhere to the engineering specifications (i.e., the degree of variation in
throughput), and the extent to which throughput is subject to breakage
or other types of damage or spoilage. Quality of throughput additionally
determines the amount of work-in-process. Work-in-process is created by
the imbalance between operational practices and commitments to customers regarding shipment volume, mix, and rate, and the reality of system

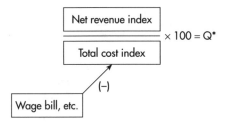

Figure 14.1   Cost cutting through downsizing – a one-dimensional strategy

capabilities for meeting those commitments. Work-in-process is made up of inventories of purchased inputs, intermediate goods, and finished product, in addition to materials in the machine processes, and rejected product to be reworked, or scrapped. Rework and scrap result from throughput identified as inferior product before it is shipped to the customer or as a return from the customer.

In addition to these direct relationships there are a number of potential relationships that are applicable. For example, the more a manufacturer reduces the variation in throughput (i.e., the closer to engineering specifications it can produce all throughput), the greater the degree of precision possible for the engineering specifications. The greater the degree of precision to the engineering specs, the higher the quality of throughput. Similarly, an enhanced ability to make timely line changeovers will support reductions in the amount of inventories that must be maintained, thereby reducing work-in-process. Improved organization of work can reduce work-in-process if, as a result, inventories, rework, or scrap are reduced. Changes in the product design may indirectly affect the level of inventories of purchased inputs, particularly where the firm's strategy is to increase the use of standardized parts. Changes in the quality of the throughput may also affect the levels of purchased inputs and intermediate inventories needed.

The denominator of the economies of quality index, total cost, is a function of labor costs, prorated investment costs, and other operating costs. Labor costs, in turn, include both direct labor (e.g., line workers, rework labor, and inventory-logistics workers) and indirect labor (e.g., administrative employees, including quality department employees). The average wage rate is a function of the weighted occupation structure and the weighted wage rate structure for the firm, or relevant parts thereof. Prorated investment costs would include amortized physical capital and human capital costs. Other operating costs would include costs such as inventory finance, transportation costs, data collection and dissemination and, importantly, the cost of repair under warranty.

Using the economies of quality index, it is a simple operation to set up an example to trace the origin of change for the one dimensional improvement, cost-cutting through downsizing, associated with mass production firms. Such an exercise is shown in figure 14.1. Reduction in size of the

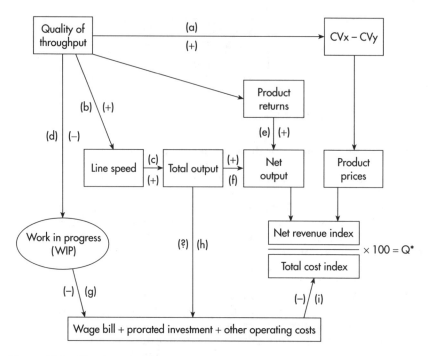

Figure 14.2 Simultaneous improvements in net customer value components

labor force lowers the firms cost of production. The basic assumption is that the smaller labor force is able to maintain output. Such an assumption may indeed be heroic, but, nevertheless, we will grant it. If total output can be maintained with the smaller labor force, then output per worker would rise and cost per unit would fall. To establish some basis for comparison, let us say that firm Y reduces it costs by 10 percent. This would yield the following index number:

$(100/90) \times 100 = 111.11$

This indicates an 11.11 percent increase in productivity for the firm.

In contrast, the continuous improvement firm, call it firm X, focuses it efforts on improving the quality of the product by reducing several aspects of product variation in critical dimensions. We can trace through the implications of this strategy by referring to figure 14.2. To visualize quality changes, we need to assume some specific product so that quality dimensions become manifest. Let us say that X and Y produce paper. If internally generated improvements reduce the variation in the thickness of unfinished paper, the customer value of the final product would be enhanced, as shown by (a). This reduction in variation will also cause an increase in total output for two reasons. For one thing, more rolls of unfinished paper will pass internal inspection and go on to be finished while the number of scrapped rolls will be reduced. Secondly, the line speed of the finishing process can be increased because the likelihood of encountering thin rolls that will tear has been reduced. These changes are represented by (b) and (c). These increases in total production of the plant yield an increase in net output (f). Net output is further increased by the reduction in returns from dissatisfied customers as shown by (e). For purposes of our example, let us assume that the improvement in quality causes net output to increase by 5 percent, from 100 to 105.

The improvements in quality will reduce total cost by reducing the scrap, the rework, and the necessity to carry inventories, all of which are represented by (d). The arrow (h) indicates that there may be some increase in the use of purchased inputs if the line speed is increased. In any case, we would expect that the overall impact on total cost would be a reduction as shown by (i). Let's assume that total cost falls by 5 percent so that the Total Cost Index moves from 100 to 95.

We now put the two sets of changes together to arrive at X's new economies of quality index (Q^*).

$$(105/95) \times 100 = 110.53$$

A straightforward comparison of the respective changes in Q^* would tell us that Y reports better numbers. If Q^* were simply a productivity measure, we would know that productivity improved by 10.53 percent (i.e., cost per unit fell by 9.5 percent) for X while Y's productivity improved by 11.11 percent (i.e., cost per unit dropped by 10 percent).[12] This perspective is misleading, however, because it overlooks what has happened to relative net customer value.

The improved quality not only increases total output and net output, it changes the nature of the output so that customers' value perceptions change, as shown by arrow (a) in figure 14.2. The changing value perceptions carry the straight forward implication that the price wedge will also increase by the same amount and creates a strategic pricing opportunity for firm X. Let's add some more assumptions to enable us to carry the example forward. In the base period, assume that a previously derived difference in net customer value has created a price wedge (CVx – CVy) of 100 minus 80 = 20, and comparative costs per unit (AC) are ACx = 80 and ACy = 80. (All prices and costs are in dollars.) Firm X is therefore enjoying a per unit profit of $20 in the base period while firm Y shows no profit on its sales.

We can now determine each firms' cost per unit after improvements (ACx′) and cost cutting (ACy′). Our previous calculations for firm X indicates that cost per unit fell by 9.5 percent from ACx = 80 to ACx′ = 72.4. For firm Y the 10 percent decrease in cost per unit means that ACy = 80 would become ACy′ = 72. To pull another reasonable number out of the air, let's assume that the improvement in the quality of firm X's product results in the customer now valuing its product by an additional 4 dollars so that the price wedge becomes (CVx′ − CVy′) = 104 − 80 = 24. Firm X now has a to make a pricing decision: Does it want to convert the increase in customer value into profits by increasing the price or does it want to pass the increase along to customers in an effort to increase its market share? If price is held by firm X at $100, customers will enjoy a higher level of net customer value while X's profit will increase to $27.6 (100−72.4). With a price wedge now at $24, firm Y will have to reduce its price to $76, thereby eroding the potential profit gain from its productivity increase.

While Y, in our example, moves to a profit position of $4 per unit (or a rate of 5.3 percent on sales), it is in the tenuous position of being held hostage by firm X. At any time, firm X can drop its price and throw firm Y into a potential loss situation. If, for example, firm X decided to hold its post-improvement rate of profit at the pre-improvement rate of approximately 20 percent, it could lower its price to 91. Its profit would equal 91 minus 72.4 or 18.6 which, relative to its price of 91, would equal a 20.4 percent profit. This would, however, create a pricing policy dilemma for firm Y because, with the difference in customer value equal to 24, it would have to lower its price to 67 (91 minus 24) to maintain its market share, or hold its price at 76 and face the prospect of losing substantial market share. If it lowers it price to 67 to maintain its market share, it would suffer a loss of $5 per unit. This is obviously an untenable position in the long run. Firm Y eventually would have to either give up some market share by raising its price to cover its cost per unit, or it would have to further cut its cost per unit to a level commensurate with the lower price.

The foregoing examples have assumed that both firms X and Y incur their costs in dollars and earn revenue in dollars. If, however, firm X had been incurring costs in yen and earning its revenues in dollars, its otherwise unassailable position could have been compromised by the previously discussed vagaries of the global monetary institutions.

RESPONSES TO THE DEVELOPMENT OF TQM FIRMS

Some MP/SM firms have responded to the challenge of the new competition based on TQM by attempting to adopt all or some aspects of the new paradigm. Others have chosen the cost-cutting strategy of the global factory approach while others have done the same through the downsizing approach. Still others have tried a mix of the three strategies. In particular, some firms that experimented with TQM fell back on the old ways and became dedicated cost cutters. It will be useful, therefore, to take a look at each of these strategies.

As already noted, cost-cutting through downsizing can be generally characterized as an attempt to cut costs by reducing the size of the firm's labor force, particularly at the ranks of middle management, but also in the ranks of blue-collar workers. It also may involve eliminating or consolidating departments or divisions. The objective is to increase labor productivity by producing the same output with fewer resources. This is believed to be possible especially where firms have become inefficient due to overstaffing. A list of firms that have engaged in cost-cutting through downsizing would read like the Fortune 500, as well as including many mid-size and small companies.

The basic weakness in the cost-cutting strategy is that it does not directly address the issue of customer value. This makes the MP/SM firm particularly vulnerable to the market share approach of a continuous improvement rival. As noted above, the internally generated improvements of the TQM firm provide for constant expansion of the customer value/price wedge which puts downward pressure on the follower firm's price and profits. This results in a persistent pressure to continue cost-cutting until diminishing returns are encountered. Such an outcome was recently acknowledged by Stephan Roach, the Morgan Stanley & Co. economist who for years espoused the view that corporate cost-cutting through downsizing would lead to greater productivity, boost the economy and lift employment opportunities to create greater general prosperity. In a recent report (May 9, 1996) to his clients, however, Roach reversed his long standing position, stating, "it's 'highly debatable' whether plant closings, layoffs and other 'tactics for improving efficiency' would result in long-run improvements for the economy and workers in general. He also suggested that corporations had put too much emphasis on 'slash and burn restructuring strategies' . . . rather than investing in new technology and worker retraining."

The global factory approach can be seen as another example of a cost-cutting strategy and is probably best exemplified by General Motors (GM) production of its "world cars." The global factory approach takes economies of specialization to its extreme, by outsourcing the production of many components to the lowest bidder in the global marketplace. The result is vertical disintegration of the firm and fragmentation of production around the world. The objective is to reduce costs by having as many components as possible produced by low bidders according to designs and specifications provided by the manufacturer. New rounds of bidding are sought each year (or production cycle) in order to pressure suppliers to lower component prices each round. For example, a GM "world car" may be designed in-house in Detroit, its frame produced by Fischer Body Co. in St Louis, the engine produced in a factory in Tokyo, electronic components purchased from a firm in Taiwan, head lights from Mexico, brake systems from China, tires from Malaysia, etc., based on competitive bids sought in the current year. A subsequent year's round of bids will likely result in some geographical changes in the origins of some of these components. While the global factory approach does not directly address quality issues, its most obvious shortcoming is the fact that it would be extremely difficult to combine it with just-in-time manufacturing.

A comparison of TQM firms with companies that use cost-cutting strategies suggests that the latter emphasize one aspect of competitiveness, cost-cutting, based on a short-term approach to employee and supplier relationships. The TQM firm, on the other hand, simultaneously emphasizes quality improvement, timely delivery, and cost-cutting, based on long-term relationships with its employees and suppliers. The cost-cutting strategy would, therefore, be most likely to succeed in markets where customers put little emphasis on improvement of product quality or just-in-time delivery and much greater weight on price. In markets where product quality is important and is continuously improved by producers, TQM would seem more likely to succeed. The nature of markets may change, however, and that is especially the case for those where quality may seem unimportant at the moment. Take for example, an industry such as paper, whose product is thought to be so standardized as to constitute a near commodity. Because that is the view at one point in time does not mean that it will continue to be the view forever. As some firm develops the capability of continuous improvement and reduces variations in the several aspects of quality, customer value differences will emerge. Furthermore, differences in ability to meet increasingly tighter delivery schedules can differentiate the products of the firms in any industry. Therefore, a firm that chooses the cost-cutting strategy based on the current environment lays itself open to possibly devastating competition if a TQM firm enters the market. In general, it appears that cost-cutting strategies alone will not support long-term viability if there are active TQM firms in the market or if there are strong prospects that one or more may enter.

PREDICTING TRENDS FOR THE TQM STRATEGY

Prospects seem good for TQM to continue to thrive in Japan. Japanese manufacturing has spent the last several years being battered by a severe domestic recession and a strong yen abroad. While the strong yen has made exporting more difficult by pushing up the dollar price of Japanese goods, the recession has greatly reduced the size of the domestic markets for those goods. In the face of those tremendous pressures, the Japanese TQM firms have resisted the temptation to engage in downsizing as a strategy for protecting short-term profits. For the most part, work forces have been kept intact with the consequent down time utilized for training, maintenance, and work on product and process improvements. This was done despite the many predictions in the West that the Japanese firms would have to drop their TQM trappings as they faced such massive adversities. This common view was based on a belief that the so-called "bottom-up" approach of the TQM firms was a luxury that could only be afforded in the flush of growing markets.

One now hears reports such as that coming from Toyota that new rounds of internal improvements in product and process will permit the firm to market models with lower prices and better performance. This, coupled with news that the Japanese economy appears to be emerging from the recession augur renewed vigor for the Japanese version of the TQM firm.

There is, however, at least one impediment to the future success of the Japanese version of the TQM firm. The troublesome problem of the yen exchange rate will continue to hang over the Japanese TQM firms, despite the recent fall in the value of the yen.[13] If this roadblock is to be removed, it will require that the Japanese government and private sector work hard to reduce the size of the balance of trade surplus. A long-term solution to this problem would appear to require a move toward a regime of freer trade. While a shift toward freer trade would provide an atmosphere in which TQM firms should thrive, it also would promote some unique problems for the Japanese economy and society. To date, for example, the potential cultural costs of changing the way goods are distributed have constituted a major brake on this needed change. Prospects of losing the small-scale farming sector have also been unappealing. So long as the trade gap bolsters the value of the yen, the Japanese TQM firms will have to engage in competitive fights with one hand tied behind their back. Even so, they will be formidable competitors.

When one asks of the prospects for TQM in firms producing outside of Japan, the analysis becomes decidedly muddy. No straightforward answer can be given because there is such a variety of firms worldwide attempting to implement a TQM strategy. There are western firms with production facilities in their domestic markets and abroad. There are also subsidiaries of Japanese firms operating in the West and South. What can be said is that the principles of TQM have not gone unnoticed by firms outside of Japan. Topics such as customer value and employee involvement have been on many executives' reading lists and jargon from TQM is part of the *lingua franca* of business. Two of the most popular aspects of TQM that have been considered are statistical process control (SPC) and just-in-time manufacturing (JIT). Consulting firms all over the world have pushed these techniques and thousands of firms of all sizes have shown interest in at least some aspects of TQM. These firms represent the full spectrum of businesses, including services, not just manufacturing. Moreover, a number of government offices and even some school systems have been implementing some features of TQM.

While the experience is mixed, it is common knowledge that many organizations are considered to have had little or no success with those soft technologies and, in fact, after a brief attempt at implementing the TQM technologies, some have reverted back to their old ways. The truth of the matter is that most MP/SM firms that have looked at TQM have approached it on a piecemeal basis, accepting some aspects and rejecting others. Some former MP/SM firms, however, have accepted the importance of making a complete paradigm shift. Harley-Davidson and Hewlett-Packard are good examples of firms that have had comprehensive make-overs from mass production to TQM firms. Those who study the TQM experience tend to agree that a continuous improvement capability emerges only when a comprehensive package of those soft technologies is adopted.

There is another aspect of MP/SM manufacturing firms that offers some interesting insights. We are referring here to the experience of the overseas subsidiaries of some major US firms. With US firms attempting to utilize TQM technologies, it might be expected that some of that interest would spill over to their subsidiaries. For example, in a study of the Brazilian electronics sector, the full sample of US subsidiaries was employing SPC to some degree and 60 percent were attempting to adopt JIT manufacturing (Bos and Cole 1994). A companion study in the maquiladora zone of Mexico (Wilson 1992) found US subsidiaries using all of the TQM soft technologies: SPC, worker suggestion systems, JIT, and supplier programs. Furthermore, in most cases the TQM technologies were used more comprehensively and successfully in Mexico than in comparable home operations. US subsidiary managers generally indicated that the frontier environment of the Mexican setting gave them more freedom to experiment than was the case back at the home base. It is also of interest that the US subsidiaries were using the TQM technologies more intensively than their Japanese counterparts.

Finally, we have the experience of Japanese subsidiaries in the US, and especially the Japanese automakers. Initially the Japanese automakers established US subsidiaries in response to the voluntary export restraint agreement negotiated between Washington and Tokyo in 1981. The major Japanese automakers, Toyota, Nissan, and Honda were the first to establish a presence in the US and were later followed by the second tier automakers, Mazda, Mitsubishi, and Isuzu. Honda made the pioneering move because the bulk of its sales were in the US (it had only a small share of the Japanese market). Given that a significant proportion of its automobile operations would likely become located in the US, Honda had little choice but to establish the subsidiary as a continuous improvement firm. Although no definitive studies allow us to make direct comparisons between Honda's US subsidiary and its domestic facilities, the US subsidiary appears to be operating as a successful TQM firm.

Toyota took a more conservative approach to entering the US market than did Honda. Toyota's first entry into US production was a joint venture with General Motors, establishing the New United Motor Manufacturing, Inc. (NUMMI) in 1984. The joint venture utilized a previously closed GM plant in California and the vast majority of its work force. Studies of NUMMI suggest that, as a TQM firm, it successfully transferred the continuous improvement techniques to the production workers, but encountered significant difficulties with middle management (Kenney and Florida pp. 117–18).[14] NUMMI was apparently enough of a success for Toyota to make the decision to establish a wholly-owned US subsidiary in Kentucky in 1988. While informal statements from Toyota officials indicate that the level of improvement generation in Kentucky is not as high as in its Japanese plants, they are nonetheless pleased with the rate of progress toward continuous improvement (Personal interview, September 1991). A Toyota executive recently remarked that, as good as they were, the US labor force of Toyota was not as good at continuous improvement as their Japanese counterpart.[15] The Toyota executive did not take the comparative quality results to mean that Japanese are inherently better, but rather that it would take a while longer for US labor to catch up to Japanese standards. Such statements suggest that Toyota's US subsidiary should be considered a qualified success as a TQM firm. Not all of the Japanese automakers, however, have been successful in transferring the continuous improvement technologies to the US. In 1985 Mazda established a stamping and assembly plant in Michigan with the intention of creating a TQM firm. Fucini and Fucini have documented the mutual disenchantment of both its workers and managers with the evolution of the organizational culture. Workers and managers have come to mistrust each other and, while production tasks are performed by teams, the teams do not attempt to generate product or process improvements.

Given the successful experience of companies like Hewlett-Packard and Harley-Davidson that have wholeheartedly adopted TQM, the accelerated efforts of US subsidiaries, and the partial success of the Japanese automakers in the US, the prospects for TQM worldwide generally look good. It should be stressed, however, that the future of TQM is not a matter of Japanese versus Western firms. Within the global marketplace, the firms that cater best to customer value considerations will, in the long run, have a better chance of succeeding than will those that single-mindedly go about cutting cost by downsizing and outsourcing.

SUMMARY AND CONCLUSION

During the 1980s many thought that the TQM firm was a uniquely Japanese-style firm that would lead Japan to global hegemony. By the early 1990s, Japan's domestic economic difficulties and the rising value of the yen were punishing the Japanese TQM firms. At the same time, their western competitors responded by adopting TQM technologies or by pursuing cost-cutting strategies that gave them new life. The flash of apparent success by the cost-cutters prompted some analysts to conclude that the TQM firm was nothing more than a passing management fad that could be thrown on the rubbish heap with all the other management fads. By the mid-1990s, however, the resilience of Japan's TQM firms, the vigor of former MP/SM firms that have made the conversion to TQM, and the anorexic experience of many cost-cutting firms has led some analysts to once again reconsider the strengths of the TQM firm.

All the short-term vagaries of the market aside, it should be clear from the above analysis that the TQM firm represents a formidable competitor that will continue to make its presence known in global markets of the future. It is neither a fad nor a panacea. The TQM firm is a new paradigm whose strengths and weaknesses we are only beginning to understand. Its strengths include its ability to utilize all the assets that its workers have to offer. To be able to utilize all its workers' assets requires that the TQM firm invest substantial amounts of resources to develop their human capital.

The result can be a loyal work force that will continuously improve the firm's product and production processes so as to more closely match the qualities that its customers want. A weakness is that the investment in human capital must be sustained even in the face of a down market. Substantial losses are likely to be incurred by the TQM firm when market demand periodically declines. The tactic of making short-run adjustments in labor employment that allows the mass production firm to sustain its profits or minimize its losses during market downturns is of limited use in the TQM firm. This has led some firms to suspend or terminate their attempts to make the transformation to the TQM firm.

Those firms that decide to take on the challenge of making the transformation must make a long-term commitment if they are to succeed. The transformation from the old mass production/scientific management paradigm to the new paradigm of the TQM firm is more akin to a marathon race than a sprint. It can not be made without suffering some setbacks, nor is there a one size fits all recipe for making the transformation. For those firms that persevere and make the complete transformation, the TQM paradigm holds the promise of helping them become market leaders. This does not mean that all TQM firms automatically will be market leaders. As we stated earlier, the cup goes to the one who does it best. Neither will the laws of supply and demand be suspended. Even the best TQM firms will be subject to the short-term vagaries of the market. For those firms that choose to not make the transformation, or poorly implement the transformation process, the likelihood is that any success will be temporary. They always will be looking over their shoulder waiting for the day when a TQM rival enters their market. In cases where a TQM rival has already arrived, they may survive but will have to be content with the role of the follower firm, which carries the threat of bankruptcy.

Notes

1 For a discussion of TQM in the context of developing countries, see Wilson, Ballance and Pogány (1995).

2 The importance of exchange rate movements is once again being felt in the US. The long-term trend of appreciation of the yen has recently reversed with the yen/dollar exchange rate moving up from approximately 80 yen per dollar in the spring 1996 to almost 115 yen per dollar in mid-summer 1997. This has sent shockwaves reverberating through US industry as it prepares for another onslaught of competitive pressure from Japanese manufacturers.

3 This approach to the concept of customer value comes from Carothers and Adams (1991, pp. 33ff). The term "customer value" is also found in Hayes, Wheelwright, and Clark (1988, p. 342), but with less formal development than in Carothers and Adams.

4 Because "sacrifice," includes nonprice elements, net customer value will be less than the consumer surplus as defined by economists.

5 It is because of the nonprice elements of sacrifice that we cannot draw the straightforward inference the net customer value is the total value received minus the price.

6 We cannot say that a customer will always choose the alternative that offers the highest net customer value. An income constraint might keep a customer

from considering a product that offers relatively more net customer value than alternatives. A particular automobile, for example, might be perceived by an individual as affording 50 thousand dollars of value while featuring a price of 40 thousand dollars or a net customer value of 10 thousand dollars (for simplicity, assuming that other opportunity costs are zero). The potential buyer, however, might be constrained by personal income level from entering that market and may possibly pay 20 thousand dollars for an automobile perceived to yield only 20 thousand dollars in value (net customer value of zero).

7   Customer value here refers to the total value provided by the use of the product less any non-price opportunity costs incurred in the purchase of the product.

8   The prototype example for the simultaneous improvements in all aspects of customer value is the development of the Toyota Production System, the original just-in-time manufacturing system.

9   The focus here is on downsizing solely aimed at cost-cutting. In this context, downsizing is not a part of a larger strategy, such as restructuring or reengineering of the firm, but rather is the whole of the firm's competitive strategy.

10   See Cole and Mogab (1995, pp. 110ff) for a comparison of the continuous improvement and the mass production approaches to the "cost of quality."

11   The use of the term "throughput," for readers familiar with it, may bring to mind the theory of constraints, expounded by E. Goldratt in *The Goal, It's Not Just Luck*, and elsewhere. As used here, throughput refers to the process of converting inputs into outputs, whereas Goldratt defines it as "the rate at which the system generates money through sales" (p. 59). Despite the difference in the definition of throughput, there is considerable agreement between the analysis here and the theory of constraints. For example, both analyses emphasize the importance of a continuous improvement strategy to enhance quality rather than a cost-cutting strategy; both see quality improvement as a means to simultaneously increasing revenues and decreasing costs; and both recommend that firms should prioritize and implement improvements based on the potential for improving revenues and reducing costs. The similarities, however, were not intentional as we had no knowledge of the theory of constraints when the Economies of Quality Index was first developed.

12   For firm Y total output did not change so that the 10 percent reduction in total cost would reduce unit cost by the same rate, 10 percent. On the other hand, firm X enjoyed an increase in total output of 5 percent coupled with a 5 percent decline in total cost. Both of those factors combine to affect cost per unit.

13   See note 2.

14   Some US makers of autoparts who became suppliers to NUMMI also report success at implementing the TQM technologies. See, for example, Walker's step-by-step account of Packard Electric's continuous improvement efforts to qualify as a NUMMI supplier.

15   These remarks followed published reports that the Lexus, built by Toyota in Japan, was top ranked in terms of quality while the Toyota Camry, built in the US, had fallen from the top ranks.

References

Bleakley, Fred R. The Wall Street Journal Interactive Edition – May 20, 1996, "Economists Shift on Downsizing Sparks Outcry in British Media."

Bós, Antonio and Cole, William. "Management Systems as Technology: Japanese, US and National Firms in the Brazilian Electronics Sector," *World Development* 22 (2): 225–36, 1994.

Carothers, Harlan and Adams, Mel. "Competitive Advantage Through Customer Value: The Role of Value-Based Strategies," in M. J. Stahl and G. Bounds (eds.), 32–66, *Competing Globally Through Customer Value: The Management of Strategic Suprasystems*, Westport, Conn.: Quorum Books, 1991.

Cole, William and Mogab, John. *The Economics of Total Quality Management.* Cambridge, MA: Blackwell Publishers, 1995.

Fucini, Joseph and Fucini, Suzy. *Working for the Japanese: Inside Mazda's American Auto Plant.* New York: The Free Press, 1990.

Goldratt, Eliyah. *It's Not Just Luck.* Croton-on-Hudson, New York: North River Press, 1994.

Goldratt, E. and Cox, Jeff. *The Goal.* Revised Edition. Croton-on-Hudson, New York: North River Press, 1986.

Hayes, R. H., S. Wheelright and K. Clark. *Dynamic Manufacturing: Creating the Learning Organization.* New York: Free Press, 1988.

Kenney, M. and R. Florida. *Beyond Mass Production: The Japanese System and Its Transfer to the U.S.* New York: Oxford University Press, 1993.

Mogab, John W. 'Industrial Policy and Protectionism in Post WWII Japan," in James, D. D. and J. W. Mogab, eds. *Technology, Innovation and Industrial Economics: Institutionalist Perspectives.* Boston: Kluwer Academic Publishers, 1998.

Stahl, Michael and Bounds, Gregory. *Competing Globally Through Customer Value.* New York: Quorum Books, 1991.

Walker, James P. *A Disciplined Approach to Continuous Improvement.* Packard Electric, 1988.

Wilson, Steven R. "Continuous Improvement and the New Competition: The Case of US, European, and Japanese Firms in the Mexican Maquiladora Industry," Ph.D. Dissertation, University of Tennessee, Knoxville, 1992.

Wilson, Steven, Ballance, Robert and Pogány, János. *Beyond Quality: An Agenda for Improving Manufacturing Capabilities in Developing Countries.* Hants, England: Edward Elgar Publishing, Ltd., 1995.

Index

3M Corporation, 221
7-Eleven Japan, 208
100 Best Places to Work in America, 117, 132

Aaker, D. A., 143
ABI/INFORM searches, 40–1
ABS Quality Evaluations, Inc, 354
academic culture, 71–101
  cross-functional cooperation, 82, 85–6, 87
  cultural change, 90, 99n
  cultural clash with total quality, 75–83, 95
  customer satisfaction, 81
  employee participation, 82
  implementation of total quality programs, 81–3
  Japan, 72, 75
  lack of importance attached to quality, 73–5, 83, 98n
  lack of literature on quality, 74, 76
  leadership, 82
  reliability and control, 82–3
  researcher-customer relations, 83–5
  skepticism of quality, 80–1
  status of students, 81
  total quality as lacking empirical support, 76
  total quality as lacking theoretical validity, 76
  see also research
accounting data, 37, 40, 65–6

Christensen and Lee study, 53–4
Easton and Jarrell study, 60, 61–2, 63, 64
Hendricks and Singhal study, 49–53
Holder and Pace study, 54–5
Lawler, Mohrman, Ledford study, 42–4
self-announcement studies, 54–5
accreditation networks, 354–5, 367
Adams, Mel, 372
Adler, P., 94
advertising intensity, 48
AEA, 124
AES Corporation, 110
Agility Forum, 124
Allaire, Paul, 99n
Alter, C., 93
American Banker, 352
American Electronics Association (AEA), 124
American Express, 205
American National Standards Institute (ANSI), 354
American Quality Foundation, 42, 347
American Society for Quality Control (ASQC), 79, 87, 88, 89, 354
American Stock Exchange, 44, 54
Amundson, S. D., 249
analysts' forecasts, 61, 63, 64
Anderson, Eugene W., 352
Anderson, James C., 10, 76, 249

Anderson, S. W., 32, 44, 48–9, 65, 66, 349
ANSI, 354
Apple Computers, 137
Applied Energy Services Corporation, 118
D'Archifari, Vanni, 359
Armstrong, J. S., 30
ARS database, 58
Arthur D. Little, 79, 346
artifacts, as manifestation of culture, 138
Artzt, Edwin, 74
Ashby, Ross, 107
ASQC *see* American Society for Quality Control
assembly line production, 106
asset turnover (assets/ sales), 50, 54
assets, return on, 115–16
  GAO report (1991), 41
  Lawler, Mohrman, Ledford study, 42–3
assets/income, 50, 53, 54, 61
assumptions, as manifestation of culture, 138
AT&T, 205
  process management definition, 184, 185–6
A. T. Kearney, 346
Athos, A., 137
audit experiences, manager perceptions, 33
automotive industry, 210, 382–3

Baba, M., 93, 107, 109
Babbage; Charles, 106
Bacdayan, P., 29

Bacon, Francis, 91, 92
Baldrige Award *see* Malcolm
  Baldrige National
  Quality Award
Banc One, 205
Bane, M., 247
Bangeman, Martin, 345
Barker, J. R., 139
Barney, J. B., 137, 150
BARRA, 117, 132
Bednar, D. A., 97n
Beer Game, 194–5
Beer, M., 134, 150
behavior
  influence of
    organizational culture,
    139–40
    TQM, 139–40, 148–9
Bekaert-Stanwick, 349, 353,
  354
Bell Laboratories, 213
Bennis, Warren, 113
Benson, P. G., 44, 249
Berry, Leonard A., 8
Black, S. A., 44
BOC Limited, 359
BOM, 278–80, 297–9, 300
Bordogna, Joseph, 99n
Bos, Antonio, 382
Bowen, D. E., 249
BPR *see* business process
  reengineering
brainstorming, 23
brand differentiation, 277
Brand, William A., 10
Brazil, 382
Brimley, Richard, 351
Brisa Bridgestone Sabanci
  Tyre Manufacturing
  and Trading, 359,
  360–1
British Standards
  Institution, 349–51,
  354
  BS 5750, 361
  BS 7750, 361, 364
  BS 7850, 346
  BS 8800, 361–2, 364–5
British
  Telecommunications,
  359
BSI News, 358
BT, 359
Buffa, E., 106, 107
bulls-eye schedule system,
  263, 264
bureaucratic control, 139,
  202
Burns, Mary Jane, 21

business metrics, 31, 47,
  115–16
business pressures *see*
  competitive pressures
business process
  reengineering (BPR),
  28
  case manager, 203–4
  costs, 191–4, 207–8
  cycle-time reduction, 188,
  191–4, 197, 201
  definition, 188–9
  elimination of checks,
    controls,
    reconciliations, 202–3
  elimination of steps not
    providing value,
    191–4
  empowerment of
    employees, 201–2
  examples of, 204–5
  execution of high level
    strategy, 190
  failure rates, 206
  high level strategies,
    189–204
  holistic redesign, 195–6
  impact of, 204
  improvements
    observation, 190
  information flow
    redesign, 194–5
  installation of
    appropriate controls,
    190
  leadership, 206
  mapping of process, 189,
    191, 194, 202, 215–17
  measurement of process,
    189–90
  objectives in terms of
    customer value, 189,
    191–4, 209
  parallel versus series
    working, 197–9
  resistance to, 206–8
  selection of high level
    strategy, 190
  soft side of, 206–8
  standardization, 199–200
  suppliers and internal
    customers, 196–7
  work organization around
    customer groups, 201
  work organization around
    products/services, 201
business results
  Baldrige criteria, 337,
    338, 339

European Quality Award
  criteria, 357, 358
  organization level,
    117–18, 131–2
business support processes,
  28
Business Week, 134, 154, 313
Businesswire, 50, 58
Butz, Howard E., 10
buying criteria, 11, 25

CAD *see* Computer-Aided-
  Design
Cadotte, Ernest R., 15
Carothers, Harlan, 372
CEN/CENELEC, 347
Centra Automotive Ltd
  (UK), 349–50
certification, 27, 348–9,
  352, 353–5, 362–3, 367
  quality certification
    studies, 48–9, 65
Champy, J., 28, 206
change, entrepreneur's
  views on, 113
change practices, 149
chemical processing
  industry, 210
Chintagunta, Arol Pradeepk
  K., 10
Christensen, J. S., 44, 46,
  51, 53–4, 65
Chrysler, 196–7, 362
Churchill, Sir Winston, 365
citizenship, Baldrige
  criteria, 336, 337, 338
Clark, K. B., 246, 248
coal industry, 107–8, 118,
  131
cognitive psychology, 108
cognitive representations,
  143–5
Cole, R. E. 99n, 100n
  American faculty, 83
  employee involvement,
    29
  Japanese quality control
    circles, 77, 91
  quality failures in USA,
    80
  quality as social
    movement, 95
Cole, William, 78, 79, 382
communication
  high performing
    organizations, 127
  TQM programs, 176–7
Compact Disclosure
  database, 55

company performance, Baldrige criteria, 336, 337, 338
company responsibility, Baldrige criteria, 336, 337, 338
company-specific results, Baldrige criteria, 332, 333, 334, 335, 336, 339
Company-Wide Quality Control (CWQC), 67n
comparison standards, 15–16
compensation policies, 116
competitive advantage
  customer value, 372–3
  dimensions of, 246, 248
  fast product development, 246–7
  mental models of, 143–5, 151
  TQM firm, 371–86
competitive analysis, 247
competitive pressures, 7, 24, 39
  European industry, 343–4
  from Japan, 27, 73, 313, 372–3
competitor orientation, 143, 144, 145–6
COMPUSTAT database, 46, 48, 50, 51, 54
Computer-Aided-Design (CAD), 222, 237, 248
concurrent engineering, 247
The Conference Board, 315
consensus, 137, 138, 149, 150, 361
consequences, customer value, 14–15, 16, 19, 20, 21, 22, 24, 25
constraints, theory of, 385n
content themes, as manifestation of culture, 137–8
contingency theory, 78, 93
continuous improvement and learning, 173, 249, 269
  electronic sensor case study, 260
  European Quality Award, 108, 344, 356–61, 366–7
  high performing organizations, 115

implantable device component case study, 266
navigational device case study, 255
QS-9000, 363
see also ISO 9000 standards; Total Quality Management (TQM)
control charts, 213–15, 217–18, 220
control samples, 38, 40, 66
  Christensen and Lee study, 53
  Easton and Jarrell study, 60–1, 63–4
  Hendricks and Singhal accounting data study, 50, 51–2
  Holder and Pace study, 54
Cooper, Antony, 217
cooperation, 249, 268
  electronic guide case study, 261, 263
  electronic sensor case study, 259
  implantable device component case study, 265
  mainframe computer case study, 253
  medical device case study, 257
  navigational device case study, 254
  network data processor case study, 267
Copleston, F., 91
corporate performance *see* financial performance
cost leadership strategy, 146
Costello, T., 107
costs
  business process reengineering, 191–4, 207–8
  downsizing, 373–4, 375–6, 378–9, 385n
  Eskildsone study, 64
  factor of competitive differentiation, 246, 248, 373–80
  global factory approach, 379
  total cost index, 374–8
Critical-To-Function (CTF) parameters, 232
Crosby, P., 46–7, 249, 250

cross-functional management, 29
cross-sectional correlation studies, 38–9
cross-sectional regressions, 42–3
CSM *see* customer satisfaction measurement
CTF, 232
cultural change, 90, 94–5, 99n
culture, organizational, 22–3, 134–52
  adaptive, 141
  behavioral influence, 139–40
  building of, 147–9
  coordinating role, 150
  core values, 147, 245–6, 248–50
  definition, 137–8, 150, 248
  different perspectives on, 140–2
  differentiated, 141
  effect on effectiveness and performance, 136–7
  high performing organizations, 112, 120, 130
  integrated, 141
  market orientation, 142–7
  strategic, 140–1
  strategically differentiated, 141–2, 146–7, 149, 150
  strong type, 140
  total quality integration, 135–6, 147–8, 149, 150
customer accessibility management, Baldrige criteria, 333, 334, 335
customer complaint management, Baldrige criteria, 333, 334, 335
customer complaints, 24
customer focus, 9, 28, 31
  customer group work organization, 201
  electronic sensor case study, 259
  high performing organizations, 111–12
  mainframe computer case study, 252, 253
  medical device case study, 257, 258

customer focus (*contd*)
product development, 67,
234–6, 249–50, 268
software product case
study, 264
customer knowledge,
Baldrige criteria, 333,
334, 335, 337, 338
customer orientation, 143,
144, 145–6
customer satisfaction
academic culture, 81
Baldrige criteria, 331, 333,
334, 335, 336, 338, 339
definition, 15–16
emphasis on, 28
European Quality Award
criteria, 357, 358
ISO 9000, 351–3, 367
"moment of truth"
experience, 178
quest for, 351–3
relation to customer
value, 15–17
surveys, 12, 21–2, 23
Total Quality
Management, 78,
351–3, 367
use of information
technology (IT),
178–9
customer satisfaction
measurement (CSM),
9, 10, 11–12, 16–17, 21,
22, 59
customer scenario analysis,
23
customer transcripts,
analysis of, 23
customer value, 7–26
adoption of shared
concept of, 19, 23
attributes, 11–13, 14–15,
16, 19, 20, 21, 24, 25
business process
reengineering, 189,
191–4, 209
changes in, 17–18
competitive advantages,
372–3
consequences, 14–15, 16,
19, 20, 21, 22, 24, 25
customer relationships,
19
definitions, 10, 372
desired end states, 15, 16,
20, 21, 25
high performing
organizations, 111–12

improving competitive
capabilities, 19–24
lean enterprises, 275–82
learning process, 19–20,
21, 22–4, 25
market orientation, 142–3
new concept of, 13–19
organization's conception
of, 10–11
process managers, 210,
211, 219–20
product development,
221–2, 234–6, 243, 244
relation to customer
satisfaction, 15–17
research, 21–2
training, 23, 25
translation of learning
into action, 20, 23–4,
25
use of information
systems, 208
use situations, 17
customer value
determination process,
22, 23, 25
customer value hierarchy,
13–19, 21, 23, 24, 25
customer value
measurement (CVM),
16–17
customer value wedge,
377–8, 379
customer-defined quality,
28
customers
future needs projection,
224, 227, 228, 232, 244
increased demands of,
7–8, 24
increased influence of, 7
ordering patterns, 296
relations to academic
researchers, 83–5
satisfaction surveys, 12,
21–2, 23
understanding needs of,
8–9, 185–6
CVM, 16–17
CWQC, 67n
cycle-time reduction, 28, 29,
67
business process
reengineering, 188,
191–4, 197, 201
Eskildson study, 64
high performing
organizations, 129
lean enterprises, 289

D2D Limited, 359
Daly, J., 32, 44, 48–9, 65,
66, 349
data, Baldrige criteria, 334,
335, 336, 337, 338
data collection plans,
217–18
Day, G. S., 10, 134, 142–4,
145, 146
Dean, J. W., 29, 44, 114,
135, 136, 148, 149, 249
debt structuring, 64
decision making
fact-based, 28, 250, 253,
254, 261, 262, 268
high performing
organizations, 112–13
Delors, Jacques, 344, 359
Delta Airlines, 202
demand forecasts, 273–4,
278–81, 302–5
demand signal processing,
281
DeMeyer, A., 248
Deming management
method, 76
Deming Prize, 108
Deming, W. Edwards, 107,
249, 371
Deming Wheel of Plan-Do-
Check-Act, 115, 315
Department of Defense
(DoD), 254, 260–1
Department of Labor, 41
Department of Trade and
Industry (UK), 354,
355
dependability, 246, 248
derating, 238
Dertouzos, Michael L., 222
Deshpande, R., 142, 143,
145
Design of Experiments, 222
Design-for-Assembly, 222
Design-for-Manufacturing,
222, 247–8, 255
desired end states, 15, 16,
20, 21, 25
diffusion, 149
disconfirmation model, 15
distance learning
technology, 124
distribution channel
integration, 275–6,
308–9
distribution channels, 7
distribution plans, 225
DJNS, 44
DOD 5000.510G, 346

Donaldson, Eric, 221
Dow Jones News Service
  (DJNS), 44
downsizing
  business process
    reengineering, 206,
    207
  cost cutting, 373–4,
    375–6, 378–9, 385n
  Easton and Jarrell study,
    62
  network data processor
    case study, 266
downtime, 285, 296
Drucker, P., 113
DTI, 354, 355
DuPont, 49
Dutch Council for
  Accreditation, 354–5
Dutka, Alan, 9, 11

EAC, 355
Eastman Chemical
  Company, 141–2, 146,
  147, 150
Easton, G. S., 48, 116, 346
  in-depth interview study,
    56, 58–64, 65, 66
  just-in-time deliveries, 34
  manager perceptions, 33
  managerial exaggeration
    of TQM, 35
  organization level results,
    117, 132
  sample selection, 32
  start date of deployment
    of TQM, 34
  TQM characteristics, 28
Eco-Management and Audit
  Scheme (EMAS), 364
Economies of Quality
  Index, 374–8
The Economist, 222
*The Economy of Machinery
  and Manufacturers*, 106
EDI, 307
education *see* training
EFQM, 345, 356, 361
Egbelu, Pius, 98n
Eisenstat, R. A., 134, 150
Eldred, 107
electronic data interchange
  (EDI), 307
electronic guide case study,
  251, 260–3
electronic sensor case study,
  251, 258–60
electronics industry, 210,
  250–68

Ellis, Vince, 359
EMAS, 364
Emery, Fred, 107
employee involvement, 29,
  31
  academic culture, 82
  high performing
    organizations, 113–14,
    118–30
  lean enterprises, 284
  relationship to financial
    performance, 42–4,
    65
employees
  Baldrige criteria, 336,
    337, 338
  behavior, 139–40, 148–9
  empowerment in BPR,
    201–2
  European Quality Award
    criteria, 357, 358
  impact of failed TQM
    programs, 135
  motivators and
    dissatisfiers, 108
  needs, 108, 113
  as owners of local
    knowledge, 93–4
  percent change, 61, 62
  TQM investment in,
    383–4
  see also team working;
    training
empowerment, 156, 201–2
EMS, 361, 363–4
EN-ISO 29000, 347, 367
Engelhard, 205
engineering faculty, 85–6,
  97n, 98n
engineering quality testing,
  256, 261
Environmental
  Management Systems
  (EMS), 361, 363–4
EOQ, 345, 356
EOTC, 355
Equiagaray, Juan M., 359
equity, return on, 42–3, 54
Ericsson SA, 359
Ernst & Young, 42, 79, 347
Eskildson, L., 64–5, 66
European Accreditation of
  Certification (EAC),
  355
European Commission, 344,
  345–6, 349, 354, 355,
  356–7, 364, 366
European Council, 343–4,
  346, 347–8

European Foundation for
  Quality Management
  (EFQM), 345, 356, 361
European Organization for
  Quality (EOQ), 345,
  356
European Organization
  for Testing and
  Certification (EOTC),
  355
European Quality Award,
  108, 344, 356–61,
  366–7
European Quality Platform,
  345
European Quality Prizes,
  356, 357
European Quality
  Promotion Policy, 344,
  365
European Quality Week,
  345
European Union, 343–6,
  347, 354, 364, 366
Evans, J., 74–5, 83, 98n
event study methodology,
  39, 44–6, 49
evolutionary economic
  theory, 92–3
exchange rate movements,
  372, 381, 384n

fact-based management, 28,
  250, 268
  electronic guide case
    study, 261, 262
  mainframe computer
    case study, 253
  navigational device case
    study, 254
Factory Response Profile,
  303–4
factory system, 106
Failure Mode Effects
  Analysis (FMEA), 285
Falkenburg, Don, 90
Farley, J. U., 142, 143, 145
fax communication, 307
FDA, 265, 362
Federal Express, 110, 118
Feigenbaum, A. V., 67n
Ferdows, K., 248
field studies, in-depth, 66–7
financial performance,
  27–70
  accounting data studies,
    42–4, 49–54, 65–6
  Anderson, Daly, Johnson
    study, 48–9, 65, 66

financial performance
(*contd*)
Arthur D. Little study, 346
A. T. Kearney study, 346
Baldrige criteria, 331,
336, 339
Christensen and Lee
study, 53–4, 65
cross-sectional correlation
studies, 38–9
Easton and Jarrell study,
58–64, 65, 66, 346
employee involvement,
42–4, 65
GAO report (1991), 41
Hendricks and Singhal
accounting data study,
49–53, 65
Hendricks and Singhal
stock price study, 44–7,
65, 66
high performing
organizations, 117–18,
131–2
Holder and Pace study,
54–5, 65
in-depth interview
studies, 58–64
International Quality
Study, 42
Lawler, Mohrman,
Ledford study, 42–4, 65
Lemak, Reed, Satish
study, 55–8, 65
market-oriented firms, 145
non-academic studies,
41–2
quality award studies,
44–7, 49–54, 356
quality certification
studies, 48–9, 65
research methods, 37–40
self-announcement
studies, 54–8, 65
stock price event studies,
42–9, 65–6
survey-based studies, 37,
42–4, 65
turnaround studies, 64–5
Finland, 355
Fiol, C. M., 145
five "S" checks, 284–5
flexibility, 246
Flint, Daniel J., 18
Florida, R., 382
flow charts, 285–6
Flynn, B. B., 44, 115, 249
Flynn, E. James, 115
FMEA, 285

focus groups, 23, 24
Food and Drug
Administration (FDA),
265, 362
Forbis, J. L., 142
Ford
accounts payable
experience, 195–6
core set of norms and
values, 147
financial performance of,
53–4
ISO adoption, 362
Japanese competition,
73
Ford, Henry, 147
Ford Q1 designated
suppliers, 46, 51, 53
Ford Q-101 Standard, 47,
53
forms, as manifestation of
culture, 137–8
Fornell, Claes, 352
Fortune 500 firms, 65
Fortune 1000 firms, 34, 42
Fournier, Bernard, 359
Fox, Tony, 351
Freeman, E. B., 30
Fucini and Fucini, 383
Fujimoto, T., 248

Gadd, K. W., 28
Gale, Bradley T., 10, 11
gaps analyses, 8
Gardial, Sarah Fisher, 13,
18, 22, 23, 112
Garwood, D., 247
General Accounting Office,
41, 42, 58
General Motors, 7, 197,
362, 379, 382
Germany, 100n
Gillespie, Edward, 350
global factory approach,
379
globalization, 346, 365–6
The Goal, It's Not Just Luck,
385n
Goldratt, E., 281, 385n
Goodard, Martyn, 351
Goodman, P. S., 135, 136,
148, 149
Goodstein, Leonard D., 10
governance, 154
Grant, R., 78–9
Great Place to Work
Institute, 117, 132
Guba, E., 100n
Gutman, Jonathan, 14

Haasen, A., 108
Hage, J., 93
Hall, Gene, 207
Hallmark Greeting Cards,
205
Hammer, M., 28, 188, 195
Harley-Davidson, 381, 383
Harratts of Wakefield, 351
Harrington, H. James,
184
Harrison, Kunlé, 239
Hartley, J. R., 247, 248
Harvard Business Review,
97–8n
Harvard Business School,
74
Hawthorne Plant, 107
Hayes, Bob E., 9, 11
Hayes, R. H., 246, 248
Health and Safety Executive
(UK), 364
Heighlein, F., 107
Heller, Thomas, 346
Hendricks, K. B., 44–7,
49–53, 65, 66, 356
Herman Miller, 110
Hertz, H. S., 32
Herzberg, Frederick, 108,
131
Heskett, J. L., 137, 138,
140–1, 147, 150
heuristics, 76
Hewlett-Packard, 381, 383
Hiam, A., 41
high performance work
practices, 28
high performing
organizations, 105–33
accountability and
responsibilities, 125–6,
129
achievement of data
driven business results,
115–17
business results, 117–18,
131–2
business valued
measurements, 129–30
communication, 127
compensation policies,
116
continuous improvement,
115
creative funding
resources, 124
customer value, 111–12
design team, 123, 124
education and training,
124, 126–7, 128

employee contributions,
113–14, 118–30
evolution, 106–8, 131
foundations, 110–17, 131
high performance teams,
123–4
implementation
effectiveness
evaluation, 130
implementation through
people engagement,
118–31
job design, 116
leadership, 113, 119–20,
122, 125, 129–30, 131
management structure,
systems and style,
116–17
organizational culture,
112, 120, 130
problem of drift, 115
reward systems, 130
skills/knowledge
requirements, 126
steering committee, 123
support systems, 129
team teaching, 124, 127
team working, 114–15,
120–4, 125–6, 129–30
theory, 108–9, 131
values and principles
versus rules, 112–13
work design, 116
work redesign, 124–5
Hild, Cheryl, 211, 217
Hinckley, S., 107
Hines, Cathy, 98n
Holder, M. E., 54–5, 65
Home Depot, 7, 140
Honda, 382
Hopp, Wallace J., 211
Hout, T. M., 246
HRM *see* Human Resource
Management
human goodness, 249, 268
electronic sensor case
study, 260
implantable device
component case study,
266
mainframe computer
case study, 253
software product case
study, 264
Human Resource
Management (HRM),
86, 118, 132
human resource results,
Baldrige criteria, 332,

333, 334, 335, 336, 338,
339
Hunt, J. G., 139
Huysse, Garry, 87, 98n

IBM, 7, 137, 359
Ichniowski, C., 67, 118, 132
ICL Manufacturing
Division, 359
impact on society,
European Quality
Award criteria, 357,
358
implantable device
component case study,
251, 265–6
in-depth interviews *see*
interviews
in-process kanban, 293
income per employee, 50,
61
income/assets, 50, 53, 54,
61
income/sales (profit
margin), 50, 53, 54, 55,
57–8, 61
inductive knowledge, 91–2,
94
Industrial del Ubierna,
359
information, Baldrige
criteria, 334, 336, 337,
338
information flows, redesign
of, 194–5
information products
industry, 223
information technology
(IT), 175–9, 208
innovation, 12, 21, 246
institutionalized principles,
148–9
integrated manufacturing,
29
interdependency, 93
interfunctional
coordination, 143
Internal Revenue Service,
191–3
International Quality Study,
42
International Uniforms
Limited, 351
interview training, 23
interviews, in-depth
manager perceptions,
33
performance impact of
TQM, 58–64

sample selection
approaches, 32, 36–7,
58–64
inventory turnover, 54
investment costs, 375
investment, return on,
Lawler, Mohrman,
Ledford study, 42–3
investors, total return to,
Lawler, Mohrman,
Ledford study, 42–3
Ishikawa, K., 77
ISO 8402, 344, 346, 347
ISO 9000 standards, 36
accreditation network,
354–5
Anderson, Daly, Johnson
study, 44, 48–9, 65, 66
benefits of, 349–51
certification, 27, 348–9,
352, 353–4, 362–3
customer satisfaction,
351–3, 367
documented procedures,
347, 352
as foundation for quality
initiatives, 361–5,
366–7
investment in, 346, 347–9
self-assessment, 323
ISO 9002, 32
ISO 14000, 363–4, 365
ISO 14001, 361
Isuzu, 382

J. Walter Thompson
Company, Ltd, 350
Jacob, R., 27, 134
Jager, Durk, 116
Jain, Diput C., 10
Japan
academic culture, 72, 75
commitment to TQM,
380–1, 383
competitive pressure from,
27, 73, 313, 372–3
development of TQM, 77,
91–2, 371
ISO certification, 348
quality control circles, 29,
77, 91
subsidiary firms in USA,
382–3
Total Quality Control
(TQC), 27, 28, 29
Japanese Union of
Scientists and
Engineers (JUSE), 77,
91–2, 100n

Jarrell, S. L., 48, 116, 346
  in-depth interview study,
    56, 58–64, 65, 66
  just-in-time deliveries, 34
  manager perceptions, 33
  managerial exaggeration
    of TQM, 35
  organization level results,
    117, 132
  sample selection, 32
  start date of deployment
    of TQM, 34
  TQM characteristics, 28
Jarrell, S. M., start date of
  deployment of TQM,
  34
Jaworski, B. J., 142, 143,
  145
Jenkins, Roger L., 15
JIT *see* just-in-time
  manufacturing
job design, 116, 334
Johnson, Marilyn F., 32, 44,
  48–9, 65, 66, 349
joint improvement teams,
  28
joint quality improvement,
  29
Jones, D., 272
Jones, N. R., 41
Joslyn, C., 107
Juan Carlos, King of Spain,
  359
Juran, J. M., 248, 249, 371
JUSE *see* Japanese Union of
  Scientists and
  Engineers
just-in-time manufacturing,
  34, 373, 381, 382

Kahle, K. M., 51
Kahn, R., 109
kaizen, 78, 361
Kaizen action lists, 294
kanban pull system, 293–4,
  306–7, 308
Kano, N., 77, 79
Kantarci, Hazim, 360
Kaplan, Robert, 74
Katz, D., 109
Kearns, David, 74
Kelman, H. C., 139
Kemeny Consulting, 168,
  169, 172, 174
Kennedy, Michael E., 223
Kenney, M., 382
Kinney, Jean, 98n
Kirchenstein, John J., 359
K. L. Ruppert, 345

knowledge
  inductive, 91–2, 94
  local, 93–4
  scientific, 77, 91
  see also customer
    knowledge; market
    knowledge
knowledge work, 114
Knoxville Management
  Development Center
  see University of
  Tennessee
Kohli, A. K., 142, 143, 145
Kotter, J. P., 134, 137, 138,
  140–1, 147, 150
Kruse, D., 29

labor, division of, 106–7
labor costs, 375
Lambert, Douglas M., 8
Lavin, Douglas, 196–7
Lawler, E. E., 29, 33–4,
  42–4, 65
lead-time reduction, 28
leadership, 31
  academic culture, 82
  Baldrige criteria, 331–2,
    337, 338–40
  business process
    reengineering, 206
  electronic guide case
    study, 261–2
  electronic sensor case
    study, 260
  European Quality Award
    criteria, 357, 358
  high performing
    organizations, 113,
    119–20, 122, 125,
    129–30, 131
  influence on
    organizational culture,
    147
  medical device case study,
    257, 258
  network data processor
    case study, 266–7
  self-assessment, 331–2
  TQM programs, 147–8,
    149, 170–1, 173–5
Lean Aircraft Initiative, 287
Lean Enterprise Systems
  Design Institute
  component level
    planning BOMs, 299
  customer demand
    profiles by product
    family, 306
  element integration, 283

factory response profile,
  304
first-level planning BOMs,
  298
lean enterprise, 276
lean enterprise measures,
  287
model-level planning
  BOM, 279
objective of rate-based
  planning techniques,
  303
process flowcharting
  symbols, 285
production scheduling,
  300
value stream alignment,
  295
lean enterprises, 272–310
  customer value, 275–82
  definition, 275
  distribution channel
    integration, 275–6,
    308–9
  implementation
    strategies, 277–81
  major components of,
    275–6
  market scope, 276–82
  performance
    measurement, 287–8,
    309
  rate-based demand and
    production planning,
    275–6, 294–305
  rate-based order
    management, 275–6,
    305–7
  supplier process
    integration, 275–6,
    307–9
  team working, 294,
    309
  training, 284, 294
lean production, 275–6,
  283–94
  baseline current process,
    284–8
  creation of
    manufacturing cell,
    288–92
  future changes, 294
  pull scheduling systems,
    292–4
learning *see* training
learning organizations,
  22–3
Ledford, Jr., G. E., 29,
  33–4, 42–4, 65

Lee, W. Y., 44, 46, 51, 53–4, 65
Lehman, Donald R., 352
Leitnaker, Mary G., 211, 217
Lemak, D. J., 32, 55–8, 65
Lemmel, Magnus, 345–6, 365
Leuliette, Timothy D., 197
Levering, Robert, 117, 132
Levi Strauss, 110, 118
Levine, D., 29
Lexmark International, 237
Liberty Mutual, 205
Lillrank, P., 77, 79
Lincoln, Y., 100n
Lloyd's Register, 354
loan application process, 198–9
local knowledge, 93–4
long-term orientation, 249, 269
    electronic guide case study, 261, 262
    electronic sensor case study, 259
    mainframe computer case study, 252
    medical device case study, 256, 258
    software product case study, 264
Lopez de Arriortua, J. Ignacio, 197
LSC *see* Total Quality Leadership Steering Committee
Lucent Magazine, 120
Lucent Technologies, 110, 118–30
    Values Statement, 119
Lutz, Robert A., 197
Lyles, M. A., 145

McClindon, Constance, 99n
McGinn, Rich, 120
McGregor, D., 107, 108, 110, 113
The Machine that Changed the World, 272
McKinsey study, 222
Madison City, 110
mainframe computer case study, 251, 252–3
Malcolm Baldrige National Quality Award, 32, 33, 36
    as basis for self-assessment model, 329–40

criteria, 249, 315–16, 322–3, 331–41
direction setting – input items, 335–7
direction setting – output items, 337–8
Easton and Jarrell study, 58, 62
GAO report (1991), 41
Hendricks and Singhal stock price study, 46
high performing organizations, 117–18
items that support the value chain, 334–5
job design, 116
leadership, 331–2, 337, 338–40
national research agenda, 86, 87, 98–9n
objectives of, 313–14
organization level results, 117–18
value chain items, 333–4
work design, 116
management
    assessment of financial impact, 37
    business process reengineering, 207
    cross-functional, 29
    customer value learning, 22–3, 25
    decisions to implement TQM, 39
    exaggerated claims about TQM, 32, 35
    knowledge of customers, 8–9
    leadership role in BPR, 207
    leadership role in TQM, 29
    lean enterprises, 308–9
    perceptions of, 33, 44
    representations of competitive advantage, 143–5, 151
    self-assessment process, 320, 322, 328
    translation of learning into action, 23–4, 25
    see also fact-based management; leadership; process management; process managers; Total Quality Management (TQM)

management structure, systems and style, 116–17
manufacturing
    decline of, 114
    organization level results, 118
    product delivery problems, 173–5
manufacturing companies, 27
market knowledge, Baldrige criteria, 333, 334, 335, 337, 338
market orientation, 142–7
market performance, Baldrige criteria, 331, 336
market research, 23
market scope, lean enterprises, 276–82
market segment, 281–2, 306
market-sensing, 142
marketing plans, 225
marketing strategies, lean enterprises, 277
Marrett, Cora, 99n
Martin, J., 137–8, 140, 141, 145
Maskell, 295
Maskill, B. F., 246
Maslow, Abraham, 108, 131
mass production/scientific management (MP/SM) methods, 372, 378–9, 381–2
Massey, Walter, 88, 99n
Masters, R. J., 137
material kanban, 293
Materials Requirements Planning (MRP) system, 297
matrix management structure, 168, 170–1
Mauss, A., 95
Mavrinac, S. C., 41
Mazda, 195, 382, 383
means-end theory, 14
medical device case study, 251, 256–8
Mehta, N. T., 142
Mejabi, B., 107, 109
mental models, 143–5
Merck, 118
metrics and measurement, 31, 47, 115–16
Mexico, 382
Meyer, M. W., 41
Microsoft, 140

Milliken, 110, 359
MIT Commission on
  Industrial Productivity,
  221–2
Mitchell, Randy, 350
Mitsubishi, 382
Mittatekniikan Keskus, 355
Mobil Oil, 348
Mogab, J., 78, 79
Mohrman, S. A., 29, 33–4,
  42–4, 65
Monden, 275, 293
Montgomery, J. C., 32, 55
Moss, Brian, 351
Motorola, 73, 110, 118, 222
MRP system, 297
multi-attribute theory, 11,
  21
multiple regression models,
  38

NACCB, 354, 355
NAM, 124
NAMAS, 354
Narver, J. C., 142, 143, 146
NASA, 46
NASDAQ, 44
National Academy of
  Science, 87, 145
National Accreditation
  Council of Certification
  Bodies (NACCB), 354,
  355
National Association of
  Manufacturers (NAM),
  124
National Centre for
  Manufacturing
  Sciences (NCMS), 124
National Institute of
  Standards and
  Technology (NIST),
  117
National Market System
  filings, 54
National Measurement
  Accreditation Service
  (NAMAS), 354
National Research Council,
  222
National Science
  Foundation (NSF), 71,
  72, 87–8, 89, 95
Naumann, Earl, 10
navigational device case
  study, 251, 254–6
NCMS, 124
Nedungadi, P., 143–4, 145,
  146

Nelson, R., 93
net revenue index, 374–8
Netas, Northern Electric
  Telekomuenikayson AS,
  359
Netherlands, 355
network data processor case
  study, 251, 266–8
New Jersey Star-Ledger, 119
New United Motor
  Manufacturing, Inc.
  (NUMMI), 382
New York Stock Exchange,
  44, 54
Nexus/Lexus, 58
Nissan, 382
NIST, 117
Nonaka, I., 77, 247, 248
Nordstrom, 138
norms
  core set of, 147
  differentiated culture,
    141
  integrated culture, 141
  as manifestation of
    culture, 137, 138, 150
  as source of concertive
    control, 139–40
  strategic cultures, 141
  strategically differentiated
    cultures, 141–2, 147,
    149, 151
  strong cultures, 140
Norsk Akkreditering, 355
North West Missouri State,
  110
Norway, 355
Novum Organum, 91
NSF *see* National Science
  Foundation
NuAire Limited, 351
NUMMI, 382

Oakland, J. S., 28
occupational health
  systems, 364–5
October 1987 market crash,
  55–6, 57
Oliver, Richard L., 15
operational impact studies,
  66–7
Orcunus, Ali Risa, 360
order management, lean
  enterprises, 275–6,
  305–7
organization level business
  results, 117–18, 131–2
organizational linkages, 93
organizational routines, 93

Osborn, R. N., 139
Ouchi, W. G., 137
outsourcing, 379

Pace, R. D., 54–5, 65
Parasuraman, A., 8
Pareto principle, 292, 297
Parr, William C., 199
participative management,
  31
partner process
  management, Baldrige
  criteria, 333, 334, 335
partner results, Baldrige
  criteria, 332, 333, 334,
  335, 336, 339
partnering, 28, 93
Pascale, R. T., 137
PCDs, 232
PDCA, 115, 315
PDS *see* Product Design
  Specification
Pearce, J. A., 30
people engagement,
  118–30
people management,
  European Quality
  Award criteria, 357,
  358
people satisfaction,
  European Quality
  Award criteria, 357,
  358
Pepper, John E., 71–2, 88,
  99n, 116
performance
  benchmarking, 40, 51,
    61, 63
performance indicators,
  292
performance measurement
  Baldrige Award, 315–16
  lean enterprises, 287–8,
    309
pharmaceutical industry,
  210
Philip Crosby Quality
  Award, 46–7
Philips Consumer
  Electronics Company
  (USA), 350
Piker, Ahmet, 361
Plan-Do-Check-Act, 115, 315
Planning Bill-of Material
  (BOM), 278–80,
  297–9, 300
planning-assessment link,
  316–17
point-of-sale data, 278, 295

Point-Of-Use (POU), 290
policy and strategy,
  European Quality
  Award criteria, 357,
  358
Porter, L. J., 44
Porter, M. E., 146
POU, 290
Powell, T. C., 44
PR Newswire, 50
practices, as manifestation
  of culture, 137–8
Prennushi, G., 67
press releases, 49
prevention focus, 28, 250,
  269
  electronic guide case
    study, 261
  mainframe computer
    case study, 253
  navigational device case
    study, 255
principles, high performing
  organizations, 112–13
printer development
  projects, 230
probit models, 48–9
problem-solving, 76, 93
  high performing
    organizations, 112–13
  TQM, 148, 149, 166–7
procedures, high
  performing
  organizations, 112–13
process, definition of, 154
process control, 31
Process Control Dimensions
  (PCDs), 232
process definition, 28
process emphasis, 250,
  269
  electronic guide case
    study, 262
  electronic sensor case
    study, 259
  implantable device
    component case study,
    265
  mainframe computer
    case study, 252
  navigational device case
    study, 255, 256
  network data processor
    case study, 266
  software product case
    study, 263
process flow charts, 285–6
process improvement, 28
process indicators, 115

process management, 28,
  208–9
  Baldrige criteria, 333,
    334, 335, 338
  customer value, 210, 211,
    219–20
  definition, 183–4, 185–6,
    211
  designed experiments,
    218–19
  multi-step processes for,
    185–9
  ownership of, 184–5,
    209
  process variation, 212–19
  statistical methods,
    212–19
  successful versus
    unsuccessful efforts,
    186–7
process managers, role and
  responsibilities of,
  210–12
processes, European Quality
  Award criteria, 357,
  358
Procter & Gamble, 110,
  116, 118
Proctor, Dominic, 350
product attributes, 11–13,
  14–15, 16, 19, 20, 21,
  24, 25
product design, 212,
  221–44
  avoidance of
    overspecification,
    247–8
  "bottom-up" testing,
    241
  case hardening, 242
  comprehensive
    evaluation/testing,
    240–3
  concurrent engineering,
    247
  configuration selection
    process, 238
  controlled iteration,
    238–9
  conversion of customer
    needs into technical
    requirements, 234–6
  critical variables, 224,
    233–4, 236
  customer criteria used in
    technology selection,
    235
  derating, 238
  design layouts, 237

design for
  manufacturability, 222,
  247–8, 255
design margin, 232,
  237–8
design reviews, 239
design without delay,
  247
Easton and Jarrell study,
  59
Failure Mode and Effect
  Analysis, 240
failure testing, 240–1
humidity tests, 242
key "design quality"
  concepts, 232–43
life testing, 240
mechanical subsystem
  testing, 242
modular designs, 247
modular subsystem
  testing, 242
"operating space," 224,
  233–4, 240, 241
parts evaluation, 241–2
preliminary evaluations,
  240
statistically designed
  experiments, 219
stress testing, 225, 240,
  241, 242
system tests, 242
temperature tests, 242
testing to specification,
  240
top-down design, 236–7
zero drawing, 237
Product Design
  Specification (PDS),
  225, 235–6, 238, 240,
  243
product development, 28,
  29, 221–44
  as an integrative process,
    222–3, 228, 244
  case studies, 250–68
  compatibility with quality,
    245–71
  customer focus, 67,
    234–6, 249–50, 268
  Customer Future Needs
    Projection, 224, 227,
    228, 232, 244
  customer involvement,
    229
  customer value, 221–2,
    234–6, 243, 244
  development phases and
    goals, 223–6

product development (*contd*)
Easton and Jarrell study, 59
Final Product Definition
and Project Targets,
225, 226, 227, 232, 236
information continuity
for critical product
characteristics, 228,
229–32
information convergence,
228, 229
Manufacturing Readiness
Review, 226
Manufacturing System
Design, 225–6, 227
overlapping stages, 247
process speed, 221, 243,
245–71
Process Technology
Selection and
Development, 224–5,
227, 232, 233–4
processes of, 223–32
Product Concept Phase
Review, 225
Product Design and
Evaluation, 225, 227,
232, 234–6, 243
Product Ideas phase,
223–4, 227
Product Infant Mortality
Tracking Program
Review, 226
Product Launch
Readiness Review, 226
Product Manufacture and
Delivery, 226, 227
Product Marketing and
Distribution
Preparation, 225, 227
Product Release Review,
225
product robustness, 221,
237–8, 243
Product Technology
Selection and
Development, 224, 225,
227, 232, 233–4, 241
role in TQM
organization, 221–3
Socio-Technical systems
theory, 109
strategic focus, 222
strategic role of fast
product development,
246–7
strategies for achieving
fast product
development, 247–8

team work, 223, 227,
228–9, 230, 244, 268,
270
Technical Feasibility
Phase Review, 224
vision of future product,
227, 228–9, 244
product improvements, 19
product process
management, Baldrige
criteria, 333, 334, 335
Product Response Profile,
302–3
product strategy, lean
enterprises, 277
production kanban, 293
production planning, lean
enterprises, 275–6,
294–305
production quality control,
28
productivity improvement,
78
profit margin (income/
sales), 50, 53, 54, 55,
57–8, 61
prototype testing, 254–5
public announcements *see*
self-announcement
studies
Pugh, Stuart, 235, 238
pull scheduling systems,
292–4
pulp and paper industry,
210
purchase drivers, 11, 25

QFD *see* Quality Function
Deployment
QS-9000, 363, 365
quality assurance
inspections, 77
quality awards
accounting data studies,
49–54
Christensen and Lee
study, 53–4, 65
Easton and Jarrell study,
63
Hendricks and Singhal
accounting data study,
49–53, 65
Hendricks and Singhal
stock price event study,
44–7, 65
implementation of TQM
studies, 32, 35–6
stock price event studies,
44–7

see also European Quality
Award; Malcolm
Baldrige National
Quality Award
quality certification studies,
48–9, 65
quality control, 28, 77
visual, 292
quality control circles, 29,
77, 91, 361
Quality Function
Deployment (QFD),
23, 222, 247
quality improvement, 28,
29, 31
quality indicators, 115–16
Quality Management
System (QMS), 154,
352–3
Quality Maturity Ladders,
325
quality values *see* continuous
improvement and
learning; cooperation;
customer focus; fact-
based management;
human goodness; long-
term orientation;
prevention focus;
process emphasis
questionnaire-based
approaches *see* surveys

R&D intensity, 48
Raad voor de Acreditie, 355
Raad voor de Certificatie,
355
RAB *see* Registrar
Accreditation Board
Rank Xerox Limited, 359
rate-based demand and
production planning,
275–6, 294–305
balancing of demand and
flexibility, 299
coordination meetings,
299
demand variability, 302–5
expectations and goals,
295
implementation
requirements, 295–6
model-level bill-of-
material, 297–9
production in quantities
of one, 296–7
production scheduling,
299–302, 307
repetitive scheduling, 297

rate-based order
management, 275–6,
305–7
Rath and Strong, 79–80
receivables turnover, 54
Reed, R., 32, 55–8, 65
Reeves, C. A., 97n
Registrar Accreditation
Board (RAB), 354, 355
Reimann, C. W., 32
Renault, 361
research
assessment of financial
impact, 37–67
barriers to faculty research
on quality, 74–5
cross-functional, 82,
85–6, 87
establishment of research
agenda, 86–7
funding, 84–5, 87–90
involvement of industry,
72, 74, 84–5
link to teaching, 74, 75
qualitative versus
quantitative, 21–2
relations of academics to
customers of research,
83–5
TQM implementation,
30–7
TQO national research
agenda, 83–90
resources, European
Quality Award criteria,
357, 358
reward systems, 130, 264
RFP process, 254
Richards, Ian, 349–50
risk-taking, 45, 120, 257–8
Roach, Stephan, 379
Roberts, H., 81, 82
Robinson, J., 74
Robinson, R. B., 30
Rokeach, M., 248–9
Roos, D., 272
Rosenthal, Jim, 207
Ross, William, 217
Rubbermaid, 118
Ruekert, R. W., 142, 145
rules, high performing
organizations, 112–13
Rungtusanatham, M., 76,
249
RVA, 355
RVC, 355

"S" checks, 284–5
safety checks, 285

safety management systems,
364–5
Sakakibara, S., 44, 249
sales per employee, 50, 116
GAO report (1991), 41
Lawler, Mohrman,
Ledford study, 42–3
sales, return on, 116
GAO report (1991), 41
Lawler, Mohrman,
Ledford study, 42–3
sales/assets, 50, 54
salesperson call reports, 24
sample selection
approaches, 30–7
accounting data studies,
49–54
Anderson, Daly, Johnson
study, 48–9
Christensen and Lee
study, 53–4
Easton and Jarrell study,
58–64, 65
Hendricks and Singhal
accounting data study,
49–53
Hendricks and Singhal
stock price study, 44–7
Holder and Pace study,
54–5
in-depth interview
approaches, 32, 36–7,
58–64
Lemak, Reed, Satish
study, 55–8
quality award studies,
44–7, 49–54
quality certification
studies, 48–9
self-announcement
studies, 31, 32, 54–8
survey instruments, 32–5
third-party assessments,
32, 35–6
Sanders, Howard D., 217
Sanders, Richard D., 211,
217
Saraph, J. V., 44, 249
Satish, P. K., 55–8, 65
Scarisbrick, John, 360
Schacht, Henry, 119, 120
scheduling
lean enterprises, 276,
294–305
mixed models, 300–2, 307
Schein, E. H., 138, 248
Schermerhorn, J. R., 139
Scholtes, Peter, 186
Schonberger, R. J., 247

Schroeder, R. G., 44, 76, 249
scientific knowledge
induction, 91
scope and domain of, 77
scientific management
(SM), 106–7, 110, 113,
372, 378–9, 381–2
Japanese lack of belief in,
77
scoring thermometers,
325–6
Scott, W. R., 94, 99n
SDCA, 115
Sears, 7
self-announcement studies
Easton and Jarrell study,
63
Holder and Pace study,
54–5, 65
implementation of TQM
studies, 31, 32
Lemak, Reed, Satish
study, 55–8, 65
performance impact of
TQM, 54–8
self-assessment, 313–42
assessment output, 319,
327–9, 330
assessment process
model, 317–21
Assessment Workbooks,
326–7
Baldrige framework,
329–40
definition, 314
design of process, 316–29
direction setting – input
items, 335–7
direction setting – output
items, 337–8
European Quality Award,
357, 360, 366–7
evaluation framework,
318, 322–4, 330
evaluators, 318, 319–20,
322, 330, 340
information gathering,
318, 324–7, 330
items that support the
value chain, 334–5
leadership, 331–2
planning-assessment link,
316–17
Process Owner, 319, 320,
322, 323–4, 326, 329,
340
purpose of, 321–2, 330
scoring issue, 325–6, 327
value chain items, 333–4

self-centered firms, 144
Senge, Peter, 194–5
service industry, 114
service process
    management, Baldrige
    criteria, 333, 334, 335
service quality control, 28
setup time, 34, 289, 296
Sharma, Arun, 8
Shaw, K., 67, 118, 132
Shea, G., 108
Shewhart control chart, 213
shining check, 284
Shoultz, Donald, 352
SIC industry codes, 50, 51,
    53
simulation testing, 254, 262,
    263
Singhal, V. R., 44–7, 49–53,
    65, 66, 356
Sitkin, S., 78, 82, 89
Slater, S. F., 142, 143, 145,
    146
Slywotsky, Adrian J., 10
Smith, Adam, 77, 106
Snell, S. A., 29, 44, 114, 249
socialization, 149
Socio-Technical Systems
    theory, 107, 108,
    109–10, 113, 131
    external factors, 112
    organization level results,
    118
software development,
    255–6
software product case study,
    251, 263–5
sort activities, 284
Southern Graphic Systems,
    201, 204
Southwest Airlines, 282
SPC *see* statistical process
    control
Spearman, Mark L., 211
Spector, B., 134, 150
Spencer, B., 93, 98n
Stahl, Michael J., 2
Stalk, G., 246
Stallkamp, Thomas T.,
    196–7
Standard and Poor's
    Corporate Register of
    Directors, 58, 346
standard work time, 290–1
standardizing activities, 284
statistical methods, process
    management, 212–19
statistical process control
    (SPC), 31, 232, 381

adoption by Japanese, 77
lean enterprises, 292
scientific basis of, 76
student training, 97n
US overseas subsidiaries,
    382
steel industry, 118, 132
Steeplechase Company
    (Cheltenham) Ltd, 350
Sterman, J., 79, 89–90
stock return data, 37, 40,
    65–6, 116
Anderson, Daly, Johnson
    study, 48–9, 65
Easton and Jarrell study,
    60, 61–2, 63, 64
Hendricks and Singhal
    study, 44–7
Holder and Pace study,
    54–5
Lawler, Mohrman,
    Ledford study, 42–4
Lemak, Reed, Satish
    study, 55–8
quality awards studies,
    44–7
quality certification
    studies, 48–9
self-announcement
    studies, 54–8
survey-based studies, 42–4
storage activities, 284
strategic planning, 30, 86
Baldrige criteria, 331,
    337–8, 339
European Quality Award
    criteria, 357, 358
TQM programs, 154,
    157–8, 161
strategy development
    process, Baldrige
    criteria, 331, 337–8, 339
stress testing, 225, 240, 241,
    242
structural equations models,
    38
students, status of, 81
Superior Product Development,
    223
supplier awards, 36
supplier improvement, 29
supplier kanban, 293
supplier partnerships, 29
supplier process
    integration, 275–6,
    307–9
supplier process
    management, Baldrige
    criteria, 333, 334, 335

Supplier Response Profile,
    303, 304–5
supplier results, Baldrige
    criteria, 332, 333, 334,
    335, 336, 339
suppliers, lean enterprises,
    296
supply-chain management,
    28
support service process
    management, Baldrige
    criteria, 334, 335
surveys
    corporate
        implementation of
        TQM, 32–5
    of customer satisfaction,
        12, 21–2, 23
    performance impact of
        TQM, 37, 42–4, 65
sustaining activities, 284
Sutcliffe, Kathleen, 89
SWEDAC, 355
Sweden, 355
systems theory, 93, 107, 109

Taco Bell K-minus, 196, 204
Takeuchi, H., 247, 248
takt time, 286–7, 289
Tastemaker Limited, 351
Tavistock Institute, 107,
    110, 131
Taylor, Frederick, 77,
    106–7, 110, 131
Taylor, P., 79
teaching, link to research, 74
teaching process, 73
team teaching, 124, 127
team working
    concertive control, 139
    electronic guide case
        study, 261–2
    electronic sensor case
        study, 259, 260
    high performing
        organizations, 114–15,
        120–4, 125–6, 129–30
    implantable device
        component case study,
        266
    lean enterprises, 294, 309
    mainframe computer
        case study, 252–3
    medical device case study,
        257, 258
    navigational device case
        study, 254
    network data processor
        case study, 266–7

product development,
223, 227, 228–9, 230,
244, 268, 270
quality improvement, 156
software product case
study, 264
TQM programs, 173–5
technology adoption, 67
technology innovation, 12
Texas Instruments Europe
(TI Europe), 359, 360
Texas Instruments (TI), 46,
110
third-party assessments, 32,
35–6
throughput, 374–5, 385n
Thurow, L., 100n
time-based competition, 28
Time-Based Demand
Profiles, 278, 306
TNT Express, 359
total cost index, 374–8
Total Design, 235
total factor productivity,
Lawler, Mohrman,
Ledford study, 42–3
total productive
maintenance program,
284–5, 296
total quality
barriers to faculty
research, 74–5
conflicts with existing
economic and
management theory,
78–9
core values, 245–6,
248–50
cultural clash with
American academia,
75–83, 95
definition, 1–2, 97n, 344
emerging theory in social
sciences, 91–4
Europe, 343–9, 366
evolutionary economic
theory, 92–3
factor of competitive
differentiation, 246
ideological fervor of,
80–1
lack of academic
literature, 74, 76
lack of knowledge of, 73
national research agenda,
74, 75, 83–90, 97–8n
perceived lack of
empirical support,
76

perceived lack of
theoretical validity, 76
product development
speed, 245–71
reinterpretation of, 90–4
scarcity of teaching on,
73, 74, 76
as a social movement, 95
US efforts at transfer,
79–80
Total Quality Control
(TQC), 27, 28, 29
Total Quality Forums, 74
total quality integration,
135–6, 147–8, 149, 150
Total Quality Leadership
Steering Committee
(LSC), 71, 74, 82
design features, 83
key objectives, 89–90,
97–8n
research funding, 88
Total Quality Management
Center, 315
Total Quality Management
(TQM)
alternative styles of
implementation, 156
case teams, 179
commitment, 148, 149
communications, 176–7
competitive advantage,
371–86
concertive control,
139–40
customer satisfaction, 78,
351–3, 367
definition, 346–7
discovery of, 8
dynamic economics of,
373–8
European investment in,
346–9, 366
European Quality Award
for Masters and
Doctoral theses, 357
Executive Quality Council
(EQC), 159–62, 163,
170, 171, 174, 176
external adaptation,
139–40
failure of programs, 134,
150
functional departmental
teams, 174
information technology
(IT), 175–9
institutionalization,
148–9

internal integration, 139,
140
key characteristics of,
28–9
leadership role, 147–8,
149, 170–1, 173–5
learning, 148, 149
Local Implementation
Management Teams
(LIMT), 161, 163,
165–6, 174
Management Executive
Committee (MEC),
158–9, 171
market orientation,
142–7
missing link, 8–9
and organizational
culture, 134–52
organizational model for
implementation,
153–80
problem-solving skills,
148, 149, 166–7
Process Initialization
Phase, 163
Process Management and
Improvement Teams
(PM&IT), 164–6,
167–73, 174, 176
Process Owners (PO),
161, 163–4, 166, 167,
170, 171, 174
product development,
221–3
Quality Improvement
Team (QIT), 166–7,
173, 174
Quality Office (QO), 161,
162, 165, 166, 174
research on
implementation of,
30–7
responses to development
of, 378–80
Steering Committee
(SC), 161, 162–3, 165,
166, 170, 171, 174, 176
strategically differentiated
culture, 141–2, 146–7,
149, 150
structure, 158–67
team working, 173–5
total quality integration,
135–6, 147–8, 149,
150
trend prediction, 380–3
see also financial
performance

Total Quality Research
    Working Council, 74–5
  national research agenda,
    83–90
Toyota, 275, 380, 382–3
Toyota Production System,
  385n
Toys R Us, 7
TQC *see* Total Quality
  Control
TQO *see* Transformations to
  Quality Organizations
trade growth, 346
Trade and Industry Index
  (TRND), 44
training
  Baldrige criteria, 334, 335
  customer value, 23, 25
  employee development, 29
  high performing
    organizations, 124,
    126–7, 128
  lean enterprises, 284, 294
  need to provide for new
    employees, 73
  TQM programs, 149, 156,
    162
Trammell, Carmen J., 223
transformation process,
  109–10, 131
Transformations to Quality
  Organizations (TQO),
  71–101
  cultural context, 75–83
  design features, 83–90
  establishment of research
    agenda, 86–7
  funding of, 72, 97n
  funding of research,
    84–5, 87–90
  historical context, 73–5
  long-range objective, 72–3
  memorandum of
    understanding (MOU),
    88–9
  national research agenda,
    83–90
  researcher-customer
    connections, 83–5
  support of cross-
    functional research,
    85–6, 87
Trist, Eric, 107, 108, 118
TRND, 44
Turkey, 360–1
Turkish Quality Award,
  361
turnaround study, 64–5

UKAS, 354, 355
unemployment, 343–4
United Kingdom, 348, 354,
  355
United Kingdom
  Accreditation Service
  (UKAS), 354, 355
University of Tennessee at
  Knoxville Management
  Development Center
  (UTK MDC), 199–200,
  202–3, 204

value chain items, 333–4
Value Line Investment
  Survey, 60
Value Line safety rank, 60
Value Line timeliness rank,
  60
value stream, 295
values
  core set of, 147, 245–6,
    248–50
  definition, 248–9
  differentiated culture,
    141
  high performing
    organizations, 112–13,
    119
  integrated culture, 141
  as manifestation of
    culture, 137, 138, 150
  organization-wide
    approach, 250, 253,
    255, 259, 264, 265
  as source of concertive
    control, 139–40
  strategic cultures, 141
  strategically differentiated
    cultures, 141–2, 147,
    149, 151
  strong cultures, 140
  TQM's
    institutionalization, 148
  see also continuous
    improvement and
    learning; cooperation;
    customer focus; fact-
    based management;
    human goodness; long-
    term orientation;
    prevention focus;
    process emphasis
Vegetius, 367
Vinck, Karel, 359
visual factory, 291–2
von Bertalanffy, Ludwig,
  107, 109

Wade, Judy, 207
Wal-Mart, 7, 140, 147
Walking, R. A., 51
Wall Street Journal, 44, 46,
  196–7
Walton, 117
Walton, Sam, 147
waste reduction, 28, 29, 64
Waterman, Robert, 118
The Wealth of Nations, 106
Webster, F. E., 142, 143, 145
Wensley, R., 143, 145
Western Electric Company,
  107
What America Does Right, 118
What Works For Me, 119
Wheelwright, S. C., 246, 248
White, B. J., 29
Wilkins, A. L., 137
Wilson, Clement C., 223,
  234, 239
Wilson, Steven R., 382
Winter, Sidney, 76, 80, 92–3
withdrawal kanban, 293
Womack, J., 92, 272
Woodruff, Robert B., 112
  attribute research, 12
  customer value change,
    18
  customer value
    definitions, 10
  customer value
    determination process,
    22, 23
  customer value hierarchy,
    13, 15
  customer value learning,
    21
  disconfirmation model,
    15
work centers, 288–90
work design, 116, 334
work groups, informal, 107
work groups, semi-
  autonomous, 107–8,
  131
work systems, Baldrige
  criteria, 334, 335
workstation design, 290
World Trade Organization,
  346

Xerox Corporation, 73,
  110, 228

Zalkind, S., 107
Zbaracki, M. J., 35
Zeithaml, Valarie, 8, 10, 142